MW01275008

DESCENT OF SOCRATES

Studies in Continental Thought

John Sallis, GENERAL EDITOR

Descent of Socrates

*Self-Knowledge and Cryptic Nature
in the Platonic Dialogues*

Peter Warnek

Indiana University Press
Bloomington and Indianapolis

This book is a publication of

Indiana University Press
601 North Morton Street
Bloomington, IN 47404-3797 USA

http://iupress.indiana.edu

Telephone orders   800–842-6796
Fax orders   812-855-7931
Orders by e-mail   iuporder@indiana.edu

© 2005 by Peter Warnek

The paper used in this publication meets the minimum requirements of American National Standard for Information Sciences—Permanence of Paper for Printed Library Materials, ANSI Z39.48-1984.

Manufactured in the United States of America

Library of Congress Cataloging-in-Publication Data

Warnek, Peter A., date
Descent of Socrates : self-knowledge and cryptic nature in the
Platonic dialogues / Peter Warnek.
p.   cm.—(Studies in Continental thought)
Includes bibliographical references and index.
ISBN 0-253-34677-0 (cloth : alk. paper)—ISBN 0-253-21816-0
(pbk. : alk. paper)
1. Socrates. 2. Plato. Dialogues. I. Title. II. Series.

B317.W37 2005
184—dc22
2005022355

1   2   3   4   5   10   09   08   07   06   05

To Zoe and Stephanie

Indeed, as a physician one might ask:
"How could the most beautiful growth of antiquity,
Plato, contract such a disease?
Did the wicked Socrates corrupt him after all?
Could Socrates have been the corrupter of youth after all?
And did he deserve his hemlock?"

Nietzsche

I am an absurd sort of physician;
for my treatment makes the illness greater . . .

(Plato's) Socrates

Contents

Preface

"For those possessing νοῦς," says Glaucon, "the measure for listening to such speeches is a whole life" (Rep. 450b).[1] We are not told here, at least not directly, what the measure of this life would be, how this whole of life might receive *its* measure. But the statement does suggest that to give one-self over to these speeches, to be devoted to receiving them and what is at issue in them, is a task that takes over one's life as a whole. It is already to allow one's life to receive a certain measure, and to let it be determined thereby as a whole in a certain way. Life, as the proper measure for listening to these strange and difficult speeches, precisely because it is a *listening,* also comes to receive its measure. In this exchange between life and speech, the measure itself comes to be measured, yet measured only by what it measures.

It thus cannot be missed that Glaucon's remark, precisely by invoking a certain measure, also leaves us to consider that very measure as it opens on to an excess or lack of measure—if, that is, the life that finds itself in this exchange between life and speech does not simply return to itself, does not simply revert back to itself in a reiteration or reflection of identity, but rather also confronts itself outside itself, already ahead of itself. The very propriety of the measure, as life, thus finds itself ruptured by this ecstatic operation that is its own *erotic* necessity, since it proves to be a movement that cannot contain itself, that never will have been in a position to know itself as such. It is as if Glaucon were to say that the measure for such listening can have no measure at all, except insofar as life itself has a measure, except insofar as a measure comes to be imposed upon us, therefore, in life's finality. The speeches to which Glaucon refers can speak, then, only as they speak to this ecstatic *time* of mortal life, because only this mortal time, the very limits of such a time, give to these speeches their alleged propriety, their sense of limit. If death, as the limit of speech, remains an ecstatic limit—simply because life as a "whole," the life that we are, will have eluded us—it is no less true that this mortal necessity as such a limit has also already encroached upon life, as life anticipates its death, lives its death. One thus speaks here of a measure or a limit only by adhering to this twofold character of the limit, this double gesture in which the limit itself is put into relief precisely by the excess it harbors.

How is a reading of Plato to unfold, allowing itself to be claimed by this erotic and mortal necessity, by the ecstatic limit announced in this statement? If this book succeeds in such a reading, the first thing to admit is that it also falls far short of achieving a thorough "interpretation" of the Platonic dialogues. This is the case, if for no other reason than for the simple fact that too many texts have been left unaddressed, and too many questions left unasked and unanswered. I have been far too selective in my approach to claim something like a comprehensive and exhaustive justification for the theses I set forward in this study. I have not managed to make the law of this selection explicit. Nor can it be said that I have responded adequately to the veritable mountain of secondary literature that exists on Plato and Socrates and that continues to be produced. What is presented here is rather only a beginning, and one made, of course, within the measure of a certain time.

Nevertheless, I would insist that this book does take a decisive step in furthering a different possible way of reading Plato. This step consists in the insight that the movement of the Socratic-Platonic λόγος must be encountered not simply as it speaks *about* nature (or φύσις), not simply as it speaks to us in a way that could then be translated into the form of propositions and assertions. Instead, what is ventured here is a reading that follows this λόγος as if it itself were a manifestation of the nature or life that is at issue in it. Such a step may seem at first to conflict with the most paradigmatic account of Socrates handed down to us, in which he is characterized as one who turns philosophy away from its initial concern with nature. But this appearance is overcome once one begins to consider how things said within the dialogues—such as Glaucon's remark just introduced—can be heard to affirm that what is at issue in our speech is not in the first place something in our possession. What is at issue in the manifestation of speech, as it is enacted in the Platonic text, entails, therefore, a certain reversal in our relation to speech, in which a different relation to nature is revealed. But this presupposes that we are able to grant to these Socratic-Platonic speeches a strange and tragic paradox, that we can allow the λόγος to open up a world that remains irreducible to our willful intent and to the conceptual or representational "content" of speech. The reversal in question means simply that as a questioner one finds oneself put into question by what is questioned. This last point is important, since I shall attempt its elaboration by assuming that cryptic Greek nature poses precisely the most Socratic of tasks, namely that of self-knowledge. The Greek experience of this cryptic nature—which I take up as nature's own withdrawal—shows itself to be grounded not in a lack but in an excess, an excess that is perhaps best likened to the blinding brilliance of the sun. But if the task of self-knowledge is a matter of one's way of belonging to this excess, even as it seems to refute the identity or ipseity of the self, how does one begin to speak of the excess as such? Is it not even somewhat foolhardy to approach this question with the sober and naive conviction that it must be explicated and made transparent to us?

If it is true, as Plato's Socrates proposes in the *Phaedrus,* that every λόγος, every well-composed speech, is to be arranged like a living thing with its own body (Phaedr. 264c), this suggests not simply that writing requires a totalitarian organization, that it demands to be composed as if it were an organic system that lives merely in the falsehood of its self-referential completeness, where every part can be for the whole because the whole is also for every part. Animal life is sustained as a living body only within and by the nature that exceeds it, living only as it is permeated by an encompassing whole, thus by relating to itself as what it is *not,* by holding itself open to its own constitutive lack of identity. The "logographic necessity" (Phaedr. 264b) of Platonic writing is rather itself a reference to *nature's* necessity. Indeed, Socrates suggests, and Phaedrus agrees, that τέχνη, or skillful and competent knowledge, with regard to anything notable becomes possible only through a prior relation to this nature that exceeds its own proper domain and that, for this reason, a worthy λόγος of the nature of the soul or of the body is not possible ἄνευ τῆς τοῦ ὅλου φύσεως, "without [relating to] the whole of nature" (Phaedr. 270c).[2]

But how, then, to speak properly of *this* encompassing relation, precisely as it grounds thought's very delineation of its own propriety? How is self-knowledge possible when it must begin by accepting that it is grounded in something absolutely prior, something that must withdraw in the very appearing of the self? It cannot simply be assumed that the "whole" at issue here is to be accomodated by considering it as yet another, more encompassing, region, as if it were still determinable through the same mode of propriety it is said necessarily to exceed. On the contrary, it seems much more the case that, as this excess opens the determination and power that is distinctive and proper to each region—in the necessity of its restriction—there is at the same time an experience that recoils upon the integrity of the region as such and apparently dissolves its totalizing pretense.

The grounding of a region, the establishing of its limits, always occurs within a "whole" that would have to precede the division and gathering that is often said to constitute the very operation of philosophy as dialectic. In the *Phaedrus* Socrates proclaims himself to be a *lover* of these divine divisions and gatherings, and suggests that the ability "to see natural unity and plurality"—ἓν καὶ ἐπὶ πολλὰ πεφυκόθ' ὁρᾶν—is tantamount to seeing the ἰδέα or the εἶδος (Phaedr. 265d–266c). In this passage, the natural joints of the body, as they allow the body to be divided into parts relating to each other as a whole, serve as a kind of paradigm for the joints of nature itself: the body, divided by nature and according to nature, opens up to us nature's own divisibility. And yet, this dialectic, in which nature opens up to us according to its natural divisions, is possible not only because the body itself already is a whole, but because, as Socrates says, this bodily whole arises only within the whole that already exceeds it, the whole of nature itself. And while this is a decisive insight, still more decisive is the expectation that the λόγος, in its likeness with a living body, would also have to be somehow expressive of this excessive ground that sustains its own making manifest and its relative determinacy. A proper λόγος would accordingly have to imply a transgressive moment in which its own simple propriety is also thereby betrayed: the shattering of the word thus is not opposed to the word but belongs to its way of disclosure.

In the first book of the *Republic,* one finds Socrates asking whether it is enough for a body to be a body—εἰ ἐξαρκεῖ σώματι εἶναι σώματι—or whether a body is not in need of something else, προσδεῖταί τινος. And he answers himself by declaring that by all means a body is in need, that a body *as a body* is only through its lack, its not being enough (Rep. 341e). But if a living body must be defined in this way, precisely by a limit that exposes its insufficiency, its own lack of self-sufficiency, then every speech, in its bodily likeness, is also able to live only by accepting this essential need for supplement, and thus also by refusing the fixity and solidity of the boundaries that would otherwise define it. Speech, as living, as life, simply in order to be at all, would have to hold itself open to what exceeds it and thereby to its own constitutive lack. And yet, to be sure, it is therefore all the more striking that Thrasymachus in this crucial passage will have to insist upon the self-sufficiency and completeness of each τέχνη, thus implicitly denying the need of the λόγος to go beyond itself in order to address what is at issue in it (Rep. 342a–b). It is the case, however, that the *Republic* as a whole is a response to this very denial, as it demonstrates that the possible success of political τέχνη hangs on establishing and sustaining a healthy relation precisely to the excessive nature within which the city and soul come to be. Socrates returns to the difficulty of this relation at the beginning of his response to Glaucon and Adeimantus. Each of us, he says, is *not* self-sufficient but in need of much, adding that this discursive starting point can also be taken as the ἀρχή of the city as such. Socrates thus begins with an assumption that has from the outset already undermined the Thrasymachian account of justice, as this account comes to be repeated and enhanced by Glaucon and Adeimantus in Book II. The tyrant is able to proceed only in the denial of this archaic insufficiency precisely as it grounds political life, the need that both lies at the origin of the city and continues to sustain it. But, arguably, unfolding this need in speeches, exposing it as the necessity of human political life, as a necessity thus bound to the task of establishing and sustaining a relation to nature, proves within this dialogue to present the greatest difficulty in human life. And it is in just this way that we confront the excess indicated in the remark made by Glaucon that concerns the proper measure for listening to these speeches. While it can be said that the Socratic λόγος begins already claimed by an excessive measure, the measure that is the need of human life itself, the *Republic* shows throughout that this need calls for an almost impossible speech, one that could address precisely this daemonic excess, that could address what is at issue in it as ἐπέκεινα τῆς οὐσίας (Rep. 509b). As beyond what is, the good has nevertheless already claimed us; it appears with the bonds of necessity yet continues to elude us, as if we are claimed by the impossibility itself. As an excessive presence it is also the obliteration of difference and concealment, and thus "present" only in its absence or withdrawal.

Let me introduce this study, therefore, by proposing that while it may belong to speech as such, whether written or not, to be always caught up in this need, in what is outside it, to be already taken over by what is beyond it, the peculiar virtue of the Platonic dialogues can be said to consist in the way in which this *ecstatic* character of speech is made explicit, rigorously enforced through its enactment or repetition: precisely what is at issue in the λόγος itself—what becomes manifest with it—demands attending to something that already lies beyond the propriety of the limit, just as the *Philebus*, for example, begins as it asks us to consider conversations that go beyond the limits of the dialogue as it is presented, or as Socrates, at the beginning of the *Timaeus*, issues in the urgency of the dialogue by recounting and reenacting speeches we have never heard. To read the dialogues is to find oneself immersed in a whole world, the total comprehension of which remains impossible but that as such already bears decisively upon the things said.

And yet, at this point a word of caution is called for. Apollo's glory always points also to the dissolution of the individual, in the necessity of a transgression that both establishes and collapses boundaries. Yet there is no question that the illusion of totality and completeness that belongs to both speech and body extends even to the way in which we might address what escapes us or overwhelms us. This possibility is grounded in a most seductive thought, the perfection of the limit through which identity itself would be constituted and preserved, definitive differences between sense and non-sense, being and non-being established. It is worth recalling that health culminates not in a preoccupation with diet and habits, but in a fullness of life that finds itself enabled and empowered without thinking of health at all. Does a living body not also sustain itself precisely in this forgetting of its dependency and frailty? Must it not even become oblivious to the loss of itself, forget its own inevitable dissolution, its own death, and be able, finally, to lose itself in such forgetting? What would become of the joy and pleasure of the body without such genius for oblivion and self-deception? The discrete and constituted individual, the very selfhood of the self, is perhaps, like Socratic wisdom, as fleeting as a dream (Sym. 175e). One can hear this point confirmed and repeated by Diotima: everything in human life that can count as the "same" or as the "self" is first of all marked by the dissolution of self, by the movement between life and death as life's regeneration, neither immortal nor simply mortal. The "immortality" spoken of by Diotima is thus based upon life, not simply as self-preservation, but more originally as a movement of loss. The *desire* for immortality itself already presupposes life's own continual tragic mortality, its loss of itself as the same (Sym. 207d–208b).

Such transgression, and the necessity connected to it, is already at issue at the point at which one announces that a thorough or exhaustive commentary on the Platonic dialogues remains impossible. This limit or constraint, this announcement of impossibility—while heard often—still has to be taken seriously, because it is neither merely an inconvenience nor philosophically incidental: it can be said that *every* reading falls short of the ideal, which is to say, of the kind of reading the dialogues themselves seem to demand.[3] And it is surely inexcusable to maintain a dismissive attitude toward the apparent "violence" of interpretation, when this would also imply the very breakdown of interpretation and the loss of communication. But it might still be possible to affirm such inevitable violence—the basic discord of finitude—if Glaucon's statement can be heard to reinforce precisely what is at stake in the reading of Plato: one's life becomes the measure of the interpretation, but only because to seriously interpret is to put one's life at stake in the interpretation. What else is there to do with one's time, the time between now and sunset? (Phaedo 61e). To be sure, it is indeed already later than we think.

We could say, then, that what we have is nothing but time. To agree with Socrates when he says in the *Theaetetus* that "it is better to accomplish very little well than a great deal in a way that is lacking (μὴ ἱκανῶς)" (Theaet. 187e) is also to affirm that whatever is put forward remains always only preparatory and provisional—which is to say, still in need of address, but also left for another time, given over to the return and repetition referred to by Socrates simply as εἰσαῦθις.[4] But perhaps this is no consolation. Such an openness to the future is without doubt still a form of constraint, because it does imply an economy, perhaps the *final* economy—even if it can be admitted at the same time that the inquiry made possible in such openness occurs only within the horizon of a certain *reprieve*, within the time and space granted as what the Greeks called σχολή. If we do have *this* time, the so-called leisure to hear what is well worth hearing, this does not imply that we have therefore made clear to ourselves the conditions for such an open time and its freedom. Perhaps, as Phaedo suggests, this time hangs in the end only on a bit of chance, on the τύχη associated with what is as capricious and as shifty as the winds (Phaedo 58a).

If we can agree that it is not possible to say everything in advance, this means also that we have yet to understand what has been said *already*. A λόγος that would be relieved of this condition, that therefore could be said to be *complete*, that would be ἱκανῶς, or σαφῶς, wholly adequate or transparent to itself, would also no longer speak to the time of mortal life. It thus can seem that interpretation—which is to say, *reading*—if its intent is only to explain or to make clear, finds itself caught in a trap: clarification for its own sake will lead us astray when it encounters the task of interpreting the obscure precisely in its obscurity, when it must do justice to the necessity of obscurity as such. Yet the question confronted here is not limited only to whether there can there be a phenomenology at the limit of manifestation, a phenomenology even of what does *not* appear, of what withdraws or withholds itself in its own appearance. Socratic ignorance insists upon distinguishing at least two causes of blindness, two ways in which an inability to see can arise, namely, not only in the lack of light but also in its excess (Rep. 518a). The task here is to address, then, not only the necessity of the obscurity, but such necessity as it occurs in a superabundant appearance that I venture here to think as Greek nature. It makes no sense at all to seek to illuminate with a shadowy light what is itself already most clear. If anything, what is needed would be a kind of sheltering that would render the blinding excess more visible to human eyes by making it *less* visible, that would thereby allow the overwhelming to become visible without the undoing and destruction of human life.

I have stated that this book only makes a beginning. This beginning is concerned with thinking the origin of Socratic practice—and so, the origin of philosophy itself—in the experience of such a need for shelter, as a "second sailing" that arises in the tragic encounter with a cryptic nature, a nature that shows itself only as an excessive whole that also withdraws in its very appearance. Yet, along with this, I am also concerned to address another closely related difficulty, which arises at the point where such a need for shelter—which, in the loss of an "originary" nature, is also an awakening to ignorance—does not then leave nature to appear only in what is wholly opposed to the realm of human things. Instead, if we may speak of Socratic "wisdom"—what Socrates in his *Apology* calls "perhaps human wisdom" (ἴσως ἀνθρωπίνη σοφία) (Apol. 20d)—such wisdom has to do with an insistence upon the necessity that nature, precisely in its cryptic impossibility, is first encountered in the task of self-knowledge and in the care for the soul, and thus also in a decisive turn that turns to and follows the disclosure or manifesting of speech.

Accordingly, this book proceeds by interrogating the figure of Socrates as he appears in Plato's text. As an appearance of nature, Socrates is thus taken as the matter of Platonic inquiry, as the tragic eruption of nature in human life. After establishing a historical context for the question of Socratic nature in Plato (Part 1), my reading takes up the *Apology, Gorgias,* and *Phaedo* (Part 2), in order to elaborate how Socratic practice sustains an inquiry into nature as itself a manifestation of nature. With such an approach, it can no longer be said that Plato simply makes "use" of his Socrates, and certainly not as a mere device for literary expression; rather, in his engagement with Socrates, precisely as a question, Plato's text exhibits the inexorable difficulty of the place of human life within nature. This placeless place or non-regional region is developed through a reading of the *Meno* and *Phaedrus,* in order to return to the difficulty of the place of Socrates in Plato's text (Part 3). Socrates himself exhibits and embodies this difficulty and, as I attempt to show, can be encountered only along with this difficulty, precisely as a tragic occurrence, but therefore also as the nature's own "splendor."[5]

Acknowledgments

Although this book was written only with the encouragement and support of numerous friends, colleagues, and students, I wish to make known the exceptional gratitude I feel toward a few individuals. I wish to thank my colleagues in the Department of Philosophy at the University of Oregon for supporting my research and affirming its importance. I also wish to thank Rob Metcalf, Alejandro Vallega, and Melissa Shew, each of whom took the time to read early drafts of the book with care, returning to me many helpful suggestions and comments. I am especially appreciative of the honesty they all brought to this task. I owe an immeasurable debt to Walter Brogan and also to John Sallis, both of whom, each in his own way, first introduced me to the world of reading a different Plato. I am honored to have benefited from the consistent encouragement, generous advice, and wondrous insight of these two men. I also feel a special gratitude toward Jena Jolissaint and Melissa Shew, founders of the "Oregon Plato club." This book has been greatly affected by the hours I spent reading and discussing the dialogues with these devoted and impassioned students of Plato. To Steph and Zoe I wish to say that your loving patience with my philosophical obsessions is truly marvelous. I am thankful both for the time and space you have given me to work and for your gentle and kind words of reassurance.

P.W.
Eugene, November 2004

PART 1. WRITING SOCRATES

1

Reading Plato with a Difference

Socrates, Beautiful and New

There is no disputing that Socrates marks a decisive turning point in Greek philosophy, and thus in Western philosophy as a whole. But is it not then all the more remarkable that this Socratic event continues to provoke our questioning, that it is still able to challenge and even subvert the most established interpretations of it? That the question of Socrates continues to assert itself, that it has not allowed itself to be put to rest, means simply that our Western philosophical tradition remains at a loss before the question of its own origins. To be sure, philosophy has always taken place only within such an impasse, has never been in a position to proceed otherwise. This predicament is, of course, due in no small measure to Plato's authorship. The Platonic text gives us our Socrates, makes him an unavoidable figure, but only by presenting him at the same time as a kind of Silenic enigma, to paraphrase the assessment of Alcibiades (Sym. 221d–222a). We now speak of "pre-Socratics" and, by lumping together these early thinkers in this way, already give a clear indication of what is at stake in the historical transformation marked by Socrates. It is no exaggeration to say that after Socrates, virtually all philosophy claims to be the continuation of his legacy, although this takes place in various ways and through quite divergent appropriations.[1] Yet the proliferation of so many divergent and opposing schools, which all nevertheless claim the title "philosophy,"[2] is sustained precisely in the dense inexplicability of the figure of Socrates himself, as if philosophy had to pass through this intensely contracted moment, to be gathered together for an instant in a single enigmatic figure, only to find itself afterward projected, dispersed, and diversified.

Socrates thus appears as nothing less than the titanic upheaval that forms the landscape of philosophy as such. But why, after nearly two and one-half millennia, have we not achieved an adequate understanding of this transformation? The ongoing voluminous research bent on resolving this enigma confirms that our understanding of what comes to pass with Socrates has not become any less controversial.³ In order to grasp the distinctly Socratic contribution to history, one can easily take refuge in a consideration of the "intellectual" and "cultural" setting that frames his appearance. Yet the mere employment of this language, the simple fact that we inevitably have recourse to it, is revealing enough. While it can hardly be said that we lack the resources for an interpretation of Socrates, at the same time the language and the conceptuality that allows us to carry out the interpretation is usually taken for granted. The difficulty confronted here, however, is not simply that we continue to be entangled in language and history as if in a net. The more insidious point turns on the trenchant expectation that in our interpretation of history we should in fact be able to liberate ourselves from the metaphysical legacy we are interrogating. And it is not to be overlooked that, as a stratagem for overcoming the tyranny of history, this contemporary project of freeing ourselves from metaphysics only repeats what is perhaps the most definitive philosophical gesture of radical modernity.⁴ The pervasive tendency to believe in a wholesale departure from history, to believe that it is possible to start over through the invention of the "new," simply confirms in an utterly daunting way that our age continues to be insidiously dominated by its own historical paradigm. The task of the liberation from history, in other words, is itself already a condition of history.

Nevertheless, this prevailing view of philosophical inquiry—the view that as a discourse it can be conjured up from scratch at any given moment—can also be seen dominating the modern approach to Socrates, precisely because it takes him to be an object to be studied and rendered transparent in such objectivity. With the achievement of such clarity it is supposed that we will be in a position to decide about what parts of Socratic thought are applicable to our own lives and what parts (perhaps unsavory) are to be rejected. Let me propose that by approaching the event of Socrates in this way—in terms of the adequacy of our comprehension, as if this event were indeed something before us we might examine, measure, and finally grasp—we already bypass what is philosophically provocative about this historical phenomenon. Not only is the goal of such an objective understanding not at all appropriate to the unfolding of the history of philosophy, but the sheer givenness of the goal shows itself as a sign for the peculiar difficulty of the event in question, its *monstrous* dimension, its encompassing character. As a figure that marks the very passage into philosophy, as the opening onto such a history, Socrates presents us not with a curiosity that has yet to be unraveled, but with an impassable threshold, a liminal determination that cannot be reduced to its objectivity, or situated within the unfolding of history merely as a sequence of events. We confront here, that is, an elemental or epochal shift, an originary event that is ongoing, that still encompasses and comprehends our possibilities for thinking and speaking.[5]

The confrontation with *this* Socrates is thus the confrontation with the uniquely historical dimension of thinking itself, in which the question of the limit always forms a *self-relation:* in being directed toward such a limit one is also directed toward oneself as thoroughly situated. The field of philosophical historical inquiry proves to be caught up in the most basic Socratic task, that of self-knowledge.[6]

To take up the historical emergence of philosophy as it is bound to this task demands, then, the affirmation of an opacity, an obscurity that belongs to thinking, that inheres in its very site. As situated, thinking never transcends this opacity or renders it irrelevant. It is to be experienced rather than simply comprehended. But if thinking is able to come to itself in this way, only by first finding itself placed (or thrown) into a situation that is not to be outstripped or surpassed, this does not at all imply that it is impossible for it to relate to this situation as such, and precisely in the necessity of this opacity or concealment. The event of Socrates, as constitutive of our historical situation, still claims us even if we find ourselves at a loss before it—claims us precisely *because* we find ourselves at such a loss. And it should be possible to address this opacity in a thematic way. What is decisive is that the phenomenon that I am calling the *descent* of Socrates has to be considered as it remains inaccessible to itself through the obscuring power of its own gigantic effects, as it traverses, pervades, and in a way defines the history of the West. While giving rise to a tradition or a lineage that traces itself back to him, Socrates is encountered only in the covering over of the very conditions of his own occurrence or genesis. This points us to a strange mimetic operation, since it must be said that Socrates dissembles himself before ever revealing himself. It is this strange inversion of the mimetic structure that I wish to consider here, precisely as it can open up a different possible way of reading Plato.

Socrates shows himself not simply as a hidden origin—somehow as a presence or an *in itself* that remains above or before history—but as an appearance that in its very appearing conceals itself, and thus as a descent that makes itself manifest only as it also marks the withdrawal of its own origin. He enacts, or rather is the enactment itself of, such a strange and paradoxical movement of μίμησις, one that first establishes the imitative order as it is traditionally conceived but in this very establishing also displaces that order, by appearing as its inversion. We are thus asked to think an event that unhinges thought at its own origins, that belongs to thought's own obscuring movement, that conditions thinking itself. By speaking of a Socratic descent I thus mean to speak both of a historical singularity and of a peculiar way of becoming manifest. It can be said that as an origin Socrates functions only through his receptivity, through his way of being appropriated. He is only an image or trace of himself—only an image, then, *of* an image. But through this imaginal doubling, the logic of philosophy, which first rigorously circumscribes the "truth" of the image, confronts itself and the possibility of its own occurrence. The descent takes place, therefore, as an imitation that does not simply refer back to something prior, that does not open up an original except insofar as this original must also be derived from the mimetic movement. Accordingly, it is necessary to adhere strictly to the insight that this descensional appearance cannot be taken simply as an image or a fiction—if this designates only the distortion of some kind of original truth—since only through the descent does the very difference between image and original, or fiction and truth, arise. The descent, in other words, as the very opening of this difference itself, as it generates the difference through which it would be thought, must also displace this thought of its own origination. Or, alternatively, if one insists that Socrates *is* nothing but his fiction, nothing but an appearance, only an imitation of an impossible original, this fiction must also be allowed to recoil on itself, as it undermines nothing less than the rigorous concept of the fictional as such. For only with this "fiction," as it presents the very passage into philosophy, the movement by which philosophy finds itself enacted, do we first have anything like a fiction.[7]

This "deconstructive" starting point implies that Socrates is to be taken up both as he determines in advance the conditions of the philosophical tradition—its linguistic and conceptual resources—and also as he belongs to that tradition, finds himself situated within it. It must be said that such a double movement both exceeds and confirms the most conventional oppositions, such as those between the determining and the determined, the external and the immanent, the strange and the familiar. The tradition in question here—precisely as it continues to claim an original identity or continuity, consisting in the transmission and the survival of a sacred content—thus shows itself in such a way that this original unity finds itself displaced by a more originary conflict or contradiction. What is important to bring out at this point is that this constitutive conflict does not simply refute the oppositions and determinations that seem to define the tradition; it also allows them to hold sway, to assert themselves most insidiously at the very moment they are directly challenged. I thus wish to think this originary conflict as it grounds, for example, the movement between fantasy (or falsity) and truth, and between image and original. But here I especially want to examine how this sense of an originary conflict, in its withdrawal from the very oppositions it shelters, can also open up for us a different way to think the place of Socrates within Plato's text.

Tradition, understood originally as *traditio,* names something delivered over, and therefore given up, de-livered in the sense of released and freed, but also handed over, surrendered, and even betrayed. Accordingly, in the repetition and continuity of conceptual and linguistic resources, conveyed in and as tradition, every transaction must also be counted as a loss, or a covering over, the confirmation of an ineradicable oblivion. It is evident, however, that these opposing senses of tradition, far from excluding one another, actually belong together and remain interdependent. The sense of "liberation" and generosity that still attaches itself to every proliferation or delivering over,[8] as an occurrence that remains irreducible to the trans-mitted and communicated content of that delivery, expresses at the same time a kind of restriction, even the necessity of such restriction: a tradition liberates, namely, by imposing constraints, the ἐποχή that promises a fu-ture only by also calling for a violent contestation concerning its origins and its possibilities for repetition. The destructuring of historical dogma thus always presupposes a more severe adherence to history.

It can be said, therefore, that the "common ground" so often mentioned that tradition seems to presuppose, as the communal horizon (or friendship) within which the truth of communication becomes possible, depends upon a prior "freedom" that first of all must be able to break with every dogmatic tenet and regulation. Betrayal can itself be a sign for a great fidelity. Because it consists in going beyond the attachment to what has been conveyed—be-yond the mere sediment of communication—betrayal as such is not at all opposed to community and friendship, but can appear even as the most stringent demand of friendship itself, the *truth* of such friendship being de-nied without it, denied without this possibility.[9] That one's self-relation can be articulated first of all as a friendship means, however, that *this* relation, no less than any other, is also sustained only in a possible betrayal that implies the rupturing of the simple identity of the self, the interrupting of the move-ment that proceeds as if it were merely the unfolding of such a simple iden-tity. This friendship with oneself—this eminently Socratic task—demands rather the affirmation of a movement that must be able to turn on itself in an originary conflict and for the sake of its openness to the future. Such open-ness, as it appears with the Socrates of Plato's text, amounts to an affirmation of the *refutative* and transformative possibilities belonging to the movement of dialogical speech.

One only has to consider the twists and turns of such questioning as it is enacted in the Platonic dialogues, for example, in the *Republic* or in the *Timaeus*,[10] in order to see that such a movement continually finds itself only by interrupting itself, thus by arriving also as the unexpected and the strange, precisely as it strips away the pretense of a self-relation grounded in mere attachment and continuity. The naive justice of a Polemarchus, as a doglike loyalty, for example, as it conspires with the established order in-herited from Cephalus, *must* fail, simply because it remains incapable of questioning the ground of its own commitments and attachments. But in undermining such domesticated obedience, how is one not delivered over to the anarchic jowls of Thrasymachus, namely, to becoming an enemy to oneself and everything opposite, including the just (Rep. 352a)? How is the rupturing of identity of which I am speaking, in other words, not simply the *faction* that destroys itself and, through its disintegration, undermines its own power to act? How does the philosopher thus not inevitably appear as a kind of frustrated tyrant?

The encompassing manifold that is said to ground the community of the friend—the *all things* that friends would have in common[11]—is opened up only as an excessive community, beyond that merely human friendship through which the making of the best city and the founding of the righteous tradition are to become possible. What Thrasymachus must accept in his encounter with Socrates, however begrudgingly, is that there can be no τέχνη that would rule over this elusive sense of what is common to all.[12] And yet, the reluctant concessions of a Thrasymachus do not avoid the inevitable confrontation with a greater difficulty. There can be no question that the great paradox and scandal of the entire *Republic* is the assertion that arises directly from the difficulties entailed by this community of friends, as it is first introduced in Book IV (Rep. 423e–424a) but then reintroduced at the beginning of Book V (Rep. 449c), namely, the *laughable* claim, the culminating third wave, larger even than the previous two, that there must be a reconciliation between the philosophical and the political (Rep. 473c–d).

What is thus decisive in the *Republic,* taken only as an example, is how such a philosophical rule—carried out in the self-questioning exemplified by Socrates—is distinguished by the way in which it promises to open the human order to an excessive nature that cannot be contained within the regionalized and specialized knowledge of any τέχνη. The scandalous reconciliation between the city and the philosopher is thus in one sense only the foreground difficulty of the much more abysmal difference that obtains between human life and the community of all things, the community that both grounds the human world and yet also exceeds it. The political problem at the center of the *Republic* lies in this estrangement of human life with nature, the nature that such life also is. And this estrangement of nature with nature proves to be the basic provocation toward the task of self-knowledge, a task that therefore opens up in the question of human life as a tragic monstrosity. But to speak of *tradition* in this way, as a possible friendship (with oneself) grounded in nature, is this not already to hand all friendship—whether human or not—over to the most cryptic of friendships, the friendship of all things?[13]

I am proposing that, if a tradition must always imply an originary betrayal, in this determination that remains *doubled* and undecidable—as a delivering over or a handing down, but also as a concealing and a falling away—then the very *ipseity* of a tradition, its claim to being, its totalizing effect, becomes impossible without something that it cannot think or pay heed to: the community of nature that *cannot appear as such.* The truth of the tradition would be constituted in its definitive moments of exclusion and forgetting that generate its apparent unity and coherence. And, moreover, this constitutive forgetting, in order to succeed, above all would have to forget itself, would have to cover over and transform the very occurrence of its own transformation. To speak of the occurrence of philosophy in this way, as a tradition constituting itself in the necessity of a concealment, means precisely that the fact of the concealment itself must withdraw, must be held under, must be allowed to refuse itself, so that the operation of philosophical thought can be enabled, can enable itself. Thought in this way, the philosophical tradition defines itself and can continue in its self-appropriation—repeating itself *as itself*—only within this self-concealing concealment that continues to shelter it from its inevitable dispersion and non-recuperation, sheltering it even from this inevitability itself. We are thus returned to a tragic insight concerning the ineluctable shattering of individuated finite being, but thereby we also attain a different relation to the limit, to the opacity and the loss with which this discussion began. The concealment, in its necessity, as it inheres in the site of thinking, also gives rise to thinking—which is to say, that to think the concealment at issue here is always to think *from* it, within it, as it.

We find ourselves philosophizing within and as such a tradition. But this point allows us to reformulate the (traditional) question that concerns whether it is possible at all to think the Socratic event in its upsurgence, which is to say, not only in terms of what it has produced or claims to have produced, not only in a complacency that accepts what comes to be attributed to the event—that is, *retrospectively*—but rather by also experiencing that out of which it has arisen. To affirm that the "arising" of the Socratic tradition, taken as Western philosophy, occurs only in this necessity of concealment, thought rigorously as a self-concealing concealment, is already to think such an arising *in the descent,* in the withdrawal of the origin. The descent, therefore, no longer descends from a pure origin, as both the sense of the origin itself and the sense of how this origin is related to what originates from it undergo a complete transformation. We still have to consider without compromise the unsettling effects of this paradoxical reversal, as it destabilizes the order of image and original, in which the image appears as though it constitutes its own origin, as if what would be first arises only with its second. The premise of such an undertaking, however, is that Socrates in this sense is *still* making his descent, a descent which even today claims us, in which not only do we too continue to participate, but which also dominates in advance our possible ways of acting and thinking, precisely as these would be responsive to our historical situation.[14]

Given the severity of this premise, the encompassing character of the departure through which this study finds its orientation, the existing norms of historical research prove here to be of little help in addressing the descent as such. The difficulty I wish to address remains irreducible to the tendency to privilege contemporary views or to employ anachronistic standards in interpretation. It does not allow itself to be alleviated simply through a more exacting philology, nor can it be overcome through preventive measures that would sort out and untangle the web of historical influences and lineages, in order thereby to save us from the application of inappropriate concepts and distinctions. Accordingly, this book is to be regarded not so much as an exercise in scholarship as an attempt at opening up the future for the experience of the descent. Seeking to account for the "philosophical position" of the so-called historical Socrates, by compiling, for example, an exhaustive catalogue of his alleged questions, methodologies, and claims, because it occurs merely at the level of doxography, will always have to remain at a distance from the more difficult task of first achieving a philosophical engagement with his practice in the sense just introduced.[15] And it is obvious that the continuing preoccupation with the relative certainty of what we can know or not know about the views reportedly held by Socrates should not be confused with being challenged or even claimed by his word and deed. One might wonder, then, whether the historiographical project of modern scholarship, insofar as it seeks primarily to *reconstruct* and thereby to recover some kind of Socratic dogma or practice, can be said to have taken us any closer to the possibility of such an engagement, or whether such a project has not actually obstructed the way to such a possibility. Nevertheless, there can be no question that an attempted renewal of this possibility means taking up, once again, the Platonic dialogues. Where else, if not first of all in the reading of Plato, is there a chance of encountering a Socrates who might still address us, who might still speak to our historical situation, whether we take ourselves to be moderns or postmoderns?[16]

Yet to turn to Plato and to offer him as the interpretive key to Socrates may appear to some as a diversion: in order to answer one question we now revert to another. One might just as readily approach from the other direction and claim that it is necessary to unravel the Platonic text through the figure of Socrates. And yet, while it is no more possible to reduce Socrates to Plato than Plato to Socrates, what is decisive is the inevitability that in meeting one of them the other is bound to show up. Like the pleasure and pain of Socrates' Aesopian fantasy,[17] they belong together, thoroughly intertwined but in an elusive difference. Emerson's comment that "Socrates and Plato are the double star which the most powerful instruments will not entirely separate"[18] implies a correlate, which is that the *difference* between them shall also never be collapsed or abolished. But if the renewal of the question of Socrates begins only in the clarification of this subtle difference, confirming an intimate bond, the indissociability of these two figures—Socrates appearing within Plato, bound to Plato yet not subsumed by him—then the question of Socrates compels us to raise again the question of how to engage Plato precisely as an author, an engagement that is always determined in advance by the way in which, on the one hand, one relates this author to his work and by the way in which, on the other hand, one conceives of the very *working* of this work, its possible actuality and presence, its way of enacting meaning and truth. How is it that we designate these "Socratic conversations" as *Platonic,* that we attribute them to Plato?[19] In what sense do they belong to him?

Because access to Socrates is already thoroughly configured by one's interpretive approach to Plato, it is all the more necessary to assess what I have just articulated as the double movement of *tradition*—as a generosity that harbors loss, as a transmission that succeeds only by betraying itself, as an appearing that appears only in a prior concealment—precisely as this double movement establishes and is established by the "community" of Socrates and Plato, their friendship or filiation. But to think or to experience the descent of Socrates as it occurs in and through Plato's text is a possibility that proves to have far-reaching and drastic implications for what is usually referred to as the *mimetic* reading of Plato, to which I am mostly sympathetic. The basic assumption of this way of reading can be briefly introduced by stating, quite simply, that Platonic writing imitates a Socratic conversation and in doing so invites or compels the reader to become involved as a participant in that conversation.[20] It is supposed that there is an intrinsic connection between the dialogue form of the text and Socratic philosophical practice, since neither transmits in a direct way a dogmatic content. Rather, both engage whoever meets them, whether as interlocutor or as reader, in a way that leads that participant to assume an utterly individuated responsibility in the encounter. The experience of the reader is thus mirrored in the reading of the experience of the interlocutor. But my contention is that the descent of Socrates takes place as an imitation that does not open up an original except insofar as this original must also be derived from the mimetic movement itself—which is to say, in a decisive sense the origin remains concealed. Thus, to claim that Plato's dialogues expose us to the "truth" of Socrates by virtue of their way of *miming* his presence is already to bypass the strange difficulty I have been making thematic, namely, that *there is no Socrates independent of this mimetic operation.* Can an imitation produce what it is to imitate? The question turns on deciding whether or how Socrates is to be located and contained simply within the Platonic imitation, such that his presence can be fixed and determined within its own proper limits, checked but thereby also freed through the horizon established by Platonic writing. How, in other words, does the Platonic text sustain within itself the difference between Plato and Socrates?

The simplicity of the thought indicates its extreme difficulty: in reading Plato and meeting "his" Socrates we are asked to attend thoughtfully to the manifesting of the strange, while letting it be neither assimilated to the order of the same nor posited over and against it, simply detached from it, as wholly other. Thus, I shall have recourse at this point to speaking of the "placeless place" of Socrates within the Platonic text by taking up the way in which he is thematized or situated as out of place, placed as lacking place, being even ἀτοπώτατος, most out of place or most without place.[21] What is distinctly tragic about this Socratic ἀτοπία becomes more clear if one considers that to speak in this context of his "placeless place" is to point not to a mere contradiction, but rather to a *doubling* that asserts itself as a necessity in the way humans "belong" to nature.

To take seriously this line of interpretation leads to a different sense of the question of a Socratic "identity," since such identity can be opened up only in the paradox of being claimed by an impossibility, of living within it. I wish to elaborate this way of being claimed, by referring to it as a good, but also more precisely as a *tragic* or Silenic good, which is to say, a good that is imposed upon human life in its inexorability and refusal. The paradox of this necessary impossibility, that precisely *as* impossible it cannot be eluded, provides us with a way to think the peculiarly erotic character of Socrates, in which, I am suggesting, he is determined as an *ecstatically* engaged questioning, a questioning that questions itself only by going beyond itself.

The spell of Socrates, his narcotic effect, is the experience of this necessity of belonging while deprived of place, the experience that we are inescapably earthbound, embodied, and grounded (descensional), but thereby also monstrously perverse, appearing even as an assault upon the heavens. The tragic doubling or twisting that becomes manifest with this figure—in the drama that leads up to and surrounds his death—does not merely expose the contradiction of his presumed "identity," long sought after by historiographers. Rather, such doubling, if allowed its originary movement, utterly deprives thinking of the previously assumed primacy of identity, exposing this identity (or selfhood) to a movement in which it proves to be first derived from the doubling, or founded upon it, grounded in it.

The Socratic imperative of taking up oneself as a task thus arises only in the affirmation of an original and necessary ignorance that nonetheless returns to itself as nature, grounded in the nature that it also is. The task of self-knowledge proves in this way to be a possibility that arises only in the doubling, confirming itself as claimed by nature and yet at a remove from it, at a loss before it. This task thus cannot be separated from the peculiar and emphatic ignorance that gives it its urgency. Such emphatic ignorance, sustained only in the doubling, does not consist in a mere lack, but is precisely what distinguishes Socratic "wisdom" as such. And this wise ignorance has a peculiar strangeness about it: it is characterized as both utterly *human* and yet, precisely for this reason, also exceptional and singular.[22] As a paradigm for human life, Socrates remains outside, the strangest of strangers because he belongs. His provocative dialogical practice proves to exemplify in this way the strangeness of the human world in its most natural belonging. This strange figure is thus a figure of transgression, but only because his transgressive ἔρως—enacted as a philosophical practice— becomes the utter confirmation of a limit. Socratic practice neither rejects nor accepts this limit, as the confirmation of a human nature, but rather through him the relation to the limit undergoes a doubling.

In this way, however, the status of Platonic authority also undergoes a transformation in encountering the strangeness of Socrates. This transformation or subversion of the authority of Platonism, considered formally, takes place through the unleashing of a basic hermeneutic principle: the text should not be protected from what it makes manifest in the course of its movement; what shows itself—in its way of showing itself—should be allowed to bear upon the assumptions that would be brought to the text. This is only to affirm that the text should be read, as far as possible, on its own terms. Yet here such a traditional principle of hermeneutics does not serve primarily to reinforce the author's patriarchy or paternity. The figure of Socrates, in other words, in his way of becoming manifest in Plato, also thwarts or undermines our naive sense of Platonic *writing,* which is to say, it unhinges the *mastery* of that writing with regard to itself and with regard to what it would address. My reading is thus concerned with taking up the peculiar way in which the Platonic text is able to make manifest (or to let become manifest) an urgency or a movement that proves to be excessive or prior to its own production and mastery, as Socrates surpasses or resists what otherwise is to be taken as simply the effects of the author's making, his poetic production, his ποίησις. This is only to say that it is a matter of experiencing the descensional event of Socrates as Plato's ownmost dispossession, the expropriating movement of his own text.

If the appearance of Socrates is to be taken as Plato's ownmost difficulty, then attending to this appearance in this way becomes a matter of not reducing Socrates to the means by which Plato expresses himself, by which he comes to express or convey his own views, his own proper thought. Plato too has to be caught up in the descent he imitates. But why is it so easy to assume that Plato is only making use of his beloved Socrates, only resurrecting him in order to put him to work in the text? This assumption relies in the first place upon the distinction between truth and fiction as an unproblematic opposition. There is no question that this distinction, along with a presumed Platonic mastery over it, operates within most readings with a kind of privileged and unquestionable status: Plato may indeed borrow from the actual Socrates, may be indebted to his former teacher in certain ways, but the Socrates we encounter in the dialogues is for the most part a Platonic invention, a product of fantasy. The assumption prevails that Plato is the final master of his text, the one who orchestrates its dramatic unfolding and who in the end must take responsibility for every-thing that appears there.

It is clear that the interpretation that proceeds in this way, as it takes the distinction between truth and fiction for granted, must also close itself off to the prior philosophical question that concerns Plato's relation to his own thinking, his own self-relation. And, in fact, it is also clear that this foreclo-sure takes place in a way that is at odds with the text, since it simply by-passes the difficulty of this question as it is actually raised and sustained in the text. What is called for here, then, is a reading that would be able to hold in abeyance our sense of our ownership of the words that we write, read, speak, and hear, which is to say, our sense of the origin of the words them-selves, and the way in which what is at issue in words becomes manifest through them. One can cling to this sense of Plato's authority, his mastery over the λόγος, in other words, only by neglecting at the same time the most decisive feature of Socratic practice, namely by refusing to let the necessity of the "second sailing" recoil on that very authority and mastery. Socrates tells us that this second sailing, as the necessary recourse to another way of proceeding, and as the interruption of an initial way, arises in response to a grave danger, a kind of blindness that he also speaks of as the sickness of misology. There is no greater evil, we are told (Phaedo 89d). I see the neces-sity of this turn to speeches, as it is thematized and recounted in the *Phaedo,* as inseparable from the emergence of the dialogical practice that is peculiar to Socrates, in which one's presumed ownership of the word must be given over to a questioning movement with another. It is important to note that the danger of misology is elaborated by Socrates through the dif-ficulty of sustaining friendship, as if to say that our relation to the word is already bound to our relation to each other. Thus, to situate Platonic au-thority outside this same necessity is already to remove it from its own philosophical difficulty; and, at the same time, it also effectively shelters the reader from the dialogical character of the text and from the dispossession such dialogical movement entails. Dialogical thinking is thus left behind in this prevailing interpretation, precisely because such an interpretation must first begin with the prior unity of Plato's own willful thought, so as to dis-cover that thought as it deploys itself throughout the text, the same thought that has simply been posited by the interpretation in advance.[23]

Even if today there is at last a consensus building among scholars around the question of Platonic "anonymity," in which it is affirmed that no single character within the dialogues can be assumed to be speaking for Plato—namely, as a kind of ventriloquized mouthpiece expressing some-thing like his sincere or considered opinion, the loudspeaker that perhaps amplifies and enhances Plato's original voice[24]—what emerges at this point is still the more fundamental difficulty that concerns how one is then to receive and respond to the manifold characters that appear within these di-alogical dramas as they address and engage one another. The decisive point here cannot simply turn on the shallow but undeniable fact that Plato does not speak within the dialogues, which is to say, *in his own name,* since this is almost too obvious to bear repeating: Plato is *almost* entirely absent as a character. But it is also the case that his absence within his own text is not at all a pure absence, precisely because the absence itself comes to presence; the absence as such is made thematic, takes place in such a way that one cannot overlook it.

Strictly speaking, Plato appears in his *Phaedo* at the death scene of Socrates—thus, in the same dialogue in which Socrates most explicitly addresses the danger of misology and the necessity of the second sailing—appearing, however, as one who does *not* appear, as one whose appearance is said to be withheld or refused through his own sickness. Plato thus appears as a figure holding a place within the dramatic world of his text, but only at its margins, barely visible, visible enough to be *not* seen. This most liminal visibility is in fact enhanced by the tentativeness with which Phaedo makes the remark, issuing it almost as an afterthought. It is as if, in a dialogue that begins by stressing the importance of one's presence to the fatal event in question, present as oneself, as the αὐτός that one is, the question of Plato's own presence could not be less important.[25] But this only has the effect of making the remark—the fact that the remark is made at all—all the more impressive. Πλάτων δέ οἶμαι ἠσθένει (Phaedo 59b). All that Phaedo says to Echecrates in passing is that he believes that Plato had fallen ill, was taken over by a lack of strength, deprived of σθένος. No details are given *about* this utterly determinant weakness or sickness, as it is recollected by Phaedo years later, and as it is alleged to hold Plato back from entering into his own text at its greatest sublimity, namely, in the imminence of Socrates' departure. The sickness is marked only as a principle of refusal: Plato is present enough only to have his absence announced and confirmed in a certain obscure necessity.

It should be recognized, therefore, that the reasonable tendency to speak of Plato's "choice" at this point, to assert his authorial decision to withhold himself from his own text and to remain silent, as if he were thereby the master over what does and does not transpire here, is tantamount to claiming that he *chooses* his sickness, that his own absence is not imposed upon him (as the text tells us) but is rather merely an effect of his production, an extension of his own designs. The absence and what necessitates it, in other words, is regarded not as a *pathos*, as something endured and undergone, but as a mere literary device.

It is all the more striking, therefore, that the traditional interpretation of this passage takes it only to confirm Plato's mastery of his text. Through an inference that derives a Platonic motive from Phaedo's words, Plato is heard to make a declaration about the character of his work and his relation to it. The passage is thus typically read as Plato's way of confirming the merely "fictional" status of the dialogue Phaedo will narrate, a point that can lead equally to a variety of further conclusions, namely, that Plato was actually not present at the death, that he was present, or that one is able to draw no conclusion at all from the passage concerning his actual presence. Others have taken the passage as Plato's way of conveying his grief, his anger, or even his fear over Socrates' death. This lack of consensus as to the import of Phaedo's remark is telling in itself. But even to state that Plato "designedly" leaves us to battle over these possible conclusions[26] already mitigates the force of the statement, as it accounts for Plato's absence in explicitly dramatic terms. Thus, if one is compelled to read the passage as indicative somehow of Platonic intent and design, such a reading would still need to consider this dramatic content itself, precisely as Phaedo attributes Plato's absence to a suffering, to an occurrence that first of all reminds us of the fragility and precariousness of human designs. Plato speaks to us as he presents the death of Socrates, saying at the same time that he lacks the strength to speak to us as he presents the death of Socrates.

Similarly, what is most striking about Plato's presence in the *Apology*—noted and made explicit by Socrates on two occasions (Apol. 34a, 38b)—is the way in which it lets a certain silence reverberate throughout the dialogues. The fact that he does show, however briefly, but again at a most decisive juncture, yet only to keep his silence, points once more to a character who *might* have spoken, just as the thematic regard for his absence in the *Phaedo* puts into relief the denial of a presence that is otherwise possible. It is thus extraordinary that the second passage in the *Apology* where Plato is mentioned by name (Apol. 38b) does, in a way, have Socrates speaking for Plato, but again only in order to confirm that such a speech could have occurred but does not. Here Socrates relays the Platonic desire that Socrates should preemptively minimize his punishment at the hands of the city by proposing a more substantial monetary fine, the payment that Socrates says is guaranteed by Plato and others. Socrates complies with this wish, although it alters neither the outcome of the trial nor the punishment inflicted upon Socrates.

The one time we can be sure that Plato does convey something to us—doing so even through the mouth of Socrates, although only through that mouth—what is revealed is precisely a desire that cannot be fulfilled, the desire to save Socrates, to ward off his death. Such a desire as it becomes apparent in the *Apology* returns us directly to the *Phaedo*, as Socrates undertakes another defense of his practice, by responding to his friends' frustration over his apparent eagerness to die (Phaedo 63a–b). We have to conclude that Plato too must be subjected to this same conflict, left unresolved by the text, but also rigorously enforced as unresolved, necessarily unresolved. This is confirmed by the dialogical and dramatic tension of the *Phaedo,* which asks us to consider that the Socratic affirmation of death would be undermined through misology. The second sailing, as a turn to the disclosive movement of speeches, is also to be regarded as a philosophical affirmation of human mortality.

Platonic speech is thus itself a strange speech, infected by the strangeness of Socrates, since it speaks only in order to enforce its own silence, to make apparent the necessity of that silence. It thus becomes possible to *hear* the silence of Plato, as his own text announces that silence. But have we therefore grasped the conditions of this silence? Do we know how it comes to be imposed upon him and thus upon us? Are we able to question the ground of this necessity? Achieving a perspective on what establishes the impossibility of this speech presupposes being able to question such a ground, for in no other way can it appear as a decision, as something contingent. Indeed, what makes the conspicuous silence of Plato *as a character* particularly important is that he is also the author of the text, that the Plato who appears as non-appearing within the text, this one who speaks through his silence, bears the *same name* as the one who signs the text.[27] His silence as a character, then, decisively transforms his silence as author, since this author is no longer simply outside his own text but has been written into it, however obscurely and elusively.

It is impossible to overstate the effects of such a transformation, since this peculiar character of Platonic sigetics is precisely what allows for the tragic appearance of Socrates himself: only within the space opened up by and preserved within this Platonic silence—a space that is opened up explicitly *as preserved* by the author's own withdrawal—does Socrates speak and act *in his own name*. The descent of Socrates thus begins in and as a Platonic writing. And the belonging together of Plato and Socrates, as a belonging together in an essential difference, turns on a decisive non-reciprocity between them: each has a different way of being absent (or silent), and thus of being present in such absence, speaking through silence: the non-writing of Socrates (and his death) gives Plato to himself as author, who then in turn speaks to us through his peculiar silence, a silence that gives Socrates his voice. The death of the author (Plato) becomes the life of Socrates, the death of Socrates becomes the life of Plato. Plato writes only (in) the descent.

I am thus pointing to what I take to be an irreducible difficulty, irreducible, that is, to the need to decide whether and how Plato is speaking or not, irreducible to whether he speaks in another's name (for instance, *as* Socrates) or does not speak at all. Instead, here it is a matter of simply grasping that his speaking finds itself both limited *and established* in and through the encounter with Socrates, in a dialogical "friendship" that displaces Platonic authority. My contention is that the tradition that begins with Plato and Socrates constitutes itself only in this original conflict in which each gives the other to be, precisely through a decisive restriction and obscuring. This conflict occurs as a dialogical exchange between writing and speech (life and death), in which the speech of Socrates interrupts the alleged autonomy of Platonic writing. This is an especially important point because the conspicuous absence of Plato as a *speaking* character—an absence made explicit in the text as absence—is almost always readily converted by the reader into his pervasive presence as author. One thus contends with his towering and commanding presence as a figure in the history of philosophy. In his silence he survives as a "superspeaker."[28] His anonymity gives way to the entire text being read as a signature.[29] The alleged 'death of the author' becomes the pretense for preserving in an insidious way the text as the transcendental field of the author's creative and godly genius.[30] Plato becomes even the name for the origin of Western philosophy.[31]

While there is widespread disagreement concerning what Plato is up to by having Socrates state what he states, and thus little or no consensus concerning what Plato means to convey through his dialogical dramas, the tradition, as it arises (or descends) from Socrates and Plato, is nevertheless obsessed with discerning just what it is that Plato is up to and what he would convey. Few readers have been able to question their attachment to this sense of the propriety of thought that is taken to ground the genuine authorship of the text, precisely as that thought would assert itself and hold sway throughout the dialogues, governing by design what comes to be manifest in them.[32] This means that even if we can get past the childish dispute over whether Plato has to "mean" what Socrates states—since it is clear enough that Socrates himself does not always, if ever, "mean" what he states[33]—we are still caught within the assumption that Plato does mean without question to have Socrates state what he states, just as it is assumed that, if Socrates speaks with irony, we are to understand that he does so "intentionally."

There is no doubt that the task of reading Plato continues to be defined primarily in terms of this possibility of *understanding* him. Plato is still taken as the name for a transcendence that can gather together the meaning of the text, even if the sense of this meaning is granted an extreme elasticity. From this point of view, it makes little difference whether what is to be understood is approached dogmatically, namely, as something *asserted*, as a position or doctrine to be decoded and deciphered propositionally, or whether what is to be understood is articulated instead as a kind of "literary" purpose that is thought to be peculiar to the dialogues as a textual genre. The reading that begins by insisting that the dialogues must be read as "literature" begins inevitably by also taking for granted the difference between literature and philosophy.[34] What is to be noted is that this very difference will always remain a philosophical determination, in which the literary can be sustained *as such* only if this philosophical determination is allowed to be reinscribed upon it. The "literary" reading of Plato proceeds only by having recourse to philosophical determinations, the origins of which take us back to Plato's text, and to words spoken by Socrates within that text. To speak of philosophy as if it were governed by literature, drama, or poetry, and to seek thereby to grant a simple priority to this literary horizon—the supposed primacy of myth—only confirms a dependency upon this pervasive philosophical conceptuality.[35] To insist that the "content" of the dialogues remains inseparable from their form and performativity is only to insist that the distinction between form and content must be accepted in advance.[36] Every reading of Plato begins in this situation: to read Plato is already, whether knowingly or not, to make a *philosophical* decision about the text.

At the risk of redundancy, let me articulate the difficulty once again as succinctly as possible. On the one hand, the project that would take upon itself the detective work of tracking down and rooting out the so-called historical Socrates—even if this project concludes by abandoning its own task and by consigning this figure to historical oblivion, while still positing in this oblivion an actuality, a kind of *in-itself*—can be carried out only if it remains originally caught in the grips of a Platonizing metaphysics. On the other hand, those who would simply assert the independence and autonomy of the Platonic word and thought over and against, or beyond, the appearance of Socrates can do so only by too readily disregarding the dialogical, dramatic, and mythic features of Plato's text, features that thus irrevocably divest Plato's voice of its own authority. What this means is that the metaphysical reading of Plato (whether doctrinal or not) and the problem of the historical Socrates can be confronted only when they are taken as correlates, as projects that imply and demand each other in a certain conspiracy of interpretations and assumptions. Either one accepts the difficulty of this hermeneutic circle or one blithely continues to bring assumptions to a text that have been derived from it.[37]

In order to interrupt the urgency of these projects, as they are wholly complicitous with the metaphysical tradition that begins with the rise of Platonism—in the descent of Socrates—Socrates and Plato must be allowed to speak *to each other* through a certain difference that has yet to be established, in which it would be possible for Socrates to appear as neither a literary device nor simply a means of communication. It is no exaggeration to say that Socrates, for whose sake Plato is said to have burned his own youthful tragic poems,[38] appears as the utterly decisive provocation on every page of the Platonic corpus.[39] There is no question that Plato "chooses" not only to include Socrates in his written dialogues, but rather to make him their central figure—*the very same* ugly old man, the same intractable and outlandish snub-nosed, exophthalmic, barefooted seducer of youths he knew. But is this fact not rendered harmless, and perhaps even irrelevant, once the dialogues are designated as fictions? Do we understand what this designation entails? The difficulty here in one sense concerns simply what is at stake in this name, "Socrates," as it appears as the *same* name throughout Plato's text. The appearance of this Socrates, as the same, means that the interpretation of Socrates in Plato will always have to involve questions that simply do not arise when one turns to what are taken as more fictional figures within the dialogues.[40]

I have stated that as a *mimetic* enactment of Socrates, the Platonic text alters the very sense of the fictive, because it transforms and enables what would be its own history and tradition, already engaging its own possible ways of being received.[41] We encounter here a work that determines the very conditions of its reading, that thus bears upon the measure of its own "truth." But once it is acknowledged that such a work is no longer simply a fiction—that it is already straining, even to the point of collapse, the strict opposition between the true and fictive, the literal and figurative—we are at a loss as to how to proceed. If we are to read Plato's work as it takes place in the descent of Socrates, the text must be liberated from the obsessions of historiography. But how, then, does such a different way of reading bear upon the uniquely historical character of philosophical questioning?

I would like to take a moment to consider how this question—as it concerns the difference between poetry, history, and philosophy—is already anticipated by Aristotle, in order to point out how this Aristotelian tradition continues to lay its claim upon modern readings of Plato. In his *Poetics* Aristotle states that it is not insignificant if the characters in a story, the figures who appear in a μῦθος, are recognized as having actually existed. What is at issue in such a case, according to Aristotle, is the use of *names,* the way names are invoked. While it is not an indispensable feature of tragedy, tragic poets, unlike the composers of comedies, "cling to actual names" (Poetics 1451b15–16). What Aristotle says in this passage is that they do this because only what is possible is *persuasive,* and what has come to be has already proven its possibility. The name of the actual is a guarantee of possibility, and possibility is an indispensable feature of persuasion. But one might then want to suppose also that the cathartic operation of tragedy, which hangs on its persuasiveness, would demand that it be attached to an irreplaceable singularity, the singularity and irreversibility that would be taken as history itself. The undoing of an individual, the *downgoing* of one who struggles courageously against necessity, if it is to be experienced in a way that would be *ethically* transformative, which arguably is the implicit goal of tragedy,[42] might seem to arise only through the presentation of something that is irreducible to the merely formal and that does not permit any substitution. And yet, this is precisely what Aristotle does not or cannot allow. We are told that it should be enough only to *hear* of the beautiful and noble *actions* that lead to destruction in order to experience the fear and pity of catharsis. And for this reason Aristotle is also able to say that it is not at all necessary for such things to have actually happened. Not the individual it portrays but that it imitates actions *of certain sort,* this is what is essential to tragic poetry. And what is decisive in these actions is thus not the singular one who suffers—not the awakening to an irreversible facticity—but rather the universal or the general that becomes thereby manifest, what is καθόλου, according to the whole.

Accordingly, Aristotle can claim that (tragic) poetry remains *more philosophical* and is therefore *superior to history* precisely because it is concerned not with the merely factical, namely, with what has actually come to be, but with the possible according to what is likely and with the necessary. "They [history and poetry] differ in that one speaks of what has come to be while the other speaks of what sort would come to be" (1451b4–5). While poetry is certainly not yet philosophy, not yet the philosophical λόγος, the distinction between poetry and history also must be rigorously upheld. This distinction would emphasize the superior status of the *poetic* operation, above mere history, because it is the operation through which *the most persuasive* stories can come to be, as it is not constrained by the merely actual but unfolds according to the likely and the necessary. From this we might conclude, then, that philosophy would be best suited to receive tragic poetry, since it is the philosopher who is best prepared to grasp what is καθόλου as it is at issue in the tragic. And yet, at this point it might also be helpful to recall how the *Ethics* makes clear again and again that action as such always concerns the singular; and on this basis Aristotle points out repeatedly that it is necessary to contend with an inevitable *imprecision* or lack of clarity in any λόγος that has as its own end right action or acting well. An ethical λόγος thus addresses something that, as singular, always must elude it. But if it is then assumed that poetry, like the ethical λόγος, also remains oriented toward the good, although in its own distinctive way, how then can poetry be persuasive by seeking to address what is general?

The use of the proper name, according to this passage in the *Poetics*, does not pertain to the individual as a singularity at all, as an irreplaceable occurrence. It is as if the proper name would belong to nobody because it must pertain to everybody. This is what the tragedians are talking about when they present Oedipus and Antigone, Iphigenia and Orestes. Aristotle says: "The general [καθόλου], that it falls to a certain sort of human [τῷ ποίῳ] to say or do certain sorts of things [τὰ ποῖα] according to the likely or the necessary [κατὰ τὸ εἰκὸς ἢ τὸ ἀναγκαῖον], is what poetry aims at in attaching names" (1451b8–10).[43] We could say that the names of those portrayed in the tragic do not, according to Aristotle, return us to the actual μίασμα in our midst, the bloody stain that has soaked the earth, the same earth that now nevertheless sustains life. Tragedy does not arise as an original expression of chthonic necessity and non-substitution, but soars to the heights of universality, detached from the irrevocable and the singular. And even though the tragedians cling to the actual, and tend to speak by name of those who actually have been, Aristotle allows himself to admonish the poets, to comment upon their excessive preoccupation with the stories and names of tradition. Writing at a time when the great tragedies of Sophocles and Aeschylus had already become a thing of the past, and thus at a time when tragedy had already met its end, Aristotle seems to speak as if the improved future of tragic poetry is still awaiting its arrival, as he offers what appears to be a kind of prescription for its more essential composition: "One ought not to seek to cling completely to the stories that have been handed down concerning those whom tragedies are about" (1451b23–25).

Aristotle, who is himself fond of taking Socrates as an example, and thus of using his name, especially when it is a matter of providing an effective analogue to the movement of nature in human life,[44] could thus be taken here to be making a strong claim, even if only indirectly and implicitly, about what would be at issue in a distinctly *philosophical* reading of the Platonic text, since that text also offers, on his own terms, a poetic presentation of the story of Socrates. According to such an Aristotelian hermeneutics, the Platonic dialogues would be persuasive not because Socrates actually came to be, because of the actual deed of his life. Whether the dialogues are to be taken as poetry, or as philosophy, at bottom it makes no difference. It seems that Aristotle would have to tell us the same thing, that what is at issue in these philosophical dramas is precisely the universal, not the singularly exceptional Socrates of history, and thus not the tragedy of that singularity, in and as singularity.

By insisting in this way that the effect of tragic catharsis not depend upon the actual at all, that it be removed thereby from what is most elusive, namely this sense of the singular, it may be that Aristotle wants to free poetry from the truthmongers and moralists who would demand of poetry that it lower itself to the standard of mere correctness and historiography. The *lying* poet had already been cleverly defended by the sophist Gorgias, on the grounds that tragedy is a form of persuasion and that persuasion depends upon deception. Paradoxically, Gorgias could conclude, in a way befitting a sophist, that the deceptive poet is *more just* than the poet who does not deceive at all.[45] Aristotle himself, however, is not far from this same position. Because he also sees the transformative persuasion that tragedy is able to enact, he recognizes the role it plays in ethical and political life. Nevertheless, one has to wonder whether defending poetry in this way, as Aristotle himself does, through what are said to be its *philosophical* virtues—as a discourse not of the particular but of the universal, detached from the actual—can succeed in preserving precisely what is tragic and poetic about tragic poetry. In Aristotle's time it may be that philosophy and poetry come to lose a certain relation to the singular and the actual, as these must be abandoned or handed over to a new sense of history. Indeed, if one sets Herodotus alongside Thucydides, what could be more blatant than that the sense of truth that is at stake in historical inquiry—history (ἱστορία) as inquiry itself—also undergoes a profound shift?[46]

But if the tragic finds itself no longer able to express the utterly singular, because such singularity is already opposed to what is καθόλου, perhaps this only confirms the death of tragedy. It thus may be that the loss of the singular is itself the loss of the tragic, if, that is, the tragic can be said to begin precisely in the ruin of the imitable or even in *the ruin of imitation as such*, with the manifestation of what refuses or breaks down the very possibility of imitation.[47] Thus, another way to speak of the tragic strangeness of Socrates, his uncanny placeless place, is to state that he appears within the Platonic text by interrupting his own imitation, that he is not simply inimitable, but rather that he enforces through his appearance the necessity of an imitation precisely as it shatters on its own impossibility. And yet, if the philosophical λόγος as it is appropriated by Aristotle comes to assert itself as the knowledge of what is καθόλου, if knowledge thus concerns only the universal—as a logic of infinite substitutability, grounded in an eidetic purity—then tragic poetry would on this account also expose the very limits of philosophy, by making manifest, in a way peculiar to it, the loss of the singular, the impossibility that the singular as such be addressed in the λόγος. But then the choice between history, on the one hand, and the conceptual clarity of what is καθόλου, on the other, already precludes or conceals this other sense of the tragic, just as it also precludes or conceals another sense of philosophical questioning. The attempt to save tragic poetry in this way, as Aristotle does, by deciding in favor of its philosophical merits, *the very fact that such a saving is deemed necessary*, becomes itself only a sign of the concealment or loss that occurs with the decline and death of tragedy and the tragic. And while it cannot be taken up here, this also prompts another question about whether *on these terms* Aristotle would be able to concede to poetry (or philosophy, for that matter) a formative or transformative role precisely in the historical, not simply understood as the alleged record of what has been but also and more decisively as the relation to the possible. Placed above or beyond what has been, through the separation of the possible from the factical and actual, it would seem that poetry already must find itself cut off from its own *life*.

Aristotle's discussion of what is at issue in the *names* invoked by the tragic poets thus reveals in an exemplary way how the difficulty of placing Socrates within Plato is already posed within the limits of a metaphysical history. The possibilities for interpretation are already established as alternatives that appear as oppositional terms defined in relation to each other. That Aristotle interprets the poetic use of names—the invoking of the names of those who have lived and accomplished deeds—by likening tragic poetry to philosophical discourse, a discourse he thereby opposes to history and historical actuality, raises the question as to whether poetry does not in this way find itself violently assimilated to the measure of conceptual universality. One already discerns here, perhaps, that the μῦθος of tragedy functions merely as an allegory for a properly philosophical truth, a truth that cannot but be said καθόλου and in a λόγος of pure propriety.⁴⁸ But what then to make of the invocation of the proper name within philosophical discourse itself? There can be no question that philosophy also makes use of historical actuality in order to be persuasive. The *endoxic* beginning of dialectical inquiry, as it affirms things more knowable "to us," must have recourse to the tradition that passes down and preserves a reliable and trustworthy relation to the truth precisely in the λόγος put forward by those held to be wise. Accordingly, it is the authority of commonly held opinion, vouchsafed by the reputation of the wise and the good, that grounds the possibility of philosophy as such. But if this *authoritarian* moment presents an indispensable feature of dialectical inquiry, such an inquiry is also no less a *questioning* that puts this authority into question precisely by allowing it to question itself on its own terms. Philosophy thus always remains the voice of commonly held opinion, even the authority of tradition, but only as it continues to demand the merciless interrogation of its own λόγος. In other words, a tradition can free itself for its own movement only by turning on itself, in a kind of betrayal. The authority of a doctrinal lineage, precisely as it descends from the names of the wise, finds itself recoiling upon its own assertions, and thereby opening up the truth that must appear as *paradox* and *aporia*.

In this context it becomes possible to hear in a different register the famous but puzzling remark in the *Second Letter*, where Plato seems to disavow all ownership of the things said in the dialogues, stating that what is found there instead belongs to a transformed Socrates, which is to say, to the *same* Socrates, but also one having become different, other. What Plato states is that the texts that bear the name Plato are in fact not his, not written by him: "There is not nor will there ever be a writing [σύγγραμμα] by Plato, but those which now bear his name belong to a Socrates become beautiful and young" (L2 314c). This remark, and the passage in which it appears, is frequently introduced along with a related passage found in the *Seventh Letter* as a way to suspend the appropriation of the dogmatic content in the dialogues.⁴⁹ The appeal to this remark in this way, however, should not lead to the neglect of what is especially puzzling about it, namely, that it does not at all amount to a simple disavowal or disowning of the text. Instead, only as it sustains the very authority of the author does the remark also question the sense of what it means to write. Here the very divesting of Platonic ownership and authority also underscores the operation itself that enacts a repetition and that therefore stands apart from what it would only repeat. What is at issue here, again, is the very sense of one's relation to the λόγος, to the origin of that λόγος, the possible mastery over things said or written in the original doubling of dialogue: in merely *repeating* another, I come to speak for that other, but also that other comes to speak for me, through me. The texts, which are written by Plato, because they do bear his name, in one sense still have to be regarded as his, cannot but be called Plato's. Is it not Plato himself who, as author, detaches himself here from his writings—attempting to do so even in and through writing—disowning them as if they were only errant little bastards, the illegitimate offspring of his proper genius? But they must be disowned precisely because they will also always belong to him, to that one corpus bearing his signature. This is the reason for the need to make clear how these same texts that belong together also belong to another, one who is supposedly *not* Plato, namely, a certain Socrates. Yet this other, proposed now as the true author, is also not simply or completely himself; the Socrates who thus writes for Plato, or through Plato, also comes to be transformed or translated, through this descent into the writing that Plato himself enacts or *mimes* on behalf of this other, who now, as the *same* Socrates, becomes other than himself, becomes beautiful and new.

It is, of course, a perfect irony of history that this text has at times been disputed as spurious. What is debated is the ownership of a text in which it is stated that there is no Platonic writing. And yet, it also has to be acknowledged that the very text which would seem to disable and suspend Platonic authority and ownership makes the Platonic effect upon Socrates all the more unmistakable and decisive. Have we become even remotely capable of comprehending the stakes of such a translation, the community that both would bind Socrates and Plato together and yet at once also hold them apart? Are we to understand that the unwritten pre-Platonic Socrates—the Socrates who would rather not write at all—remains merely an old and ugly man? How does Socrates appear, then, in this very alteration, as he appears between himself (is this the proper Socrates?) and the Plato who would transform him, giving him a makeover, as it were, making the old and ugly become young and beautiful?[50]

If one now returns to Aristotle's *Poetics* in order to assess the much-discussed passage near the beginning of that text which states that "Socratic speeches" (Σωκρατικοὶ λόγοι)—which is to say also, Platonic dialogues—are to be considered as a form of μίμησις or imitation,[51] one discovers that the passage appears in a different light. It is clear that in Aristotle's time the "speeches" of Socrates had themselves come to be *a kind of text,* even a genre unto themselves, and were thus already delivered over to their repetition, and to a certain loss of propriety.[52] But an imitation, it seems, will always be an imitation of something. And to the extent that the imitation is to become explicit precisely *as* an imitation, it still must hold this indicative or referential moment that points beyond itself. The question for a reading that takes this mimetic character of the Platonic text as its starting point thus becomes: how does this excess and its supposed priority show itself and hide itself precisely in the imitation? And, more importantly, how can it show itself *as hiding itself*? In other words, can the loss of what is imitated, or the ruin of imitation as such, show itself in the very movement of imitation? Yet this is precisely the riddle of Socrates in the Platonic text: such a self-showing, as a hiding, presupposes that the movement of imitation sustain itself by virtue of a difference, that it enact a self-differing relation, a doubling that must take the same beyond itself and its mere identity.

This doubling of the origin has already opened the way to an interpretation of the famed "second sailing" of Socrates. But I have stated also that the second sailing of Socrates must bear upon the reading of Plato. If the dialogues can be said to bring Socrates to appearance, to make him present by presenting, through a mimetic operation, the "original" Socrates, this presentation (as if it were a kind of image) also does not simply return us to the origin, does not simply return us by rendering that origin present to us, by rendering it visible without distortion in the transparency of the imaging itself, in a reduplication or recreation of simple identity. As an imitation of Socrates, as a kind of *second*, what is decisive about Platonic writing—if for now, despite Plato's own testimony, we can risk the assertion that such writing does indeed exist—is the way in which it shows that such an origin, as *first*, only appears in a kind of *doubling*, in a second. The effect is that the very ipseity or presence of the origin is always already ruptured, taken away from it, as it shows itself to be always already lost in an other.[53]

The turn to the λόγοι, strictly speaking, cannot come *after* some other way of encountering beings, a fantastic encounter in pure αἴσθησις. What becomes evident, instead, is that the very manifesting of what becomes manifest will always already have been bound to the disclosive movement of the speech. Thus, the imaginal doubling of Platonic imitation, if taken only to confirm the traditional hierarchy between image and original, is as mistaken, and perhaps as necessary, as the likeness Socrates proposes between image and word.[54] That Socrates presents this likeness, as if in a certain necessity, only then to recant its appropriateness, demonstrates dramatically in this context that the descent of Socrates does not indicate the descent from a pure origin. What is decisive (and I shall return to this) is that the very manner in which Socrates imaginally presents the operation of speech, as if it were simply an image, finds itself interrupted by its own operation.

The Platonic dialogue, as a written text, as what is itself called a *dead* word, does not simply bring the original Socrates back to life, allowing his living speech to resound once more. As *mimetic*, it does not, as is so often said, "immortalize" Socrates.[55] Its achievement consists rather in letting the life of Socrates show itself in its passing away, in its already having been claimed by its mortality, only as a written or rewritten life. The speech of Socrates lives through its death, through its dying—which is to say also, through Platonic writing. As an "origin" Socrates arrives only after he has been lost, in his repetition, as he only arrives posthumously, precisely through his departure, having already departed. Socrates *is* dead. (Has this been grasped?)[56] He is thus Socratic, even *properly* Socratic by displacing or withholding the very sense of his own propriety, in this necessary "having become other" that also proves to be the ineluctable feature of the Platonic-

Socratic dialogue. This doubled λόγος reveals this intimate bond between life and death, and between speech and writing, as if the Platonic corpus is to be read only as a visitation upon the dead, as if it were itself a kind of *katabasis* to the underworld. But this descent does not actually succeed in bringing the dead back to life. Instead, the dead Socrates—appearing even as a kind of Teiresias, alone possessing νοῦς—remains still only a fleeting shadow, forever ungraspable.[57]

Socrates, then, does indeed belong to Plato. The two belong together, to each other. When one reads Plato, nothing is more certain. But such *belonging*—the effect of an appropriation, enacted by Plato—has to be considered as if it were more like an intimacy or a proximity, which, far from simply abolishing difference, first lets difference prevail, become manifest. I am reluctant to call this intimacy or kinship between Socrates and Plato, this "belonging together of the strange," a friendship or a community, if only because of the overriding tendency to interpret friendship first of all in terms of a commonplace familiarity and predictable loyalty. One cannot simply presume to be able to speak of this friendship, this community, when what is first of all in question here is the sense of the common itself.

This chapter began with the historicity of the event of Socrates precisely as it bears upon possibilities for reading of Plato. The historical problem of Socrates and the possibility of a mimetic reading of Plato prove to be related issues. If the text can be counted as a Platonic *deed*, if this λόγος is no less an ἔργον, then it should be possible to submit the ground of this work or deed to a *philosophical* interrogation. But where else are we to find the resources to carry out such an interrogation except in and through a reading of Plato, a reading in which we meet Socrates? The drama of Socrates' dialogical practice in the city can thus inform our way of reading Plato. This is to say, however, that Socrates, as a figure within the text, is not only mimed by the text, but appears already himself to be miming Platonic writing, as an effect of that writing. The question of the *nature* of Socrates—the question of how nature becomes manifest with him—thus needs to be brought to bear upon our sense of nature as that nature manifests itself in Plato's work. But before turning directly to the reading of Plato, let us first consider in greater detail how the tradition has assessed Socratic nature.

2

Socrates and the Retreat of Nature

Suffering a Simple Teacher of Ethics

I began this discussion taking up the way in which historical understanding finds itself at a loss before the event of Socrates. There is a way in which the entire philosophical tradition remains caught up in the descensional appearance of Socrates, even as that history produces its image of Socrates. Yet Socrates is not just subjected to this operation, not merely an effect of it. He appears also as its originator, as one who withdraws in his own appearance. As this strange appearance, Socrates holds a placeless place, indicating an uncanny and tragic doubling of nature in human life. Attending to this doubling of nature in the figure of Socrates leads to a different way of reading Plato, just as this way of reading Plato proves to open up the doubling itself. Before pursuing this reading further, I want now to show briefly how the most traditional account of Socrates, far from denying this descent, can also be seen to consist in its continual confirmation, whether knowingly or not.

Regardless of how one engages the historicity of philosophical inquiry, it would be absurd to claim that there is a lack of resources for an interpretation of Socrates. It is evident that an entire tradition has already succeeded in defining and constituting itself in a powerful and thorough appropriation of this event, an appropriation that at a certain level remains unquestionable and even in many ways unrecognized. It is then not at all a matter here of first establishing an interpretation, since this is already long since accomplished, but of finding a way to interrogate the dominant and prevailing account in its complacency and self-assuredness. This is precluded, however, as long as the interpretation to be interrogated and interrupted remains oblivious to the way in which the text it submits to interpretation has already infiltrated and anticipated the assumptions it would bring to the text.

With certain attendant risks, therefore, a preliminary formulation of the traditional interpretation of Socrates can and must be offered, so that it might serve as a guide for this inquiry and open up its topic. Yet it would be unfair to say that I am seeking to test the validity of such an interpretation, as if it were something like a tentative hypothesis, in need of evidence, critique, or supporting arguments. Such a goal would have to assume in advance a certain transparency (or self-knowledge) with regard to the matter that is at issue in the interpretation, a transparency that has never been achieved. If Socrates marks an originary event in which philosophy is thought to have first established itself in a kind of self-relation (as a saying of the *same*), first discovering or inventing itself in that relation, then the interpretation of Socrates can no longer be considered, as it usually is, as if it were merely the elaboration of an incidental historical detail, as if it were an independent or isolated claim. The traditional interpretation of the historical significance of Socrates as a philosopher, an interpretation that is brought to bear upon him again and again, is more decisively the activity of a self-interpretation, a retrieval that enacts or reenacts this moment that it takes to be constitutive of philosophy, confirming that moment, as it is thought to have occurred first with or in Socrates, by repeating it and reinscribing it upon itself.

Because I want to interrogate the descent of Socrates in this way, as a double movement that both establishes the tradition and is established by it, the task cannot be merely to compensate for the neglect of the tradition as it has interpreted Socrates, so that now we might acquire a better picture of who he was and what he actually believed. Strictly speaking, it cannot be decided whether the tradition has an "accurate" or "correct" view of the Socrates who descends, since questioning such "correctness" can occur only through an encounter with the entire tradition as such. We have to enter into a different order of questioning at this point, and begin by admitting that the measure is lacking for assessing the descent. To introduce and to repeat the Socrates who both establishes and is established by the philosophical tradition is also already to concede that he asserts himself with a certain necessity. And it is this necessity itself that must be questioned.

According to what is by far the most prominent and commanding interpretation, repeated by many authors in many texts, stretching from antiquity to the present, beginning already with Xenophon and Aristotle, the transformative turning point marked by Socrates is thought to consist in a turn away from the original matter at issue in philosophy, namely in a decisive turn away from φύσις or nature. This turn, as an aversion or a *turning away*, however, is also determined as a kind of *reversal*, in which, precisely in the turn away, philosophy is also thought thereby to *turn toward* something else, to open up, then, a new region of philosophical inquiry, a region that subsequently comes to be spoken of in various ways, but that can be said to be primarily the concern with ethical, political, or even simply *human* matters—an articulation, then, of what is good in human life, as the possible ways in which that life might flourish. Such a turn toward human things, as the abandonment of the more meteorological, cosmic, or elemental questioning of prior philosophy, is thought to be evident above all in the Socratic emphasis upon the task of self-knowledge and the care for the soul.

According to the most traditional account, then, Socrates is said to mark a reversal that is also a revolutionary beginning. It is important to emphasize, however, that this revolutionary beginning, as a reversal, is not to be viewed simply as a restriction or *narrowing* of the matter at issue in philosophy. At the same time, problems arise if one tries to think of it as an expansion or a *broadening* of that matter. But neither can it be said that Socrates simply makes philosophy more selective and refined, by increasing the subtlety of its distinctions, by pointing out a sub-discipline within the general area of research already marked out by earlier inquiry. What is decisive is that, as a reversal, as a turn away from nature, Socrates does in a way still preserve or sustain nature, but he does so only through a seemingly impenetrable transformation, by determining nature precisely *in the reversal itself.* The reversal enacted in Socratic inquiry thus does not simply turn away from nature but brings about a *doubling of nature,* a movement through which nature comes to be opposed to itself.

We have to interrogate this reversal as such, not only what begins with it, but its necessity. Yet this opens a great difficulty. For already it might be wondered whether the reversal in question can actually be said to occur because philosophy (as a distinctly *human* practice) *chooses* to turn away from nature, or whether, instead, it must not somehow be said that it is first of all nature itself that—*in its fondness for self-concealing*—retreats, thus refusing itself, and thereby first establishing the opposition between nature—that is, nature itself—and what is eventually taken to be other, the properly human, the opposition in terms of which the reversal as such is first able to find its articulation. Let me make it unmistakably clear that it is not my intent or desire to decide this question one way or the other. I am more intent upon opening up and attending to how such a question can refuse to be decided. For in such a refusal, the emergence of Socratic philosophy is definable not simply in terms of what it says or does not say *about* nature. Instead, the dialogical practice of Socrates in the city—itself irreducible to a possible discourse *about* nature—also has to be thought as *of* nature, precisely as a movement occurring in and as nature's own cryptic withdrawal. The very passage into philosophy, therefore, its genesis or birth, can be thought also as an event of nature itself.[1] Yet it is not to be overlooked that this nature must somehow precede the nature that comes to be determined *by* philosophy, cannot be identified with the nature that thus comes to be restricted within the boundaries of one way of disciplined questioning, as one region to be delimited among other regions.

Here admittedly we confront an impasse or an abyss, an interruptive moment of impossibility, an intransigency. For at the point at which one allows oneself to wonder in this way, it becomes exceedingly difficult, if not downright impossible, to account for this archaic nature precisely in its retreat or refusal. This nature, originally confronted by Socrates, from which he is said to turn away, and which somehow must precede the reversal in question, must somehow not yet be determined by the opposition that only first comes to be established in the reversal, in the retreat. If such a nature cannot yet be said to be simply opposed to the realm of human things, simply because it must somehow be prior to or before the nature that is so opposed, then to speak here already of only a Socratic *ethics,* along with a corresponding non-engagement with physics, as if the meaning of this is unproblematic, only achieves at the very beginning precisely the closure and covering over of the difficulty that remains to be taken up. To say, for example, that Socrates is "exclusively a moral philosopher,"[2] that he is the first "political philosopher,"[3] only makes apparent, precisely by way of its stark omission, the very question that is in need of address.

Before anything more is to be said about the traditional interpretation of Socrates, it is necessary to pause long enough to let this difficulty announce itself as such. As a central concern of this study, the difficulty at issue can be said to concern a concealment at the origins of philosophy, the failure to experience a loss, the concealment of this loss. But such "failure" can also be considered as a certain intensification of the experience of the loss, since it has to do with a kind of loss of loss — a doubling, then, of loss. By speaking of a "cryptic" nature I do not mean only to speak of a concealed origin, but already to indicate this doubling itself in which nature retreats and also conceals itself in its retreat. The revolutionary moment marked by Socrates is thus founded upon this necessary concealment and its doubling. How then to think the loss — the loss as such — that is implied in the event of Socrates, in the turn from an impossible nature? Can the emergence of philosophy, its very appearance, be thought precisely in this refusal — can it be thought, that is, *philosophically* — when the loss, or the loss of the loss, must first be reckoned as what enables that very thought, as what enables philosophy itself?

To pose *this question* is simply to pose the question of the possibility of a philosophical engagement with Socrates *in his descent,* as it was articulated in the introductory chapter. It is clear that such an engagement can occur only at the limits of philosophy, at a point where philosophy can no longer make complete sense of itself. This is only to admit that the question of self-knowledge arises in a way that cannot be detached from the question of nature's own manifestation, its cryptic withdrawal. I have proposed that Socrates — the figure of Socrates as he appears in the Platonic text — *is* this question. The Platonic text opens up a response to this most questionable provocation precisely by repeating the provocation itself, and as such amounts to nothing less than the invitation to the reader to take up an extreme possibility, to give a philosophical account of the origins of philosophy and the philosopher through such withdrawal, through nature's self-concealing.

It must be admitted in the first place that the Platonic text itself seems to corroborate to the point of utter incontrovertibility this traditional interpretation of the event of Socrates, especially in certain key passages that are adduced repeatedly throughout history and yet that still deserve the most attentive and subtle reading. Again and again well-known passages are enlisted, above all in the *Apology, Phaedo,* and *Phaedrus,* that seem to support this account of Socrates. Yet it can be shown that what is decisive in the Platonic text about this turn from out of nature, as it turns then, in a way previously unheard of, to human (political) matters, is how it also cannot be dissociated from a simultaneous turn to the λόγοι, a turn to the manifesting movement of speech. And thus it can be shown how this very turn to speech comes to sustain a still more intimate relation to nature, precisely as it attends to nature's own way of becoming manifest. It is especially evident, although seldom noted, that in such a turn, as it sustains this relation to nature, the dialogical practice of Socrates cannot be opened up or elaborated except by attending to the peculiar way in which this practice finds itself between the earth and the heavens, thus affirming a necessary directedness toward the heavens while remaining bound to the earth.[4]

If the enigma of Socrates poses the difficulty of thinking the obscure origins of philosophy, then this origination can be encountered as itself a movement of cryptic nature, arising as nature itself, but always in the λόγος. The assumption of the mimetic reading is that Plato's writing offers to us a "direct" encounter with this Socratic strangeness and in such a way that we ourselves, as readers, can find ourselves drawn into this strangeness and put into question along with it. In order to approach Socrates, in other words, *the question of our own nature must arise,* since the interpretation itself cannot be carried out without at the same time confronting in the very movement of the λόγος the ignorance of ourselves as the nature we are. The task of reading Plato mimetically can thus be posed with greater determinacy: Socrates, written by Plato, poses to us the task of self-knowledge as the possible way of nature's own manifestation. The question raised by Socrates, as the question that he is, is not simply a question that we are asked to consider. Rather, in the asking we must find ourselves placed into question.

Philosophy, perhaps, will never have been in a position to think the retreat or refusal of nature, the nature spoken of by Heraclitus, which he says loves to hide. The concealment of this retreat occurs no doubt through the patent unquestionability and pervasive self-evidence of nature itself as it announces itself in the archaic word that defines philosophy in its origins: φύσις. The word speaks of philosophy itself in the obscurity of its origins.[5]

It succinctly expresses both the difficulties and the achievements of philosophy prior to Socrates. Spoken at the birth of philosophy, the word itself speaks of birth and generation. As it names what is originally at issue in original philosophical inquiry, as it speaks of the first matter, naming it, it also speaks of the origin itself: the ἀρχή of the all, of the many, in the sense of both the beginning and the sustaining ground, the originary and the originating movement of what comes to presence from out of itself, and what returns to itself, as if through a self-healing relation, a cycle of regeneration, always already on the way only to itself.

As such an original name—original in this double sense, *for* the origin, *at* the origin—it can be thought to name the matter most proper to thinking. Thus, *prior* to all thinking, prior to the word, to its own proper name, φύσις would have to be given to thinking in a way proper to it: originally. As that to which thinking itself is given, so that thinking itself can first be given to itself, given simply to think, the thinking of φύσις would demand not simply the thinking of thinking, not simply the thinking of thought's own origination, whereby thought simply gives itself to itself, in a *reflection* whose trajectory by now has been rehearsed perhaps exhaustively.[6] The thinking of φύσις originally would demand another thinking, a thinking *of* the origin, in a way that thinks from it, that thus would let the origin become manifest in a way that would be proper to it, by preserving its necessary concealment.[7] The very saying of the word, then, if said originally, would already demand a translation of thinking in which thinking allows itself to be transposed, taken outside itself, into nature.

An original saying of the word, it seems, would demand that the word be simply translated into itself, into what the word itself already says, at the beginning: not a mere name, but a way to open up the matter. Here perhaps it is best to follow the advice of Plato's Timaeus, who tells us, at a decisive moment in the dialogue named after him, that "the greatest thing is to begin all matters at the beginning according to φύσις" (Tim. 29b).[8] Where else to begin, except at that ἀρχή that is κατὰ φύσιν? But if φύσις is to provide the measure for the most proper beginning, the beginning at which one ought to begin—the *natural* beginning, we might already want to say—how does one then begin at such a beginning when the very matter, to begin with, is φύσις itself?

It might be supposed that all translations of φύσις, at least to start with, should on some level be resisted, held in abeyance. Above all, the most established and traditional translation seems to offer no help at the beginning, even if at the same time we are already inevitably dependent upon it, already making use of it, still making use of it. But it is clear that the conventional translation also poses great dangers, since it is likely only to perpetuate the conviction that an original philosophical inquiry into Greek φύσις must mean asking how the Greeks conceived of "nature," as if an original repetition of this question simply amounts to elaborating the historical shifts of an idea or a concept, as if repeating the beginning of philosophy as it arises in the question of φύσις is simply a matter of asking how the Greeks interpreted, albeit differently, a phenomenon that is already plainly evident to us and that thus remains one and the same throughout history, throughout the various interpretations of it. Nevertheless, these dangers in themselves are not enough to reject outright the strategic advantages of working with such a traditional translation, since the effect of such translation also opens up the possibility that an original repetition of φύσις will have a transformative effect upon our own modern way of thinking, and thereby our relation to nature. It is thus a matter of hearing the way in which our modern word does not wholly belong to itself, so as to let it be translated back into such a strangeness, expropriated into its own obscure origins.

But in order to enact such an original repetition and translation, it would not suffice simply to discern the different ways in which the word φύσις comes into "use," as if in this way what is at issue in φύσις can then be gathered together and made clear. Such a procedure cannot succeed, so long as it manages to avoid the more difficult task I have been emphasizing: in order to encounter the origins of philosophy, precisely a philosophical encounter with the question at issue in that origin must be attempted. And only in the failure or impasse that must be confronted in such an encounter does it become possible to open up the origins of philosophy in a different way.

Whether we consider the fragments of Heraclitus, or the other so-called *physiologoi* or *physikoi*, the surviving texts of the sophists, or even the group of texts that come to us under the heading of the Hippocratic Collection, this word, φύσις, with its family of forms and meanings, plays a pervasive and decisive role. Even Parmenides, who is singled out in Plato's text by Socrates, as an exception (Theaet. 183e), and who Aristotle tells us at the beginning of the *Physics* was *not* investigating nature at all, because he was not concerned with beings in their movedness,[9] cannot be utterly removed from the discussion concerning the investigation into nature. This is revealed in the simple fact that Aristotle begins his *Physics* precisely with a refutation of the Parmenidean "one." But this supposed refutation does not so much abandon the unity of being as it seeks to show how the unity itself already calls for thinking that unity precisely in its manifold character. If the Parmenidean thought of the unity of being were irrelevant to the investigation of nature, there would be no need to engage it at all. But since the engagement with Parmenides does provide, in fact, the most decisive way to mark out what is at issue in the investigation into nature, it is necessary to reconsider whether and how the poetic thought of Parmenides nevertheless does open up the Greek experience of nature.[10]

If all early questioning was organized *around* the inquiry into nature, and was able to engage in a dispute *about* it, this was possible only because nature was *already* disclosed in a decisive manner, and thus in a certain way unquestionable. In order to take up its inquiry, thought had to be already predisposed toward nature, claimed by it in advance. What is named here, then, concerns both what is already given and also what is sought after. Early questioning is already sustained only in this inevitable, necessary, but also *paradoxical,* circularity. This is the sense of the paradoxical fragment of Heraclitus: φύσις, precisely as what is most evident and unhidden—that which never sets—nevertheless loves to hide.[11]

This can still be seen in the way that Aristotle ridicules the attempt to demonstrate *that* there is nature. That there is nature is not and cannot be in question and therefore cannot be demonstrated or made clear. It cannot be made clear simply because in a decisive way it is *already* the most clear. Only on the basis of this *limit* concerning what can be made clear through demonstration, through the disclosive movement of the λόγος, does Aristotle's investigation proceed; only then can it encounter the questionable. The questionable is thus based upon this prior relatedness to nature, which is itself in a certain way beyond question. The inquiry—inasmuch as it does seek what is not evident and moves toward obscurity from out of clarity—thus takes place only in the aftermath of a self-evidence, taken up only as it is *already* operative. "Progression" here has then also the sense of a falling away from an original unquestionable clarity: the movement from the "that" or "how" to the "what" of something, the knowledge of its cause and origin. The thinking that takes up what is not already evident is thus decisively determined by this preestablished limit that sets it in movement, that makes it possible. The inquiry that would establish nature, that would ground this ground, that would attempt thereby to establish *that* it is, would be most foolish, according to Aristotle, because it would demand that one proceed *from* what is not evident *toward* what is already most evident. Aristotle tells us that such a procedure can be likened to reasoning about colors while lacking the power to see.[12] In attempting to use obscure things to illuminate what is already clear, this inquiry (of the fool) denies itself the possibility of achieving what is most important: giving an account of the *way* in which nature is *already* clear, attending to its way of self-showing in a way that is appropriate to that self-showing. But it should be noted that this clarification of clarity occurs then precisely by also insisting upon a proper obscurity.

Nature, as most evident and most unquestionable, and the entire Aristotelian engagement with it, is thus grounded in a certain enabling limit that would mark the difference between darkness and clarity, between folly or blindness and philosophy, that would mark, therefore, the very folly and blindness *of* philosophy, the folly and blindness that philosophy must always guard itself against. What is at stake in this difference? And how does one venture to mark such a limit without risking blindness, without becoming a fool oneself? To transgress this limit is either not to see what is already most visible (to admit one's blindness), or to act as if one did not see what is already most visible, as if one were blind, and thus to play the fool. Aristotle's refusal to attempt a *demonstration* at this point has to be heard, however, as a basic affirmation of the limit itself. The limit, itself determined by nature, by its evident unquestionability, precisely because it is a limit, also intimates or betrays the ineradicable obscurity or opacity harbored in the clarity and the unquestionability itself. The question of this limit and its obscurity, a kind of darkness hidden in the brightest light, is not utterly suppressed; it is marked by the refusal, by the need to articulate the refusal as such. And the very fact that Aristotle makes the refusal explicit, that he actually does refuse, even if in the mode of ridicule, already betrays the limit itself, as it would be imposed and secured by its own self-evident clarity. How else would one proceed to mark such a limit, except by ridicule and by speaking of blind fools? The clarity is thus only in the imposition of the limit itself, and to establish the limit is simply to privilege the clarity. Such privileging of this clarity, along with the refusal to address *its* attendant obscurity, must be taken, however, also as an interpretive decision. Established thematically *as* impossibility, the limit does not remain unsaid or unthought, but is set forward and affirmed as an enabling and instantiating impossibility, at the point at which questioning must cease, but also at the point from which it can begin, can only but begin. This is the point at which thinking would be given to itself, would be able to lay claim to itself.

In limiting, determining, and provoking inquiry in this way—both the most clear and the most obscure—nature makes up the preoccupation of Greek thinking. In order to locate the very inaugural event of philosophy itself, it is assumed almost without exception that one should locate that very site at which the question of nature is first opened. This is already an ancient tradition. Simplicius, for example, appealing to the commonplace authority of a tradition that had already been established in his time—going back through Theophrastus at least to Aristotle—writes of Thales and the turn to nature as *the* decisively inceptive moment, an inception so decisive that it leaves its past in oblivion. Thales is the "first" because he first turns to nature, but he is also the "first" because precisely in this turn he effects an eradication of the past.

> It is a tradition that Thales was the first to turn the Greeks to the study of nature, as has been maintained by Theophrastus as well as many other researchers. For Thales so surpassed those who preceded him that everyone has forgotten them.[13]

The historical event of the turn to nature corresponds to the upsurge of the philosophical tradition. But Simplicius only indirectly suggests the troubling implication: how does one then think that out of which the event emerges? In terms of what does one begin to think this beginning? Can the beginning, inasmuch as it is a beginning, have a past? Or can it be a beginning only by erasing, obscuring, and covering over its cryptic origins?

We confront again a strange "anachrony" of the beginning. The beginning shows itself by having the *telos* that appears only later, being an "effect" of the beginning, reinscribed upon it. It shows itself thereby through a reinscription that has to eclipse itself and its own past. The history of the beginning would seem to proceed only by virtue of a necessary forgetting, the ἀποκρύψαι mentioned here by Simplicius. Where does one stand when one *first* turns to what has to be *already* evident? Can one think or imagine the impossible scene that gives rise to such a beginning? How, then, did nature *first* come to be given, first show itself? How could it *become* what is most unquestionable, most clear, such that it finally becomes impossible to account for its becoming unquestionable, as Aristotle attests? Must we conclude that the turn *to* nature, its discovery, was able to take place only because, in a certain sense, it never did take place, never could have taken place? How did Thales first open his eyes, appearing as one who could see in the midst of the blind?

By virtue of the retrospection that comes from out of the future and from out of the "truth" that nature will determine and guarantee, that it will have determined and guaranteed, from out of a future that thus reconstructs the past, positing the necessary *presence* of nature, its always already having been before any possible discovery, before any progression or movement—precisely thereby, the beginning as such seems denied. The *turn* to nature never took place, since there can be nothing "before" the turn to nature. One turns to nature "for the first time" only when one returns, turns to nature *again,* turning to nature only because one is already turned to nature. The beginning withdraws into the obscurity of an impossible past: a past without beginning because the beginning begins by having no past. The beginning, taken as the "first" turn to nature, demands both the affirmation of the past, so that it might at all be possible to speak of the *turn to* nature (and so demarcate where philosophy begins over and against pre-philosophy or non-philosophy), and its denial, since the turn is indeed the "first." The past is affirmed precisely in its being lost, erased.[14]

The turn to nature that is said to mark the instantiation of philosophy is readily correlated in this way with the movement from myth to reason, whereby all myth is understood to find its truth and fulfillment in the λόγος of philosophy that takes up nature. Having always already been the anticipation of that λόγος, myth would then have to be, essentially and always, the allegory for nature, for the λόγος of φύσις. Myth (and metaphor) are nothing but allegorical physiology. Myth, itself a kind of λόγος, would remain the story that only prepares the way for the truth, the λόγος that will, in the end, liberate itself from myth, the liberation that begins as the turn to nature. The freedom (ἐλευθηρία) that is repeatedly associated with philosophy and philosophical questioning presupposes or anticipates this turn from myth to nature, this translation of myth that is effected in the λόγος and that lifts the "wonder" of myth into its truth, freeing human life from the naive and superstitious.[15]

A time *before* nature would have to be a strictly mythical time—and therefore an impossible time—both in the sense that such a time can be presented or recalled only mythically, by telling myths, and in the sense that there would be only myths in this time, that the myths told about this time would have to tell of a time when myths were myths not *of* anything but only myths, when images were not images *of* anything, but simply images: the image as its own image, the tautegory of its own truth. But once myth and image are handed over to this fantastic time, to this unthinkable or "unprethinkable" origin, in which myths and images no longer refer to another truth, and no longer await their translation into this truth, we no longer know what is meant by myth, by image, or even by time. We thus *almost* are compelled to suppose that nature was always there, in advance, at the beginning. It must have always already been there, yet somehow hidden, neglected, shrouded in myth and poetic images.

Simplicius and all the later accounts of the history of philosophy stand within the shadow of Aristotle's original projection of the history of philosophy from out of its beginnings. Yet Aristotle's text itself betrays the difficulty or the impossibility of accounting for the beginning. The turn to nature—taken in the definite sense of the turn to the question of a primary "matter" (ὕλη)—characterizes those who "first philosophized."[16] And Thales is indeed preserved as the "pioneer" or the founder (ἀρχηγός) of this kind of philosophy.[17] And whereas this is only the report or *rumor* that Aristotle *receives,* there is also the further report—or at least that is the way it is presented by Aristotle—that Thales, the *first* philosopher, as he turns to nature and matter *as* water, is already anticipated by those who came before, and who are believed to mark *another* earlier beginning. The time of this "before" cannot be extracted from its mythical or "theological" dimension: it is, in fact, also the beginning of "theology." Aristotle stops short of making any definitive claims about this beginning. But he does leave open the possibility that the beginning of philosophy made by Thales—who himself is reported to have said that "all things are filled with gods"[18]—is made possible by yet another ancient beginning. The beginning of philosophy recedes into the obscurity of hearsay and myth.

> Some think that even the ancients, who lived long before the present generation and were the first to theologize, had similar beliefs about nature, for they represented Ocean and Tethys as fathers of generation, and the oath of the gods as being by water or Styx (as the poets call it); for that which is most ancient is most honorable, and that which is most honorable is that by which one swears. It remains unclear whether this doxa about nature happens to be original or ancient; at any rate, Thales is said to have spoken out in this manner concerning the first cause.[19]

The more explicit demarcation of the beginning, which is itself never-theless handed down and thus subject to the limitations of what it means to be handed down, leads to another consideration that cannot have the same kind of clarity. There are those who speak of the "ancients" who, "long before the present generation" (πολὺ πρὸ τῆς νῦν γενέσεως), were al-ready engaged or concerned with nature, were already anticipating philos-ophy, but doing so by virtue of a concern with the gods. This *doxa* about nature, in which the inquiry into nature is brought back to a mythic en-counter with gods, has to be left as it is, in its obscurity, standing outside or *before* the present time. Its origin does not belong to *this* generation. The extreme *epochal* alterity of this myth concerning the mythic origin of philosophy—which is itself presented through a kind of myth that ac-counts for myth and its origin—demands that Aristotle press on to the re-port that is given of Thales, to that point where philosophy proper begins. It demands that the report of this ancient origin of philosophy be raised only in order to be put aside, with its authority thereby suspended. Less a thorough consideration, the topic is only briefly opened in order to be closed again, so that the distinction or difference between myth and phi-losophy, or between theology and philosophy, can be preserved. But the difference is preserved even as myth and philosophy are also exposed to their common origin, or to the *rumor* of a common origin. What is evident here is the operation of an assimilation or translation of myth *to* philoso-phy, even as Aristotle also has to admit thereby that myth and theology are *already* philosophy.

Aristotle will again take up the "theologians" as he is engaged in work-ing out philosophical difficulties that concern the origin of things.[20] But again he will do so only to dismiss the worthiness of myth for the task at hand. There is something inherently confused and contradictory about Hesiod's mythic characterization of the gods, their taking ambrosia and nectar and thereby *becoming* immortal, since this mythic account of the be-ginning, or of the becoming of the gods, if it is an attempt to explain these gods *as themselves the origin of things,* cannot make clear why they would then need sustenance to be that origin and cause, that is, why they are thus dependent or reliant upon a beginning that precedes them. The mythic ac-count of the beginning only exposes the impossibility of returning to that beginning. It exposes the failure of myth: "it is not worthwhile to take seri-ously those who indulge in mythical sophistications or subtleties [μυθικῶς σοφιζομένων]." Yet this pronounced disregard for the "wisdom" of myth is also marked by the acknowledgment that the theologians, as those who do indulge in myth, do not, for their part, take philosophy into account. There is, then, the concession of a certain untranslatability, an admission that the clarity of myth is of a different kind: the theologians do not speak so as to be clear "to us" but say only what they find convincing. It should be no-ticed that this statement, made by Aristotle, bears a striking resemblance to a remark made by the Eleatic Stranger in Plato's *Sophist*. It is all the more remarkable, therefore, that in that dialogue, the stranger is not speaking about early poets, but rather about those who discoursed about being (Soph. 242c; see also Theaet. 180d).

Philosophy and myth, Aristotle thus insists, as they both turn to the question of the origin, have themselves a common origin. But this common origin, while it does not permit confusing philosophy and myth, also brings myth to philosophy and preserves myth for philosophy, and precisely in this way preserves philosophy for itself. Thus, whereas Aristotle's own ontology must include and to an extent culminate in theology, this philosophical or ontological theology is, however, already anticipated in a mythic tradition. Thus, too, the thought of the "unmoved mover" (in Met. Λ8, 1072b1 ff.) finds its precedence in an ancient myth that takes the heavenly bodies as gods and that asserts that "the divine encompasses or includes all of nature" (περιέχει τὸ θεῖον τὴν ὅλην φύσιν). Yet the mythic heritage that is bequeathed from the "ancients of very early times" (παρὰ τῶν ἀρχαίων καὶ παμπαλαίων) to us, as those who come after (τοῖς ὕστερον), not only is a thought *about* the divine, not only concerns the place of the divine in nature or of nature in the divine. It is itself believed to be "divinely spoken." Remarkably, Aristotle states that the "rest" (τὰ λοιπά) of what comes to us, the entirety of what gets handed down in the tradition beyond this divine myth concerning the divine and nature, is only "added mythically" for the sake of persuading the many, and because it is useful for laws and convention.

If one strips away this supplement, this encompassing addendum that would shelter human life from the purity of a divine word, that would preserve a space for mere νόμος, there is only this myth that has survived and prevailed throughout the repeated destruction in every age of art and philosophy. Without the supplement that serves popular convention and law there is only the one myth about nature and the divine that is itself something that comes to us from the divine, as if the divine were itself to speak through myth. Thus, Aristotle himself offers us nothing less than a story about the transmission of myth that literally surpasses philosophy, that both survives the death of philosophy and is "believed," therefore, to have a divine origin. Its survival throughout the ages beyond the creation and destruction of philosophy and art, as it attests to this divine origin, also confirms the philosophical theology presented in Aristotle's text. This theology—presumably, the theology proper to philosophy—appeals in this way to the authority of an ancient and divine myth. And yet, once more, Aristotle will appeal to mythic and divine authority by also marking the limits of its clarity. "The *doxa* of our forefathers and of those who were first [τῶν πρώτων] is evident to just this extent."[21]

When it has spoken of its own origins, philosophy has always had to look to myth and poetry. Philosophy continues in this way to account for its own genesis, as the birth of the λόγος from out of metaphor and myth. Philosophy, as it has issued a warning over the dangers of the obscurity and unaccountability of the power of myth, has also constituted itself in this warning. The delimitation and translation of myth is essential to the founding of philosophy. When philosophy comes to tell this story of its own origin, it tells a story that—under the pretense of *not* being a myth itself—accounts for the movement from myth to λόγος. It tells a story that assigns a definitive status to the story, a story that therefore presumes to transcend every mere story, that presumes to transcend the story as such. And yet, this story, too, cannot but end up as a kind of myth, because all myth, even as it tells the story of the origin, fails to account for its own origin. The origin of myth itself (or of a myth, or myths) always recedes into obscurity. It is only heard, handed down, received, and repeated. This is no less true even when an account of the origin of myth is given: the origin of this myth of myth still withdraws. But is this not also the secret of its power? The one who utters the myth is never its author, only the vehicle of its transmission, a moment of its repetition. The authority of myth derives rather from the fact that it has no author, no localizable authority, the source of its authority coming from the source itself, as if it were divinely spoken.[22]

It is this same tradition of interpretation and commentary, as it tells us that philosophy begins in the turn to nature, that tells us also that Socrates marks yet another beginning, a new beginning in philosophy. This account of the historical event of Socrates is thus indissociably connected to the interpretation of philosophy prior to Socrates. Only through nature's self-evidence, as it is at issue in early philosophy, does the Socratic turn *from* nature become in any way understandable. This account, arising primarily in the Hellenistic age, but again already confirmed in Xenophon and Aristotle, has it that with Socrates philosophy not only loses its exclusive preoccupation with nature, but actually turns away from nature altogether, thus away from the investigation into divine or heavenly matters. Socrates is said instead to have asserted the primacy of other questions, such as that of the care of the soul and of human life in the polis. In this context, it has become almost mandatory to cite Cicero's by-now famous phrase, when he declares that Socrates brought philosophy "down from the heavens into the cities of men."[23] Diogenes Laertius, repeating the account of Demetrius of Byzantium, writes: "he thought that theorizing on matters of nature was not our concern but discussed ethical matters in the workshops and the market-place; Socrates sought 'the evil and the good that is done in a house.'"[24] Socrates is said to bring about what could be called a certain *domestication* of philosophy. Xenophon, who is both utterly reliable and deeply misleading, writes: "He did not even discourse on the nature of all things [περὶ τῆς τῶν πάντων φύσεως] as did most of the others; he did not discuss the so-called cosmos of the sophists, the necessity of the heavens. He would even seek to demonstrate that the concern with such things is foolish. . . . For his part, he was ever discussing human concerns [αὐτὸς δὲ περὶ τῶν ἀνθρωπίνων ἀεὶ διελέγετο σκοπῶν]."[25]

It is worth noting how in this passage, as well as in other passages,[26] Xenophon suggests that the issue for Socrates in this regard is the question concerning where such inquiries into nature might lead, what their *use* might be, and, most importantly, whether these inquiries might exclude or preclude the possibility of pursuing other inquiries. *Why* is the inquiry into nature foolish? The answer given is that it must lead to a neglect of other things, things more human.[27] In other words, the issue involves the operation of a certain restricted economy in philosophical inquiry, an economy that establishes a limiting relationship, if not even a relationship of exclusion, between different concerns or different regions of inquiry. This economy, because it is restricted and restricting, also thereby establishes certain constraints upon human life, seeming to set limiting conditions upon the humanly possible. These limits, the restrictions at work in such an economy, shed light on the "freedom" from the necessities of life that Aristotle also associates with the origin of both philosophy and myth, and the "leisure" (σχολή) that allows philosophical practice to be detached from the production and instrumentality that otherwise is thought to be essential to all knowledge and practice. The question of the Socratic turn thus concerns the extent to which precisely this emphasis upon "human things" does not also challenge the possibility of such an open freedom, by opening up the necessity of a certain economy within which it will also be sought after.

Aristotle corroborates the prevailing interpretation of what is distinctive about Socratic inquiry when in his *Metaphysics* he gives an account of the history of thought leading up to his own thought and work. Plato is presented as having taken the decisive step beyond the "materialist" thought of the so-called *physiologoi* by advancing to the "look," to the εἶδος, or the ἰδέα. Yet this decisive Platonic advance is also linked to Socrates, even indebted to him. Socrates, Aristotle says, *sought definitions* and "was engaged in ethical matters, but not at all in nature as a whole" — Σωκράτους δὲ περὶ μὲν τὰ ἠθικὰ πραγματευομένου, περὶ δὲ τῆς ὅλης φύσεως οὐδέν (987b1–2).

According to Aristotle, what is thus distinctive about Socratic inquiry, over and against the earlier concern with nature, is its engagement with the ethical but, at the same time, also its emphasis upon "definitions" (ὁρισμοί) and upon what is badly but perhaps inevitably translated as "the universal" (τὸ καθόλου). The concern with the ethical, as a departure from the physicist's inquiry, arises along with this new emphasis upon definition, what Aristotle also refers to as the whatness, "the what it is" (τό τί ἐστιν). The two developments are connected. Precisely because of his engagement with the ethical, an engagement that is "about ethical virtues" (περὶ τὰς ἠθικὰς ἀρετάς), and precisely "in connection with these" (περὶ τούτων), Socrates was the "first to seek to define universally," or according to the whole (ὁρίζεσθαι καθόλου ζητοῦντος πρώτου).²⁸ And yet, Socrates seeks the universal, the whatness or definition of a thing "with good reason" (εὐλόγως): for he sought to prove something, he sought to syllogize (συλλογίζεσθαι ἐζήτει) (1078b23–24). Aristotle names "inductive" arguments (ἐπακτικοὶ λόγοι) and defining universally as the distinctive contributions of Socrates: it is "just" to give credit to Socrates for these. But these are also intimately connected with his turn to the ethical, a turn that is also therefore, according to Aristotle, connected with or concerned with the ground or origin of ἐπιστήμη or scientific, regionalized knowledge (περὶ ἀρχὴν ἐπιστήμης) (1078b27–30). Aristotle's characterization of the historically transformative moment that is marked by Socrates suggests therefore that the inquiry of disciplined knowledge (ἐπιστήμη)²⁹ — which we take to be the very establishing of the differing regions of inquiry — with its delimitation, definition, and conceptualization, established in the λόγος that arises by ἐπαγωγή,³⁰ emerges along with a certain turn to the ethical. This is a turn that also turns to the disclosive and demonstrative power of the λόγος or the syllogism. As it moves somehow beyond the preoccupation of those whom Aristotle calls "physicists," it thereby creates a difference within philosophical inquiry itself.³¹ This traditional determination of Socrates, or rather of the historical significance of the rise of Socratic inquiry — as marking the rise of science, of ethics, *and* the turn away from the exclusive concern with nature — has continued to have a decisive influence on scholarship, even though contemporary scholarship may be less uniform in its interpretation.³² Hegel, in his *Lectures on the History of Philosophy,* provides a brilliant and notable example of this tradition. He confirms this account, repeating the ancient histories, but expressing its truth in his own modern philosophical idiom. With Socrates, he says, "the spirit of the world begins a reversal."³³

The tradition has always had difficulty drawing the line between Socrates and Plato, although the need to draw this line is almost always affirmed. We have begun to see how this need is grounded in a very definite assumption concerning what it means to read Plato's dialogues. Socrates, before Plato but already anticipating the advance of Plato, marks thus not only the turn *to* ethics, but also thereby the movement *away from* physics. The decisive development from the "physiologists" to Socrates, and from Socrates to Plato, is understood as a movement from a preoccupation with nature to an ethical or political concern, and then, finally, from this concern to a regionalized philosophical inquiry, which (logically or dialectically) distributes and organizes philosophy along the lines of both ethics and physics.

Socrates turns to ethics but at a point where the regions of philosophical inquiry have yet to be established, because the capacity to regionalize explicitly has yet to be established. This capacity is often taken as the decisive contribution of Plato. Again, according to Diogenes Laertius, "in early times it [philosophy] discoursed on one subject, namely physics, then

Socrates added the second subject, ethics, and Plato the third, dialectics, and so brought philosophy to perfection."[34] Socrates creates or institutes a new field, but he does so without dialectics, that is, somehow at that point where philosophy is still *imperfect*, without the means to articulate what it is doing and how it will organize its inquiry. The tradition, therefore, has to understand Socrates to be, in an important sense, *already* Platonic, already therefore a dialectical thinker, even though dialectics (understood as the regional distribution of philosophical thought) is to mark the actual advance belonging to Plato. Plato in this regard is the "first." The advance of Socrates, the advance that is proper to Socratic practice, is itself something that can be articulated only if one already assumes this initiating Platonic contribution.

There is, however, a repeated and pronounced hesitancy in this regard in traditional Plato-interpretation. Schleiermacher, for example, will almost give full credit to Plato for bringing philosophy to its complete form but, at the same time, virtually take that credit away. It is not clear in Schleiermacher's text whether the reserve that he shows regarding the achievement of Plato is attributable to the fact that philosophy in his view had already achieved its divisions, or whether such divisions were only to come later. While emphasizing the need to keep the whole in view, he writes that not only was the division of philosophy into different inquiries not unknown to Plato, but in fact "he may be looked upon as the first originator of it *to a certain degree,* still hardly any of his writings are confined to any one of these compartments in particular."[35] Thus, we should not look for a physics and an ethics in Plato as distinct inquiries. "Now if Plato ended with separate expositions of the several sciences, it might then be supposed that he had also advanced each for itself in gradual progression, and we should be compelled to look for two separate classes of dialogues, an ethical and a physical series. But as he represents them as a connected whole, and it is ever his peculiar theory to conceive of them generally as essentially connected and inseparable, so also are the preparations for them united in like manner, and there are therefore not several unconnected and collaterally progressing series of Platonic dialogues, but only one single one, comprehending every thing in it."[36] The dialogues always address the whole and can always, therefore, be read as either ethics or physics because they are both. Or rather, insofar as they can be read as either ethics or physics, they must be read as both.

Sextus Empiricus announces the advancement of Plato but also with a marked hesitation. When he raises the question of the proper subjects and divisions of philosophy, he points to Plato as "virtually"[37] the first, as the "founder," the ἀρχηγός, who addressed and divided philosophy in its most complete terms, as ethics, physics, and logic.

> These thinkers [those who come before Plato], however, seem to have handled the question incompletely, and, in comparison with them, the view of those

who divided philosophy into physics, ethics, and logic is more satisfactory. Of these Plato is, virtually, the pioneer, as he discussed many problems of physics and of ethics, and not a few of logic.[38]

Yet Plato "discusses" physics, ethics, and logic precisely by means of Socrates, through the mouth of Socrates, as he has Socrates (and others) carry out conversations that open up these questions. The Socrates in Plato's text is, therefore, the Socrates that Plato wanted to portray, Plato's Socrates, not Socrates himself, and thus a kind of fiction.

> Socrates turned aside from physics to the study of ethics. . . . Plato, however, ascribes to him every division of philosophy,—logic, in so far as he is introduced as an investigator of definitions and divisions and etymology, which are logical themes,—ethics, because he discusses virtue and government and laws,—physics, since he is made to philosophize about the universe and animal creation and the soul. Hence, Timon censures Plato for thus decking out Socrates with a host of sciences: for Plato, he says, "suffered him not to remain a simple teacher of ethics."[39]

The traditional interpretation of Socrates in his relation to nature presupposes the *difference* between Socrates and Plato. What is strange here is that in a decisive sense Plato must precede Socrates in order for Socrates to hold the place that he must, which is to say, in order to be able to account for the emergence of Platonic philosophy.[40]

We have also seen, if only in a preliminary way, how our interpretive access to Plato and Socrates is determined in advance by the work of Aristotle, by his appropriation of the history of thought preceding him, and by the conceptuality and philosophical structure that he employs in that appropriation. Without doubt Aristotle takes up and reiterates the emphasis upon the ethical and the political that is characteristic of Socratic practice. But at the same time it seems that he departs from this Socratic movement or even that he develops a kind of counter-movement to it, to the extent that he understands himself to be recovering the pre-Socratic inquiry into nature. Yet Aristotle overcomes the presumed Socratic indifference to nature not only by asserting or reasserting its philosophical primacy, but also by establishing and setting conceptual boundaries to "physics," as the special inquiry into τὰ φύσει ὄντα, namely as an inquiry into beings considered in terms of their ability to move and be moved, where the ἀρχή of movement is to be found in beings themselves. Such an inquiry thus inquires into a region that, for its part, has a kind of independence. And yet, at the same time, Aristotle's conception of nature does not only recover the pre-Socratic tradition of those who inquired into nature; he himself accounts for his advance beyond this tradition by pointing to the introduction of the "look" into nature itself, that is, precisely by introducing something of Platonic or, perhaps, *Socratic* origin.[41]

The task now is to make plain how the Platonic Socrates can be seen enacting the doubling that has been introduced. This will be carried out through an examination of only a few key texts: the *Apology, Gorgias, Phaedo, Meno, Phaedrus,* and to a lesser extent, *Republic* and *Theaetetus.* In each of these texts the question of a Socratic appearance will be taken up in the context established by the dialogue. In this way, it becomes evident that the figure of Socrates appears only in a certain conflict or difference, over and against others, but also in a self-differing relation that as such sustains his questioning practice.

Part 2. Dreams, Oracles, and Silenic Affirmations

3

The Purest Thinker of the West and the Older Accusations in the *Apology*

If we are related to what withdraws itself, then we are drawn along with the self-withdrawing, in the enigmatic and thereby elusive nearness of its claim upon us. If a human is properly drawn along, then that one is thinking, however far that one may be removed from the self-withdrawing, and even if the withdrawal also remains, as ever, veiled. Socrates, in the time of his life, up until and into his own death, did nothing other than place and keep himself in the pulling draft of this drawing. For this reason he is the purest thinker of the West. Because of this he wrote nothing. For whoever begins to write from out of thinking inevitably has to resemble those humans who seek refuge in the lee before this overpowering draft. It remains a strangely familiar fact of a still concealed history, that all thinkers of the West after Socrates, their greatness notwithstanding, have had to be such refugees. Thinking turns into literature.[1]

"He wrote nothing," Heidegger states confidently. One might well wonder, however, where Heidegger believes himself to have met this Socrates. Is this not a good *phenomenological* question, the question, namely, of access? How does the phenomenon appear? How does it show itself? Does Heidegger refer here to the so-called historical Socrates, a Socrates who would wish also to remain outside all texts? And should we be surprised that Heidegger introduces this elusive and transcendent non-writer in order to concede to him a singular *purity* of thinking—doing so in a *text* that devotes itself to thinking, namely, to what calls for thinking, to the question at issue in thinking, the question of what it is to think, to be called to think? But in Heidegger's statement one might also already hear a peculiar appropriation of what I am taking up as the traditional interpretation of Socrates, assuming, that is, that the famous Socratic "turn away from nature" can be thought to arise first of all in the movement of nature's own refusal and withdrawal.[2] To be sure, Heidegger himself wants to think the way in which thinking can be said to be thinking only in its being drawn along in such a self-withdrawal. And to place oneself in the withdrawal of the self-withdrawing is precisely what is said here to make the thinking of Socrates pure.

Yet this purity is also spoken of here by Heidegger in terms of time, as a distinctly Socratic time: the time of life and death. The purity is thus already determined, at least implicitly, by an inescapable economy, in a restriction of time in which thinking can replace or resist other possibilities. The purity consists, that is, in the way in which Socrates is thought to have spent his time (or not spent his time), the way in which the time of Socrates, his life and death, can be defined in philosophically *heroic* terms, perhaps even as a courage: Socratic thinking is pure because he did nothing else "up until and into his own death" but place and hold himself in the veiled withdrawal of the self withdrawing.[3] Socratic purity, his purity as a thinker—that he places himself in the withdrawing—proves to be bound to at least two things: the fact that he did not write and his courage as a way to death. Although Heidegger does not speak of it explicitly, it is possible to see here a reference to the σχολή that is thought to be definitive of philosophical life and necessary to it, a σχολή that would be connected, then, both to human mortality and to Socratic non-writing. There is thus a need for a renewed interrogation of the so-called leisure of the philosopher in terms of the distinctive way it comes to temporalize life and inquiry, thus bringing to bear upon the movement of inquiry the mortality of human life. Far from being mere "leisure," as if it were an escape or a reprieve from life's burdens, philosophical σχολή shows itself to be the space or time within which the *necessity* of human life can first be encountered.[4]

According to this passage, Socrates stands as a liminal figure, at the beginning of a history of writing, but as an exemplary exception to that history, outside it, or prior to its inception, prior to the necessity that comes to be imposed upon all subsequent thinkers, the necessity that all of them, however great, still be writers, that precisely *as* thinkers they nevertheless seek refuge in the shelter of the written word. After Socrates, thinking turns into literature and loses itself, loses its purity.[5] And in this *contaminating* transformation, the thinkers who come to writing *from out of* thinking must now inevitably "resemble," or even be equated with—*gleichen*—the rest of humankind: these are the fallen thinkers, their "greatness notwithstanding." Heidegger does not find it necessary to address here the question of the community for whom such an equation or resemblance is established. But if Socrates thus marks the descent of thinking, stands at that moment of descent of human life, into human life, it is necessary to ask: how does he appear and for whom? After Socrates it can seem as if the thinker (as thinker/writer) is no longer a thinker, no longer thinking at all, but rather only seeking shelter. Accordingly, Plato then would be the first contaminated thinker, the first thinker/writer, the first one to lose his purity. He would be the first thinker who comes to writing from out of thinking and thus first comes to resemble all those who merely seek shelter. After Socrates (and *since* Plato) all thinkers come to be claimed by the same great necessity. "*Since Plato . . .*": it is worth mentioning that with this little phrase Heidegger again and again singles out the figure who would mark the inception of metaphysical thinking, the transformation of truth into correctness and of φύσις into a region of being. Socrates, in contrast, the thinker who remains pure, is the exception to this rule of history, as a thinker unlike all others, the paradigm that thus establishes the rule without being submitted to it, thus living and dying at the very limits of the humanly possible, while also marking those limits precisely through his own withdrawal from history, the beginning of which he is therefore thought to mark in a different way. Socrates marks the beginning because everything *after* him has changed, whereas with Plato everything *before* him, everything that thus cannot be said to be *since* Plato, comes to be claimed and established in a different way. The very *difference*, then, between Socrates and Plato would be determined in the beginning of such a history, as also the very difference between thinking and writing, between the thinking that is pure and the writing that proceeds from out of thinking.

And yet, it should be obvious that the Heideggerian assertion concerning the superlative purity of Socrates as a thinker utterly resists appropriation; it does not allow itself to be readily adopted or taken over, cannot easily be made applicable and relevant. It thus cannot be presented as if it were already available for exchange, as if it were a matter of simply granting and accepting what is said here, thus letting it be repeated, inserted into an economy, put to use. The statement, by speaking of the uttermost purity of Socratic thinking, as such thinking would be drawn along precisely in the self-withdrawing, also already speaks of the very withdrawal of Socrates himself, his elusive and enigmatic character. Socrates, it turns out, as the purest of thinkers, is no less enigmatic than thinking as such, the very paradigm of the thinker and the enigma of thinking. The assertion can therefore be raised only as a troubling provocation, because it demands a continued questioning both of Socrates and of the very character of thinking as it would show itself, or hide itself, with him.

But if one would then turn to the Platonic text, precisely in order to take up and to elaborate the question posed in this way, how does such a purity of thinking establish itself or present itself in connection with Socratic non-writing and death, as such death has already infringed upon life and the supposed purity of life? It can be said that this most enigmatic but purest of thinkers appears in the Platonic text as a thinker bound to a peculiar dialogical necessity, in which Socratic inquiry shows itself to be always already bound to the movement of speech as manifestation, in a questioning engagement with others. In order to open up what I am calling the doubling of nature as it becomes manifest with and in the figure of the Platonic Socrates, this dialogical necessity, the questioning turn to speech, must be addressed as such. The question before us as we proceed remains: How does Socratic dialogical necessity, arising in a peculiar ignorance and in the affirmation of the task of self-knowledge, prove to be, then, a necessity of nature itself?

Among Platonic texts, *The Apology of Socrates* seems to provide the clearest and most incontestable example of how Socrates disavows the inquiry into nature. The *Apology* is also distinctive no doubt by virtue of the way in which it seems to offer a direct account of Socratic philosophical practice and the origins of that practice. Less a dramatic dialogue, the text seems to present Socrates as he speaks for himself, as though the text were simply a straightforward record of the speech given by him at his trial. Scholars have thus been in large part willing to agree that the Socrates confronted in this text must be sharply distinguished from what is supposed to be Plato's own philosophical position, a position that finds itself articulated nevertheless by Socrates—by *another* Socrates—in Plato's text. Accordingly, when Socrates, in what have come to be called the middle and later dialogues, makes a statement that appears to contradict what is said in the *Apology* (and in what are taken to be other early dialogues), such a discrepancy is readily viewed as a way to discern Plato's own departure from the position that he originally only inherits, thought to be properly Socratic.[6] Even Schleiermacher, who opened up entirely new possibilities in textual interpretation by insisting that it is a mistake to ask whether Socrates (or anyone else) speaks for Plato, nevertheless finds himself wondering whether the *Apology* can have anything to do with the "thoughts" of Plato.[7] And Charles Kahn, who also argues a strong thesis in this regard ("Even where the inspiration of Socrates is clear, the dialogues are all Platonic"), stops short of taking on the question of the *Apology*. "I shall not dispute the status of the Apology, which is after all not a dialogue and may have preceded the creation of the dialogue form."[8]

And yet, while few can fully resist the temptation to question the genuinely *Platonic* character of this speech, almost never is the *Apology* taken to be a direct and accurate transcription of the word of Socrates. Whatever Socratic "truth" one may find here—and almost all who seek this truth agree that this is the place to look[9]—it is also generally acknowledged that this speech comes to be heavily mediated by Platonic writing, transformed, however decisively, through a Platonic reception and repetition. But for the most part this only results in the necessary concession that Plato contributes a kind of "artistic refinement," bringing a rhetorical and poetic form to what otherwise can be taken as essentially Socratic "content." It seems that even in those accounts that appeal to a more phenomenological sense of the truth, as one finds it enacted in a portrait, for example,[10] there is still the risk of implicitly reverting to this insidious distinction between form and content. Throughout these differing readings what is assumed is that Plato, as artist, is able to enact through his own writing a decisive withdrawal of himself, to withhold himself so that

Socrates, the actual Socrates, can come forward and speak to us, so that, to speak in a way that echoes the *Phaedo,* he *himself* would be present. I am not suggesting here at all that such an approach is "incorrect," only that it ought to be considered along with the fact that the dialogues themselves, as they continually revolve around the question of the self in its relation to itself, also alter the very sense of what it would mean for "Socrates" to be present. What is at issue here, in other words, has to do first of all with the concrete "how" of the self-showing that occurs in this Platonic portrait. I have already discussed how a distinctive Platonic *silence* becomes audible when Socrates remarks that Plato is present (Apol. 34a, 38b), just as a certain Platonic *presence* becomes apparent at that very point in the *Phaedo* where Phaedo mentions in passing Plato's weakness and sickness (thus implying his absence) during the death of Socrates (Phaedo 59b).

The dominant interpretive approach to the *Apology* is thus perfectly suited to support those readings that seek to establish and to distinguish in historiological terms the doctrinal position of Socrates over and against that of Plato. The approach that dedicates itself to deciding this very question has also assumed a decisive understanding of the λόγος in which its possible truth is determined in advance only by returning and restricting that truth to the intent and will of its author, whether this be the speaker who is Socrates or the writer who is Plato. Thus far, I have merely stressed that this obsession with the question of ownership and propriety is grounded in a sense of authorial identity that can be given priority and precedence over and against whatever difference and opposition might appear. It is all too easy to assume in advance that Plato must have a coherent metaphysical doctrine, or at the very least a clear project that is to be conveyed through the dialogues as properly his, as his own. When the doctrine, and its owner, is nowhere to be found, or is found only in incomplete form, this either is said to reflect badly upon Plato as a philosopher or sets into motion new research now bent upon resolving the appearance of contradictions. One of the easier ways to account for such contradictions is to suppose a Platonic "development," a movement that contains within it different philosophical positions and transitions as they are evident in what is supposed to be the chronological progression of the writing.[11] I have stressed that this approach, as compelling as it may seem, utterly excludes the encounter with Socrates himself as a philosophical provocation, as the enigma that is actually encountered by the dramatic characters in the Platonic text. A related assumption here is that paradox and contradiction can refer only to imperfect expressions of philosophical rigor. Gregory Vlastos, for example, in insisting upon the insuperable difference between the Socrates who appears in the *Apology* and the Socrates who appears perhaps first of all in the *Meno* and *Phaedo,* even goes so far as to allow himself the most preposterous and unphilosophical anachronism imaginable, when he speaks of the *brain* of Socrates, which he supposes, if it had to hold all the "positions" presented by Socrates in the Platonic text, would have to be schizophrenic.[12] But if Socrates is to be encountered in Plato's text, he must lie somewhere between Heidegger's purest of thinkers and Vlastos's brain-bucket.

Why is the *Apology* granted this special status, in which it almost always lends itself to being taken as more Socratic and therefore as less Platonic? Even if in the end one would want to insist upon the utterly distinctive character of the *Apology* among the texts of Plato, it certainly cannot be said that the *Apology* lacks a mythic horizon or a dramatic context altogether. On the contrary, it can be shown that without this horizon and this context the speech presented by Socrates becomes utterly senseless. What would become of the "content" of the *Apology*, insofar as it is thought to be essentially Socratic, if it were no longer situated within the dramatic context of the public trial, as this trial presents a decisive moment, a total transformation of the relation between Socrates and the city of Athens? It may be, in fact, that the very force of the claim that in this text Socrates shows himself to be a "moral philosopher," or a "simple teacher of ethics," someone who turns away from natural inquiry in favor of strictly *human* things, is something that first has to be considered by taking seriously the peculiar conditions under which the claim is made, the distinctive constraints of this situation, the time and place within which Socrates is speaking, as inexorable limits come to bear upon the possibilities of that speaking. It may be that the *lack of privacy* of this event makes another kind of discourse impossible: the philosophical conversation that takes place only among friends, that both establishes and is established by such community. And, moreover, how would Socrates account for his practice, if in doing so he were to make no reference to his interpretation of the strange oracular pronouncement concerning his wisdom?[13] It is certainly the case that this supposed wisdom, spoken of by the god, is already in play as Socrates responds to the oracle, in the very manner of his responding. This human response to the oracular pronouncement is thus not simply produced by the god, in a divine command, but is rather grounded in a prior dialogical necessity that is already characteristic of Socrates and his supposed wisdom. And yet, if this enigmatic *human* wisdom of Socrates, confirmed by the god's oracular word—but also confirmed only in the Socratic interpretive response that would *test* and examine the word, through a dialogical practice—reveals the peculiar character of Socrates' continued inquiry into nature, it is also the case that precisely this "wisdom" does not permit itself to be fully addressed within the context of the public trial, within the limits of that time and place. The dramatic setting and the mythic horizon of the *Apology* thus thoroughly determine the way in which Socrates becomes manifest in the text.

It cannot even be rightly said, as it often is, that the Socratic λόγος presented in this text is not engaged in a certain kind of dialogue. Meletus finds himself interrogated and refuted by Socrates (Apol. 24c–28b).[14] But it is also not incidental that Socrates, in this dialogical exchange, by distancing himself from the teachings of Anaxagoras, supposedly disavows his inquiry into nature. The dialogical dimension of the defense, as it establishes the context of what is said, is thus not to be bypassed, although this has not stopped commentators from simply applying the distinction between "ethics" and "natural science" as an unproblematic way to interpret Socrates' remarks.[15] It is true that we do not hear the speeches of the accusers, except insofar as they are recalled and retold intermittently by Socrates himself in his own defense.[16] But Socrates is responding nevertheless to precisely these accusers, and thus engaging them as interlocutors, even as the Platonic text suppresses or silences their actual speech, allowing them to speak only indirectly, as Socrates would recapitulate and recover what he takes to be relevant in their speaking. The speech of Socrates thus makes its way by virtue of this restricted repetition of speeches that have already been made — not only by repeating and invoking the speeches made by his accusers at his trial, but also, more importantly, by speaking of those stories and allegations about Socrates that have been circulating for a long time and that are responsible for the most entrenched opinions about him. Thus, it must be asked: How does Socrates manage *to speak the truth*, as he insists he must, in the context of these entrenched convictions held against him? What Socrates asks of the "men of Athens" is that they rise to the task of being judges, namely, that they attend solely to whether what he says is just or not. This is the ἀρετή of a judge, just as the ἀρετή of a speaker is to speak the truth (Apol. 18a). And yet, how does the peculiarly *dialogical* situation force a reconsideration of this correlation between "truth" and "justice" that the *Apology* is said to reveal?

What must be considered most carefully is the way in which the emergence of a dialogue in such a public context finds itself severely limited precisely by that context itself. To begin by asserting that the *Apology* does *not* belong to the dialogue form is only to preclude in the most preemptive way the very possibility of encountering the great difficulty raised by the text, which concerns namely how Socratic dialogue, and the disclosure it makes possible, remains deeply incompatible with the conventions of public speaking, conventions that prove also to be bound to constraints of time. If Socrates appears as a stranger or a foreigner to the law-courts and to public speaking, because he does not speak the language native to this setting, this fact must also be allowed to bear upon the very conflict that his speech would address, the truth it would make manifest that pertains to the place of philosophy in the city, the conflict in human life between the philosophical and the political. The trial of Socrates, insofar as it would put philosophy on trial — in order to assess a possible wrongdoing or injustice, a certain ἀδικεῖν — also becomes the trial of Athens. What is to be decided in this trial, then, concerns not only whether philosophy is a good in the city, whether and how it is to be counted as a *human* good, but also whether and how Athens is able to receive and sustain that good.[17] The *Apology* has to be read as a deeply dialogical λόγος that is already enacting its own impossibility, as it attempts to speak its truth in a situation that already limits its very way of speaking, threatening to render dialogue altogether impossible. How does nature appear in the city? The *truth* this stranger would speak has to be heard as it also bears upon the very sense of the stranger's strangeness—of what it means for the strange to appear at all—as that truth would address the conflict or incompatibility between city and philosophy, which in turn opens up the relation between human life and the whole that exceeds, surrounds, and sustains it. The political question of philosophy, a question that inevitably attaches itself to philosophical questioning, is always also a question of the place of human life, or the lack of that place, in nature.

The dialogical practice of Socrates in the city makes explicit a truth that I have introduced in terms of a *tragic* necessity, that nature claims human life through a doubling, a doubling that also makes manifest nature's refusal. But what is this truth, if not that those who are thought to be wise by the many have in fact proven in their encounter with Socrates to be ignorant, which is to say, *not* wise? The slander against Socrates proves to be grounded in the way in which he has undermined a conventional wisdom, betrayed his tradition; his truth has exposed an alleged human certainty as flawed and untrue. One then has to consider that the very telling of this truth, its way of becoming manifest, also occurs only as it confronts the way of speaking through which such conventional wisdom otherwise continues to affirm and express itself. And if this public way of speaking, allied with the wisdom of tradition, now finds itself ruptured by Socratic practice, his tragic truth, it is no less the case that this strange Socratic truth remains constrained precisely by that prevailing way of speaking. The *Apology* thus unfolds as a dialogue at the limits of the dialogical, a dialogue that both insists upon the necessity of such dialogue and demonstrates its political impossibility.[18] Moreover, every other Socratic dialogue is for this reason also inevitably related to the *Apology*.[19]

This liminal dialogue between city and philosophy takes place at the point at which Socrates attempts to refute the older accusations. These accusations are said to be much more dangerous and more difficult to address than the official charges now brought against him. Socrates takes the official charges to be grounded in these older accusations, based upon the widespread opinions that circulate about him. Meletus, says Socrates, is counting on these commonly held prejudices when he brings the charges against Socrates (Apol. 19a–b). And although it has to be noted how the difficulty of engaging such long-standing and deep-seated opinions, according to Socrates, consists in the impossibility of engaging them *dialogically,* this is also precisely where one must begin, if one is to proceed ἐξ ἀρχῆς, from the beginning (Apol. 19a). First of all, says Socrates, there is the hearsay, the rumor, all the talk (φήμη), the prejudice and slander (διαβολή). Word has gotten around, has been circulating since long ago, already many years (πάλαι πολλὰ ἤδη ἔτη) (Apol. 18b). These numerous and longtime accusers got hold of the Athenians when they were still children, thus at a time when the Athenians were receptive in a certain way and could be easily persuaded. The age of the listener thus sets limits upon the way in which speech may be received, just as age also seems to dictate a certain way of speaking: it would not be fitting for Socrates at his age to speak like a youngster and present fabricated speeches (Apol. 17c).[20] The difficulty of dealing with the persuasive power of the older accusations is also connected to its way of perpetuating itself, its way of recycling its own convictions. Those who ended up persuading others had first been persuaded themselves. The concealing of nature's concealment, taken here as the political appropriation of the philosopher in the city, is thus sustained in a kind of self-perpetuating λόγος that refuses to question itself and what is at issue in it. But this self-perpetuating movement, in which humans appear to themselves in a concealment, namely, as wise when they are not, is no less nature's own movement, nature's own way of concealing its very refusal.

What has to be recognized, therefore, is that the first question taken up in the *Apology* concerns the question of this operation of a certain diabolical persuasion, the way in which a pernicious speech has come to reveal but also to conceal Socratic practice, and the way in which Socrates, through such a movement of persuasion, has made a name for himself, the way in which he has acquired his reputation, his ὄνομα (Apol. 20d). The question of the name of Socrates, of what is at stake in this name, thus shows itself as the place to interrogate nature's manifestation in human life. It is nothing other than *this very name*, the most questionable of reputations, as Socrates himself takes it up in the *Apology,* that is also associated with the investigation into heavenly and subterranean things. The first time Socrates repeats the older accusations, he says: "There is a certain Socrates, a wise man [σοφός ἀνήρ], a thinker of heavenly things, a seeker of all the things beneath the earth, and one who makes the weaker λόγος the stronger [τὸν ἥττω λόγον κρείττω ποιῶν]" (Apol. 18b).

Socrates draws the deadly conclusion that will be derived from this slanderous report concerning his name. Those who spread this report and who thus accuse Socrates are said by him to be δεινοί—that is, terrible, clever, dangerous—because those who listen to them suppose that the ones who seek these things are not at all attentive to the gods, do not in their customary way encounter the gods, do not recognize the gods as gods: οὐδὲ θεοὺς νομίζειν (Apol. 18c). It must be noted how Socrates, simply by marking this supposition as such, the belief, namely, that a relation to the divine is opposed to natural inquiry, only puts the supposition into question. The question is thus raised only implicitly that concerns how natural inquiry would have to exclude the νομίζειν in which the gods would be encountered. The question of such a νομίζειν, of the νόμος that would be excluded through the inquiry into nature, is not taken up directly.[21] But the numerous accusers, those who have taken over the name of Socrates, in characterizing him in this way, as one who studies heavenly and subterranean things, know that those who listen to them already take the study of nature, the concern of this "wise man," to conflict with the human relation to the divine.[22] Their persuasion, therefore, its way of being terribly clever, depends upon this, since the presumed *impiety* of Socrates is not directly stated in the simplest formulation of the slander.

The so-called wisdom of Socrates, his name and reputation, are said here to concern an inquiry defined primarily by what that inquiry seeks, heavenly and subterranean things, but also by its clever and uncanny relation to the persuasive power of speech, the ability of speech to conceal and mislead, to make what is weaker be stronger, appear stronger, become stronger. Thus, the theme of persuasion in the *Apology* both pertains to the operation by which the accusers have managed to establish the deep prejudice against Socrates—*they* have persuaded the Athenians, and thus, says Socrates, *they* are terrible and clever, δεινοί—and also pertains to the way in which these accusers, in their persuasion, actually characterize Socrates and Socratic practice. Socratic practice amounts to a certain ποίησις, a making in the λόγος that renders strength out of weakness: Socrates is said to make the weaker λόγος stronger. Precisely as it is formulated in this way, however, the accusation harbors a great difficulty that remains unaddressed within the *Apology*. Yet this difficulty pertains to the very matter we are concerned with, namely, the manifestation of Socratic nature in and through dialogical speech.

At the very beginning of his speech Socrates remarks at the most outlandish lie told by his accusers, that the judges should be on their guard since Socrates himself is a terribly clever speaker: *his* speech is said to be δεινός. But the question is neither raised nor addressed here concerning how the same λόγος that is said to be both weaker and stronger, that brings the weaker and stronger together, making the weaker stronger, is to be determined as such, as either weaker or stronger. And the more one puzzles over this older accusation, the stranger it becomes. In being persuasive and terribly clever, does Socrates actually transform his weaker λόγος, turning it into something that is actually stronger? How, then, does this persuasive transformation occur? Or is it the case that his "stronger" λόγος only *appears* to be stronger, that is, by virtue of its being merely persuasive, while in truth remaining weaker? It should be noted that the determinations "weaker" and "stronger" are comparatives. And so, one could also hear the accusation to say that Socratic dialogue, as a *refutative* practice, makes the originally stronger speech of his interlocutor weaker than his own; in his refutations, as he displays the ignorance of his interlocutor, Socrates makes his own speech stronger by making the speech of another *weaker*. Socratic strength would thus always be predicated on the relative weakness of another. Nevertheless, this in itself still does not settle the question of how the comparatives as such are first to be determined. With regard to *what* is a λόγος taken to be strong or weak? If Socrates only makes something appear to be weak when it is in truth, or by "nature," strong, as he undermines the conventional wisdom of prominent Athenians, this could indeed be called a form of degeneration or corruption, and as such could be said to be a wrongdoing, a kind of ἀδικεῖν.

The liminal dialogue enacted within the *Apology* thus hinges on a series of questions: Is it supposed that Socrates only *persuades* others to take what is weaker as stronger, or does the accusation mean to say that he actually gives strength to something that is inherently weak, to what was *before* weaker, making it stronger by adding something to it, transforming it in truth? What is the experience of Socratic refutation (or Socratic wisdom) such that this insidious strength can be attributed to the Socratic λόγος itself, a strength that would only mask its more profound weakness? Yet how would this alleged weakness be covered over by the clever Socrates while still being obvious to all? One has to conclude that the Athenians who condemn him are, in fact, quite unpersuaded by the weak/strong Socratic λόγος. But if Socrates is able to force or to compel his interlocutor to agree with him, to give that interlocutor no choice but to assent to convictions that nevertheless remain unpersuasive, above all to that very interlocutor, how can this happen?

Socrates in the *Apology* does not address this question directly, the question that concerns where the measure of such strength and such weakness is to be found. He does not address what occurs through dialogical refutation, except to say that it exposes an ignorance, a failed wisdom. Perhaps the situation of the *Apology* precludes the possibility of such an address taking place, and this would confirm its tragic structure. The rift that opens between Socrates and the "men of Athens" proves to be no less abysmal than the incompatible communication that takes place between Sophocles' Antigone and Creon. And yet, regardless of how one finally comes to answer the question, the possibility of taking it up presupposes that there would indeed be operative, however obscurely, an elusive measure for the λόγος and its presumed strength, even if one wanted to insist that such a measure would have to be referred back only to the λόγος itself, precisely to its own persuasive movement in the city. That Socrates neglects this question in the *Apology* does not make the question irrelevant or unimportant. On the contrary, the entirety of Socratic practice can be viewed as it hinges on this question, and as it points toward the nature that exceeds the mere persuasive movement of speech. But if the question arises in other dialogues it should then be possible to let its way of appearing inform the reading of the *Apology*.

Thus, very briefly, one reads in the *Phaedo*, for example, as Socrates accounts for his "second sailing," that Socratic inquiry is always grounded in a certain hypothesis. But making the hypothesis explicit, far from being the arbitrary positing of a logical assumption, actually demands an affirmation of the λόγος as it already imposes a decisive claim upon the speaker. What Socrates says in that text is that in each case the λόγος that is taken over is the one that he finds to be ἐρρωμενέστατον, or "mightiest" (Phaedo 100a). And if, through questioning, this λόγος should prove to be in need of a λόγος, if an account must be given of this hypothesis itself, this, says Socrates, only involves recourse to still another hypothesis (Phaedo 101d). The Socratic hypothesis is thus so far from being something like a thought experiment that it opens up precisely an inevitable dependency upon speech in its priority, the impossibility that one might detach oneself from what allows one to begin thinking, speaking, and even acting.[23] What the hypothesis points to is the necessity of taking up in an explicit way the presuppositions that have already asserted themselves, not by attempting to ground them in a pure and unshakable beginning, but by attempting to see what issues from them as they have already claimed us.

It should also be recalled how the *Republic* begins, with Polemarchus and his gang arresting the very ascent of Socrates and Glaucon, challenging them to submit to his demands if they are unable to prove stronger (κρείττους γένεσθε) (Rep. 327c). The Socratic response to this challenge, as it introduces the possibility of persuasion as a third option, thus also raises the question of the possible strength of such persuasion and the question of how such strength would assert itself. Is the Socratic λόγος itself a kind of strength, or is it an alternative to strength as such? The forbidding reply of Polemarchus, which proposes, in the form of a question, that persuasion utterly depends upon the receptivity of the listener, would suggest that the Socratic λόγος is *not* a kind of strength at all. In this same text, Thrasymachus will tell us, in posing the decisive difficulty that sets into motion the entire questioning of the *Republic*, that justice is nothing other than what benefits the stronger (τὸ δίκαιον οὐκ ἄλλο τι ἢ τὸ τοῦ κρείττονος συμφέρον) (Rep. 338c). Socrates manages to keep the Thrasymachian wolf at bay, succeeds only in charming him like one charms a snake, by pointing out that what is still needed in such a formulation of justice is an adequate account of what would constitute such strength and thereby such benefit. And yet, if Socrates succeeds in holding the wolf at bay, by showing that he is not able to offer such an account, only in Book II, in the renewed exchange with Glaucon and Adeimantus, does it then become clear that such an account would have to be able to address precisely the relation between nature and city, and thus between nature and νόμος, as this relation is bound to the difference between what is and what only appears to be, what is only held for true. If Thrasymachian strength is held at bay by the Socratic λόγος, this is accomplished only by opening up the entire questioning that becomes the dialogue of the *Republic*, that addresses the difficulty at issue in that dialogue. That Socrates succeeds in only *subduing* Thrasymachus—not converting him—shows how the characterization of Socrates that is first introduced in the *Apology*, as one who makes the weaker λόγος stronger, is attached to the difficulty I am calling the Socratic doubling of nature. It turns out, in other words, that an account of the very strength of the stronger λόγος would have to account for the way in which this strength has already made an implicit appeal to the relation and the difference between the human political realm, the realm within which such strength would appear and become persuasive, and the natural realm that would ground such strength. What would have to be addressed, in other words, is the very *grounding* character of such a ground. In doing so, such an account would have to address whether these realms are simply opposed or, if related, in what way they are related. Socrates demonstrates, however, in the doubling of nature, that this relation can hold the opposition within itself: the political realm, as νόμος, can presume to be detached from a natural determination only because this difference is already claimed as a movement of nature itself. The Socratic task of self-knowledge, as it turns on nature's concealment, thus proves to have inescapably a political dimension.

But if nature and the inquiry into nature must be opposed to every possible relation to the gods, as the accusers imply, then this exhaustive disjunction between the natural and the divine might also be bound up with an opposition between what occurs by nature and what allows itself to be determined merely through the power of persuasion, an opposition, then, between the natural realm and the realm in which νομίζειν and νόμος prevail. But then the gods, too, would have to be subordinated to the effects of persuasion.[24] And those who accuse Socrates of *not* believing in the gods could do so *only because they themselves already no longer believe*, only because they themselves recognize the gods as a matter that is reducible to political expediency, an expediency that has no place in nature, that means little or nothing outside the walls of the city. The charges brought against Socrates, as they are grounded in such deep-seated and long-standing prejudices, thus depend upon a powerful and insidious disjunction between nature and the human realm, as that human realm is thought to be determined primarily by νόμος, πίστις, and δόξα.

The accusers speak of a certain Socrates. But is this not the same controversial *name* or reputation constantly invoked and taken up by the Platonic text? Leo Strauss points out,[25] as does John Sallis,[26] that the *Apology of Socrates* is certainly distinctive in that it is the only Platonic text in which the *name* of Socrates appears in the title. The Platonic dialogues as a whole also continually present themselves as engaging and challenging the persuasive and vehement undercurrent that would judge Socrates, that has already presumed to be able to judge him. Such an engagement (but can it be called a dialogue?) must be read, in fact, as a question that is always at issue in the text, the question that concerns what is at stake in this name: Who is Socrates?[27] The apparent frustration of the Socrates who appears in this *Apology* is that, while his very name is at stake—and thus it becomes necessary to make a defense—the names of his long-standing and numerous accusers remain wholly indeterminate and elusive. It is this lack of the name that also prevents dialogue, or at least makes impossible a direct and explicit interrogation of those who accuse and slander him.

> But what is most unaccountable of all [ἀλογώτατον] is that it is not even possible to know or speak their names, except when one of them happens to be a maker of comedies. And all those who persuaded you by means of envy and slander—and some also persuaded others because they had been persuaded themselves—all these are the most impossible [ἀπορώτατοι]; for it is not even possible to call any of them up here and refute them, but it is necessary in defending myself to fight clumsily with shadows, as it were, and to refute [ἐλέγχειν] when nobody answers. (Apol. 18c–d)

Socrates identifies here, precisely by referring to this impossibility, a need to let the refutative movement of speech reveal the truth. We shall return to this question most explicitly in the next chapter, in the treatment of the *Gorgias*. The reference Socrates makes to the comedy of Aristophanes is also important, and it occurs one more time in the *Apology*, as Socrates again explicitly distances himself from this poet's portrayal of him: "a Socrates being carried about there, saying he was walking on air and foolishly speaking a lot of other foolishness, about which I know nothing" (Apol. 19c). This disavowal of the comic Socrates who would *detach himself from the earth* is also already connected to the prior widespread assumption that concerns what is taken to be a necessary disjunction between the human belief in the divine and the study of nature.[28] As one of the μετεωρολόγοι, Socrates would indeed soar into the heavens, but it is already assumed by many that he could do this only because the heavens are devoid of gods. It is worth anticipating at this point also how Aristophanes is mentioned in the *Phaedo,* as Socrates speaks of the way in which what concerns him philosophically finds itself dramatically projected but thereby also distorted. Not even a maker of comedies, remarks Socrates, would say that Socrates, on the very day of his death, in telling stories about how philosophy begins in the fact of human mortality and extends itself into that mortality—as it inquires into the soul "itself in accordance with itself"—is making speeches about matters that do not concern him (Phaedo 70c). This is to say that the investigation into subterranean and heavenly things is not unrelated to the way in which Socratic inquiry is bound to the question of the soul and human mortality. It may be that our mortality is most intimately connected to our relation to the earth and the heavens.

The discussion of the older set of accusations, as they come to be explicitly formulated by Socrates himself, serves as a way to bring to the popular opinions that surround Socratic practice a determinacy that they otherwise would not have. This determinacy, introduced by Socrates, also makes possible the examination of these opinions in the λόγος. They can be interrogated as they are brought into an arena of an explicit dialectical scrutiny, held accountable to the very account they give. The truth Socrates promises to speak in his *Apology* thus begins by attempting a recovery and a transformation of his reputed wisdom, which is meant originally only as a slander: there is a certain Socrates, a *wise* man. . . . Thus, it is utterly significant that Socrates himself, in accounting for his reputation, does, in fact, begin by attributing that reputation to a wisdom. But if the so-called wise Socrates is now able to show that this peculiar wisdom is not simply the inquiry into the things of nature, in the way that his many accusers would contend, how does such wisdom nevertheless sustain itself in an engagement with nature? In other words, how does the Socratic engagement with nature, as nature itself shows itself in a certain necessary self-concealing, find itself opened up in the *Apology* precisely through the articulation of Socratic wisdom as a kind of self-knowledge?

If it can be said that Socrates knows himself, it is no less true that he himself also experiences or undergoes the seductive power of the speech of his accusers. We see this quite clearly if we return to the very beginning of the text, which opens with Socrates addressing the effects of the accusers' persuasion. While not himself persuaded, Socrates also does not remain *unaffected* by the speech. He concedes, in fact, even if with an unmistakable irony, that he has come close to forgetting himself, close to forgetting who he is, such is the persuasive power of the accusation. But if Socrates is able to be so affected, how will this speech—which we do not have the privilege of hearing, from which we are thus sheltered—have to be heard by others, by those whom Socrates repeatedly addresses simply as the "men of Athens"?

> How you, men of Athens, have suffered [πεπόνθατε] from my accusers, I do not know. I for my part almost forgot myself, so persuasively did they speak. [ἐγὼ δ' οὖν καὶ αὐτὸς ὑπ' αὐτὸν ὀλίγου ἐμαυτοῦ ἐπελαθόμην· οὕτω πιθανῶς ἔλεγον.] And yet, in what they have said they have spoken not a word of truth. (Apol. 17a)

The speeches that we do not hear, the ones made by the accusers, as they set the stage before Socrates makes his entrance, are said by Socrates to cause him almost to forget himself, almost to lose himself as he tries to find himself in what they have said. In this way, the text opens by opening up a difference between the untruth or falsehood, as a persuasive speech, and a true λόγος, but by conceding to speech apart from this difference a certain power as "mere" persuasion. While the accusers have said nothing true, from Socrates we are to hear or to listen to the whole truth. "From me you

will hear the whole truth [ὑμεῖς δ' ἐμοῦ ἀκούσεσθε πᾶσαν τὴν ἀλήθειαν]"
(Apol. 17b). But this listening or hearing, which can receive the truth but
also can be persuaded by the lie, is therefore characterized as a kind of
πάσχειν: "I do not know how you were affected, πεπόνθατε." And what is
raised as a possibility in such utter receptivity or passivity has to do with
the way in which speech can bring about a certain λήθη in the listener, can
effect a concealing, as that listener can be affected by speech, can come to
suffer what is disclosed through it.

Thus, if it is clear that Socrates does *not* succumb to the speeches of the
accusers, his admission that they spoke persuasively is also not to be simply passed over on the grounds that it is meant only with irony. The irony
itself points instead precisely to the need to respond to the peculiar power
of the accusing but false λόγος, the fact that there is indeed a certain difficulty in resisting its persuasion. What becomes evident in this way is that
Socratic self-knowledge—which in the *Phaedrus* appears as inseparable
from a kind of sickness for the hearing of speeches (Phaedr. 228b)—always
remains bound in some way to this simple persuasive power of speech,
that the task of such knowledge cannot be taken up independently of this
disclosive movement of speech as persuasion.

The λόγος can persuade even when it is untrue. What is it that enables
such a false λόγος to achieve the persuasion that renders it virtually indis-
tinguishable from the true λόγος, that allows it while false to appear *as
true?* The difficulty that confronts the reader in this question of a false
yet persuasive λόγος thus comes to be repeated in the charge made against
Socratic persuasion, namely that he makes the weaker λόγος the stronger,
a charge that now appears to bear upon the Socratic relation to nature.
Accounting for the possibility of a persuasive falsehood, as it is introduced by Socrates at the very beginning of the text, must therefore also
bear upon the way in which Socrates himself *appears* to the Athenians,
insofar as he is taken by them to be one who deceives and corrupts. The
speech is said to be a ψεῦδος because it does *not* reveal Socrates. It conceals him, however, not simply through a covering over, but by misleading, by actually *showing* him to be something, which is to say, something
he is not. Thus, the ψεῦδος can be persuasive because it does enact a certain pretense, the *showing* that conceals precisely in the showing, while
also not showing precisely the concealing that it is. This twofold structure of the persuasive movement of false speech, which obviously remains dependent upon the truth in one respect, also *in another respect*
must precede the distinction between the true and the false: in order to
be persuasive it must also be *possible* for the λόγος to be false. And it must
be said, then, that every persuasive λόγος, whether true or false, must first
of all appear as true if it is to be persuasive at all. If the ψεῦδος in this way
shows itself to depend upon the truth, because it must *seem* to be true, it
is also the case that every true λόγος remains dependent upon this prior

and undecidable showing, as the pure appearance that it cannot bypass or dismiss.

The true λόγος, no less than the successful ψεῦδος, must *seem* true. The contradiction consists, then, in the fact that the ψεῦδος, as a concealing, can reveal itself *as a concealing* only when it *no longer* is able to conceal. The ψεῦδος reveals itself *as such* only when it is no longer able to be precisely what it would reveal itself to be. The point at which the ψεῦδος comes to be discerned and thus distinguishable from the true speech is precisely the point at which it is *no longer* persuasive. It thus must be said that something is obscured in this movement in which the lie comes to be exposed, a movement of obscuration that is only indirectly expressed in the phrase "no longer." What is obscured is nothing less than the persuasive power belonging to speech, in which it is able to bring about the πάσχειν that cannot be fully determined or accounted for simply in the difference between the true and the false. This point returns us to the thematic starting point of this study: the movement of tradition is also a movement of showing, a doubling in which its transmission (disclosure) is grounded in a prior concealment that also must remain concealed. The descent of Socrates, in other words, as the originary contestation over the origin of philosophy, is enacted in the very first lines of the *Apology,* raised as the question of a possible self-knowledge precisely through the disclosive movement of speech, precisely as this movement precedes the traditional mimetic structure of the difference between origin and (false) image.

It turns out, however, that the *wisdom* of Socrates, as it comes to be revealed in his practice and as it remains bound to the disclosive movement of the λόγος, shows itself to be such that it cannot be accounted for simply in the difference between the speech that proves false and the speech that would be true. Such a practice (and such a wisdom) proves to be irreducible to this difference because such a difference as such still remains dependent upon the utter disjunction between what is and what only appears, a disjunction that correlates also to an interpretation of nature's way of becoming manifest. The peculiar receptivity of Socrates shows itself instead to consist in the way in which he is able to attend to the simple manifesting of speech in its disclosive movement, as it makes possible a certain self-showing, while neither insisting upon a dogmatic attachment to things said nor abandoning speech to the indeterminacy that would render speech a mere means to political advantage. It is in this middle position—as an affirmation of the doubling—that we find the Socratic genius for refutation, his astonishing ability to expose ignorance without himself having a positive knowledge over the matters in which the refutation takes place. Socrates thus traces the accusation made against him, that as one who is wise he makes the weaker speech stronger, back to the practice of refutation or ἔλεγχος. "On each occasion those present suppose that I am wise concerning that in which I refute another" (Apol. 23a). In this way the *name* of Socrates thus becomes the name of one who is wise; his name or reputation is synonymous with being wise: ὄνομα δὲ τοῦτο λέγεσθαι, σοφὸς εἶναι (Apol. 23a).

Those spoken of here are the same ones who suppose that the inquiry into nature implies the absence of the gods. They are the same ones who also take Socratic refutation to consist simply in a superior knowledge. They are unable to see how dialogical questioning, as a refutative capacity (making the weaker speech stronger), is also bound to a peculiar ignorance and to the affirmation of that ignorance in and through dialogical engagement. For this reason, both the Socratic turn to the λόγοι and the reinterpretation Socrates gives of his reputed wisdom in the *Apology* must be related to the necessity of nature's concealing, precisely as that concealing poses the task of self-knowledge. If this task is able to sustain itself only in a certain turn toward the disclosive movement of speech, what must be addressed is how this same movement occurs also as nature's own way of becoming manifest.

4

The Good, the Bad, and the Ugly

Nature, Rhetoric, and Refutation in the Gorgias

Before I proceed along these lines any further, I would like to interrupt this reading of the *Apology* long enough to insert a discussion of the *Gorgias,* and in particular the accusation made by Callicles against Socrates as it is issued near the very center of that dialogue, namely that in his *refutative* encounters with Polus and Gorgias, Socrates exploits and yet covers over the difference that prevails between what holds according to φύσις, or nature, and what holds merely according to νόμος, or convention (Gorg. 482cff.). An elaboration of refutation (ἔλεγχος) in this context reveals how the Socratic turn to dialogue, and to the necessity of dialogue, is intimately bound to a transformation of nature and the human relation to nature. Socratic refutation in the *Gorgias* can be said to enact a kind of *dialogical justice* that unfolds only in the affirmation of the human good as it is inexorably bound to a prior community, the friendship that arises from out of the belonging together of all things. The dialogue demonstrates that it is this community that returns Socrates to the task of self-knowledge as a possible friendship with oneself.

What Callicles says can be heard as an attempted summary of what occurs through Socratic refutation: "And this, take note, is your wise ploy for working evil in speeches: when one says something according to convention [κατὰ νόμον] you respond according to nature [κατὰ φύσιν], and when one speaks of what is according to nature, you respond with what is according to convention" (Gorg. 483a). Now while it is the case that in this dialogue Socrates both flatly denies the opposition as such and denies that he exploits the opposition in his refutations (Gorg. 489b), it is nevertheless worth recalling how Aristotle will account for this very stratagem, the one that in Plato's text Callicles attributes to Socratic refutation, as a piece of sophistry.[1] Callicles, however, raises this objection against Socrates as a way to deprecate what he takes to be a distinctly *philosophical* practice. Closely connected to the charge that philosophy exploits the distinction between nature and human convention is the further claim that philosophy leads to a corruption or a degeneration of human life. It is the ruin of humans, the διαφθορὰ τῶν ἀνθρώπων, especially if the one who takes it up continues to pursue it beyond youth.

The relative benefit or harm philosophy holds for human life thus comes to be articulated by Callicles within the *nature* of human life, precisely as that nature is bound up with a movement of *aging,* and cannot be determined in abstraction from such movement. Philosophy is thus said not only to present a distorting interpretation of nature—by covertly exploiting the distinction between nature and convention—but to be itself a degenerate form of nature. Callicles thus asks Socrates to dispense with philosophy and to move on to "bigger things" (Gorg. 484c–d). It becomes clear that this means that Socrates should cease refuting: παῦσαι δ' ἐλέγξων (Gorg. 486c). Philosophy can be compared to lisping and the playing of tricks, which Callicles states are endearing when found in youth but become disgusting if encountered in one who is older (Gorg. 485b). But what is most debilitating about philosophy, when it is pursued beyond the years appropriate to it, consists in the way it produces "ridiculous" and "unmanly" individuals who are unable to defend themselves in public. Philosophy is thus something *shameful*—and we might also say, ugly— because of the political ineptitude that it brings about. Callicles challenges the wisdom of an "art" (τέχνη) that renders one utterly incapable of saving oneself "from the greatest dangers" (ἐκ τῶν μεγίστων κινδύνων) (Gorg. 486b).

> For as it is, if someone got hold of you or of anyone else like you and took you off to prison on the charge of injustice when you were not unjust [φάσκων ἀδικεῖν μηδὲν ἀδικοῦντα], you know that you wouldn't have any use for yourself. You would be dizzy and agape with nothing to say. You'd go to trial facing a no good accuser and be put to death, if death is that to which that one would condemn you. (Gorg. 486a–b)

In the *Apology*, Socrates himself raises this very objection against himself and responds to it, namely that he should be ashamed of getting himself into such trouble. "Are you not ashamed, Socrates, of having pursued such a pursuit that now, from this, you are in danger of being put to death?" (Apol. 28b). The Socratic response to Callicles can thus be seen as a repetition or a prefiguring of the *Apology,* since both texts must present nothing less than a defense of philosophical inquiry and practice. What is at stake in this defense is thus also the question of Socratic beauty over and against the apparent "shame" of philosophizing. It is important, then, that Callicles not only attacks Socratic philosophical practice as a dysfunctional or degenerate appropriation of nature, as a corruption of nature, but makes clear that this has to do more precisely with an inability to defend oneself by means of speech in a public context such as a trial. It is important to note, therefore, that Socrates responds to this attack in the *Gorgias* by speaking of it as an opportunity to undergo a certain testing of himself. It is evident, in other words, that the challenges posed by an attack from one who is presumed to be wise (Callicles) come to be interpreted by Socrates also as an opportunity to take up the task of self-knowledge (Gorg. 486d–487a).

With regard to the questions that have just been raised in the *Apology*, the *Gorgias* provides an excellent place to undertake a consideration of the charge made against Socrates that through his refutations he makes the weaker speech stronger, especially as that charge can be explicated only through a Socratic relation to nature. But the *Gorgias* also presents a dialogical interrogation of rhetoric itself with self-professed rhetoricians who find themselves having to confront the question of the truth of persuasion while being denied the chance to employ rhetorical devices in their own defense. Socrates thus insists throughout the dialogue that the conversation proceed by means of brief speech (βραχυλογία) rather than lengthy speech (μακρολογία).[2] The *Gorgias* stands in stark contrast, then, to the situation of the *Apology*, almost as a kind of inversion of it, since the *Apology* as a public speech is determined precisely by the impossibility of refutation through dialogical questioning. The dialogical refutation that does occur in the *Apology*, as, for example, when Socrates calls Meletus to the stand, only demonstrates how this more careful way of proceeding, as it is distinctively Socratic, finds itself easily overwhelmed by more lengthy speeches and by the deep-seated prejudices against Socrates that have been circulating already for a long time. Yet it is also the case that Socrates proves to be no more persuasive in the *Gorgias* than he is in the *Apology;* the *Gorgias* does *not* portray the persuasive power of Socratic refutation at all but rather only confirms its extreme political failure. The dialogue also thereby sheds light on how the prevailing hatred of Socrates—the deep-seated prejudice against him—comes to be, as Socrates speaks of it in the *Apology*.

In the *Gorgias* Socrates repeatedly interrupts his own questioning at crucial junctures, in order to make explicit how he views his interaction with others, as that interaction is bound to speech and dialogue. He puts into relief the way in which his own practice must be distinguished from the more combative agenda that would first of all seek victory in the λόγος at the cost of coming to a better knowledge of what is at issue in that λόγος. Socrates declares to Gorgias that he is one who enters into dialogue (διαλέγεται) "desiring to know that about which the speech is" (βουλόμενος εἰδέναι αὐτὸ τοῦτο περὶ ὅτου ὁ λόγος ἐστί) (Gorg. 453b). His questioning, he says, is not directed at Gorgias himself but the λόγος and the possibility of revealing what is at issue in it (Gorg. 453c). Why does Socrates persist in asking questions where things seem already clear or evident (δῆλον)? "I ask my questions for the sake of thoroughly retracing and following through on the λόγος, not because of you (οὐ σοῦ ἕνεκα, not because I am aiming at you), but to prevent us from habitually grabbing recklessly at the things each of us has said, so that you may elaborate and follow through on what is yours according to what you have set down [τὰ σαυτοῦ κατὰ τὴν ὑπόθεσιν]" (Gorg. 454b–c).

Dialogue thus seeks to work against the hasty anticipation of what is said, and so amounts to a shift in the *time* of speaking, in the way in which inquiry must be allowed to take its time. When rhetoric comes to be distinguished from teaching, because rhetoric brings about only conviction and not knowledge, Socrates states that this has to do with the constraints of time, that one cannot manage to teach a crowd on such great matters ἐν ὀλίγῳ χρόνῳ, "in a short time" (Gorg. 455a). Similarly, when in the *Apology* Socrates accounts for his chances of overcoming the deep prejudices against him, he says that he would be surprised if this could be done ἐν οὕτως ὀλίγῳ χρόνῳ, "in such a short time" (Apol. 19a, 24a, 37b). And when Socrates at one point pauses in order to reiterate his own desire in the conversation, it again becomes clear how such engagement through refutation, as another way of proceeding in speech, cannot be abstracted from the question of time or the possible openness of time in σχολή. At this point Socrates anticipates his refutation of Gorgias but expresses a certain fear and asks whether he should not abandon the matter, since Gorgias may take it as a personal attack, may mistake Socrates' desire as it is directed at the matter for mere contentiousness (Gorg. 457e). Socrates himself claims to be one who is just as pleased to be refuted, if he says something not true, as he is pleased to refute another if that one happens to speak untruly (Gorg. 458a). But when Gorgias affirms his own willingness to engage Socrates in this way, the question then becomes one of time and whether such a continuation might not detain those present who are wanting to do something else, who may be βουλομένους τι καὶ ἄλλο πράττειν (Gorg. 458c). Likewise just before the point at which the conversation with Gorgias is abruptly overtaken by the brash Polus, Socrates does not revel in the refutation of Gorgias, but only affirms the difficulty that has been now opened up. Socrates proclaims, swearing "by the Dog!" that a thorough examination of the issue, an inquiry that would be namely ἱκανῶς, is something that demands οὐκ ὀλίγης συνουσίας, no brief meeting, a being together that must perhaps extend beyond the time allotted to us (Gorg. 461b).

The *Gorgias* begins with Gorgias himself, at the prompting of Socrates, defending his own τέχνη—the τέχνη he both practices and also presumably teaches to others (Gorg. 449b)—as the art of rhetoric, which he initially claims to be only that art that has to do with λόγοι or speeches (Gorg.

449d), but which he then must concede to be also the ability through speeches to bring about persuasion (πειθώ) in the listener, or in the soul of the listener (Gorg. 452e–453a). What is most decisive here, however, is that Gorgias is asked to account for this rhetorical skill in the same way that one would account for any other τέχνη, which is to say through a determination of its ἔργον and its δύναμις, its work and its power. And since the other arts, as differing forms of expertise, are no less bound to the λόγος, the question becomes one of determining as precisely as possible the peculiar matter over which rhetoric can be said to have its own proper expertise and authority. It is the same with all the arts, says Socrates. Each of them is concerned with the λόγος, some more so than others, but each is concerned with the λόγος only as that λόγος happens to deal with the matter (περὶ τὸ πρᾶγμα) that is proper to each art as such (Gorg. 450a-b). The question thus becomes: *With regard to what* does rhetoric have its authority and power in the λόγος (ἡ περὶ τί ἐν λόγοις τὸ κῦρος ἔχουσα ῥητορική ἐστιν)? (Gorg. 451a). Where is one to look for the region that would ground the κῦρος that is unique to rhetoric? When Socrates presses Gorgias to respond to this question he at first can only say that rhetoric concerns τὰ μέγιστα τῶν ἀνθρωπείων πραγμάτων . . . καὶ ἄριστα, "the greatest and the best of human affairs" (Gorg. 451d). But if Gorgias's rhetoric is to distinguish itself as an art in distinction from all other arts, even those that make similar claims about having to do with what is of paramount importance to human life, such as the arts that deal with health or with the acquisition of money, it becomes necessary to give a more precise account of that with which the rhetorical art is concerned. Thus, finally, Gorgias makes a most important concession: "Well I am speaking of that sort of persuasion, Socrates, that takes place in the law-courts and in other mass-gatherings, as I already just said, and it is concerned with the things that are just and unjust [περὶ τούτων ἅ ἐστι δίκαιά τε καὶ ἄδικα]" (Gorg. 454b).

The demand that Gorgias account for rhetoric as a τέχνη leads to the claim that his persuasive skill amounts to a kind of expertise concerning matters of justice. But if rhetoric is able to reveal justice (or the lack of justice) to the listener, in the way that the healing art is able to reveal health or the lack of it, it would seem then that persuasion is a form of teaching. Yet it can hardly be said that the listener who is persuaded is actually required to learn justice in order to be persuaded. And how could it be asserted that the one who achieves an expertise in this persuasive art becomes thereby knowledgeable concerning justice? It would seem that if persuasion is a teaching, then becoming convinced (πεπιστευκέναι) is the same as having learned (μεμαθηκέναι) (Gorg. 454c).

Gorgias readily agrees that there is a difference between πίστις and ἐπιστήμη, between trust or conviction and discursive knowledge. The difference can be said to lie in the way that πίστις can be false and still be a πίστις, whereas a false knowledge is no knowledge at all. Thus, even to say that knowledge as such is true is already to enter into deeply misleading formulations, if truth here is meant as something that is simply opposed to the false. To assert the *truth* of knowledge does not serve to distinguish it at all, in the way that asserting the truth of an opinion can distinguish it from a false opinion, since the truth proper to discursive knowledge differs from opinion as such, whether that opinion be true or false. In the *Meno* Socrates insists that this is one of the very few things he claims *to know,* namely that there is a difference between knowledge and (right) opinion (Meno 98b). This Socratic knowledge concerning the very character of knowledge, as it arises in the determination of a difference that sets knowledge apart from the way things for the most part show themselves to human life, must be taken as a indispensable feature of Socratic refutation. The truth proper to ἐπιστήμη cannot be thought simply as a superior form of πίστις, since the determination that would distinguish them from each other opens up an unbridgeable difference, a difference marked by an abyss. To say that knowledge is more true than conviction, trust, and opinion is like saying that a circle is more round than any square. The truth of πίστις is *necessarily* related to its possible falsehood, and this concerns the very way things become manifest thereby: such becoming manifest can be affirmed only through the accompanying affirmation of this possibility. Trust, even if true, remains a form of ignorance, which is to say, utterly separated from knowledge.

And yet, despite this, the peculiar power of rhetoric is that in a public setting it can appear more knowledgeable than even the expert or specialist, that it thereby enables the speaker to be more compelling and persuasive to the audience regardless of what is at issue in the speech. Gorgias proudly declares: "There is no matter about which the rhetorician could not speak more persuasively before a multitude than any craftsman" (Gorg. 456c). Gorgias readily agrees that while rhetoric is indeed able to produce conviction in the listener in a way that surpasses even the persuasive power of the specialist, this ability also depends upon the ignorance of the listener. Persuasion succeeds only where the listener is a *non*-knower. If the one who is sick can be more easily persuaded by the rhetorical non-physician (Gorg. 456b), it is also the case that the physician as such, as a knower, is not susceptible to this persuasion (Gorg. 459a). And yet, it is apparent from the very beginning of the dialogue that the certainty that must be afforded to each and every τέχνη, as a reliable and knowing relation to what is, depends first of all upon the way in which each art must be strictly confined to its own domain or region: the knowledge that is τέχνη is defined by its περὶ τί τῶν ὄντων, by the way in which it has a boundary or limit that both restricts and grants it its authority, its κῦρος over its own proper matter. But the justice addressed by rhetoric pertains to all the arts, proves to be at issue in all regions within which human life confronts its own reliable and productive engagement with nature while being reducible to none of them.

If it is not possible, strictly speaking, for each human being to attain a mastery over the totality of these arts, if no one can be counted as an expert in *all* matters, then human knowledge, as necessarily fragmented or regionalized in this way, also cannot provide the measure for justice. In other words, the power of persuasive speech (as rhetoric) to bear upon matters of justice is predicated upon the limits of knowledge as τέχνη and the way in which justice remains irreducible to the regionalized expertise of any one τέχνη. Rhetoric can be said to live only in this *tragic* necessity, that a basic ignorance defines human community, that what is *common* to all the arts remains elusive because it must remain something that cannot be rendered transparent in any particular art. But this would mean also that there is no τέχνη or ἐπιστήμη that could ground the authority of νόμος as such. It would mean, then, contrary to what Socrates will tell Polus (Gorg. 464b–465c), that there is no τέχνη for political matters and for matters concerning life or soul—that unlike the gymnastics and healing arts that pertain to the body, the alleged arts of νομοθετική and δικαιοσύνη remain absent. It would appear, then, that the authority of justice can be determined only according to νόμος. For if νόμος too, like justice, must remain outside or prior to the regionalized certainty afforded to τέχνη and ἐπιστήμη, then every νόμος (as an expression of νομίζειν) must likewise be returned to πίστις and δόξα. The life of justice would be inseparable from its way of being grounded in persuasion. But precisely for this reason, perhaps, such πίστις and δόξα must still account for itself, must still submit itself to the dialogical questioning that would interrogate it as a λόγος.

The refutation of Gorgias, as an example of a Socratic ποίησις, the alleged making in which the weaker speech becomes stronger, consists at this point only in exposing an apparent contradiction. On the one hand, Gorgias insists that rhetoric and justice remain independent of each other, since he admits that the persuasive ability of the rhetorician is something that may be *used* either justly or unjustly. The relation rhetoric holds to justice is thus determined in its use or χρῆσθαι, but the sheer persuasive power itself does not in itself have to be directed toward what is just (Gorg. 456c–457c). In this sense, neither is justice determined by rhetoric, nor does rhetoric have to submit itself to justice. Rhetoric can be unjust and still be rhetoric, and there is a justice that would be able to remain untouched by the persuasive manipulations of rhetoric. But, on the other hand, Gorgias also finds himself claiming that one will necessarily learn about justice while learning rhetoric, if, that is, such a one does not already know justice beforehand (Gorg. 460a). It is important to see that Socrates connects this last claim to Gorgias's earlier statement, which is made as an attempt to account for rhetoric under the assumption that it is to be regarded as a τέχνη, namely, that the speeches made through this art always (ἀεί) concern what is just and unjust as that over which or about which they have their proper expertise (Gorg. 460c). As a τέχνη, how could rhetoric not submit itself to its matter as the measure of its own success? If it is possible to disregard the knowledge of justice at issue in rhetoric, then it would seem that rhetoric is no longer to be taken as a τέχνη at all. And since it is agreed that it is not possible for one who actually *knows* justice not to want also to be just (Gorg. 460b–c), this appears to contradict the possibility of using rhetoric for unjust ends. As a knowledge of justice, rhetoric would already have to demand the just use of rhetoric, would already have to submit itself to a prior justice, to the very priority of justice. The use would follow from the truth or the knowledge that makes the art the art that it is.

Precisely at this point Polus is no longer able to contain himself. He interrupts the conversation and attacks Socrates, whom he accuses of rudely shaming Gorgias into a contradiction (Gorg. 461b–c). According to Polus, the *shame* of Gorgias is, in fact, decisive for the apparent refutation, just as it is for Callicles when he comes to account for the refutation of both Gorgias and Polus through the disjunction between nature and convention or law (Gorg. 482e). But what is shameful here? What grounds the shame? What makes it possible? According to Polus, Socrates has shamed Gorgias into the refutation because no one would admit to not knowing what is just, noble, and good. Gorgias's concession that he will teach these things to others, if for some strange reason they do not already know them, is only a concession based upon the assumption that these things are already quite evident to everyone and that they are not in need of being taught at all. Would it not indeed be shameful to admit that one lacks even common sense? (Gorg. 461c). In the *Meno* we learn that Gorgias is well known and even admired for his refusing to claim that he teaches any kind of ἀρετή (Meno 95c). It is also the case that to claim an ability to *produce* individuals who are good would seem to make one responsible, even if only indirectly, for their actions, their deeds, whether just or unjust. And yet, the refusal to be willing to teach something that is supposed to be already evident could be taken as shameful not only because one thereby seems to admit an ignorance concerning the self-evident. In refusing to address explicitly and carefully what is thought to be already plain as day, already available to everyone, the persuasive speaker also preserves the possibility for a deception that exploits this presumption that justice is self-evident. What would be shameful, therefore, is not simply the admission that one cannot teach justice (because of ignorance) but rather the admission that one cannot teach justice because it is justice that the effective speaker must be able to manipulate and exploit. The Socratic refutation is thus irreducible to the appeal to rationality.[3] Rather, the character of the Socratic refutation of Gorgias certainly allows for this indeterminacy of the shame. If Gorgias admits that he only invents or manipulates justice, then his persuasion would be exposed as a lie, would be betrayed, since such a justice would lack legitimacy, would no longer be just. But if he admits that his rhetoric, as an actual knowledge, only submits itself to its matter, grounded in the authority of a prior justice, how does this still give *power* to the persuasive speaker? What would be left for Gorgias to teach?

The younger and more aggressive Polus, who, as Gorgias's student, also claims to know everything his teacher knows, in now responding to the Socratic λόγος, will have to proceed in a way that is more shameless, less affected by this shame. The operation of shame—even through the desire to resist it—pervades this dialogue as a πάθος. But it also appears throughout the dialogues in general. The beautiful Alcibiades, for example, remarks that Socrates is the only one who has ever brought him to this kind of self-awareness as it is reflected back upon oneself and through another (Sym. 216b). And Socrates himself is by no means immune to the experience of shame. In the *Phaedrus*, for example, he delivers his first speech on love with his head covered out of shame, as if shame induces the desire to be less visible. The operation of shame, as it arises in the *Gorgias*, already points to the *communal* or political horizon within which the conversation takes place, and thus already indicates the power of *appearance* that prevails within the human realm, the way in which what is said also remains inexorably connected to the way the speaker appears to others. The importance of one's appearance in connection with the possible affirmation of justice becomes explicit also in Book II of the *Republic*, as Glaucon and Adeimantus ask Socrates to defend the justice in the soul "all by itself, without regard to wages and consequences" (Rep. 358b). The decisive character of one's own *visibility* as a way of grasping the necessity of justice becomes apparent above all in the story of Gyges, as told by Glaucon. And while Herodotus tells a different version of the same story, in which it becomes clear that this tale is also bound to a tragic necessity, leading to destruction, in both versions of the story, Glaucon's and Herodotus's, what is decisive is the way in which one's being visible establishes an inexorable bond between humans.[4] Such visibility, however, is never unambiguous, but is continually modulated through ways of self-concealing and veiling, whether this concerns the way one becomes visible simply to others or the way one becomes visible *to oneself* through one's visibility before another. In hiding from the other, one also hides from oneself.

Are the shameless retorts of Polus now also to be heard as emblematic of those students from whom Gorgias wants to keep his own distance, when he states that he is not to be blamed if *unjust* use is made of his rhetorical art? (Gorg. 457a). Why is Gorgias so intent upon making this point, if not because his students have garnered unsavory reputations? But it is important then to notice how, in the transition from the conversation with Gorgias to the more shameless discourse of Polus, the question of the good, as a human possibility, as it is at issue in both rhetoric and philosophy, becomes more explicit. It also becomes more clear in this way how the possibility or impossibility of such a human good already has involved a relation to nature, is itself a manifestation of nature. If the refutation of

Polus in the end still hinges on a certain shame, on his inability to proceed utterly without shame, how does the question of this shame and its apparent necessity open up the Socratic relation to nature?

It is Socrates who provokes the transition to the explicit discussion of the good, by offering an emphatic delimitation of rhetoric and its power. What is decisive is that Socrates states that rhetoric has no account of the nature (φύσις) of the things with which it works, no λόγος of their way of coming to be, and so cannot speak of their cause (αἰτία), and for this reason cannot be an art (Gorg. 465a; also 501a). Rhetoric is not an art, not a τέχνη, but only a way of being familiar, a conversancy with things that seeks gratification, merely an ἐμπειρία. Just as cooking, as it seeks to gratify or flatter taste, must not pretend to be a healing art (must not present itself as an actual knowledge of what is healthy and how one becomes healthy), rhetoric, too, should not be confused with justice. It is instead only flattery or κολακεία disguised as justice (Gorg. 465b–c). Socrates expects that Polus, because he is familiar with the work of Anaxagoras, will grasp the necessity of this distinction between what is pleasant and what is healthy (Gorg. 465d). The role of Anaxagoras here is important, especially given the way he appears in other dialogues, most notably those treated in this book. In all of these passages where Anaxagoras appears, one finds a thematic discussion of the strange Socratic relation to nature.[5]

Thus, the power of rhetoric, as Socrates accounts for it, can be said to be grounded in the seductive charm of pleasure, but more precisely it is a pleasure that arises out of flattery. Such flattery can be viewed as a counterforce to the shaming ἔλεγχος of Socratic dialogue, but both have power by bringing about a certain self-awareness in the listener. In the case of flattery, the self-awareness is unhealthy because it induces a self-satisfaction with regard to oneself. Shame, on the contrary, as a πάθος that is radically positive, can have a healthy effect precisely because it awakens one to the task of self-knowledge, a task that is thoroughly intertwined with one's presence before others, with one's being accountable to them. But Polus understands rhetoric to bring about a power that is comparable to the power of the tyrants. Like the tyrants, the effective rhetoricians have the power to put to death whomever they want, can take money away from anyone and expel anyone from the cities (Gorg. 466c). The response of Socrates, namely that such individuals, like the tyrants who act unjustly, do not have power, Polus finds to be both shocking and laughable. To assert such a thing is monstrous, unnatural, ὑπερφυής (Gorg. 467b). And although he seems unable to take seriously the distinction that Socrates draws at this point, that doing what seems best (ποιεῖν δόξῃ βέλτιστον) does not have to mean doing what one wants (ποιεῖν ὧν βούλονται), he also, like the Thrasymachus in Book I of the *Republic,* cannot refute the distinction and thus the difficulty opened up with it. The procuring of what is wanted, the "making" of it, as a form of action, already implies a relation to that for the sake of which (οὗ ἕνεκα) such action is undertaken. Socrates here resorts to the paradigmatic example: health. One takes φάρμακα (drugs) not simply because it is good to do so, but rather for the sake of health. In such a case one does not simply want the drugs, but rather it is obvious that wanting the drugs depends upon and is connected to the desire to be healthy (Gorg. 467c). Likewise, Polus must agree that when someone is put to death, or expelled, or deprived of property, this is not carried out because it is taken as a good in itself (Gorg. 468b). What only serves as a means, as an intermediary (τὰ μεταξύ), has to be regarded as something done for the sake of something else. Socrates proposes, and Polus agrees, that these intermediate things are done for the sake of what is good, for the sake of good things (ἕνεκα τῶν ἀγαθῶν) (Gorg. 468a).

But it should be recognized that Socrates in this way also makes explicit a conflict that points to an unmistakably tragic condition of human life: it is possible to do what *seems* best and yet thereby to do what one does *not* want. One can do what seems best and still bring about great harm, even to oneself, *above all* to oneself. It may be, in other words, that humans do not know what is good for them, do not know themselves well enough to secure what is to their benefit. Here it is important to stress, however, that this tragic not-knowing, as it seems even to define human life, proves also on Socratic terms to be grounded and confirmed in a prior relation to the good. The dialogue assumes this, in fact, and one can say that without such a prior and basic relation to the good, the tragic alienation of human nature from itself makes no sense.[6] Precisely as what would be most proper to life, as what would even define the life of that life, the good may be not only elusive but actually unattainable. For if the *knowledge* of the good remains unattainable, then our doing would be utterly dependent upon that form of ignorance that is mere opinion—and the possibility of human happiness utterly exposed to the whims of chance or fortune. The good itself, while not unattainable by necessity, would also remain in a basic way concealed from human life, withheld from it—withheld, that is, precisely as it nevertheless presents or reveals itself as the defining possibility of life. The tragic character of Socratic philosophical practice would consist in this double movement, in which the good, while not impossible, appears as something most difficult, at the very limit of the possible, verging on impossibility.

If it turns out that no humans can affirm the good that is the singular obsession of Socrates, the obsession that therefore would itself mark his extraordinary singularity, his way of being exceptional among humans, then what appears at first as a most commonplace observation, that it is possible for humans to do what they do *not* want, becomes at once a more drastic and comprehensive determination of human life.[7] Only at this point, perhaps, do the most paradoxical claims of Socrates achieve their full effect. In his conversation with Callicles, for example, Socrates interprets what has been achieved in his exchange with Polus: it has been agreed, he claims, that "no one does injustice wanting to do injustice (μηδένα βουλόμενον ἀδικεῖν), but all who do injustice do it not wanting to do it" (Gorg. 509e). Such a scandalous claim, which must be set alongside the similar statement that the knowledge of ἀρετή must itself already be ἀρετή, is a claim that can be received only through a consideration of the incomparable determination of knowledge put forward by Socrates. Because a knowledge of the good cannot be extricated from the task of self-knowledge, what has to be grasped is how such knowledge can emerge only at the extreme limit of life, as something next to impossible. Socratic ignorance insists upon precisely the extreme difficulty of an actual knowledge of what is most important in human life. Such a claim, therefore, cannot at all amount to a simple "intellectualizing" of virtue, as is sometimes said.[8] Precisely because it insists upon the near impossibility of the self-knowledge in question, this claim can be heard only as it asks us to confront once again the inevitably tragic question that concerns whether and how, or to what extent, the human good is available at all. It becomes necessary, in other words, to alter in the most decisive way the very sense of knowledge itself, and thereby to attend once again to the difficulty and danger that the task of such knowledge poses.

Polus seems undaunted by this tragic thought of a contradictory desire and the danger it entails. And when, as a way of responding, he challenges Socrates to admit that the tyrants are enviable because they can transgress justice with impunity, Socrates insists, against this, that to do wrong (ἀδικεῖν) is the greatest of evils (μέγιστον τῶν κακῶν) (Gorg. 469b), worse even than suffering injustice (ἀδικεῖσθαι) (Gorg. 469c). Moreover, Socrates insists, while the wrongdoer is certainly wretched (ἄθλιον), such a one is less wretched if, as a wrongdoer, that one can "give justice" or pay the penalty for the wrongdoing. Socrates thus proposes that this possibility of such a διδόναι δίκην—to grant what is right—presents itself as a good for the one who has transgressed against justice. The things Socrates is saying make no sense to Polus: they are ἄτοπα, totally out of place, incomprehensible to him (Gorg. 473a). For, according to Polus, the possible good of the wrongdoer, what is good for the one who is unjust (ὁ ἀδικῶν), requires that such a one is able, precisely as a wrongdoer, to escape punishment altogether. According to Polus, there is nothing to be redeemed in justice itself for the wrongdoer since such a justice is only a punishment that brings harm.

The exchange between Polus and Socrates gives rise to a most basic disagreement, a conflict between two incompatible and contradictory positions. It must be recognized, however, how this conflict also arises out of the prior encounter with Gorgias, as it makes explicit the unspoken difference already at issue between Gorgias and Socrates. The conflict, as it comes to this explicit formulation, seems to demand that one of the positions give way, that one of the two assertions concerning the good in human life find itself refuted. This conflict also returns us to the *Apology* and to the way that Socrates is accused of undermining conventional wisdom through refutation, through a dialogical practice that is experienced by the Athenians as a way of making the weaker λόγος stronger. The *Gorgias* thus provides a way to consider the dialogical limits of the *Apology* and to assess, in a way that remains impossible through a consideration of the *Apology* alone, what is at stake in the conflict between Socrates and Athens, or between philosophy and the city.

And yet, if the conflict between Polus and Socrates demands that one of them be refuted, it is also evident at the outset that there are two distinct senses of refutation at work in this exchange, two entirely different ways of understanding what it would mean for an assertion to find itself refuted. Moreover, Socrates makes it clear that this difference between these two ways of undergoing refutation—as nothing less than the difference between rhetoric and dialogue—is not unrelated to the more explicit conflict that has now arisen between Polus and Socrates, as it concerns the power of rhetoric to transgress justice and thereby the question of how such transgression bears upon the possible good in human life. It can be said, in other words, that the dialogical engagement of Socrates appears as itself an enactment of the very position put forward by him, that the Socratic way of affirming justice, as it runs counter to prevailing opinion and convention, is itself thoroughly bound up with his peculiar relation to the disclosive movement of speech. If justice can heal the soul, as Socrates proposes, then such healing also demands nothing less than the Socratic turn to dialogical speech, which also shows itself as a decisive receptivity to the transformative possibilities of refutation. It is for this reason that Socrates asks Polus to submit himself bravely to the λόγος, just as one would submit oneself to a physician (Gorg. 475d).

Polus's attempted refutation of Socrates consists simply in an appeal to something that he takes to be already unquestionable to everyone, namely the good life of Archelaus, who, as the tyrant of Macedonia, cannot be anything other than unjust. According to Polus, Socrates should consider himself refuted simply because there is no one among humans who would hold the view that Archelaus is unhappy as a wrongdoer. This passage puts into stark relief the way in which the utter singularity of Socrates becomes apparent, his exceptional position among humans. "Do you not think that you are refuted, Socrates, when you say such things that no human whatsoever would accept?" (Gorg. 473e).

The experience of encountering Socrates as utterly exceptional is portrayed in this way throughout the dialogues. In the last chapter we saw in a preliminary way that attending to this sense of Socratic strangeness in the *Apology* leads to an interpretation that must contend with very different questions than those that concern themselves merely with the content of Socratic teaching. The question of Socrates, the question of his singularity, remains irreducible to the views or positions he appears to hold, precisely because the *place* of his appearing, as political or distinctly *human,* always shows itself as a limit that already lays claim to the possibilities of that appearing. What shows itself in this way thus shows itself also as it withdraws in its appearing: Socrates as out of place or most out of place. We shall return to this peculiar strangeness of the Platonic Socrates—his disruption of the sense of the human good, as an appearance of monstrous or tragic nature erupting from within the political itself, thus belonging to the political *as* a manifestation of nature, belonging to nature as a manifestation of the political—by seeing how it is confirmed in other dialogues, notably, the *Phaedo, Meno, Phaedrus, Theaetetus, Republic,* and *Symposium.*[9] There are many passages in the dialogues that speak of Socrates by referring to his utter singularity, the question of his monstrosity. We shall take up these passages one by one. But it is important to see from the beginning that they all point to a Socrates who, precisely as preeminently human, also establishes this humanity through his remarkable exceptionality, his aberrant inhumanity. Who, then, is the monster? Consider, for example, the passage in the *Symposium* (Sym. 221c), where the drunken and effusive Alcibiades declares: "There is no one like him among human beings, neither among those of old nor among those now, and this is what is wholly worthy of wonder."[10] But this same sense of the inhumanity of the philosopher can be heard to be expressed by Socrates himself at the beginning of the *Sophist.* The philosophers roam about in the cities of men as strangers, looking down on human life (Soph. 216c–217a). In the *Theaetetus,* in a decisive passage at the center of that dialogue, Socrates puzzles over the strangeness of the philosopher, represented famously by the clumsy Thales, precisely as one who appears in the city as a stranger, and as one who is entirely incompetent when it comes to dealing with "down-to-earth" human concerns; Socrates even declares that the philosopher in this sense is one who wonders before the question of what belongs to human nature and, as such a one who wonders, is also hardly aware of who it is that actually counts as a human being at all, hardly aware of whether one's neighbor is not in fact some kind of monstrosity (Theaet. 174b).

There are many such passages that should be taken as interpretive caveats in the attempt at addressing Socratic nature in its relation to nature. At this point, in the *Gorgias,* we confront the most astonishing assertion, put forward by Socrates, that despite the fact that no human is able to agree with him, despite the fact that he is utterly alone in his assertions, nevertheless all human life is in accord with what he is asserting. The dialogical refutation, in other words, enacted by Socrates, while it does not simply impose a claim upon the interlocutor, does begin by returning explicitly to the tragic determination of the good as it has already been raised by Socrates, namely that it is possible for the good to hold sway as the good in human life and yet also to remain concealed from human life. Thus, although the Socratic claim about the good of justice conflicts with prevailing opinion, Socrates says, "I think that you and I and all other humans suppose that doing injustice is worse [κάκιον] than suffering it, and that not submitting to justice [μὴ διδόναι δίκην] is worse than submitting to it" (Gorg. 474b). What Socrates is saying is remarkable: the entire community of human life, insofar as it must be said that it disagrees with him, does *not* know itself, does not know what it wants, as nature remains estranged from nature.[11] The exceptional singularity of Socrates, his extraordinariness, that he is alone among humans in his assertions about justice and the human good, thus seems to conflict with this remarkable statement, in which it is asserted that all humans do agree with him, and even must agree with him.

But this presumption that lays claim in advance to an agreement, that claims a certain necessary community, is also only the *promise* of Socratic dialogue, and thus something deferred, only an anticipatory relation that first of all must be encountered as it poses and presupposes a great task. The promise can arise only through the wondrous appearance of Socrates himself, who not only insists upon but enacts this unheard-of undertaking, supposedly encountered by everyone as exceptional, even as outlandish and monstrous, as a perversion or corruption of nature.

It must be noted that Polus's manner of refutation—the way of refutation that belongs, as Socrates says, to the law-courts—does not require this undertaking, and so cannot make any promise of such community. What is more important in such rhetorical refutation is the sheer *number* of witnesses that can be brought forward, without regard to whether a coherent account can be given of what is thereby said. This sort of refutation, Socrates says, is worth little as a way to the truth, since the number of witnesses, no matter how great, is no assurance against the falsity of what they assert (Gorg. 471e–472a). Socrates admits that many would indeed support Polus, Athenians and foreigners alike, including the entire family of Pericles (Gorg. 472a–b). But for his part he refuses to accept this authority on its own and declares that he is concerned only with the opinion of his interlocutor, the one with whom he is engaged: "If I for my part do not produce you yourself as a witness who consents to that about which I am speaking, I think I have accomplished nothing of worth with regard to what is at issue in the λόγος; nor do I think you have, unless I am your sole witness and you bid farewell to the many others" (Gorg. 472b–c).

If one wanted to assess the reasons for Socrates' total failure to persuade anyone in this dialogue to agree with him, to agree namely that it is necessary to affirm justice as an unconditional good in human life—a good even for the one who as a wrongdoer must be punished—such an assessment would have to begin by considering how the possibility of Socratic persuasion, as it would occur only through a peculiar kind of refutation, depends first of all upon a dialogical exchange that is able to suspend or interrupt the way of interaction in speech that otherwise prevails and that is thoroughly exploited by rhetoric. There can be no question that such a suspension or interruption of the contentious speech of rhetoric, if it were to take place for Polus or Callicles, would also require a shift in the way in which they view what is good for them precisely as they participate in this dialogical exchange. The matter of knowing what it is for a human to fare well, the matter that concerns, namely, the human good—about which, Socrates says, to have knowledge is "most fine" (κάλλιστον) and not to have knowledge "most shameful" αἴσχιστον (Gorg. 472)—proves then to be inseparable from the way in which this matter as such must be opened up through dialogue. The Socratic affirmation of justice already presupposes a certain way of questioning, just as that questioning cannot proceed without the prior affirmation; the "truth" proclaimed by Socrates can become persuasive, that is, only through the dialogical exchange that he both insists upon and attempts to enact. It thus must be concluded that the most extreme and scandalous Socratic assertion in this dialogue, namely that just punishment (διδόναι δίκην) is an actual human good, is a truth that cannot be elaborated or approached at all without already involving the dialogical self-knowledge of the one who would assert or receive it.

But if Socratic self-knowledge must be thought as a decisive relation to nature, then the necessity of dialogue, as it is precipitated in and by such self-knowledge, is also a necessity that arises from nature, as a necessity of nature. Polus and Callicles, precisely because they refuse dialogue, also refuse to accept how the question they are discussing concerning the good of justice confronts them with a basic task and puts them into question. When Socrates invites Polus and Callicles to enter into such a dialogical engagement, he also asks them to take up the task of self-knowledge, to affirm the task as such. But it becomes clear at such a point that assuming this task as one's own also means becoming receptive to the transformative possibilities of refutation as they can arise only in and through dialogue. The philosophical practice of Socrates, as a refutative practice in the city, as an operation that appears to make the weaker account stronger, and as it thus poses nothing less than this task of self-knowledge, is the demand that human life expose itself to nature, to the nature that it is and that becomes manifest through speech. But then the trial of Socrates, far from demonstrating that his practice has nothing to do with nature (as he appears to claim), is throughout a confirmation of the Socratic turn to nature precisely through this affirmation of a dialogical necessity.

The refutation of Polus makes explicit that his way of interacting with Socrates cannot be separated from what he would assert. While he claims that suffering injustice is "worse" or "more evil" (κάκιον) than doing it, that ἀδικεῖσθαι is worse than ἀδικεῖν, he also concedes, at the prompting of Socrates, that doing injustice is αἴσχιον, more shameful, more disgraceful, uglier, than suffering it (Gorg. 474c). But because he cannot sustain this distinction between τὸ κακόν and τὸ αἰσχρόν, between the bad and the ugly,

Polus proves unable to account for shame in a way that does not return to what Callicles soon refers to as nature. If what is bad in unjust action is merely the shame of it, in distinction from the bad that comes with suffering injustice, one still has to account for this shame itself as something undesirable or bad. Good and evil thus still emerge for Polus as the final measure of what is beautiful and what is ugly or shameful. And Socrates exploits this point to draw the conclusion that if doing injustice is more shameful, it also must be more evil, κάκιον.[12]

According to Callicles, however, Polus's concession that ἀδικεῖν is αἴσχιον, that doing injustice is more shameful than suffering it, is something that Polus admits only through shame, "being ashamed to say what he thought" (Gorg. 482d–e). According to Callicles, Polus has gotten himself into the same condition as Gorgias; he shares the same πάθος (Gorg. 482c). Thus, in order to save the account begun by Gorgias and Polus, Callicles must come close to insisting that shame is completely unnatural, that the self-relation opened up through one's interactions with others, the place in which injustice appears, functions only as a kind of inhibition or concealing of true nature, the nature that would find its perfect expression only in the life of the tyrant. And yet, even Callicles refuses to abandon justice altogether, since he also returns the violence of the tyrant to another justice, the justice that he attributes to nature herself:

> But I think that when a man comes to be who has a sufficient nature [φύσιν ἱκανὴν γένηται ἔχων ἀνήρ], he shakes off everything, breaks through and escapes, stomps upon our boundaries and deceptions, our charms and laws, all of which are against nature [παρὰ φύσιν]; the slave rises up, shows himself as our master, and there shines forth the justice of nature [τὸ τῆς φύσεως δίκαιον]. (Gorg. 484a)

The tyrant thus does not simply abandon law and justice but is rather a primary instance of nature's way of rupturing merely human law, merely human justice. The tyrant acts according to the law of nature, κατὰ νόμον τὸν τῆς φύσεως (Gorg. 483e).[13] But how does this defense of the tyrant also find itself enacted by Callicles, precisely in his interaction with Socrates?

The dastardly and specious Callicles proves by the end of his interaction with Socrates that he cares little for dialogue, that he refuses to expose himself to its transformative possibilities. More than once he admits that he has intentionally deceived Socrates, although it is unclear whether such prevarication on his part is also not simply a ploy to avoid being held accountable to his responses. And while he begins assuring Socrates that he is acting as a friend, he finally admits at that point where the conversation breaks down that he does not care at all about what Socrates has to say (Gorg. 505c). But Callicles' refusal to enter into dialogue with Socrates is due to a more comprehensive refusal to accept the possibility of dialogue as such. Callicles is incapable of affirming that anyone could enter in the sort of dialogical exchange proposed by Socrates. He continues to interpret Socratic refutation as a form of combative speech. The Socratic affirmation of refutation he identifies with a "love of victory" (Gorg. 515b). He thus acts just like those described by Socrates in the conversation with Gorgias, who in being refuted are unable to accept it as a good, since they take it as only an attack (Gorg. 457d).

In the end, Callicles gives up entirely on the conversation. The expectation is that Socrates can continue on his own. While there is no longer any resistance to the Socratic demonstration that the fulfillment of every possible desire must lead to an irredeemable life and the most frustrated form of bondage, it is clear also that Callicles remains unpersuaded. The fact that such persuasion is precluded by this utter refusal to engage in dialogue corresponds to the account of tyranny offered by Socrates. The paradigm of the incurable tyrant indicates that it is possible for the human good to be irretrievably and utterly concealed (Gorg. 525c). And yet, it must be emphasized that such a demonstration makes little sense without the account of the soul as it belongs to a cosmic order, an order that Socrates speaks of as a fourfold community and friendship of all things: "The wise say . . . that sky and earth, and gods and humans, are held together in community and friendship, in orderliness and moderation and justice, and for this reason they call this whole a cosmos" (Gorg. 507d–508a). This important passage should be heard as an elaboration of what Socrates says at 482c concerning the promise of philosophy, the promise of a harmonious self-relation. The possibility of such a self-relation, grounded in nature, granted by nature, is finally only asserted mythically, in the story that Socrates tells at the end of the dialogue. And yet, despite the demonstration, the great paradox of the dialogue remains, which is that while Socrates insists upon the necessity of what he says—since he has found that every other assertion can be made only by becoming "ridiculous"—Socrates himself remains ridiculous in the eyes of Callicles and those like him.[14]

It is of particular importance in this regard to return to the famed δεύτερος πλοῦς or "second sailing" of Socrates, his well-known insistence upon the turn to the λόγοι as the necessity of the recourse to a "second best way," as Plato has him speak of it on the day of his death, and to reconsider how this turn does not so much abandon nature, or even the sensibility of nature, as much as it makes evident that the question of nature remains inextricably entangled in nature's way of appearance or manifestation. This emphasis upon the way of nature's manifestation, however, not only means that the *human* good cannot be successfully pursued if severed from such manifestation—a point that certainly bears upon every productive concern with health, and even also upon every concern with justice—but, more decisively, it means first of all that nature's way of manifestation is always already bound to a certain necessity or limit, *a limit that does seem to be grounded somehow in nature's relation to the horizon of the political or historical.* The failure of Socrates to persuade his interlocutors is not an incidental fact, something merely regrettable. The death of Socrates, his condemnation by the city, is instead the confirmation of nature's self-concealing doubling. The tragedy of Socrates from this perspective arises through a conflict of nature itself and thus remains irreducible to the claim that Socrates was right although misunderstood. The tragedy of Socrates is the shattering of identity itself because truth is delivered over to a dialogical necessity in which nature can withhold itself.

It is of the greatest importance, therefore, that this relation to the political and historical be articulated carefully and submitted to the most rigorous interrogation. It would be utterly premature, for example, simply to assume at this point that such a limit, in its necessity, boils down to something like a corruption or domestication of nature, that it amounts already to a loss of nature's purity and wildness through the distorting projection of merely human concerns and valuation. Even if the trajectory of Western metaphysics is such that it does lead to the near total expunging of nature, through an encompassing and globalizing technological imperative, it is all the more necessary to forestall the assumption that already sees in the appearance of Socrates the beginning of such an expunging of nature. Such an assumption, to begin with, must already take for granted the distinctly modern divide between nature and culture—as this is bound up with the distinction between "what is" and "ought to be," between facts and values—and in such a way that this divide comes to be simply imposed *anachronistically* upon archaic Greek experience. If anything, a unique opportunity presents itself here: to develop a historical genealogy of this divide in its apparent unquestionability, so as to expose it to its limits and to its contingency.

How then to forestall this assumption, which is no doubt as seductive as it is misleading? In the figure of Socrates a drama unfolds in which nature opens up to human life in the necessity of a certain *doubling.* This doubling of nature can be addressed, to begin with, by speaking of the paradoxical relation that the "good" retains to human life. While it is evident in the dialogues that the good *as such*—the so-called universal good—is irreducible to the *human* good, the question of the human good is also never simply restricted to itself, to its total self-sufficiency, as an isolated region, set apart. The place at which the question of the human good can first be raised as a question is also a place at which it must lose the very sense of its own self-containment and purity, its independent or distinct identity. But this is also only to insist that the dialogues remain irreducible to the task of imparting a knowledge of the good programmatically or dogmatically, that instead the question of the good once raised already implies being claimed by a task. The human good—in the full sense of both "being good" and "living well" — is still a regional question; it thus demands to be grounded. It thus becomes possible only as its very boundaries are ruptured, as it thereby opens itself to the excess that arises within it and that points beyond, to another place. The doubling at issue here is thus not at all grounded in human deficiency, but in the exuberant abundance, in the "demonic excess" of the good itself.

5

Silenic Wisdom in the *Apology* and *Phaedo*

We saw in chapter 3 that the deep-seated prejudices against Socrates can be traced back to the way in which his refutative practice is taken by many as a claim to wisdom (Apol. 23a). Socrates, in "making the weaker speech stronger," appears to many as arrogant and hubristic. We have just seen how the *Gorgias* offers an exemplary demonstration of this movement of ἔλεγχος that is referred to in the *Apology*. The utter failure of that conversation appears to lie initially in a basic conflict or disagreement concerning the very character of refutation itself. But more fundamentally the conflict between rhetoric and dialogical inquiry proves to bear upon the way in which the human good can be addressed in speech, a good that proves to be inseparable from the place of human life in nature. This conflict continues to escalate in the dialogue, as it moves from the conversation with Gorgias himself to the conversations with Polus and Callicles, until it becomes clear that the disagreement is also bound up with a basic difference concerning human life as it belongs to nature. This irreconcilable difference, as it appears in the *Gorgias,* concerns the very manifestation of nature as it takes place in speech and as it concerns the good. The justice that Socrates pursues through his dialogical inquiry is grounded first of all in the community or friendship of all things, of "sky and earth, gods and humans" (Gorg. 507e–508a). The possibility of a Socratic justice is not only not to be abstracted from this natural community, but rather the very inquiry itself into justice, the possibility of first asking the question, is already the assertion of this natural cryptic community. Socratic justice, as it confirms nature's friendship, becomes the promise of Socratic dialogue only because this dialogical λόγος has always already assumed it in advance as the very condition of its movement. The good in human life, as the good proper to that life, cannot be dissociated from nature as a whole, no more than the λόγος itself can be wielded for mere political expediency.

The strangeness of Socrates, his utter exceptionality, the very thing that Polus and Callicles cannot accept, lies in the insistence that the dialogical movement of speech—as an occurrence of aporia and refutation—is nature's way of becoming manifest as justice. But this radical affirmation of the disclosive movement of speech also entails a decisive dispossession, in which it is necessary that one accept that the λόγος is no longer simply the means by which one expresses oneself. The affirmation of the healing power of justice entails the abandonment of the desire to be "right" in an ecstatic openness to the experience of refutation. Such an affirmation of the healing λόγος, as it also involves this πάθος of a certain healthy shame, thus anticipates or repeats the necessity of the "second sailing" as Socrates speaks of it in the *Phaedo.* By way of anticipation, it can be said, in the language of the *Phaedo,* that Polus and Callicles offer further examples of those who suffer from the sickness of "misology," precisely because they view the λόγος as something that is merely at their disposal. Socrates tells us that it is "not possible to suffer a greater evil than such a hatred of speeches" (ὅτι ἄν τις μεῖζον τούτου κακὸν πάθοι ἢ λόγους μισήσας) (Phaedo 89d). Such misology, as an inability to love, closes itself off to the good, but not simply by abandoning the good. Rather, the foreclosure at issue in misology consists in a way of actually claiming the good as self-evident. The good is thus not simply withheld or absent in misological speech, but conceals itself in a certain showing, in a deceptive presence that shows the good as it is not.

In the *Gorgias* Socrates attempts to persuade his interlocutors that the persuasive power of speech is grounded in nature and nature's justice, an issue taken up also in the *Phaedrus.*[1] The Socratic transformation of nature entails a transformation of the self: one's self-relation must be exposed to its own ignorance, its own tragic failure to know what is good for it, precisely as this good is grounded in a nature that exceeds it and yet has also already claimed it. The breakdown of the *Gorgias* is thus attributable to the incapacity on the part of the interlocutors to accept this very transformation. What is most telling in this regard is that Socratic irony, because of this breakdown, cannot be experienced at all as a provocation to engage this cryptic nature, as it becomes manifest in speech, but is instead viewed as only the pretense for a not-so-veiled arrogance.[2] Has the philosophical tradition, to the extent that it takes Socrates to be the master of his irony— just as it takes Plato to be the master of his writing—not also proven itself incapable of responding to the Socratic provocation toward nature's crypic manifestation? I have been claiming that this refusal on the part of the tradition can be thought as a refusal of nature itself, which is to say, that the concealing of nature's concealment unfolds in and as the descent of Socrates.

I want to return now to the *Apology* and take up the oracular word that concerns Socratic wisdom in order to make some preliminary observations that will allow me to connect the emergence of this strange "wisdom" to the way in which Socrates in the *Phaedo* speaks of his practice emerging in a certain necessity. The "second sailing," as it comes to name Socratic practice, can be thought as an ongoing movement that is continually conditioned by an encounter with impossibility. Such a practice, then, continues only as it returns to this transformative impossibility, in a repetition that sustains its necessity, that lives in its refusal. It may seem cumbersome to speak of a necessary impossibility, but such a phrase indicates the way in which this decisive Socratic impossibility does not simply refer to a mistaken byway—some kind of errant experiment Socrates might have and should have avoided—but is instead to be recovered or recollected as an originating withdrawal, a concealment in which nature refuses itself in its very way of becoming manifest. The turn to speeches then has to be thought as the confirmation of this concealing movement, as it sustains and intensifies the necessity of the concealment itself.

It is indisputable that the Socrates who is encountered "directly" in the Platonic text will always have to exceed whatever paltry Socrates comes to be produced by those intellectual historians who nobly restrict themselves to the "facts" and to doctrinal positions. One can admit this without hesitation and still affirm that the Platonic Socrates remains nevertheless irreducible to a mere Platonic invention. The task of human life, according to this (Platonic) Socrates, arises only in and with the posing of the ancient Delphic task of self-knowledge. A thoughtful interpretation of the Platonic reception of Socrates thus requires that this reception be considered as it repeats the posing of this originary task. The Platonic dialogues thus enact a translation of Socrates *into himself* but only as they sustain and repeat without compromise the primacy of this task as a task. This recollective reception or translation of Socratic practice does not take place, therefore, as the transmission of content, but rather first of all *as the posing of a question,* simply because the text itself makes plain that this Socrates remains a question to himself, a question that can be posed and taken up only as a practice, as an interpretive movement in the λόγος that takes time. Because Socrates appears in the dialogues in this way, the dialogues themselves should be read as they repeat a way of questioning, or as they insist upon a form of *inquiry*—which is to say, as they expose themselves to the descensional necessity of thinking. Yet to confront Socrates and the question of the nature of Socrates as this descent is to be thrown back upon oneself as a task and on the question of one's own nature, since the structure of Socratic questioning is such that those who come to ask it must find themselves as questioners put into question by it.

And yet, if the achievement of the Platonic "masterpiece" is that it is able to reveal something radically other and strange to its own production, that it is able, like all great poetry, to release something excessive or prior to its own intent or design—without simply contradicting itself[3]—in no way does this then lessen the demand, imposed upon the reader, to take everything in the text, to the most minute detail, as meaningful and necessary, as if it were the *unnatural* and total suspension of the accidental.[4] On the contrary, it must be asserted at the beginning that only under the presumption of such complete meaning, such totalizing necessity, does it become possible to encounter what breaks forth from within the text as utterly uncanny and strange. The illusion of perfect beauty, the illusion of the harmonious whole that would be the Platonic cosmos, in its absolute suspension of all errant cause—as if constructed through a purely noetic vision[5]—must always be the starting point, precisely because only in this way, through a moment of failure or breakdown, or in the manifestation even of the "ugly," shameful and discordant, does the insuperable or "incommensurable" rift between nature and the purely geometric open up.[6] Precisely through these limits, however, through the discourse that allows these limits to be imposed upon it, it becomes evident that there is no calculus or proportion that would exhaust or comprehend Socratic ἔρως. Such ἔρως appears rather as the incommensurable remainder.

It cannot be said, therefore, that the Platonic text simply takes over the life of Socrates, since it also comes to be undone and unraveled by that very life and its death, perhaps even in a love for that life, as a singularity not to recovered or recuperated. The death of Socrates gives birth to Platonic writing, a writing that gives birth to Socrates. I have already discussed how Plato's work can be read as it accounts for its own possibility by referring to a Platonic sickness. And although this sickness remains decidedly indeterminate, it does point to the limits of the author, even implying perhaps a Platonic convalescence through the writing that would have the courage to affirm the death of the beloved. The parting words of Socrates thus can also be heard to speak to this decisive Platonic sickness. I shall have to come back to this. But does this mean that Plato, like many other Greeks, wants to count the dead as happy, even to count *only* the dead as happy? Perhaps like Solon and the tragic heroes he also draws the final conclusion that it is only death that shelters us from life.[7] Aristotle, who takes delight in stating the obvious, already saw the contradiction such a view seems to contain: it would indeed be contradictory to find the good of human life only in death, since this implies precisely the *impossibility* of such a good, amounts to the very denial of that good itself.[8] And yet, despite the Aristotelian rebuke—later amplified by Nietzsche—one must still ask: is it not the case that death does insinuate itself into the good of life, simply because life as such will never have cut itself off from death—no more than health can ever be said to be the mere absence of sickness? The Socratic affirmation of death that one finds most powerfully enacted and articulated in the *Phaedo* is so far from being a denial of life (in Nietzsche's sense) that it becomes apparent in the dialogue that only in the affirmation of its death does human life affirm itself at all. If there is sense in this statement, it is to be found in the recognition that human life (and its good) is caught inexorably in a tragic impossibility. This "impossibility," as the extreme philosophical articulation of nature's cryptic manifestation, thus does not simply imply the denial of the good in human life. Rather, the "second sailing" of Socrates, because it is able to affirm the *necessity* of the impossibility, continues to hold itself in it and open to it, *as* impossible. The *Phaedo* is a dialogue that demonstrates from beginning to end how the Socratic affirmation of speech, his love of speeches, can be an affirmation of life. The ecstatic Socratic λόγος, if it is to hold itself open to the good (of life), must be the life that must hold itself open to the good (of death).

If one were to attempt at this point a provisional but admittedly paradoxical formulation of the essence of tragedy, perhaps the best thing to say is that it consists precisely in such a necessity of impossibility, and thus in the way in which human life finds itself already claimed and sustained by what must remain forever withheld from it. Plato, the magisterial puppeteer, the consummate storyteller, puts Socrates on stage as a wonder, as strange and uncanny, but nonetheless as an appearance of nature. And it would seem that as an appearance of nature Socrates would only exemplify human life, as that life belongs to and arises from the whole that surrounds it. The good that would be most proper to human life can only be determined accordingly, through the way that life belongs to the whole and finds its place within it. This prevailing sense of the good thus hangs on the allotment or the dispensation of a divine nature. And yet, this very sense of the good—as that toward which all things aim—as it arises in nature's undeniability, precisely as what is most natural, also shows itself as something strangely denied to human life.

This denial is exhibited in the paradox of Socrates himself. If he reveals human life by being a kind of exemplar or *paradigm* for that life, he does so only because he also appears as its singular exception. He thus reveals the possibilities of human life at its limits, and in the necessity of those limits, at a point where it must be said that the possible verges on impossibility. When he is said to be ἀτοπώτατος, most strange, most out of place, this also can be heard to say: *most without place,* most lacking a home, most without a site of belonging. Yet what must be noted is that this outlandish appearance, attributed to Socrates, always confirms a double meaning, since it serves to set him apart from the rest of human life as it also confirms the *atopic* character of human life itself—that is, the very monstrosity of human life in nature. Socrates appears, then, as a figure risking *hubris* and transgression, who by his life places the very nature of human life into question. The miraculous or wondrous monstrosity of Socrates can be said to consist precisely in his way of sustaining this terrible tragic contradiction as nothing less than the condition of human life, in a "wisdom" and practice that continually confirms the contradiction. He is monstrous (and wondrous) because he holds himself within the contradiction and affirms it as such, "in the time of his life, up until and into his own death," as Heidegger says.

But this contradiction is *accomplished* only through a dialogical practice in the city. The tragedy of nature is thus inevitably political. And although this practice is likened to the practice of the midwife, the healer, and even the wizard, Socratic practice itself remains irreducible to any recognizable expertise, foreign to any τέχνη that would then allow itself to be codified and directly communicated, transmitted, and received in a teaching. The work or task of human life, as it comes to be addressed and enacted by Socrates, cannot be rendered transparent in a skillful productive knowledge. This is to say, however, that the work of human life cannot be found in the knowledge that otherwise appears to be most proper to human life, the distinctive accomplishment of that life. Even when there is the appearance of such a claim to knowledge on the part of Socrates, the content of the claim—what the claim is about—is such that it can also be heard to bring about an ironic displacement of the very force of the claim. When, for example, Socrates states that he has expertise concerning "erotic matters" (Sym. 177d, Phaedr. 257a), or when he asserts unequivocally to know the difference between opinion and knowledge (Meno 98b), or even when he states that he knows that he does not know, it becomes clear in each of these cases that there is also a movement that recoils upon the very sense of the claim. Such ironically charged assertions on the part of Socrates concerning his own expertise or knowledge are thus intensely paradoxical. The claim to such supposed "knowledge" only makes Socratic ignorance more emphatic and questionable, since what is indicated in them is first of all an awareness of an unmistakable absence, lack, or failing.

As Socrates sustains a relation to this absence, and holds himself in it, the absence thus also comes to reveal the demonic excess that proves to have already claimed him in advance. Socratic practice thus arises only within this excess, by sustaining a relation to it. It is this excessive claim, a way of relating to the whole, the community or kinship of all things, that makes it necessary in the *Gorgias* and in the *Republic,* for example, that he defend the life of justice as a good while at the same time insisting upon a radical ignorance concerning justice as such. What is most remarkable is that this ignorance does not at all conflict with the correlated insistence upon the good of justice. On the contrary, the two prove to be intimately bound together in the same excessive Socratic ἔρως, as if the inquiry concerning justice, the very necessity of that inquiry, is already grounded in and demanded by the excessive insistence upon its good, as Socrates is *already* claimed by the good of the life that must follow justice.

One has to begin with the fact that such an excessive whole—as it goes beyond the determinable region—always appears in the context of a rigorous delimitation of τέχνη, since through this delimitation the possibilities

for *regionalized* knowledge are set against the possibility of another relation to nature, characterized by this peculiar ignorance and its excessive
movement. But if the Platonic presentation of Socrates is a text that must
be encountered and interpreted as a *liminal* discourse in this sense, it is
also necessary to gain an appreciation for how and why it is incontestable
that τέχνη plays such a fundamental role in human life, so as thereby to
make clear its original necessity as a paradigm for philosophical discourse.
The decisive importance of this paradigmatic knowledge is underscored
by Callicles when he remarks that Socrates cannot stop talking about cob-
blers, fullers, cooks, and doctors (Gorg. 491a; cf. Sym. 221e). Many scholars, some brilliant, have debated and puzzled over the meaning of the
pervasive analogy with τέχνη in Greek philosophy.[9] But it cannot be disputed that the reliance upon this analogy must first of all be referred to the
most basic determination of τέχνη, which is that it is itself a way of being
grounded in nature, that it names primarily a certain unquestionable
knowledge, a knowing relation in and with nature, a basic and reliable
comportment toward it (Phaedr. 269e–270a). As a productive engagement,
which is always oriented toward a determinate task and which thus com-
pletes itself always within the clear boundaries of a preset region, τέχνη is
thoroughly beyond dispute, as much as it continually proves indispensable to human life. Only at this point, however, precisely as the necessity of
this paradigm makes itself evident, does it then also first display a basic *inability* to address its own way of being grounded in nature. In the paradigmatic knowledge of craft or art we see both an unquestionable human
relation to nature and its structural failure to address that relation adequately. Only at this point, then, by virtue of this curious mingling of its
necessity and failure, can something show itself that is prior to or beyond
the knowledge otherwise dominated by τέχνη.

The account Socrates gives of his experiences with the craftsmen
(χειροτέχναι or δημιουργοί) in the *Apology* remains the best starting point.
Unlike the politicians and the poets, the craftsmen, Socrates concedes, are
indeed found to be knowledgeable, and therefore in a certain respect can
even be said to possess a sort of wisdom. But, Socrates adds, their consistent failing is to mistake their regionalized expertise for a greater knowledge of what can be assigned to no region or domain of productivity at all.
They take themselves, he says, to be "most wise in great matters" and this
stupidity or errancy (πλημμέλεια) ends up obscuring the wisdom they do
have (Apol. 22d). Socratic "wisdom"—which is to say, his peculiar ignorance, as it grounds his practice—has no expertise in the sense in which it
can be found in the craftsmen, but this ignorance thus also preserves therefore a relation to the nature that exceeds every region, and that—it must
also be added—must not be said to be the totality of such regions, as if
such totality could itself be deemed a kind of region, the region of all regions. Thus, although Socrates is certain about the competency of the one

whose expertise concerns the well-being of horses, the possibility of this same kind of expertise with regard to human life cannot be assumed, despite the conviction of Callias that Evenus will make his sons better. Certainly, Socratic practice does not begin by making any such promises (19e–20c). The continuous Socratic reliance upon τέχνη thus does not simply privilege this paradigmatic form of knowledge; it exposes a necessity by confirming the indispensability of such knowledge, but precisely in order to let something else appear at the limits, at a point of failure or aporia.

This is an especially important point, if the reliance upon productive knowledge, as a basic and indisputable way of nature's disclosure in human life, can also be shown to play a constitutive role in the appropriation of nature that has come to be inseparable from Platonism. If Socratic aporetic discourse resists as much as it insists upon the "idealization" of nature—in the privileging of the "look" and in the search for the account of the defining "what"—then such discourse at the same time also still preserves the possibility of another relation to nature, one that is, strictly speaking, not determinable within the limits of the metaphysics of Platonism.[10] In this regard, however, it becomes crucial to consider how the Platonic text accounts for the *origins* of Socratic wisdom, the way in which Socrates comes to the dialogical practice that sustains itself in its emphatic ignorance while nevertheless holding itself open to what makes itself manifest in speech, through a movement governed by postponement and withdrawal.[11]

To claim that the Socratic insistence upon the εἶδος—upon the necessity of the search for it—arises in what can only be called a tragic necessity, in his downgoing, is to point to an awareness of inexorable limits that determine human life. In saying this, one also accepts that the Socratic relation to the limit cannot be rendered clear in an eidetic vision as it is ordinarily conceived. But if Socratic practice is nevertheless claimed by what *exceeds* these limits, by no means does this entail the abandonment or the denial of the limits as such, in a simple transcendence, but rather only first of all confirms the inexorability of the limits themselves. The confirmation of this inexorability thus can be thought as a *descent,* since in confronting the limits in question one experiences oneself as determined and encompassed by them. A consideration of the way the Platonic text accounts for the origins of Socratic wisdom and practice bears out that the insistence upon the εἶδος does not simply establish the opposition between the sensible and the intelligible, for example, but also occurs through a moment that cannot, strictly speaking, be situated *within* that opposition, made sense of simply in terms of the opposition. This is not to suggest that one may then proceed as if one has dispensed with the opposition. The opposition as such continues to maintain a kind of inevitability, even as it becomes manifest as an effect of a strange excess. This is the strange moment of Socrates that, in its refusal to be wholly determined metaphysically—even as it remains caught up in the necessity of metaphysics—puts into relief the distinctive character of the excess in question.[12]

By considering the emergence or generation of Socratic practice—as it confirms this sense of descensional appearance—it becomes possible to see how the Socratic relation to nature can be said to exceed or precede the regionalized nature of the Platonist. Here it is my intention only to make some preliminary observations concerning the necessity of the "second sailing" in order to show, in particular, how this necessity reveals precisely the tragic doubling that defines Socratic wisdom and that imposes upon him the task of self-knowledge. I shall make these preliminary observations, however, by relating this necessity of the second sailing first to the oracular pronouncement concerning Socratic wisdom as it is developed in the *Apology* and then to the dream Socrates mentions near the beginning of the *Phaedo.* I then will offer, in this context, some more explicit indications of how I take the second sailing to confirm a tragic good. I will do this by interpreting it as a kind of "Silenic" wisdom. These observations are thus a far cry from providing something like a comprehensive reading of the *Phaedo;* my goal here instead is to open up a general orientation toward that which would make such a reading possible.

It is well known that in the *Apology* Socrates accounts for the origins of his dialogical practice in the city—the practice that brings him to his trial and his death—by speaking of a divine command. But the first thing to note in this regard is that this divine command is issued enigmatically, in the oracular word that is reported to have proclaimed to Chaerephon that no one is wiser than Socrates (Apol. 21a). The oracle, if it does issue a command, also does not tell Socrates what to do in unambiguous terms, does not give him straightforward instructions at all. Thus, it is not possible to account for Socratic practice simply by tracing it back to a divine imperative. It cannot be said that Socratic practice, as it has given rise to the slander and prejudice (διαβολή) against him, is simply due to his obedience to the god's command. Instead, it must be emphasized that Socrates himself understands his practice first of all as a way to *interpret* the oracle, as a way to test its meaning, to determine what the god is saying.

What is decisive, then, is that the practice must already have established itself by first of all refusing to accept the divine word—by not simply accepting what the word only appears to say. Rather than simply obeying the divine word, by accepting its *apparent* meaning—which is, namely, that Socrates is the wisest—his philosophical practice begins by insisting that the possibility of a genuine obedience to the god calls for an interpretive response. This response, while it must appear to reject the oracle, also cannot amount to its simple rejection. What Socrates says is that he proceeded "with great reluctance" after being at an impasse or in aporia "for a long time," and that finally (and reluctantly) he went to one thought to be wise *in order to refute the oracle* (Apol. 21b–c). But it becomes clear that if the word of the god is to be received this apparently defiant response on the part of Socrates becomes necessary, in which the god's word is resisted, but thereby also granted a decisive indeterminacy. It is the allowance of this indeterminacy that establishes the space within which Socratic practice unfolds. Because the difficulty raised by the oracle goes beyond the alternatives of its simple acceptance or rejection, the interpretive response of Socrates demands that he hold himself in an openness toward the oracular claim without becoming indifferent to it. Socrates must challenge the word, attempt even to *refute* it, precisely so that the word may nevertheless be accepted, received.[13] Must we conclude, then, that the second sailing has already been launched before the priestess of the Pythian god has uttered one single word?

The oracle must be *received,* but it is apparent that such a reception requires more than a simple compliance, does not at all call for a mere passivity. This is so because what is commanded by the oracle cannot be transmitted directly, cannot be imposed upon the listener, simply in the content of what is said. Such reception thus becomes possible only through the peculiar receptivity of Socrates, through which he is able in advance to hold himself in a certain self-relation, through which he is already able to know himself, to know that he is indeed *already* claimed by the very task that the oracle would ask him to take up. The oracle makes clear that it does indeed speak the truth, but only because Socrates himself proves his wisdom precisely through his way of responding. The truth of the oracle is confirmed, therefore, only because it anticipates the Socratic response; and Socrates can respond in the way that he does only because he is *already* determined by his peculiar wisdom. It would seem, then, that the origin of the command, the source of the imperative to take up philosophy, to take philosophical questioning to the citizens of Athens, can be located neither in the oracular pronouncement nor simply in the Socratic response, since the oracle only provokes Socrates to do what he is already prepared to do, only confirms that he ought to do what he would do anyway. It is evident that the oracle, as Socrates interprets it, has to be regarded more as an encouragement that he continue in his practice than as a divine command to alter his life. But it can only encourage him in this way like the dream Socrates mentions in the *Phaedo,* by testing him, by calling for a response. One can get lost in this dizzying circle: the oracle is *interpreted* as a confirmation of the interpretation that is brought to it. The oracle tells Socrates that he is wise because he is able to question the oracle, but he questions the oracle because it tells him that he is wise.

This interpretation of the oracle, however, determined in this way, in and by the response itself, first of all has to remain a *questioning* that does not simply reside in such a circular confirmation: it demands that the question be settled *through a practice* that takes Socrates outside himself. The response, as the call to a practice, must be able to suspend the apparently inevitable closure belonging to interpretation, must be able to resist the way in which understanding has always already anticipated itself, has already run ahead of itself in what is to be understood. It is only because Socrates does take the meaning of the oracle to be obscure, to be difficult to discern, only because he *is able* to take it in this way, that this divine word for its part is able to speak, to pose its task—which is to say, to issue its command or imperative. The task posed by the oracle can be said, therefore, to consist in the first place in nothing other than the interpretation of the oracle itself—precisely as it has already laid claim to Socrates and the matter of who he is among humans. The riddle of the oracle concerns the oracle itself, but precisely as it lays claim to Socrates. But then, in order to take up this interpretive task, precisely in order to carry out such an interpretation of the oracle, it is also necessary that Socrates engage in his questioning practice in the city. According to Socrates' own account of the origins of his questioning and refutative practice in the city, it must be concluded that every Socratic dialogue that takes place in the city is to be heard as the attempt at settling this question: What does the god mean to say by declaring that no one is wiser than Socrates? "Thus I am still now going around in accord with the god searching and questioning anyone I think to be wise, whether that one is of the city or is a foreigner. And when that one does not seem to be wise, I give aid to the god and demonstrate that that one is not wise" (Apol. 23b).

The dialogues are thus to be taken first of all as a form of inquiry, a way of posing the question that concerns the nature of Socrates and his wisdom. And yet, because Socratic practice must be able to respond to the oracle in an openness, by keeping it undecided, must it not then be concluded that this questioning dialogical practice as such *precedes* the oracular command? It is not the god who tells Socrates he is ignorant: "For I am well aware that I am not wise either much or little" (Apol. 21b). It thus cannot be said that Socrates engages in dialogue simply because he is commanded to do so by the god. Instead, the possibility of first receiving the divine word in the way that he does, precisely as the injunction to philosophy and to dialogue, is already grounded in a prior ability, already presupposes that Socrates be dialogically responsive. The command to engage in dialogue, in other words, can be heard only by one who is *already* engaged in dialogue, can be received only by one who is *already* claimed by the command. How does this initial receptivity come to be? Can one be persuaded to listen?[14] The oracular pronouncement that Socrates is wisest, that none is wiser than he, is true only because he is able to receive it aporetically, as a riddle, as he is also able thereby to suspend its truth and to seek its refutation. It must be concluded, therefore, that the Socratic response in this way does not at all solve the riddle of the oracle but rather only confirms it precisely as a riddle: the riddle of the oracle is itself only *the oracular expression of the riddle that Socrates already is,* the question of his dialogical practice as a wisdom.

Because the oracle only takes for granted a Socratic relation to the λόγος, at most confirming it but not bringing it into being, it must be said that the story of the oracle that Socrates tells does not present an adequate account of the origins of his practice.[15] Like virtually every story Socrates tells, this story also speaks of origins while enacting a necessary withdrawal. The story suggests, in fact, that another account of the origin of this practice is called for. But if one takes what is said in the *Phaedo* as a more originary account, as Socrates speaks of the necessity of his "second sailing," the question then arises: Why is it not possible for Socrates to speak of this other origin at his public trial? The interpretation of his wisdom that is offered in the *Apology* must nevertheless be related to what is said in the *Phaedo,* precisely as it is revealed how Socratic ignorance arises in a youthful encounter with nature (Phaedo 97c, 97e, 99e). Socratic ignorance proves to be first of all grounded in a failed encounter with nature, but in that failure there is also the demand for the dialogical practice that Socrates speaks of in his *Apology.* That Socratic ignorance arises from out of this encounter means only that his dialogical engagement with the oracle already presupposes this peculiar relation to nature.

The question Socrates asks—How can the oracle be true, as it undoubtedly must be, when he knows that he is *not* wise?—thus can be heard as it opens onto another question: Could it be that this non-wisdom is still a certain kind of wisdom? Let me propose that this question, as it crosses over into a blatant contradiction—that is, non-wisdom *is* wisdom—already speaks of the doubling of nature that becomes manifest with Socrates. The doubling itself already poses the contradiction: the Socratic turn away from nature is itself the way of sustaining or retrieving a more original relation to nature. Socratic ignorance, which only confirms the self-concealing withdrawal of nature itself, also has to be thought as a movement that turns toward nature in a more originary way, in a way that would be appropriate to human life.

The contradiction of this wisdom establishes an intolerable condition and demands *movement.* The search for its reconciliation becomes the unceasing drive of Socratic practice. Deprived of knowing what the god wants, Socrates must still act. While he cannot rest assured that he has the god on his side, and cannot presume to be acting on divine authority, he also will never be released from the inexorable claim imposed upon him by the oracle. His practice thus turns out to be both the posing of this question that concerns the meaning of this oracle, as it announces his superlative human wisdom, and the forever incomplete answer to that question. And yet, the condemnation of Socrates by the city of Athens, because it must be regarded as the condemnation of his dialogical practice in the city, amounts to nothing less than the condemnation of his way of interpreting the oracle, if not the outright rejection of the oracle as such. It cannot be overlooked that the Socratic interpretation of the oracle also implies a statement about the hubris of the city of Athens: the Socratic gadfly is sent by the god to make the citizens aware that they are not wise, that they are not what they take themselves to be. And Socrates does prove the god irrefutable, since he proves through his practice that no one is wiser than himself, that no one is wiser than this one who is not wise at all. But this means also that Athens's condemnation of Socrates amounts to the city's assertion that Socrates has failed to refute the Athenians and has failed to know himself, that Socrates, alleged to be wisest of all, is not at all wise, does not know his own wisdom or lack of wisdom.

Thus, before any conclusions can be drawn concerning the precise meaning of the oracle, it is already necessary for Socrates to have *staked his life upon his response,* since the response itself has already demanded of him that he confront the city in this way. The questioning response, in its openness to the oracle, thus already constitutes a kind of interpretation that intervenes upon the city. And the interpretation cannot be dissociated from this political deed. Because the practice and the act of interpretation cannot be separated, the response has also already laid claim to the supposed knowledge that Socrates would have of himself. The response can only be the response that it is by already laying claim to that knowledge. It is nothing other than this Socratic self-knowledge that both puts the divine word into question and is put into question by the divine word, as that word speaks of a superlative wisdom.

And so, even when, in the *Apology,* Socrates does seem to make definitive or conclusive claims concerning the oracle and its meaning, these claims must not be abstracted from the way in which they have emerged, namely from the fact that his life has been solely dedicated, perhaps even in a certain kind of *purity,* to the very task of interpretation. The interpretation of the oracle amounts to nothing other than an affirmation of the need to continue questioning, "in the time of his life, up until and into his own death," as Heidegger would say. The divine imperative that Socrates receives cannot conclude in doctrinaire assertions because the reception is constituted only in this need to return to a more thorough questioning of what the god wants. If Socrates can indeed be said to be the "purest thinker of the West," it is precisely because of the way his dialogical practice is able to expose itself in its ignorance to the necessity of this return to questioning and the beginning of questioning, even as it extends into death and the uncertainty of death. And, in fact, the affirmation of ignorance in the context of death can only be taken as a kind of *courage,* inasmuch as fear, according to Socrates in the *Apology,* consists in the false presumption of wisdom and knowledge. "To fear death . . . is nothing other than to take oneself as wise when one is not; it is taking oneself as knowing what one does not know. For no one knows if death does not happen to be the greatest of all human goods" (Apol. 29a.; cf. Phaedo 68d–69b). Death, as the greatest of all goods, the good that we have in common, thus has to be thought alongside that other Socratic claim, namely, that the hatred of the λόγος is the greatest of all evils.

Socratic wisdom can be said, then, to consist also in the paradox or contradiction of such a courageous ignorance, a paradox or contradiction that can be confronted and confirmed only through the questioning practice that is protracted, that must unfold in a time of postponement and deferral, holding itself open even to the possible good of death. When Socrates introduces his wisdom in the *Apology* this is already evident, since what he says is that his wisdom, announced by the god, is *not* wisdom at all, or rather is only a *human* wisdom, ἀνθρωπίνη σοφία (Apol. 20d). It is the failure of the Athenians to grasp the peculiar character of this distinctly human or mortal wisdom that leads to the prejudice against Socrates, since his capacity to sustain the questioning movement of dialogue—inseparable from his refutative capacity—can be taken by them only as a knowledge that presumes to be simply the opposite of ignorance. But it is said that death imposes a factical ignorance on all human life, while the fear of death Socrates takes to be a kind of denial of such ignorance.[16] The refusal to confront this ignorance can be seen as the refusal to confront death as death. Strangely, Socrates shows that the fear of death is anything but the fear of the unknown; instead, such fear becomes simply the denial of death itself, a way of closing oneself off to life's mortality.

What sets Socrates apart from the rest of humankind can be said to be his way of affirming that he is only human, that his wisdom does not approach the wisdom that would be "more than human" or divine. He is most strange, in other words, through a paradigmatic or exemplary wisdom that is utterly peculiar to him, but this peculiarity also confirms his humanity. The singular gives rise to a logic of the synecdoche, where one is able to stand for all only because at the same time as one it remains in itself, distinguished and set apart. Such a logic lets the singular stand for the whole only by also making explicit the operation by which the whole will have been *reduced* to that very singularity. Yet this is the contradiction of Socratic wisdom, presented as a paradigm, since this reduction can never be completed. The paradigm, that which proves to be "like" all the others, precisely by virtue of this remarkable and encompassing likeness, remains unto itself, in an inimitable singularity. What is paradoxical about Socratic wisdom, as merely human, lies in its impossibility: if the difference is to be abolished between the exemplar and that of which it would be a mere example, precisely the difference itself must be insisted upon. Socrates is preeminent and exemplary because he is also the singular exception. Socratic singularity thus must enact the ruin of imitability, and in this tragic enactment Aristotle's logic of infinite substitution is refuted.[17]

Socrates is thus a figure of utmost moderation, an affirmation of the limit, but such moderation already demands a certain hubris and transgression. The same tragic necessity plays itself out again and again: to mark the limit is already to surpass it. *On the one hand,* the superlative wisdom of Socrates seems to achieve a reversal and is reducible thereby to the simple truth that human wisdom is worth little or nothing and that only the god is truly wise (Apol. 23a). If Socrates does prove wiser than the rest, it is only to the extent that he knows the truth concerning this poverty of human wisdom. But is this such a slight difference? Does this difference itself not establish the very possibility of Socratic practice, a questioning practice that enacts nothing other than a demonstration of the truth about the insignificance of human wisdom, that it is worth almost nothing, only very little? It must also be acknowledged, then, that the practice itself demands, *on the other hand,* that the failure of those who would present themselves as wise be exhibited or made plain. Socratic dialogue thus becomes the means by which the god displays human failure, and dialogical refutation becomes the breaking of hubris, the collapse of wisdom as a human possibility. And it must not be overlooked that it is this demonstration that leads Socrates to his death. The practice, as such a demonstration, thus only reveals what the god wants to convey, is carried out in the service of the god—so says Socrates. But because the Socratic paradigm both exemplifies human life and stands apart from it, Socrates thus exhibits human life in its own proper monstrosity. What Socrates says is that the god, by speaking of the superlative wisdom of Socrates, in saying that human wisdom is worth little or nothing, is also *producing a paradigm,* only making an example of him—παράδειγμα ποιούμενος (Apol. 23b). So that the hubris of Athens be displayed, Socrates must be destroyed.

This divine ποίησις that is said to transform Socrates into such a monstrous but paradigmatic figure can be correlated exactly to the "making" that appears in the accusation in which it is claimed that Socrates *makes* the weaker λόγος the stronger. The one making calls for the other; they imply each other. Such a divine making is, however, only the confirmation of the same contradiction that opens the tragic character of all human life. The singularity of Socrates lies in the fact that he would be nothing special at all. And this already intimates his great transgression. Socrates articulates his merely human wisdom in a way that also makes evident its *inhumanity:* it is this very practice, carried out in the service of the god, that is said to deprive him of the σχολή to engage in political matters, and that forces him also to neglect what he calls here τὰ οἰκεῖα, his own interests, what is properly his own. The refutative practice (philosophy) is exposed, then, to an economy of time, in which there is also a lack of σχολή for other matters. After he explains that his dialogical practice continues as the same interpretive response to the god's oracular pronouncement concerning his wisdom, Socrates states: "And through this business [ὑπὸ ταύτης τῆς ἀσχολίας] I have the σχολή neither for any matters of the city worth speaking of nor for my own interests [οὔτε τῶν οἰκείων]" (Apol. 23b).

The dialogical practice in the city, his philosophical music, is all-consuming, demands the utter neglect of other things. And this purity, as it would establish the preeminent humanity of Socrates, appears most unlike human life. His dialogical engagement in the city is thus spoken of as a divine gift, precisely because it is *not* human to neglect τὰ οἰκεῖα, one's own interests (Apol. 31b). But this inhuman or monstrous neglect of his own affairs is already established in the economy that would set the σχολή of philosophical inquiry apart from the rest of life, setting it apart, however, precisely as the time of life and death proper to Socrates.

Situated within a certain emphatic ignorance, irreducible to any τέχνη, Socratic practice is thus excessive precisely in its resistance to being situated within any domain or region over which it might claim to have a knowing power or mastery. This strange excess, as the insistence upon what is non-regional or non-regionalizable, becomes apparent first of all simply in the way in which Socrates is able to induce perplexity and seems to stupefy those who encounter him, his refutative ability. Such perplexity is consistently encountered by the dramatic participants in the dialogues as *singularly* Socratic, and thus as otherwise unheard-of. Yet it is also the case that this perplexity is not simply unleashed upon others, imposed upon them by Socrates. Socrates himself consistently claims to suffer the very same perplexity to which his interlocutors come to be subjected in their encounter with him. As the decisive πάθος of Socrates, this perplexity thus always comes to be directed toward the other, or raised with the other, only because it is also a self-questioning, a questioning that is bound, namely, to the task imposed upon human life by the first inscription at Delphi: γνῶθι σαυτόν. The strange excessive ignorance of Socrates thus finds itself expressed in this cryptic injunction, which, as it is paired with that other Delphic injunction, μηδὲν ἄγαν, "nothing too much" (Prot. 343b), must be heard in two ways. This doubling of the Delphic imperative, which as an inscription is already twofold, is then a redoubling of the imperative, a doubling of a twofold. This redoubling brings to word what I have been calling the tragic doubling of nature.

The inscription first of all can be heard as the demand given to human life that it not forget its proper place, which is to say: such life must not take itself to be a god, must not rival the god. In this sense, the second injunction would only confirm or corroborate what is already pronounced in the first. It would reiterate and even amplify the sense of the first imperative: know yourself, which is to say, do not exceed your position, remain in your proper abode, for the consequences of transgression are certain and terrible. The two imperatives belong together and confirm each other. But such an interpretation, while in one sense always correct and compelling, must also assume that human life is already in possession of a capable knowledge of its place, that such a knowledge of the good is attainable and available to it without a movement of questioning and seeking. The assumption would be that the possibility of such a belonging and non-transgression, while depending upon a self-knowledge, would not demand in the first place the most difficult and risky engagement. A second interpretation thus asserts itself, which recoils upon the first, where self-knowledge appears not as a given, but as a task, where the possibility of such an *autognosis* only insists upon the need for self-examination and self-questioning. Autognosis, as a task, is first of all a seeking, an *autoscopy*. This second interpretation thus suggests that taking up such a task brings with it precisely the danger that is then brought to word in the admonishing character of the second injunction: in order to find oneself, precisely in order to know one's place, is it not necessary, finally, to transgress one's own proper limits, and thereby to risk challenging the god, to seek one's own destruction and undoing? The oracular disclosure of oneself, which remains unquestionable, leads always, it seems, to the tragic descent or undergoing of human life, since only in the transgression of the limits of the properly human can those very limits be made plain, can what the god thus demands be satisfied. The god demands, it seems, something impossible, both moderation and transgression *at once.* The two injunctions—*know thyself* and *nothing too much*—articulate the very contradiction of human nature as it is bound to its own self-questioning within the nature that it is and that also exceeds it.

Socrates has no time, no σχολή for anything, except the affirmation of the good of life. But this πάθος, which appears as a temporal restriction, also calls for the courage that can affirm this same good as the good of death. And such courage is itself an affirmation of human ignorance in the necessary turn to dialogue and the λόγος, as a protracted movement open to refutation. This *inhuman* practice, as it is able to neglect or forsake τὰ οἰκεῖα, what is one's own, what is in one's own interest, is the obsession with the task of self-knowledge. Socrates, obsessed with himself and the task of self-knowledge, has no time for his own interests. Presumably, this same temporal restriction—which is both the "purity" and the πάθος of Socrates—is intimately bound to his refusal or his failure to become a writer, as Heidegger suggests. Socrates, it seems, has no time to write precisely because all he can do is affirm the good of life in a dialogical practice that holds itself open to the good of death.

The only occasion in Plato's text where Socrates is presented as a writer occurs in the *Phaedo,* thus in the same dialogue that presents Socratic practice as a second sailing.[18] And it is not at all insignificant that this is also the dialogue in which the death of Socrates is dramatically presented. The question of Socratic authorship is raised as the worries of a certain Evenus are relayed by Cebes to Socrates about his having become a poet. Socrates is said to have "intensified" or "set to verse" (ἐντείνας) some of the λόγοι of Aesop and composed a hymn or proem (προοίμιον) to Apollo (Phaedo

60d). Socrates has mentioned Evenus in his defense speech as one who is new to town and is regarded by others as a teacher of wisdom and who for a fee teaches that wisdom to others; in the actual passage in the *Apology* it is clear that Evenus is supposed to have an expertise concerning the human good in the same way one who cares for horses is an expert (Apol. 19e–20c).[19] In the *Phaedo*, it is stated that this Evenus, as one who is thus alleged to possess a τέχνη that Socrates himself lacks, is concerned now that Socratic poetry might compete with his own. But Socrates' reply to Evenus appears strange and oblique, since it concludes with an abrupt affirmation of the good, but this good is the good of death. And in this way the dialogue turns to what becomes its explicit and thematic preoccupation, the question that takes up the time remaining, the time that concludes with the death of Socrates. Because of this conspicuous finality, it must be acknowledged that every word spoken in the dialogue finds itself transformed into deed. It is often pointed out that the persuasive power of the *Phaedo* consists in its dramatic connection with utter finality. Yet if what is said *about* death in the dialogue has to be understood first of all in relation to what happens and to what is done, it then becomes clear through this discussion of a possible Socratic writing that the deed of Socrates, his ἔργον, is also not simply reducible to the fact that he courageously continues to converse until he is overtaken by the φάρμακον.

It is worth asking: Why is the question of Socrates as author (or poet) raised in this dialogue at all? And how is it to be understood that when he is asked about this written work Socrates wants to talk about death and the good of death? What is this connection between Socratic writing and death?

At first Socrates tells Evenus, who simply wants to know what Socrates is up to as a poet, that his intention has not been to rival Evenus at all but rather only to test a certain recurrent dream, as it has been addressing him by name: "Socrates . . . make music and work at it [μουσικήν ποίει καὶ ἐργάζου]" (Phaedo 60e). Socrates admits that in the past he took this oneiric imperative only as an encouragement to continue what he was already doing, to continue with his philosophical practice, which he still affirms as the "greatest music."[20] But he also admits that now, while awaiting his death, he has begun to second-guess the simplicity of his earlier interpretation. Perhaps the dream has been not simply encouraging him to continue, as he assumed beforehand, but has been asking him to alter his practice, to do something else. This most astonishing admission on the part of Socrates makes it clear that Socrates views his time in prison, this temporary reprieve from death, as the opportunity to address what might be unfinished business. And he even suggests that this may be what the god wants in giving him this brief interstitial time, since he says that he has made the poems in order to acquit himself of a possible impiety (Phaedo 61b).[21]

This remarkable passage in the *Phaedo* that refers to a Socratic poetry and writing thus must be considered in the context of Socratic practice as a whole, his dialogical practice in the city. It must be viewed, in other words, as a continued interrogation of Socratic wisdom. Socrates himself invites us to do this, since he presents his writing as a possible alternative to his practice, and thus as a way to interrogate and examine the very purity of that practice, what he calls here a kind of philosophical music.[22]

Presumably, this writing of poetry, as a possible alternative to the dialogical practice in the city that Socrates articulates in the *Apology,* and that he enacts in the *Gorgias,* would not have led to death in the same way: it would be a different way to prepare for death, a different affirmation of death. Because it is such a fundamental questioning of his practice, there can be no mistaking that this Socratic turn to writing and to poetry—which the dialogue raises only briefly in order not to speak of it again, and thus in order to move on to the more pressing matter of death—does indeed give Socrates a way to examine how it is that he finds himself in prison, now condemned to die. But it is no less the case, therefore, that the "apology" Socrates offers to his friends in this dialogue (Phaedo 63b), carried out on behalf of his philosophical practice as it is bound to the λόγος, also amounts to the continuation of his self-interrogation or self-examination. The dialogue relayed in the *Phaedo*—recounted by Phaedo himself from memory because he *himself* was present when Socrates died—is in fact throughout an enactment and a continuation of the peculiar self-examination that is characteristic of Socratic philosophy, as it seeks to affirm the death that is brought about by that practice and shows itself to be inseparable from it.

This is confirmed in the dialogue most explicitly as Socrates offers an account of the origins of his own practice by speaking of it as a δεύτερος πλοῦς, as a "second sailing" or "second best way" (Phaedo 99d). What arises in the dialogue as the need to address something having to do with the σοφία or wisdom that is called the ἱστορία περὶ φύσεως (Phaedo 96a), namely as an investigation of nature that concerns the "cause of generation and degeneration" (Phaedo 95e), becomes, as Socrates proceeds, an account of the origins of his philosophical practice, an account, then, of the *generation* of Socrates himself. What Socrates relays in this regard are the things he has undergone, his experiences: τά γε ἐμὰ πάθη (Phaedo 96a). The question of our death and the good of our death shows itself in this way to be grounded in our relation to nature, and to demand an explication of the generation and degeneration of natural things. But what begins as the inquiry into nature finds itself returned, through a certain inexorable necessity, to the question that bears upon the nature of Socrates himself: "I concluded with the opinion that I was naturally unfit [ἀφυής] for this way of looking into things" (Phaedo 96c). This account of his own questioning journey, as it transforms or departs from its initial trajectory, from nature itself to the nature of Socrates, is thus also returned to how this practice from its very beginning is bound to its death and its way of dying. It is revealing, therefore, that Socrates speaks of the great failing of the causality of Anaxagorian νοῦς precisely in terms of its inability to account fully for what has brought Socrates to prison. Anaxagoras's way of neglecting the question of what is right or best shows itself also as the neglect of death, the neglect of the deeds of one's life in its mortality and its way of being claimed by justice. It thus becomes clear that the δεύτερος πλοῦς emerges as a way to take up the question of the good, but only as a self-examination of one's mortal actions. Anaxagoras, whose inquiry into nature is contrasted in the *Apology* with Socratic inquiry (Apol. 26d), shows up again in the *Phaedrus* as the teacher of Pericles, at a point where Socrates wants to stress the dependency of τέχνη upon nature (Phaedr. 270a). The shadow of Anaxagoras cannot be simply dismissed; it remains as a marker for an impossibility. This is to say, however, that the Socratic "betrayal" of Anaxagoras, as it opens up the way to the Socratic second sailing, also sustains an openness to nature's concealment.

But this means that the enactment of this mortal self-examination is also something that arises through a certain failure: the "second sailing" of Socrates is a movement that turns to the λόγοι from out of *another* approach to nature, an approach in which nature reveals itself through its refusal. And if the refusal remains irreducible to an unfortunate detour, it must be concluded that the concealment of nature and human mortality are intimately bound together. We confront our mortality in the concealment of nature, because we confront nature as mortals. But how, then, can the turn to poetry and writing, as it is only briefly discussed in the *Phaedo,* be considered as another modulation or manifestation of this *same necessity* that inititiates this δεύτερος πλοῦς, and that leads to the dialogical practice in the city as Socrates speaks of it in his *Apology*?

At the same time, one also cannot overlook how utterly misleading Socrates' account of his own practice appears to be in this passage in the *Phaedo* that deals with Socratic writing. Here Socrates would distance himself from the telling of stories and at the same time oppose such storytelling to the λόγος itself.

> So first I made a poem to the god whose day of sacrifice was at hand. And taking note that a poet if he's to be a poet, has to make stories, not arguments [ποιεῖν μύθους, ἀλλ' οὐ λόγους], and that I myself was not a storyteller [καὶ αὐτὸς οὐκ ἦ μυθολογικός], therefore after the god I turned to the stories of Aesop, the ones I had at hand and knew—whichever I chanced on first—and made them into poetry. (Phaedo 61b)

The Socratic statement on its own terms is perplexing enough, if one tries to discern by means of it what makes a poet a poet, and what makes poetry something that could be distinguished from philosophy and the philosophical λόγος. A ποιητής, as poet, is not just a maker, not just a ποιητής. The poet must make stories, not λόγοι, says Socrates. It is often pointed out how the Greek word ποίησις has this slippery duplicity, in which it has both a more general sense, which refers to making as such, and a more narrow sense, which refers only to poetry, or the making of poetry. This interpretation of the word, in which the part comes to stand for the whole, must take the ποίησις of the poet to be a making in an exemplary but peculiar sense, since it would have to stand for all other forms of making while also being distinguishable from them. Like Socrates himself it would be the paradigm that twists open any possibility of simple identity. Thus, just for this reason, precisely because it would stand for production as such, it may be that poetry also already must mark a decisive break with the merely *human* sense of production. In the *Phaedrus,* for example, Socrates makes clear in a famous passage, both thematically and performatively, as he himself invokes the Muses and is taken over by a kind of poetic madness, that poetry remains irreducible to τέχνη and human cunning (Phaedr. 245a). The difficulty that inheres in this duplicity of the word ποίησις is taken up explicitly by Socrates in the *Symposium* (Sym. 205c), and it is constantly in play in the famous censuring of poetry that one finds in the last book of the *Republic.*

Socrates says in this passage in the *Phaedo* that he *makes* the stories of Aesop into poetry, thus transforming into poetry stories that precisely *as stories* should already be poetry. It should be noted that while Socrates speaks in this passage in the *Phaedo* of Aesop's own *stories,* these stories have just been introduced into the dialogue by Cebes not as stories at all, but rather as λόγοι (Phaedo 60d). Perhaps Socrates should be taken to mean that in this poetic transformation he sets the stories to verse and meter, since when Cebes introduces the poetry of Socrates he does suggest this. But even Cebes does not speak explicitly of verse or meter. Some English translations, however, insist on rendering the text in this way, despite the fact that Socrates himself does not speak here of meter at all, but of the making of stories. Aristotle, for example, will insist that meter is not what is essential to poetry. Otherwise, even Empedocles could be called a poet. "There is nothing in common" (οὐδὲν κοινόν ἐστιν), says Aristotle, between Homer and Empedocles: one is a poet, and the other "gives [or makes, poetizes] an account of nature" (τὸν δὲ φυσιολόγον μᾶλλον ἢ ποιητήν) (Poetics 1447b17–20). After Socrates draws the distinction between μύθοι and λόγοι, suggesting that this distinction opens the decisive difference between the poet and the philosopher, he then proceeds to characterize poetry with a word that combines these two words together, making them into one: Socrates knows that he is no μυθολογικός, no storyteller, no mythologist.

It is certainly difficult to grasp what Socrates could be saying when he claims here not to be a storyteller, not to mythologize, since such a disavowal blatantly contradicts countless passages in the Platonic text. Socrates makes a similar claim in other passages. Notably, in Book II of the *Republic* he sharply distinguishes the founders of a city (οἰκισταί) from those who are poets (Rep. 378e–379a), and he does so after likening himself and his companions to those who "tell tales within a tale" (ἐν μύθῳ μυθολογοῦντες) and who with σχολή would educate the men in and with speech (Rep. 376d). But in order to overturn such a disavowal of poetry as it appears in the *Phaedo*, one does not have to appeal to other dialogues, or wait for the fantastic cosmic story Socrates will soon tell in this same dialogue about the many regions under the earth, and those between earth and sky (Phaed. 107d–115d). (Like the *Gorgias* and the *Republic*, the *Phaedo* ends with a story told by one who denies himself as a storyteller.) While Socrates can be seen performatively to contradict his own disavowal of storytelling, he also appears to contradicts himself in this very passage, as he begins to take up the task of accounting for the good of death, which he says will involve precisely μυθολογεῖν, the telling of stories about the journey to that other place (Phaedo 61e). What Socrates states quite clearly here is that his philosophical practice, as the making of a music that affirms and prepares for death, also demands a poetic engagement with myth, the telling of tales. Socratic affirmation seems to demand such tales, all of which, without exception, can be heard articulating the place of human life within the cosmos.

At the same time, it is important to note that when Socrates discusses Aesop he also appears to be quite indifferent to which stories in particular he has taken up and made into poetry. After the poem to the god, it seems to matter little which stories come to be poetized: it is a matter of chance, of τύχη. We thus cannot say which stories he has appropriated, nor do we know how he has made them into poetry. The fact that Socrates turns to Aesop is not given any special importance, although Nietzsche, more than two thousand years later, will see it as a sign of Socratic vulgarity. This "music-practicing" Socrates, who in the final hour of his life would choose Aesop as his literary predecessor or counterpart, thus marks for Nietzsche the death of tragedy and the irrevocable loss of the mythic. Nevertheless, one cannot but see such an interpretation as rash, if not dismissive, given that what occurs in the Socratic transformation of Aesop is left entirely undeveloped in the dialogue. The way in which Socrates invents his own Aesopian fable about the relation between pleasure and pain does not suggest at all that his appropriation of these utterly commonsensical stories would simply revel in their shopworn wisdom. It is clear instead that these stories would be returned to inexorably aporetic structures of life, such as the life of the body (ψυχή) in the conflict between pleasure and pain, their being joined together while held apart.

And yet, what is still more astounding is the way in which this Socratic disavowal of storytelling is itself already thoroughly overtaken by the mythic horizon of the god who has granted Socrates this opportunity to become a poet and writer, the god to whom Socrates also composes his hymn. Within this horizon we again confront the question of Socratic purity, along with a certain demand that is unmistakably Apollonian, the impossible demand that life and death be kept apart. Phaedo tells Echecrates, who wonders why such a long time passed between the trial and Socrates' death, that it was a matter of chance, of τύχη. He gives the explanation: the very ship that Theseus sailed to Crete, and that now every year is sent to Delos, did not return quickly, since it was detained by the wind. And until this ship returns from Delos, from the birthplace of Apollo—the island on which, it should be noted, both birth and death are prohibited by Apollo himself—it is the custom of the Athenians, Phaedo says, "to keep the city pure during that time and to execute no one publicly" (Phaedo 58c). Presumably, both birth and death displease the god. The time granted to Socrates, the time in which he also experiments as a poet and writer, is thus held to be a *pure time* in which death would be prohibited by divine order, but it is nevertheless a time between birth and death. If the *Phaedo* must be read both as a retelling and as a reenactment of the journey of Theseus,[23] in which Socrates plays the part of the heroic founder of Athenian greatness, and Phaedo himself plays the part of Ariadne, the young woman who betrays her own family only then to be betrayed herself, abandoned to Dionysus on the lonely island of Naxos, how does one then do justice to the supposed Socratic purity, as it shows itself to be thoroughly entangled with this mythic and tragic tradition? Theseus, the ultimate Apollonian hero and greatest of all monster slayers, also shows himself to be a hidden co-conspirator of none other than . . . Dionysus? Theseus can be taken even as a sign for the strange affinity these two gods, Apollo and Dionysus, have for one another.[24] But is this not also the case with Socrates himself? What Socrates finally tells Cebes to relay to Evenus comes as a shock to all who are present. Socrates recommends to Evenus, "if he is sound-minded [ἄν σωφρονῇ], to follow me as quickly as possible" (Phaedo 61c). Socrates, who is asked only about his reasons for writing, seems to deflect this more direct question with an utterly Silenic affirmation: *it would be best to die soon.* Humans, Socrates says, are better off dead, but it is only the god who can postpone or enact this good.

This connection between writing, the good of death, and the purity of Socrates can be approached only through the matter of how one is to spend one's time. The *Phaedo* itself, far from offering convincing proofs of the soul's immortality,[25] is instead a demonstration of what constitutes philosophical σχολή. And yet, within the restriction of such an interstitial temporality, the space opened and defined only by postponement, one also confronts the greatest of difficulties: namely the task of self-knowledge. Such σχολή is not simply a question of how Phaedo and Echecrates have the leisure to recount and to hear (with great pleasure) the last conversation Socrates has with his friends (Phaedo 58d), but rather it is first of all a question of how death has already infiltrated and determined the possibilities of life, perhaps even eclipsing those possibilities. The entire dialogue unfolds within the certainty of death, both for humans as such and for Socrates. Whatever the λόγος "demonstrates" here, it remains wholly dependent upon this unshakable and arresting fact. Thus, the Apollonian dream of a life without death must give way to the tragic necessity that time is indeed all too short for mortal human life. It is already too late, and whatever choice one may have, it occurs only by virtue of a certain reprieve, granted by the god, or perhaps what can be spoken of only as a matter of chance. Socrates thus becomes the storyteller of his own story, both presenting the purity of life and disrupting that purity through its inevitable repetition and transmission. Socrates agrees to entertain the question that his friends now find so scandalous, that the philosopher is on such good terms with death. They have not heard anything like this from Philolaus, at least not anything clear (σαφές). Socrates says:

> Now certainly I too speak of them only from hearsay [ἐξ ἀκοῆς]. What I have heard by chance [τυγχάνω], however, I don't begrudge telling. For perhaps it's especially fitting for somebody who's about to emigrate to that place to examine and also to tell stories [μυθολεγεῖν] about the emigration there [ἐκεῖ]—what sort of thing we think it is. For what else would one do in the time until the setting of the sun? (Phaedo 61d–e)

How has Socratic σχολή been claimed from the beginning by its death? The practice that determines Socrates and the course of his life, as it leads to prison and to death, and as it begins in and as an interpretive response, as the testing of the very meaning of the oracle, is said in the *Apology* to arise as a way to confirm certain dreams. "I have been commanded to do this by the god, as I say, by means of oracles and dreams and in every other way that divine dispensation [θεία μοῖρα] has ever commanded a human to do anything" (Apol. 33c). If it is this same command that Socrates speaks of in the *Phaedo,* as he approaches the hour of his death, he thus comes to ask himself whether through his original interpretation of the dream—which he connects to the oracle and its command—he has not neglected a task, not failed to do precisely what the god has enjoined upon him. It is this question that he takes up in prison through the writing of poetry. The original Socratic interpretation of the god's command is said by Socrates himself to impose upon him the need for a certain kind of exclusion, as if it is the awareness of a kind of economic necessity, a restricted economy within which some things must be abandoned in order to preserve something else, what Heidegger would ask us to think as purity, since it leads also to the definitive lack of leisure, the lack of time for anything except what the god bids Socrates to do. In postponing his death perhaps the inscrutable god is giving Socrates one more chance before his death to do what he must do, to do what he has not yet done. But then, Socrates, by questioning his own philosophical practice in such a fundamental way, on the very eve of his departure, is also inviting us to entertain a great suspicion concerning the very purity of that practice, as it would neglect both poetry and writing. The *Platonic* text makes explicit how the alleged purity of Socratic practice, a purity that announces that it has no time for anything else, also cannot detach itself from the question of its non-writing, and is even still haunted at the end of its life by the possible need to write. The three themes of σχολή, death, and writing thus cycle through each other, in the question of a Socratic affirmation of human life, a life that unfolds within a certain measure.

The wisdom of Silenus, which in our time Nietzsche brings powerfully to word in his early work on the origins of tragedy, can certainly be heard expressed throughout the poetic tradition that Socrates confronts and appears to censure.[26] That this tradition must be banished from the city he makes in the λόγος, banished by Socrates himself, is something that can best be understood, perhaps, first of all through a consideration of the way this tradition articulates and affirms the birth and death of human life, the *regeneration* through which the place of human life in the world is both opened up and put into question. To ask about this Socratic confrontation with poetry is thus to ask about how the place of human life can be defined through an inexorable privation, the necessity that reveals the home of human life as a site of not belonging, as a place out of joint, out of place. It remains to be seen how the confrontation with this poetic tradition—the confrontation, then, between philosophy and poetry—reveals not only an antagonism and a difference, an "ancient difference," as Socrates says near the end of the *Republic,* but also an intimate bond, one established precisely in the matter of human deathliness, as the paradoxical good we share in common. But it also may be the case that this friendship, the bond that would be grounded in such an abyssal and tragic good, is such that it already brings about a discord, even the necessity of a betrayal in the repetition that must venture to speak for the dead.

I have claimed that in the Platonic dialogues the good arises first of all as a question only because it is already manifest in and as a certain imperative, as a task. It is therefore promised or made available—since it already claims human life—while at the same time remaining withheld from that life, opened up then precisely through an undeniable refusal and withdrawal. The peculiar Socratic receptivity that becomes manifest in this withdrawal can be said to be a way of being claimed by a good that is "beyond being." But this exceedingly difficult thought is inseparable from the way it comes to be embodied and enacted precisely in the enigmatic figure of Socrates himself, as he makes his appearance in the city, *as he descends.* His philosophical life, his life and death in the city, as presented by Plato, reveals the human as the animal for whom it is indeed possible to know nature in a way that bears decisively upon the "health" of that animal, but this "knowledge," if considered then simply in terms of the *difference* between human life and the natural, also arises in an emphatic awareness of ignorance, as the good of nature—the good as nature—is revealed also in its being refused or denied to human life.

It is well known that Nietzsche, in the *Birth of Tragedy,* interprets the appearance of Socrates and the rise of Socratic philosophy through the death of tragedy, and that he attributes that death in part to the effects of an excessive Socratism. Nietzsche thereby emphasizes the way in which in the appearance of Socrates something occurs that is utterly unprecedented in the Greek world. But for Nietzsche "this most questionable appearance of antiquity"[27] represents the first "theoretical human," a violent assault upon instinct and nature, and is therefore only a sign of sickness and decline. Here I must forgo a discussion of how precisely on Nietzsche's own terms Socrates enacts a powerful continuation and reinscription of the problem of tragedy and the tragic hero. I only mention in passing that Nietzsche himself speaks of this "music-practicing" Socrates precisely as a reconfiguration of the confrontation between Pentheus and Dionysus.

Yet, despite Nietzsche's apparent insistence to the contrary—or perhaps because of it—Socrates, the Platonic Socrates, does not at all have to be interpreted as simply the rejection or the overcoming of the tragic. It is possible, in fact, to see in Socrates—in the philosopher whom Hegel speaks of as nothing less than "the tragedy of Greece"[28]—a creative appropriation of that obscure and oracular "wisdom of Silenus" that Nietzsche himself eloquently brings to word as the decisive riddle and insight of Greek tragedy. Nietzsche puts Silenus himself on stage, letting him address human life: "Oh, miserable ephemeral race, children of chance and suffering, why do you compel me to say to you what would be most beneficial for you not to hear? What is best of all is utterly unreachable: not to be born, not to *be,* to be *nothing.* But the second best for you is—to die soon."[29]

What is decisive about such "wisdom" is not simply that it seems to impose a final condemnation upon human life, but that it reveals how that life can relate to itself through something that is always already lost, unattainable but also unrecoverable. In proclaiming in this way that what is best (for human life), namely never to have been born, is *impossible,* Silenus does not just deny the good to human life, but instead reveals something about the limits within which human life is able to relate to its ownmost possibility: such possibility is conditioned or determined by the impossible as such. The impossibility spoken of by Silenus, precisely as what is best, is thus not simply closed off to human life. Instead, the difficulty here has to do with considering how *only in such impossibility* can what is best actually come to reveal itself, precisely as impossible. Both Silenic and Socratic wisdom demand attending to the intensely paradoxical way in which the good shows itself, through a strange constitutive refusal and loss.

The Socratic encounter with nature, as it makes manifest this constitutive impossibility, can be seen enacting a repetition of what is proclaimed and encountered in these tragic words of Silenus. This impossibility no doubt will always also have to refer back to and bear upon human life and the nature of human life in its possible flourishing and happiness. Nietzsche, after all, has Silenus couch his words in a certain reluctance, since he states that there is a great advantage in *not* hearing this wisdom. And although human life is better off not hearing precisely what concerns it most of all, Midas will nevertheless compel the sylvan god to divulge his secrets. How, then, can one approach this violent and encompassing appropriation of human life, which does indeed appear to be a final condemnation of that life and its possible natural belonging, as it speaks of that life through an eternal "too late," and thus as monstrous and out of place? Must it not somehow be heard as an extreme provocation, as the greatest stimulus to a life that still seeks its place in nature, precisely because it is itself nature, still something *of nature*? Socrates can be interpreted, then, as a sustained response to that provocation. But how does his response still also echo and even amplify that very provocation itself?

Silenic wisdom speaks of the *birth* of human life as the way in which what is best comes to be determined. But this birth, it turns out, is approachable only through the impossibility of its *not* having occurred. The necessity of having been born, the condition of one's life, is therefore also what deprives human life of its ownmost good. Precisely *as a mode of time,* something becomes manifest in birth as necessary yet unrecoverable, not to be redeemed. The words shatter the view from nowhere: it is indeed impossible never to have been born, but only the animal who is in fact *already* born and who thus knows itself *as born* can confront this inexorable limit to its self-knowledge and self-mastery. The very manifestation of what is best thus occurs with necessity, but in this necessity of its manifestation it must also refute itself, enforce its own unattainability. To know oneself as born is to confront the factical and contingent necessity of one's life, but this is already to be able to think one's own utter lack of place, one's own monstrous presence. Here there is then indeed the encounter with oneself as nothing, the encounter with one's own nothingness, but through the inversion of birth as a burden, this nothingness appears as something denied. Thus, the most terrible moment of this wisdom is not announced initially, but comes only at the point at which there is then recourse to a "second best," a "second" that is now modulated in the language of possibility: the second best is possible, can be attained: it is only to get beneath the cold earth as soon as possible, to die soon.

But if the happiness of human life hangs on the enigmatic good of dying, if it can be confirmed only in death, it is also the case that this "second best," as possible, cannot be detached from the original riddle out of which it emerges, the riddle that is posed and imposed first in terms of impossibility, since in one sense the second best comes to be second (and thus possible) only through its relation to that original limit of the impossible, within which it is established and which it can never outstrip or surpass. As a member of the wretched race, one thus learns from Silenus, as does Midas, that one's relation to death, as one's ownmost possibility, is bound tragically to the inexplicability of birth and coming to be. Our death, the death proper to each of us, as the good we have in common, is already announced in the eternal "too late" of birth, the very birth that marks our limit, our ownmost impossibility, just as the mortality of each makes manifest the strange contingent necessity of having been born.

There can be little question that Socrates' own affirmation of a second best way, the opening to a necessary doubling, as the turn to the λόγοι, becomes a way to affirm the human good in its mortality. Socrates, in a deeply enigmatic and troubling way, also speaks of the good of dying. Is philosophy not said to be even the practice of dying, nothing other than the preparation for death? But in the *Phaedo* this account of philosophy can be demonstrated only through the Socratic deed, in which meeting the fear of death (and thus affirming or even living life as mortal) requires nothing less than being healed of the most dangerous sickness, the greatest of evils, namely, the possible hatred of the λόγος.

Can the λόγος address the time of mortal human life? The Minotaur confronted by Socrates and his companions, it turns out, is not simply the fear of death, but proves to have (at least) two horns.[30] At this point it is worth considering the suggestive connection that Socrates makes in the *Phaedo* between misology and a certain inability to have friends. Both come about in the same way, he says (Phaedo 89d–e). If one sees such inability for friendship to be grounded first of all in an inability to be a friend to oneself—and thus in a kind of self-loathing—then the disease of misology is grounded in a corrupted or degenerate self-relation, which is to say, in a failure to take up the task of self-knowledge. This same failure is addressed in the *Republic* as the "sickness" of injustice, which is taken up as the failure to enact the community of friends, those who would have "all things" in common. It is in the context of this failure that the Socratic affirmation demands here that we blame not the λόγος but only ourselves (Phaedo 90b–91a). His final encouragement to his friends—his final apology on behalf of the philosophical life—hangs together, therefore, with the need to confront a whole host of related difficulties: the fear of death and misology, injustice, alienation from oneself and others.

This Socratic necessity of a "second best way" must be brought to light as it is determined precisely in the encounter with the impossibility and loss that it cannot surpass or think through. In what way is it at all possible, in other words, to see not only what is hidden, but what induces the most severe blindness by virtue of its overwhelming clarity? How is it possible, in other words, to see or experience the concealment that occurs in such an excessive disclosure? What still has to be considered here is how the turn to the λόγοι arises precisely in the blinding impossibility of nature's own manifestation. Human nature proves to be submitted to a doubling, but only in the doubling of nature itself, as nature's own way of becoming manifest.

PART 3. KINSHIP OF NATURE

6

Teiresias in Athens

Socrates as Educator in the Meno

In this chapter I shall restrict my discussion primarily to a reading of one dialogue with a view toward opening up how the doubling of nature, as it opens up the "kinship" of all things, also imposes upon human life the task of self-knowledge. Because the *Meno* does not seem to provide conclusive answers to the questions it raises thematically, it is often taken to be an *aporetic* or skeptical dialogue. Despite the fact that a number of possible answers are entertained, the questions prove in the end to be only more difficult, not only for both Meno and Socrates, but also, perhaps, for the reader. Neither the question that concerns the "what" of ἀρετή nor the question that concerns how ἀρετή comes into being seems to find a satisfactory or clear answer. Socrates has indeed departed, run out of time, and apparently without making available a true knowledge of what concerns us humans most of all, our own good.[1] It seems that, from the standpoint developed in the *Meno*, knowledge of this kind might even be unattainable, or at least something that defies communication and transmission. But if the knowledge that cannot be taught or conveyed is not knowledge at all, which is itself an assumption granted by both Meno and Socrates within the dialogue, then what we are left with instead is only the errant and unreliable alternative of right opinion (ὀρθὴ δόξα). Wandering through our own life without intelligence, we can at best hope to be something like the blind wayfarer who only happens to stumble onto the right road.[2] It is thus easy to conclude either that the dialogue is merely propaedeutic to actual philosophy—which is thought to be about conveying essential knowledge in the form of clear and direct propositions and

119

providing satisfactory answers to questions such as this one concerning ἀρετή—or that it simply demonstrates, from a skeptical vantage point, the futility of such an endeavor.

It is obvious that this conclusion regarding the dialogue can be contested, since it is grounded in prior assumptions about the proper task of philosophy and the role of *aporia* within that task. Most importantly, however, it is also grounded in prior assumptions about what is at stake in a philosophical reading of Plato's dialogical and dramatic text. My intent in this chapter is to show how a careful reading of the *Meno* can itself work toward an overturning of these more trenchant assumptions about the very character of philosophy. But if my aim therefore is to work against those readings that are on the hunt for something like an explicit doctrinal position in the Platonic text, this does not then mean that all hermeneutic prejudices can be dispensed with preemptively, or by edict. Rather, a beginning must be made somehow that would allow such prejudices to be aggressively interrogated through the reading of the text, as an ongoing task. The ideal of an "unprejudiced" reading can still orient the interpretation, but it can do so only as something that has yet to be attained. But, again, if it is to be possible to read the text on its own terms, this means only that what comes to be revealed through the reading must also be allowed to bear upon and possibly transform the very way in which the text is read.

Let me suggest, however, that this can occur in a reading of the *Meno* only if we first attend sufficiently to how the response of Socrates, precisely as an ἔργον, as something enacted, is indeed particularly appropriate, *in its very manner of responding,* to the matter at issue in the questions put to him by Meno. What must be considered is how the *possibility* of what is best in human life (the possibility, namely, of ἀρετή [Meno 77b–79a, 88e–89a]) requires first of all encountering the *aporetic* structure of the knowledge of this possibility. If the dialogue concludes that ἀρετή does not come into being simply from out of itself, as if through a kind of innate generation, neither is it the case, strictly speaking, that it can be taken as something made, a thing *produced*. We could say that whatever possibility there is for political or ethical education, it opens up as a possibility only in the dismantling of the basic pretenses concerning how one comes to knowledge. In an indirect way this point is dramatically and powerfully expressed precisely by the wholesale failure of Socrates as Meno's "teacher." In the end one will have the suspicion not only that Meno has not learned anything at all, but also that he has not become better in any way. The reasons for this failure can be seen to lie partly in his own refusal to alter his assumptions about how learning and self-transformation can happen. Yet the fact that Meno does indeed remain stuck, that he cannot undertake the movement of learning as self-transformation, is intimately connected to the explicit and thematic question concerning the possible teachability of ἀρετή. What must be asked, then, is something twofold: How, to begin with, does the dialogue remain unable to address adequately this most important possibility? And yet, how then, precisely through such failure, does it nevertheless reveal something about ἀρετή as a human possibility?

If the dialogue makes evident that the possibility of the best in human life arises only through a necessary appropriation of limits and *impossibility*—and, moreover, even in an encounter with the inability of the λόγος to *communicate* or transmit the knowledge that is at issue here—then it is also the case that the reading of this dialogue cannot simply proceed as before, as if unimpinged on by this revelation. Rather, the impossibility itself must be taken up into the reading and allowed to recoil upon the interpretation, altering its most basic methodological assumptions.

Formal skepticism, it has been said many times, is no less a version of dogmatic metaphysics, perhaps only a step along the way to unhappy consciousness. And it may at first seem like a paradox to say that the text itself is able to resist or even refuse all doctrinal interpretations, since this too can be taken as exceedingly doctrinaire and dogmatic. But is this refusal not precisely the riddle of Platonic writing as it presents Socrates? If a questioning *repetition* of the dialogue is not at all incidental to its "meaning," then it may be that this refusal must be encountered in such a way that it offers a great provocation to the reader, not only to question more deeply into the matter at issue in the dialogue, but also to consider oneself and one's own relation to that matter.[3] We have considered in this context the ancient Delphic inscription that declares that interpretation hangs upon self-knowledge. In the next chapter I shall discuss how Socrates himself makes this very point near the beginning of the *Phaedrus,* in a passage that also draws together the question of human nature and the divine dispensation (θεία μοίρα) that comes to figure prominently in the discussion of correct or right opinion at the end of the *Meno* (Phaedr. 229c–230a).[4] Accordingly, whoever would venture an interpretation of a Platonic dialogue is thus also confronted with a peculiar task. Repeating the questioning movement of the dialogue, so as to allow the questions to become actual, appears to involve a dangerous rewriting of the text, in which the text is allowed even to *rewrite itself* as the interpretation advances. But to enact such a repetition is also to allow oneself to be translated thereby into that rewriting, to be exposed to the transformative effects of the questioning movement. What the *Meno* provokes us to wonder over is how, at just such a point of transformation, ἀρετή might also arise as an actual possibility in human life, even in our life, as something that might claim us as an actual question or task. The fact that Socrates responds to Meno's question by putting Meno's own character at stake in the questioning is wholly consistent with this understanding of what is demanded by a philosophical reading of Plato's text.

In order to clarify this different sense of the philosophical character of the dialogue, namely as a pharmacological provocation, even as a kind of *narcotic* sting, it is necessary to attend to the way in which the question posed by Meno, which concerns the teachability of ἀρετή, itself undergoes a transformation through the encounter with Socrates. This transformation also involves a transformation of the sense of nature in the dialogue. By attending to the way in which the interpretation of nature is altered, we can rethink the question with which the dialogue begins, the question that concerns the possible ways in which ἀρετή might come into being. We can say in advance, with certain risks, that the transformation of nature, effected in the course of the dialogue, transforms the question of learning (and also of teaching). More exactly, the relatively naive opposition with which the dialogue begins, between what arises through teaching (or practice) and what arises by nature, is displaced in the course of the dialogue, exposing a more basic kinship between learning and nature. In this way, however, the dialogue also *puts us into question* as we attempt to learn from it. A careful reading, in other words, compels the reader to ask about his or her own kinship with nature, with the nature in which all things are said to be συγγενής, together in their coming to be.

The dialogue, therefore, does not simply rule out all human capacity to effect an ethical transformation through the λόγος, whether in oneself or another. It suggests instead that such a possibility first of all hinges upon our own self-questioning, enacted in ἀνάμνησις, recollection. But if what is disclosed through such recollection is not to be simply conveyed, as though it were a message imparted, what then is the significance of saying that it can only be incited or stirred up through Socratic questioning or, perhaps also, through the pharmacological contagion of Platonic writing? In order to make a beginning here, I shall consider how the dialogue ends with a cryptic remark made by Socrates about the possibility of a πολιτικός among the Athenians who would indeed have the power to reproduce, namely *to make* another into such a πολιτικός (Meno 100a). Here the mythic voice of Socrates tells Meno that such a one would also be the singular exception, among the living like Teiresias is among the dead: according to Homer, Teiresias, alone among the souls in Hades, possesses νοῦς; he alone has that kind of vision that sets him apart from the rest, who only flit about like shadows. The *mantic* or oracular vision of one who is otherwise blind stands here for the exceptional capacity of a political educator.[5] The concluding passage thus returns the reader to the μῦθος of the *Republic* and to the subterranean imagery that pervades the dialogues. Socrates, it seems, is always on his way down, making his descent, even as he enjoins us to keep to the upward way. We have occasion, therefore, to ask about the inevitably mythic register of the educational λόγος, which presents itself as a descensional movement, precisely as it seeks (and fails) to effect an ethical transformation in Meno, the same Meno who departs without being initiated into the mysteries (Meno 76e).[6] The dialogue thus can be read as it offers another dramatic portrait of the earthbound *katabasis* of Socrates, his questioning practice in the city. Are we, then, to discover Socrates himself as such a Teiresias in Athens?

The abruptness with which the *Meno* begins is often noted. Without explanation or provocation, and thus with no indication of the dramatic context, the dialogue simply begins with the question, put to Socrates, that concerns how ἀρετή might come into being, whether it can be taught and learned, or, if not teachable, whether it is acquired by practice, or whether it comes to humans by nature or in some other way (Meno 70a).[7] We have no idea what prompts Meno to put this very question to Socrates on this occasion, whatever the occasion may be. The dialogue does not account for the context within which the question comes to be, a question that for its part asks about how ἀρετή itself comes to be. The abruptness is such that it becomes next to impossible to say even that the question arises *within* the opening scene, since the scene first opens in or with the posing of the question, as if this encounter between Meno and Socrates has been put on the barest of stages before an audience of onlookers, and as if the conversation were therefore presented simply for us, the readers, as nothing other than a response to this great question. But then the abruptness of the beginning has to do not simply with the lack of a dramatic context, but also with the precise way in which the question of ἀρετή finds itself posed at the beginning.

The question does not simply ask about the origin or cause of ἀρετή, but it asks more precisely about the *region* out of which ἀρετή might emerge. It already presents certain regions—however indeterminate these may at first be—as the possible ways to account for that emergence. The dialogue begins, therefore, by articulating an *assumption* about which regions offer the most appropriate way to address the question. The pre-given alternatives already offer possible answers. The question itself and the manner in which it is posed thus assume these various regions of origin as they stand in relation to each other, as they might exclude one another. Most notably, the foremost suggestion is that there are grounds for looking into whether ἀρετή can be *taught*.

The question that opens the dialogue can thus also be heard to ask about the limits of learning and teaching. If it turns out that ἀρετή cannot be taught, how else might one account for its presence? What determines the limits of the teachable? What stands over and against those limits, marking those limits?[8]

Nature is named here as *one* such possible region, as one region over and against which there are other regions. While learning and practice seem to be opposed to each other, nature is opposed to both of these, opposed to what is acquired[9] or produced, to what might supplement or even alter nature, whether through learning or through practice. The region of what arises by nature would then be distinguished from that movement of development that is distinctly *human*, that can take place only after birth, with education, or perhaps merely through habituation and convention. The region of what arises by nature would be distinct from the way one might acquire the productive knowledge of τέχνη, for example, although this would not yet have to mean that what arises by nature may not also bear upon that decidedly human development, may not also unfold in the time of human development after birth. One may in fact be predisposed by nature toward becoming in a certain way, toward becoming accomplished in a particular art, for example, but that possibility would still have to be fulfilled through learning and being taught. At any rate, the dialogue itself suggests that whatever comes to human life by nature would have to be apparent already *in youth*, discernible at the time of youth. The fact that ἀρετή is not discernible in this way is given in a later passage as grounds to dismiss nature as the region of its origin (Meno 89b).

The posing of the question about the origin of ἀρετή is thus possible insofar as it seems to take for granted a basic opposition between nature and what arises as other than nature, as it appeals to an opposition that is especially prominent among the remaining texts of the sophists but that is repeated throughout Greek literature and the dialogues.[10] The question that Meno poses, however, does not ask about the opposition itself. But in order to respond to the question, as it is thus posed within the framework of this traditional opposition, one must already take a certain stance with regard to the opposition itself. The posing of the question itself, in fact, already presupposes a certain clarity with regard to the opposition.

And yet, at the same time, it has to be noted how the question, as it is posed by Meno, both at the beginning of the dialogue and in a later passage (Meno 86d), also leaves room for the possibility that ἀρετή might also come into being "in some other way" (ἄλλῳ τινὶ τρόπῳ). Such a third way—presumably a way not exhausted by the opposition between what is granted by nature and what is acquired or produced through human agency—is, however, left at this point undetermined. Presumably, however, to the extent that the opposition presented here is taken to be an exhaustive and exclusive one, such a third alternative would also have to transform the meaning of the initial opposition itself.

The manner in which Meno poses the question already suggests that the tradition to which Socrates is asked to respond establishes a certain opposition between the productive power of human agency and the generative power of nature to which that agency is otherwise subjected. We might risk, therefore, with reservations, a translation of Meno's question into a more *tragic* tone: do we humans have any say in whether we live a good life, or are we simply subject to the whims of chance, or to what is granted merely by nature, *by the very nature we are,* which thus both allows us to be and at the same time also is already opposed to what lies within our power?

Does the question then not demand the greatest caution? Despite Meno's professed conviction to the contrary, the question is not easy, but instead χαλεπόν, *difficult*—verging, that is, on the impossible. How to respond appropriately to a question of this order, when the terms of the question have been set down in advance by the very authority of tradition? The difficulty is enhanced by the dramatic situation in which Socrates finds himself. The young Meno believes himself to be well prepared for his encounter; he has studied with the famous Gorgias, and has already made a career of sorts out of distinguishing himself by discoursing on this topic. And it is clear that he hopes with this question perhaps to embarrass the famous Socrates, who has gained a reputation for wisdom.

The initial Socratic response to the question has become quite familiar to us. It defines in one sense the very gesture of philosophy. With an unmistakable irony, he defers here to the presumed wisdom of his interrogator. How can such a question be answered if the one being asked the question lacks the prior knowledge of what ἀρετή is, the knowledge of its τί ἐστιν (Meno 71a–b)? And in asking this question, Socrates emphasizes that he is not after any particular ἀρετή. Whereas Meno attempts to account for ἀρετή with respect to the particular differences of one's age and one's praxis or work (ἔργον) (Meno 72a), the kind of knowledge Socrates wants is not restricted to the ἀρετή of this or that person. He wants rather to know what ἀρετή itself is, *as such,* not partially but *as a whole* (κατὰ ὅλου) (Meno 77a, 79b, 79d),[11] and he wants to know it in such a way that it can be said, put forward *in the* λόγος. Just as there is one health or strength that is the "same" for both men and women, there should also be such a single εἶδος of ἀρετή, regardless of age or sexual difference (Meno 72d–73a). One must be able "to look off toward"[12] this εἶδος, if one is to be able to answer the question that concerns the *"what"* of ἀρετή. Socrates thus wants Meno to stop making many out of one (Meno 77a).

Yet it is strange that both Meno and Socrates then continue to talk about the ἀρετή that is distinctly *human.* This seems to run against what Socrates claims to want. For it might be asked, would not even that peculiarly human ἀρετή—assuming for the moment that an adequate λόγος of it might be achieved—still not only amount to a *part* of ἀρετή and not to ἀρετή *as a whole*? Would one not then still be speaking only of one of a greater manifold and certainly not of ἀρετή *as such,* in the same way that one might speak of *human* health but certainly does not mean thereby to speak of health *as such*? But if the question of the unity of ἀρετή is excessively simplified when it is taken as a question concerning only the human good, this cannot at all be a mere oversight, precisely because the question concerns what grounds the very difference between the regions of νόμος and nature, and what comes into being through practice and learning.[13] Is it not the case that what opens up the possibility for a properly ethical-political discourse hangs on making clear the distinction between what takes place according to the measure of human life—by νόμος, by τέχνη, and so on—and what takes place through nature itself? How then do we understand the implicit emphasis upon the human here, to the neglect of all else, given that ἀρετή as such is supposed to be at issue, and that ἀρετή as such is not at all restricted only to human life, but rather to each being insofar as it is defined by its proper ἔργον? In other words, what does the political *per se* have to do with the work of a horse, for example, or the work of the eyes?[14] We might, then, already hear the echoes of another order of questioning: How do humans belong to nature as a whole? And how does the properly human good remain to be reconciled with the good as such, the good itself? Yet, we might also say that in this way the Socratic response also only draws out how Meno's opening question, as it takes for granted the distinct regions from which things emerge, already harbors these very difficulties.

Moreover, connected to this, there is indeed something alarming and even blatantly false about the claim that this kind of knowledge that concerns the "what" is needed beforehand, before anything can be said about the matter in question.[15] Socrates asks: "If I don't know *what* it is, how could I know anything about it, i.e., how could I know it such as it is?" (ὃ δὲ μὴ οἶδα τί ἐστιν, πῶς ἄν ὁποῖόν γέ τι εἰδείην) (Meno 71b). This interrogative claim, if it is taken to mean that one must be able to offer an adequate account of "what" something is prior to any "knowledge" of it in any sense whatsoever, is as mistaken as the other blatant falsehood proposed here by Socrates, namely that all Athenians profess like him to know neither what ἀρετή is nor how it comes to be. The fact that Meno simply bypasses this deep absurdity, however, in one sense already poses the greatest difficulty of the dialogue. When Socrates draws the analogy between, on the one hand, the need for the knowledge of the what and, on the other hand, the need to be acquainted with Meno — *to know who he is* — we might hear Socrates also asking Meno another question: "What are you after by asking me this question about the genesis of ἀρετή, Meno? Do you yourself know yourself well enough to know here what is wanted? And if it is true that we are already claimed by this question about ἀρετή, if it indeed concerns each of us most of all, how is it that we are also unable in advance to account fully for this being so claimed? What task is already implied in asking oneself if one can learn (i.e., be taught), when such learning concerns our very own flourishing and our way of life?"

The dialogue thus presents a strange meeting of the private (regional) senses of the good and the more formal knowledge of what is as such good. How are we to make sense of every regional good in its relation to the whole? This seems to be an inescapable conflict, arising in every attempt to address the good. Socrates suggests, and Meno agrees, that Meno's beauty, his wealth, and his nobility are things derived from his character, from who he is (Meno 71b). And this statement is made as a way to bolster the claim that a possible knowledge of the genesis of ἀρετή must first be grounded in the prior *eidetic* knowledge of what it is, as if φρόνησις, directed at the human good, were in this way to depend upon that other sense of wisdom the

Greeks called σοφία. But both of these statements make as little sense as Socrates reproaching himself for his own ignorance about ἀρετή—"I blame myself for my total ignorance" (71b)—or, likewise, holding Gorgias responsible, as the "cause" (αἴτιος) of "wisdom" (σοφία) in Thessaly (Meno 70b). The absurdity of this kind of correlation is especially apparent as Socrates immediately continues by insisting also that he has never met anyone possessing such a knowledge concerning the what of ἀρετή, although he has even met Gorgias himself (Meno 71c).[16] And although he admits to only vague memories of his encounter with the sophist, the effect of such a lapse is only to direct the inquiry back to Meno's own responsibility in the conversation, to compel him toward a more difficult self-questioning, and to deprive him of any easy answers to the question of how ἀρετή might come into being. The effect, then, is to raise the question of what is most at issue in one's own memory, to disrupt the overwhelming and obsessive power of one's memory, and to awaken one to the task of recollection.[17] "Let us leave Gorgias alone, since he is absent. But Meno, by the gods, what do you yourself say ἀρετή is?" (Meno 71c–d). It is thus all the more curious that at 76b the matter of Gorgias's viewpoint on ἀρετή returns, in a passage, however, where Socrates also suggests that it is Meno's youth and beauty that predispose him toward his tyrannical comportment in the λόγος (Meno 76b–c), as if now his character is, on the contrary, to be regarded *as an effect* of his attributes.

The Socratic claim that he has yet to meet anyone with a knowledge of the "what" can be related to the later claim concerning the factical absence of the teachers of ἀρετή. Here again the limits of the λόγος are made manifest as it confronts its own ἔργον, as what becomes manifest in the λόγος recoils upon it, transforming thereby what it says, what it has already said.[18] At first the question of the teachability of ἀρετή seems (in the λόγος) to be dealt with conclusively in that section of the dialogue where Socrates has introduced the possibility of proceeding "from out of a hypothesis" (ἐξ ὑποθέσεως). Since ἀρετή is guided by φρόνησις, and φρόνησις is knowledge (ἐπιστήμη), and only knowledge is teachable, then ἀρετή itself *ought* to be teachable, or rather even *must* be teachable. But then, almost immediately, such a conclusion is overturned. Socrates remarks that he has never met anyone who in fact could teach it. "In any case I have often searched and tried to find out whether there are such teachers of it, but in all such efforts I am not able to find any. Indeed I have searched with many people and above all with those whom I believed to be most experienced in the matter" (Meno 89e).[19] Such remarks, like the one at 71c, must be taken quite seriously.[20] While they seem to refer to only a contingent and even anecdotal fact, they can be heard as they point to Socratic practice as a whole, to his sustained engagement with the citizens of Athens, with the statesmen, the poets, and the craftsmen, as Socrates himself presents it in his *Apology*. In this way, they cannot but reveal the limits of human life itself. In this context it should be recalled how

Socrates interprets the oracular pronouncement that concerns his own peculiar "human wisdom." Only the one who knows that such wisdom is
"worth little or nothing" can be said to be wise at all. We saw that this interpretation of the divine word, in which the god speaks of Socrates as only an
example or paradigm, is also inseparable from his questioning practice in the
city. The interpretation of the divine word can unfold only in that human
encounter.

Socrates' insistence upon the need for a knowledge and a λόγος of the
"what" catches Meno off guard and is effective enough.[21] The turn to the
λόγος, through this insistence that the "what" be addressed in dialogue, demands that one scrutinize the very discourse that makes possible the asking of the question.[22] Through such insistence Socrates is able to reverse
the direction of the interrogation and thus manages to displace the authority of a tradition that would demand that the question be posed within
those oppositions that Meno seems to take for granted. What has to be
noted above all is how Meno continues to frame the question of ἀρετή in
exclusively "political" terms. This is clear if one considers Meno's three attempts to respond to Socrates' question (Meno 71e, 73d, 77b). Of these,
however, the last is by far the most decisive, since it is here that Meno begins to confront the way in which his own desires must be reconciled with
a sense of the good that may not be immediately apparent in the desire itself, in the regional good that dominates Meno's thinking.

After this exchange of questions and answers, and after Socrates himself
has provided examples of what he is after by stating what figure and color
are,[23] Meno is still left with the original task of stating what ἀρετή is. He is
now at an *aporetic* standstill. Meno, who begins by asserting the utter non-
difficulty of knowing what ἀρετή is[24] and who claims to have spoken about
ἀρετή persuasively and with confidence many times in the past, finds himself now in the encounter with Socrates to be at a loss. He thus likens
Socrates, both in appearance and otherwise, to a torpedo fish, as he likens
himself to one who has been benumbed and stupefied by its narcotic sting.
Finding himself before the impossible task of saying what ἀρετή is, of addressing ἀρετή as a whole, he takes himself to be under the pharmacological spell of a kind of wizard, who, by means of the λόγος, has reduced him
to a state of perplexity (Meno 80a–c).[25]

Socrates, however, does not play along with Meno's game. He insists that
he, too, does not have knowledge of ἀρετή, does not have a knowledge that
would allow him to say what it is. If the torpedo fish is torpid while causing
others to be torpid, then Socrates admits to being like it: he finds himself fac-
ing the same aporia.[26] Whereas Meno may have known ἀρετή before this encounter, Socrates insists, however ironically, that he only remains ignorant.
What is decisive is that Socrates insists that it is precisely a certain relation to
impossibility that enables him to have this effect: "For it is not from having
easy access to matters that I am able to block access to others (bring others

to *aporia*); but it is from being more at an impasse myself than anyone else that I bring others to an impasse" (οὐ γὰρ εὐπορῶν αὐτὸς τοὺς ποιῶ ἀπορεῖν, ἀλλὰ παντὸς μᾶλλον αὐτὸς ἀπορῶν οὕτως καὶ τοὺς ἄλλους ποιῶ ἀπορεῖν) (Meno 80c–d). The Socratic λόγος thus operates through such a relation to aporia, attuned to it. And such aporia first becomes evident in the raising of the question of the τί ἐστιν.

Meno, despite his stupor, still believes that he did have knowledge of ἀρετή prior to the meeting with Socrates. The aporia is thus seen by him as only a momentary loss, a temporary setback, one therefore that, presumably, will be overcome once the spell of Socrates wears off. In an important sense, the handsome Meno is undaunted. He regards the limitations of his own λόγος as a result of something that Socrates *has done to him.* He sees himself as one who once knew ἀρετή, who once had such knowledge but who has now forgotten. He thus characterizes his situation in such a way that it resembles the very situation that is presented in the myth that Socrates is about to tell concerning recollection. Socrates even ironically allows Meno the possibility that "before" (πρότερον) Meno may have indeed known ἀρετή (Meno 80d). Rather than being simply at odds with Meno, the myth is thus profoundly in accord with his own understanding of his situation. It is not surprising, then, that he eagerly receives the myth, wanting to learn more about it and what it implies. Yet this very eagerness can also be seen as what obstructs or hinders his learning.[27]

Meno, who begins by asking a question about the genesis of ἀρετή and the limits of learning, does not yet see that the very possibility of posing that question already demands of him that he enter into the *movement* of learning, a movement that also demands following the disclosive power of the λόγος in dialogue. He is, however, hardly as ingenuous as he pretends to be.[28] It is above all doubtful that he has a sincere desire to come to know how ἀρετή might be possible in human life. And arguably, one cannot actually ask the question about the origin of ἀρετή unless one is already engaged in a concernful seeking—if, that is, such asking is to be anything more than lip service, a feigned λόγος. Socrates thus forces Meno to confront the fact that the possibility of asking about the possibility of ἀρετή—and thus, presumably, the possibility of *having* ἀρετή, of living a life of ἀρετή—is already grounded in the prior question of how one might question, how one might seek knowledge. Before the question concerning the origin of ἀρετή and the limits of learning can be asked, therefore, it must already in a decisive sense be answered, even if matters remain obscure as to *what* ἀρετή actually is.[29]

The Socratic thesis that declares ἀρετή to be "knowledge" thus does not at all resort to an "intellectualizing of virtue," if this is to have the meaning that ἀρετή can be acquired in the same way one learns a τέχνη. But the text does insist upon precisely the connection between ἀρετή and the *search* for knowledge, a search that is to be undertaken in dialogue, by following the disclosive movement of the λόγος.[30] The dialogue at the very beginning provides a clue that this search is a matter of an *ethos*. It is Gorgias who has "habituated" or "accustomed" Meno and his fellow Thessalians to the "habit" (τὸ ἔθος . . . εἴθικεν) of answering every question fearlessly, in a manner that befits those who know (Meno 70b–c).[31] This remark is particularly striking since we also learn that Gorgias, remarkably, does not at all claim to teach ἀρετή, but only to make clever speakers (ποιεῖν δεινούς) (Meno 95b–c). Meno, however, does not yet have any sense of his ignorance, has not yet encountered the impossibility that would make the movement of learning possible, that must be presupposed at the beginning of that movement. Thus, far from proposing that "virtue" be "intellectualized," if anything, the dialogue suggests that it is knowledge that must first be brought into the arena of the "ethical," in the more original sense of the *habitus* of practice.

If such an interpretation is not granted, then one must struggle with the way in which the dialogue at first begins by posing its initial question, which in its most basic formulation concerns the genesis of ἀρετή, but then continues with the subsequent discussion, which makes up the body of the dialogue and which concerns the possibility of knowledge and learning. The abiding question must be: how can the latter issue—provoked as it is by the Socratic ignorance that insists upon the thematic discussion of the τί ἐστιν of ἀρετή—be taken as precisely a response to the question Meno poses at the outset? Moreover, how does Socratic practice, as not only a movement in the λόγος but as an ἔργον, show itself to confirm this way of responding to Meno's question?

It is important, then, to see how the famous myth of ἀνάμνησις that Socrates will tell does not at all resolve the aporetic difficulty that Meno faces but rather makes that difficulty still more severe, more devastating. The myth not only does *not* offer a way to ground the possibility of the movement of learning, it actually insists in a certain way upon the impossibility of grounding that possibility. It demands, namely, that the sense of ground be granted the obscurity that is appropriate to it. It does this precisely by invoking nature in a manner that displaces the regional nature that is named in the opening lines of the dialogue, the nature that is opposed to learning and practice. Nature, namely, will be invoked in the myth in order to insist upon precisely the impossibility that would grant the movement of learning. Thus, the myth—to the extent that it is a response to the opening question of the dialogue—seeks to reconfigure both the movement of learning and what might arise by nature, such that these can no longer simply be placed in opposition. To be sure, Socrates does defend the myth because it *encourages* those who hear it to take up the task of learning (Meno 81d–e, 86b–c). And it must always be remembered that Meno begins by flatly denying his own ignorance. The myth is thus encouraging as it makes manifest the necessity of a certain ignorance and as it places that ignorance in the context of a nature that cannot simply be opposed to what is produced through human agency. The necessity in question is thus not simply a limit that confines or restricts human life but has to be thought as an enabling limit, an impossibility that makes possible.

With a kind of formulaic cleverness, Meno presents the problem to Socrates, who has just declared that he himself does not know what ἀρετή is. According to Meno, the very thing that would seem to call for learning, and thus in one sense make it possible, namely ignorance, seems also to preclude it. If one is ignorant of what is to be learned, one cannot *begin* to learn, cannot undertake the search for that thing of which one has no knowledge. For, supposing that this something happens by chance to be found, Meno asks, how will one know it as the thing that one formerly did not know? Learning, taken as the movement from ignorance to knowledge, seems therefore to be impossible (Meno 80d).

Socrates responds to this "eristic" argument (Meno 81d) by restating it and adding to it the correlative implication that Meno has neglected. For the argument implies not only that ignorance refutes learning, but that knowledge, too, makes learning unnecessary and impossible: one has no need to inquire into something if one *already* knows it. The argument leaves one with the conclusion that the very thing that must be presupposed for learning, both ignorance and knowledge together, precludes the possibility of the *movement* of learning. If one assumes that ignorance and knowledge must exclude one another, then the fact that learning seems to require both of these refutes the possibility of learning altogether. Socrates in this way points out what is eristic about the argument. But he also points out how the argument can deny the possibility of learning only by grounding itself in a certain assumption about knowledge and the relation that obtains between knowledge and ignorance (Meno 80d–e). It is in this context, then, that the earlier remark made by Socrates must be considered, that contrasts eristics with dialogue (διαλέγεσθαι) and dialectic (Meno 75c–d). The movement of dialogue is characterized as a movement that begins by seeking agreement rather than by attempting to gain the upper hand in the λόγος; and thus it is a movement shared by φίλοι, friends (Meno 75d).[32] This filiation or kinship that is presupposed in the possibility of following the λόγος together confirms that the proper starting point is the position not of superiority and confidence, but of openness and caution.

The further Socratic response to this eristic argument, however, involves the appeal to the myth, to things heard from wise men and women, to hearsay concerning divine matters (περὶ τὰ θεῖα πράγματα) (Meno 81a). The reference to the divine here already suggests that the myth may be connected to the conclusion of the dialogue, where origin of right opinion shall be returned to a divine dispensation: θεία μοῖρα. The soul being deathless, having been born many times, has *already* acquired knowledge concerning all things. What is called learning and seeking is in fact the *recollection* of something that, while it has indeed been lost or forgotten, has also somehow been encountered, thus known "before" (Meno 81c).

The Socratic response thus redirects the questioning by means of the myth. This response, as it translates the argument into the dimension of the mythical, however, far from offering an account of how learning first of all becomes possible, actually assumes from the very beginning that learning has already taken place. The myth that is to ground the possibility of learning in recollection does not at all account for the absolute origin of the movement of learning. It does not give an account of how the soul, starting from a state of ignorance, from a state of complete isolation, might first come to know things. Rather than account for the acquisition of knowledge, it actually presupposes it.[33] It is because the soul has *already* come to know all things, and thus is *already* related to them in a certain way, that it can *again* come to know them.

Meno, who wants to know how it is possible for knowledge to come into being from out of ignorance, and who also appears to be concerned with the origins of ἀρετή, now hears a myth that has the effect of reversing this movement by implicitly raising the question that concerns how it is possible for ignorance to come into being from out of the plenitude of knowledge. This suggests that the difficulty of addressing the possibility of learning, of accounting for the movement from ignorance to knowledge, does not have to do primarily with an attempted overcoming of the disjunction that was assumed to prevail between ignorance and knowledge in Meno's account. The myth suggests that the more relevant question has to do with the genesis of ignorance: How is it that we can be ignorant at all? In what way are we ignorant?

The possibility of learning (recollecting) is secured only to the extent that we have already forgotten. It thus becomes a matter of opening up the sense of this "before" (πρότερον), of taking up the way in which it belongs to the soul to be already involved in all things. It becomes a matter, namely, of asking about the sense of the assertion that supports the myth, that avers the *kinship* of all nature, of all φύσις (τῆς φύσεως ἁπάσης συγγενοῦς οὔσης) (Meno 81d).[34] But if the question posed by the myth concerns not so much the possibility of knowledge, but rather the possibility of ignorance, then it can be said that the myth also poses the question that concerns the possibility of the disjunction of things in such an encompassing kinship. Given the radical and prior kinship that precedes all movement, and that guarantees the possibility of knowledge, how are there discrete beings at all? And how, then, do the opposing regions themselves arise that were presupposed and operative in the posing of the question with which the dialogue began, regions that were proposed as distinct regions of genesis, and that included, among others, nature?

The possibility of coming to know, otherwise named learning, which initially is simply opposed to the movement of what arises by nature, is now shown, through a cryptic and mythic discourse, to be a possibility grounded in nature itself, or rather in the kinship that is basic to all of nature. The genesis of ἀρετή otherwise would have to be thought in terms of the division between that kind of genesis which is thought to be distinctly human, as it arises through the *transmission* of knowledge, no doubt in the λόγος, through teaching and learning, and that *other* kind of genesis which seems to have nothing at all to do with this human realm, since it is always there in advance, in the very birth, radically granted and incalculable. The kinship of all with all is nothing other than the precondition for the transmission in the λόγος, which as it turns out, is therefore *not* a transmission at all, not the conveyance of knowledge from one soul to another, but *recollection,* an awakening precisely to that kinship. The question of the possibility of *movement,* not only in the realm of knowledge, but especially in the realm of the *ethos*—if we grant for now that on some level these realms are to be held apart—is shown to be a possible movement of nature, a movement within nature, a movement only as it already is held in the whole that holds all things together in a certain kinship. Movement in such a whole will have always already anticipated itself in the kinship, in the way all things are together in their possible coming to be.

And yet, why does this response of Socrates, which attempts to affirm the possibility of the movement of learning, but which also clearly raises more questions than it resolves, take the form of a myth? The introduction of the myth is marked by a dramatic pause, rushed over by Meno, as Socrates begins to recollect this myth that tells of the movement of recollection.[35] The myth succeeds in assuring the possibility of the movement of learning by placing the soul in relation to an immemorial and seemingly endless past in which all things—named the kinship of nature as a whole—find themselves gathered together into a common origin.[36] The myth does not attempt to account for this kinship of the whole itself but begins with it already there, established in advance. It does not dispute or question the kinship but affirms and takes it up as the *whole* out of which forgetting and remembering first become possible. It thus marks a kind of necessary *limit* to memory and remembering. The myth functions so as to insist that the beginning itself can never be remembered, recollected, because it is precisely its *having been forgotten* that first establishes the possibility of remembering, the repetition whereby one comes to things *again* after having been with them *before.*[37] Remembering can only begin with a certain kind of forgetting already in play. The soul that can recollect all things, *if it is to be able to recollect anything,* must never remember how it became possible first of all to recollect all things. The possibility of remembering can be granted only through first affirming this aporetic condition of human life, through affirming the impossibility of another kind of memory. The myth as myth thus says something about how it is possible to address the beginning: every beginning is possible by virtue of a strange erasure of the past, the past that would deny the beginning as the beginning.[38] The human relation to the origin will always open up, therefore, a kind of paradoxical primacy of the λόγος, in a δεύτερος πλοῦς or "second sailing," which in one sense also shows itself as "first." The λόγος "begins" only by beginning again, in the repetition of what already is, above all and especially at that point where it resolves to begin precisely "from the beginning," ἐξ ἀρχῆς.[39]

By asking Meno to account for ἀρετή as such, Socrates thus encourages Meno to establish a more original relation to the origin as such. At the same time, Meno is encouraged to take up the task of inquiring into ἀρετή, as if the very activity or practice of such an inquiry might be necessary if the way to ἀρετή itself is to be opened. Socrates would then respond to the question of how ἀρετή comes into being by attempting, as best he can, to *show* Meno the only possible philosophical way to ἀρετή, as the way that turns to the λόγος. One might then even be tempted to say that the confrontation with ignorance and impossibility—sustained in dialogue—would be the *precondition* for the actual movement to ἀρετή, except that this is contradicted by the presence of "good" citizens who have become good without philosophy. It seems undeniable that ἀρετή as a possibility can also occur independently of such a philosophical confrontation with aporia, just as it is also the case that health does not first of all depend on the physician. To be sure, if one were to insist that it does, this insistence is likely to become an actual hindrance to the healing.

While the Socratic strategy does establish a connection between knowledge and ἀρετή, it should not be overlooked that the question that Socrates raises in response to the opening question posed by Meno is never fully addressed in the dialogue; the question that concerns the *what* of ἀρετή will receive no satisfactory treatment, will remain unanswered. And despite the conspicuous absence of such a knowledge of the *what,* and despite Socrates' protests in this regard, Meno will continue to insist that Socrates undertake to account for the origin of ἀρετή (Meno 86c–d). Even after it has supposedly been demonstrated that learning is not at all a matter of teaching, not a matter of *transmission* but of recollection, Meno still wants Socrates to undertake to teach him about the origin of ἀρετή, as if the Socratic demonstration of ἀνάμνησις only further strengthens Meno's conviction that Socrates can tell him something about the origin of ἀρετή (81e–82a).[40] He will continue to press the old man for answers (Meno 76a).[41]

Socrates does indeed agree to take up the task that Meno imposes upon him, but, given the lack of the knowledge of what it is, it is agreed that ἀρετή is to be investigated only "by means of a hypothesis," *beginning from out of a hypothesis* (ἐξ ὑποθέσεως) (Meno 86e–87c).[42] By assuming what is only a provisional understanding of ἀρετή, and based upon that provisional understanding, the inquiry will move forward, as if toward knowledge. The inquiry moves, therefore, by virtue of an understanding that explicitly takes up its own ignorance, that is grounded in the limits of knowledge. But the hypothesis is not simply a tentative starting point and therefore subject to revision. While it must also anticipate and affirm the necessity of its own failure, neither is it arbitrarily set down.⁴³ The hypothesis is in fact an assertion of something that is *in one sense* more clear than what is sought; it is thus a knowledge on the basis of which it is possible to proceed. But its eventual failure is not at all a setback. Rather, such failure only confirms its hypothetical character and is bound up with the disclosive movement of the λόγος: through the dialogical testing of the hypothesis what is at issue in the λόγος becomes manifest precisely as the λόγος also shows itself to be inadequate to the matter. It is thus above all necessary to note that the hypothesis, as it seeks to sustain an explicit relation to the necessary concealment of the λόγος, also already operates by virtue of an anticipatory disclosure. The movement of the λόγος from out of the hypothesis thus still sustains the recollecting character of learning proposed by Socrates in the myth. The turn to the λόγος turns in this way from out of the affirmation of the impossibility that is necessitated in the cryptic kinship of nature.

Without the availability of a precise knowledge of ἀρετή, it is agreed that, if it can be determined whether ἀρετή is knowledge, a certain knowledge (ἐπιστήμη τις) (Meno 87c), then on this basis it will be evident whether it is teachable. The hypothesis thus becomes possible by virtue of an established insight into the relation between knowledge and teaching. *Since knowledge is the only thing that can be taught to humans,* if ἀρετή is knowledge (ἐπιστήμη), then it must be teachable, and if it is teachable, then it must be knowledge. Precisely this insight allows for the hypothesis to be taken up that asserts that ἀρετή is knowledge.⁴⁴

Socrates thus again, for a second time, brings the question of the origin of ἀρετή back into the context of the question that concerns the possibility of knowledge. The ἔργον of the dialogue repeatedly demonstrates that the concern with the possible genesis of ἀρετή cannot be divorced from the aporetic question of its "what." The hypothesis itself, which connects ἀρετή and knowledge, attests to this. And Socrates will never actually abandon the hypothesis itself. Yet the matter of determining whether ἀρετή is knowledge opens up a whole host of difficulties that the dialogue does not seem to anticipate. At first it appears that ἀρετή must be knowledge, since it is good *in itself,* since it does not depend upon anything else in order to profit the one who has it. Ἀρετή appears, then, to be φρόνησις. The claim is made "with regard to all things" (κατὰ πάντων) that everything that would be good in human life depends upon the good of the soul and everything that would be good in the soul depends upon φρόνησις (Meno 88e–89a). Φρόνησις, and thus ἀρετή, would accordingly be at the origin of the good life, the best possible human life. A series of inferences are thus drawn. Since ἀρετή as human excellence is φρόνησις or native intelligence, and such native intelligence is ἐπιστήμη, is discursive knowledge, and since discursive knowledge can be taught, then ἀρετή is teachable.

And yet, a problem remains: Socrates asserts that he has yet to find someone who is actually able to teach ἀρετή (Meno 89e).[45] How, then, does one
account for this factical absence of those who are thus able to teach? While
the teachability of knowledge is itself not challenged, the question as to
whether ἀρετή is knowledge is also left undecided. At this point, however,
it is unclear exactly why the misgivings arise, whether they are due to a
concern over whether ἀρετή can be said to be φρόνησις, or whether they
are not instead due to a concern over whether φρόνησις can be said to be
ἐπιστήμη. In other words, it may be that a decisive difference prevails between φρόνησις and ἐπιστήμη. While the connection between ἀρετή and
φρόνησις seems evident enough, the question that concerns the teachability
not only of ἐπιστήμη, but of φρόνησις in particular, has yet to be addressed.[46]

The brief exchange with Anytus serves to demonstrate the inability of
commonly held opinion to account for the transmission or regeneration of
ἀρετή in the city. Whereas things are unproblematic with regard to the learning of the arts, there seems to be no one in the city who can properly take up
the task of teaching the youth how to live a life of ἀρετή. Whereas it is clear
to whom one should go, in order to become a doctor, a cobbler, a flautist,
and so on, Anytus reacts in dismay at the prospect that the sophists should
be regarded as the *experts* on the good life: "for they show themselves to
bring about the ruin and corruption of those who spend time with them"
(Meno 91c). Socrates, it should be noted, withholds his judgment on the
sophists. He only wants to know how Anytus has come to his opinion of
the sophists, when he himself has had no contact with them (Meno 92b–c).
And moreover, how is it, for example, that Protagoras was able to be so successful as a sophist, enjoying a good reputation and long life? (Meno
91d–92a). At the same time, it does become clear that, even if ἀρετή must be
hypothesized as knowledge, it cannot be transmitted to others in the same
way it is possible to teach τέχνη. Whatever ἀρετή is and however it comes
into being, it is clear that it is of a different order than the productive activity that is governed by the arts and thus cannot be transmitted in the same
way.[47] And the *endoxic* solution that Anytus proposes with regard to the
transmission of ἀρετή shows itself to be entirely inadequate and no less troubling than the reliance on the sophists. He claims that any fine and good
Athenian one happens to meet would be an excellent teacher of ἀρετή. When
asked by Socrates how these Athenians came to know how to teach ἀρετή,
and from whom they learned this ability, Anytus only regresses to the authority of the older generation: they learned "from those who came before"
(παρὰ τῶν προτέρων) (Meno 93a).[48]

The precise question that Anytus neglects does not have to do with
whether any Athenians have ever had ἀρετή. Socrates does not wish at this
point to dispute that there are and have been many good Athenians. The
precise question concerns how ἀρετή might be passed on, transmitted from
one generation to the next, and thus preserved in the city, allowed to regen-

erate or reproduce itself (Meno 93a–b). The question deals with how the city might undertake to save itself by cultivating and fostering the possibility of the ἀρετή of its citizens. And because many examples can be cited of those who, presumably, were good but who did not produce sons of equal quality (e.g., even Anytus himself [Meno 89e–90b]), the question arises why these "good men" would have allowed this to happen if they were able to prevent it. Why is it that the reproductive and regenerating movement from father to son—what is, in one sense, the movement of nature, since "it is from a human that a human is generated"—does not also produce a continuation of ἀρετή, does not reproduce or regenerate itself in the movement of that nature? While Aristotle will account for and delimit nature precisely as a regenerating movement, as a way to nature, like a self-healing doctor,[49] the bad son can indeed come from the good father.[50] Even the good themselves, it seems, do not know how to teach ἀρετή.

The dialogue recoils on this indisputable fact. Meno has been brought to the extreme point where he now begins to *wonder* at the problem before him. He wonders whether there are "good men" at all and how they might ever come into being (Meno 96d). This recoil demands that Socrates reassess the initial claim that everything that is good in human life comes from knowledge, or finds its *guidance* in knowledge. And yet, in redirecting the conversation back to this question, he also makes a remark concerning what is most important in the inquiry: "Above all (παντὸς μᾶλλον) we must look to our own intelligence (προσεκτέον τὸν νοῦν ἡμῖν αὐτοῖς) and try to find one who by some means would make us better" (Meno 96d). There are other passages, most notably in the *Phaedo* and the *Republic,* where the need for such an other is introduced in a similar way.[51] Always, however, this occurs with an undeniable emphasis upon how the encounter with such a teacher—a Teiresias in Athens, we might say—would not alleviate our own responsibility but would pose, precisely in the encounter, also the task of self-knowledge. How is self-knowledge possible, then, through the dialogical encounter with another?

The claim that the life of ἀρετή comes only from knowledge appears to have been mistaken, for those who lack knowledge but who nevertheless have "correct opinion" are also able to give "correct guidance" (ὀρθῶς ἡγεῖσθαι). The verb ἡγεῖσθαι recurs throughout the dialogues, at decisive moments, and plays an especially important role in the dialogical movement of the *Republic.* It conveys the sense of an *anticipatory* grasp that allows for the following of the persuasive and disclosive movement of the λόγος. It can have both the sense of "to believe," in the sense in which one might hold an opinion, and also the meaning "to lead" and even "to rule," or "to give guidance."[52] It is significant, then, that the sense of the ἡγεῖσθαι of correct or true opinion is introduced by means of the image of a journey (Meno 97a–b). Such "orthodoxy," however, implies a certain danger, since not only is it unreliable, but it can actually take on a life of its own, and run away with itself, like a runaway slave or a statue of Daedalus (97d–e).[53] And yet, Socrates also affirms that correct opinion can *become* knowledge, and he again refers to the movement of ἀνάμνησις—which he now designates as a movement that, *through the* λόγος, secures opinions to their causes (αἰτίας λογισμῷ) (Meno 98a). Socrates thus, in effect, continues to encourage Meno to turn to the λόγος and to follow its disclosive movement. By following its recollecting and disclosive movement, one can trace opinions to their origins, and thus one can come to knowledge. The possibility of undertaking the *movement toward* knowledge is, then, already grounded in an ἀρετή that, for its part, is grounded in correct opinion. But such an *orthodoxy* must still turn to the λόγος and take up a movement from out of a concealed or impossible origin.[54] We should not overlook, however, that Socrates—while insisting upon the *difference* between knowledge and opinion, between knowledge and the forming of images or likenesses (εἰκάζειν)—does not presume himself to have knowledge of such things: "And, to be sure, I speak as one who does not know but only speaks of what is likely, by means of images [ἐγὼ ὡς οὐκ εἰδὼς λέγω, ἀλλ' εἰκάζων]" (Meno 98b).

The dialogue thus returns again to the question of the *origin* of ἀρετή, but now it has been translated into the question that concerns the origin of correct opinion. Again, the question is posed, this time by Socrates, in terms of the possible regionalizing of the origin with which the dialogue began, a regionalizing that would oppose nature to what is acquired (Meno 98c–d). And again, the region of nature is refuted as such a possible origin (Meno 98d).[55] Socrates thus convinces Meno that ἀρετή comes into being neither by nature nor by being taught, but is instead granted through what might now be named the "third way," to which there was reference at the outset of the dialogue, what Socrates calls at this point "by divine dispensation" (θεία μοίρᾳ) (Meno 99e, 100b). The great rulers are "divine," in the same way soothsayers and poets are divine. It is revealing, however, how other passages in other dialogues connect poetic inspiration and madness to both nature *and* θεία μοίρα.[56] By introducing "divine dispensation" in order to account for the possibility of ἀρετή, Socrates thus undercuts the very opposition with which Meno begins, between what is by nature and what is acquired. The opposition itself proves to be incapable of accounting for such a possibility. Ἀρετή, which is divine, is neither human nor of nature (in the regional sense).[57]

The dialogue ends, however, with Socrates emphasizing that such an insight has been arrived at by following the λόγος. He then returns to the need that he referred to at the beginning, the need to inquire into the question that has been left unanswered and unaddressed, the question that concerns the *"what"* of ἀρετή (Meno 100b). Presumably, such an inquiry into the εἶδος of ἀρετή would only sustain and repeat the turn to the λόγος that Socrates has already enacted throughout the dialogue. Socratic ignorance arises in the encounter with the impossible origin that is the kinship of all nature, and in such aporetic necessity turns to the recollecting and disclosive movement of the λόγος. Thus, the question arises: How is such a turn also bound up with the θεία μοίρα that is said here to account for the generation of ἀρετή?

The non-regional or placeless origin, the obscure kinship of all with all—which grounds the possibility of learning—must emphatically differ from the nature that is introduced in the opening lines of the dialogue, as what designates only *one* region over and against others, and which the dialogue seems to refute as a possible ground for ἀρετή. This other nature, the cryptic or *lethic* nature, brought to word in the myth, must, however, also *not* differ from the regional nature, from the regionalized nature. It cannot differ, that is, if it is to name the cryptic kinship of all with all. It cannot even be said that it would *enclose* all the regions, if through such closure it would come to name only another region, perhaps a master region. Such closure would, in other words, violate its necessarily cryptic character. Such a master region, moreover, would also promise the possibility of a master τέχνη. This nature—the nature that loves to hide—cannot be the region of all regions, if region *as such* is first granted only in what might be called the self-concealing of nature, a self-concealing that shows itself in the mythic discourse offered by Socrates.

Both nature and θεία μοίρα name, then, a concealed origin that lacks every region and that must retreat from the defining divisions of philosophical inquiry as dialectic. But in this lack or retreat such divisions also become possible, such as the division between physics and ethics, a division that we moderns almost always take for granted, and that can perhaps already be recognized in Meno's question. The Socratic response to that question can be seen as an attempt to show how the possible genesis of ἀρετή must exceed both the region of physics and the region of ethics. While not reducible to "physics," the concern with the good in human life can also never divorce itself from the inquiry into nature.[58] This is already indicated in the hypothesis that asserts ἀρετή to be knowledge. The possibility of human ἀρετή arises only in the possible movement from one region to the next, in a movement that is granted by virtue of the kinship referred to in the myth of ἀνάμνησις. But this means that such a movement also occurs only with the relinquishing of the claim to that kind of productive knowledge and expertise that the Greeks called τέχνη.[59] This relinquishing is nothing other than Socratic ignorance. Granted by the divine, such a movement also remains distinctly human—at best it is only correct opinion. Divine dispensation thus has to be thought as a gift from out of impossible or cryptic nature, a gift that grants the Socratic movement of recollection in the turn to the λόγος. The opposition between the natural and the divine that is assumed by the Athenians who condemn Socrates proves to be misplaced, is opposed to what Socrates himself assumes. Such a gift can also be given to the city: Socrates himself, fastened to the city by the god, is himself commanded by θεία μοίρα (Apol. 33c). Are we to listen, then, to Socrates as the true "teacher" of ἀρετή? And are we persuaded?[60]

There is the suggestion, finally, offered by Socrates, that Meno, as the houseguest of Anytus, might be able to persuade the latter of what he himself has been persuaded of and, in this way, bestow a benefit upon the Athenians. The suggestion is, then, that matters have indeed in some way been clarified. But is Meno truly persuaded? And of what is he persuaded? We have to wonder how Meno will repeat (or transmit) his encounter with the torpedo fish. We do know that Anytus has no small part to play in the condemnation of Socrates by the "men of Athens," the condemnation that delivers Socrates to his own last φάρμακον. Has Meno, then, been healed at all? And what benefit have the Athenians received? Are we to conclude that this is the fault of the doctor? But then where is the true πολιτικός to be found, who might be able to reproduce himself, replicate or repeat himself, *make* another, one like himself?[61] As a movement of nature, this "making" would also have to be a form of regeneration, and could not be dissociated from the repetition that belongs to nature.

7

Typhonic Eros and the Place of the *Phaedrus*

The *Phaedrus* will always offer one of the indispensable starting points for taking up the way Socratic philosophical practice situates human life within nature, both in its relation to nature and also as it shows itself to belong to nature, showing itself to be *of* nature. Such a relation and such belonging can be said to be revealed, however, through a *tragic* rupturing of boundaries. The dialogue can be read as it establishes, but also as it transgresses, the boundaries between the human and the natural or divine, as it both insists upon and undermines the rigor of those boundaries, as it thus puts into question the place of human life in nature: nature out of place in nature. Thus, what becomes evident is not simply the human estrangement from the natural, but rather nature's own estrangement from nature, from itself. At the same time, in this context, the dialogue offers an occasion to consider how Socrates accounts for his own relation to the persuasive and disclosive power of speech through a discussion that begins by taking up the role of the erotic in human life, a topic that Phaedrus near the beginning of the dialogue and without explanation suggests is especially appropriate to Socrates (Phaedr. 227c).

What is the character of this Socratic kinship with the erotic? At the very end of his famous palinode (παλινῳδία), a song of atonement that would—through a transformative repetition—forestall the impending blindness to be suffered by one who has committed an offense against the divine, Socrates will address divine ἔρως as a "friend" and speak with gratitude of his own τέχνη, the expertise and proficiency in the erotic as the gift he has received from ἔρως (Phaedr. 257a). In this passage Socrates will also connect this erotic art to philosophy itself, inviting both Phaedrus and Lysias to turn to such a "friendship with wisdom," "to make life be utterly directed toward ἔρως through speeches that love wisdom" (ἁπλῶς πρὸς Ἔρωτα μετὰ φιλοσόφων λόγων τὸν βίον ποιῆται) (257b). In the *Symposium* Socrates claims to know (ἐπίστασθαι) nothing except τὰ ἐρωτικά, what concerns matters of love, what has to do with the erotic (Sym. 177d; see also 198c–d, 207c; also, Rep. 475a, where Socrates allows himself to be taken as an example of one who is erotic as a paradigm for the philosopher). A similar statement is found in the *Theages* (128b). In the *Lysis,* Socrates speaks of himself as inferior and useless in other things, but insight into erotic relations he has received as a divine gift (Lysis 204b–c). These statements, which concern a privileged relation to the erotic, stand as extreme provocations, and demand the most careful consideration. They invite us to ask about the very limits of Socratic philosophical practice, about that practice itself at its limits as it might be determined in and through such an erotic relationship. It is especially evident both in the *Phaedrus* and in the *Symposium* that the erotic itself has to be defined first of all through a relation to an absence, as a relation, therefore, of lack and wanting. But it is also indisputable that this is not the only way in which ἔρως appears in the dialogues.

Let me propose that the fact that ἔρως appears in diverse and mutually conflicting ways throughout the dialogues, above all in the *Phaedrus* and *Symposium,* may have to do with a necessity at issue in human ἔρως itself, a necessity that pertains thus to human life. Both Phaedrus and Socrates agree that love as ἔρως is ἀμφιβητήσιμος, something about which humans can hold opposing opinions (Phaedr. 263c). One could say that the dialogues address a conflict in human life that is bound to the erotic character of that life. And the dialogue form offers a particularly appropriate way to let such a conflict show itself, to let the irreconcilable become manifest as such. But what is at stake in this conflict? In the *Sophist* the stranger speaks in passing of the erotic art as a kind of hunting (Soph. 222e). But how could this be the erotic art that Socrates speaks of in the palinode as his own? If anything, the palinode refutes precisely the conception of love as a predatorial and consuming activity, in which love resembles the relation between wolf and lamb or the desire for a satisfying meal (Phaedr. 241c). Near the beginning of the *Lysis,* however, Socrates himself seems to confirm this sense of the erotic, as he warns Hippothales, who is *mad* with love, about prematurely and excessively praising Lysis, speaking even of an "erotic wisdom" in strategic and calculative terms, as if it were, therefore, comparable to a kind of hunting or capture. "And so, whoever is wise in erotic matters, my friend, does not praise his beloved before he catches him. . . . And what sort of hunter, in your opinion, scares away his prey as he hunts, making it harder to capture?" (Lysis 206a). Yet, again in the *Lysis,* Socrates will then also account for his own erotic desire in a much different way, although still in terms of desire (ἐπιθυμία) and acquisition (κτῆσις). But then in a striking passage, he speaks in this dialogue of his own singular desire, which both surpasses all other desires and distinguishes him from others. This singularly Socratic desire is the desire for the friend: "Now it happens that since childhood I have desired to acquire a certain something, just as others desire other things. For one desires to acquire horses, another dogs, another gold, and another honors. Now I for my part am quite tame with regard to these things, but am altogether erotically oriented toward the acquisition of friends" (Lysis 211d–e).

When it comes to friends, to the acquisition or generation of friends, Socrates admits here to being πάνυ ἐρωτικῶς, wholly and utterly claimed by an erotic disposition, having been this way ἐκ παιδός, since childhood. We noted in the *Apology* that Socrates also says that his δαιμόνιον has been with him "since childhood." And in the next chapter, we shall also take up the passage in the Republic (Book X) in which Socrates says Homer has been a friend since childhood. Despite the excessive desire for the friend, in the *Lysis*, Socrates goes on nevertheless to declare, precisely in this same passage, not only that he lacks the friend, but that he is "so far from this possession" that he does not even know how one becomes a friend to another (Lysis 212a). In the context of this passage it is also worth recalling how Socratic ἔρως shows itself in the well-known passage in the *Charmides* (Charm. 155d–e), where Socrates recalls being overtaken by the bodily beauty of Charmides, almost completely forgetting himself as he peers inside the cloak of the handsome youth.

The erotic also plays a decisive role in the *Republic,* at its very beginning, as that dialogue first turns to the discussion concerning justice: an old man's worries about death arise as the desires of his body leave him. The *bodily* life of Cephalus, the arms dealer, who is also the father of the Lysias mentioned in the *Phaedrus, now* becomes something most dreadful as he finds himself returning to the stories he was told as a child, about souls suffering justice in Hades for past deeds. Cephalus has begun to think about his body just at the point where he almost no longer has one. The aging of Cephalus, the degeneration of his body, makes possible a renewed receptivity to stories, to what is disclosed in the story. Justice thus appears as a question of debt opened up before death, even at the threshold of death, but also precisely in the questionable opposition that Cephalus would establish and insist upon at this point in his life, the opposition that disjoins the pleasures connected with the body and those having to do with speeches: "I want you to know that as the other pleasures, those connected with the body, wither away in me, the desires and pleasures that have to do with speeches grow the more" (Rep. 328d). It is telling that Cephalus identifies Socrates as the one who can now relate to him, to his desires and pleasures of speeches, because now he sees himself being more able to relate to Socrates. But Cephalus sees himself relating to Socrates only by virtue of the pleasure of speech being opposed to that of the body. Now that his body is no longer a distraction (in the way that it had been) he wishes Socrates would visit more often. In the withering

degeneration of his body, in his old age, Cephalus would like to visit
Socrates, but, as it is, he cannot *move* at all, can no longer make his ascent to
the city. It must be said that the very condition for entering into a philosophical conversation is what now also prevents Cephalus from doing so.
For Cephalus now it is the right time, but also already too late. From the
point of view of this "head," it would seem that if Socrates is able to relate
to the pleasure of speeches, he too must no longer be claimed by Sophocles'
"savage master." And yet, it is evident that Socratic questioning in the *Republic* opens up the question of justice precisely through the interruption of
this simple Cephalic disjunction, which opposes the body to the λόγος and
philosophy. But, in the *Phaedrus* also, ἔρως and the λόγος do not appear simply opposed to each other. It can be said instead that the disclosive movement of speech is always imbued with desire, just as human bodily desire
can sustain itself only in speech, in the repetition of speech.[1]

Thus, at the beginning of the *Phaedrus,* it is impossible to dissociate the
ἔρως peculiar to Socrates from the desire in dialogue and for speech. If the
encounter between Phaedrus and Socrates can be said to be erotic, can be
cast in erotic terms, this encounter is also thoroughly determined by the
passion each of them suffers, each in his own way, with regard to the pleasure and desire having to do with speeches. Thus, Socrates recognizes himself in Phaedrus, but with a difference. And, in one sense, the task of
reading the dialogue amounts simply to discerning precisely *this* difference. Upon hearing that Phaedrus is willing to repeat a speech he has heard
from Lysias, a speech concerning the erotic, Socrates confesses to his own
desire to hear. This peculiar *desire for hearing,* as a form of receptivity peculiar to Socrates, is what Socrates says allows him to be led by Phaedrus,
to be held captive by him: "I for my part am so desirous of hearing [ἔγωγ᾽
οὖν οὕτως ἐπιτεθύμηκα ἀκοῦσαι] that, even if you slowly make your way to
Megara and, as Herodicus recommends, return right after you reach the
wall, I won't be left behind by you" (Phaedr. 227d).

But Phaedrus has a different desire: he wants to use Socrates for a re-
hearsal, even though he begins by feigning coyness, by pretending that he
is in no position to recite from memory (ἀπομνημονεύσειν) what Lysias, a
most terribly clever man (δεινότατος), composed at his leisure (κατὰ
σχολήν) and with much time (Phaedr. 228a). This is what Phaedrus claims
to want more than money. Socrates will tell Phaedrus that ἔρως is the master of both of them (Phaedr. 265c). But if Phaedrus has to be regarded as
erotic, he also wants to oppose his own pleasures and desires to the pleasures of the body, which he calls "slavish" (Phaedr. 258e). The ἔρως of Phaedrus, like that of Socrates, thus can be said to hold a special relation to the
λόγος. But unlike Socrates (and more like Cephalus), Phaedrus views the
desire and pleasure having to do with the λόγος as unrelated to the bodily
intertwining of pleasure and pain (Phaedr. 258e). We saw that in the
Phaedo, in another dialogue that can be heard repeatedly emphasizing the

pleasure of the λόγος and of hearing the λόγος, Socrates speaks about the wondrous and strange nature of this intertwining through a pseudo-fable that would have been attributable to Aesop (Phaedo 60b–c).

How does the pleasure of the λόγος make itself manifest in the *Phaedrus*? Phaedrus has been attempting to memorize a speech since early morning. Having compelled Lysias to repeat it many times, he finally took the writing itself and now has gone over it on his own repeatedly. It is only now, *having grown tired,* that he is going for a walk in order to continue his practicing, bringing the writing along with him (Phaedr. 228a–b). We should ask: Can one possibly imagine Socrates doing such a thing? The repetition of the λόγος, in the way in which Phaedrus enacts it, leads to his bodily fatigue, leads him even to consider the advice of a physician. Phaedrus, too, thus endures a kind of sickness or obsession having to do with speech, but unlike the peculiar receptivity of Socrates, this is an obsessive passion for memorizing so as *to impress others with what he is able to say.* Phaedrus, who is carrying the speech of Lysias with him, would now rather practice on Socrates, pretending not to have the writing in his possession at all, than fess up to having the speech so that it might be repeated but also examined.

If Socrates recognizes himself in Phaedrus, as he *looks at him,* as he listens to what he says, it is because he too shares an obsession for the λόγος. "If I don't know Phaedrus, I have forgotten myself, yet neither of these is true" (Phaedr. 228a). There can be no doubt that this statement indicates a great difference. It is not that Phaedrus and Socrates share an identity, but that they are held together in the most intimate of differences, an utter proximity that opens up the greatest distance. The "knowledge" of Phaedrus, which affords Socrates a certain insight into the situation, presupposes at the same time the prior relation Socrates holds to himself: if Socrates has not forgotten himself, he knows Phaedrus.

This supposed "knowledge" of Phaedrus, which is grounded in a Socratic self-relation, will also prove, however, to be connected to the knowledge of truth and of nature that Socrates will speak of later in the dialogue as what grounds the possibility of persuasive manipulative speech. The truly effective speaker, a speaker who has mastered the λόγος, Socrates will ask Phaedrus to accept, would not merely be concerned with human opinion, but also would have already turned to nature and to truth, would already have to know nature and, above all, the nature of the soul of the one being addressed. Just as every art betrays a certain dependency upon nature and as knowledge is always actually a form of subordination to nature, it is proposed that rhetoric needs philosophy. This seems to be what Socrates wants Phaedrus to accept, and his persuasive questioning can be heard to be directed to achieving this acceptance. But if rhetoric itself is nothing less than an art of *leading or guiding life,* a kind of ψυχαγωγία, "an art of leading souls by means of speeches" (τέχνη ψυχαγωγία τις διὰ λόγων) (Phaedr. 261a, 271c), then this eminently political art of persuasive *psychagogy* also cannot restrict itself to the merely political.[2] The *prior* relation to the whole that it presupposes is not yet exhausted in a familiarity with the mere opinions of the soul, in a conversancy merely with the way things seem to the audience. If rhetoric is to be taken as a τέχνη, it presupposes a tremendous task, a task that seems at first to have nothing to do with Phaedrus's overpowering obsession for speech and the way such obsession understands itself. Rhetoric, as a kind of pharmacology of the soul, is like all great arts: it demands μετεωρολογία. The rhetoric that would be a τέχνη presupposes, like medicine, the prior knowledge of "the whole" that is nature (Phaedr. 270c). It is thus decisive that the inquiry into ἔρως, which dominates the first half of the dialogue, culminates in a mythic account of the nature of the soul, an account that grounds the differences that prevail within that nature. This myth, presented in the *Phaedo,* performs, in fact, a certain translation, by projecting the erotic into a kind of "physics" of what is light and heavy, and by articulating thereby the cryptic manifestation of nature through and in terms of the question of self-knowledge. The palinode can thus be seen as an interruption of the narcissism that constitutes political rhetoric, a subverting of the view that the λόγος is merely the means to expression and a function of political expediency. It can be said, then, that Socratic ἔρως confirms the necessity of the second sailing as it works against the misology spoken of in the *Phaedo.*

Socrates has not forgotten himself, nor does he not know Phaedrus. Socrates and Phaedrus both have an erotic relation to speech, an ἔρως that becomes manifest in speech and that is directed toward speech. But the feigned coyness of Phaedrus (as he witholds the speech of Lysias) reveals that his desire and the pleasure he seeks is quite different from the Socratic attachment to the disclosive movement of the λόγος. Such coyness puts into relief, by virtue of its difference, the unmistakably *ironic* comportment of Socrates, the secret that Socrates keeps *without hiding anything.* Socrates himself more clearly characterizes what is at stake in his own erotic longing: he speaks of himself here as ἡ τῶν λόγων ἐραστής, as the lover of speeches. It should be noted that Socrates will also later speak of himself as a friend of speech, as a kind of philologist, φιλόλογος (Phaedr. 236e). This passage thus invites a comparison with the discussion of misology found in the *Phaedo* 89d. One who is a lover of speeches is now to hear a speech that concerns love. And it is this fact, that, as Socrates puts it, he is "sick for hearing speeches" (Phaedr. 228b), that Phaedrus would now attempt to exploit by pretending that he does *not* have the desire he does in fact have. Socrates offers to Phaedrus an account of the situation that proves to be accurate: "When the lover of speeches begged him to speak, he became coy, as though he did not desire to speak [ὡς δὴ οὐκ ἐπιθυμῶν λέγειν], even though he intended to do so in the end, even if he had to force himself upon unwilling listeners" (Phaedr. 228c). Why does Phaedrus pretend that he does not have the desire to speak? What advantage does he gain through this pretense, by withholding Lysias's writing, when his desire is so intense that, if his strategy of coyness were to fail, he would then even force himself on Socrates? Phaedrus will insist, however, that it is Socrates who in all of this holds the upper hand, suggesting even that it is Socrates who now holds Phaedrus captive. This play, between seducer and the seduced, between captor and captive, this difficulty of deciding who is leading and who is being led, is suspended for a moment when Socrates asks Phaedrus to reveal what he is holding in his "left hand" beneath his cloak. That Phaedrus's deceptive strategy fails at this point, however, does not yet alter his desire, his "left-handed love" (*Phaedr.* 266a). If it is the case, as Phaedrus asserts, that Socrates forces him to speak, Socrates also forces him to do only something he already intends and wants to do from the very beginning. The ἔρως of Phaedrus shows itself to be characterized by a certain insistent intent upon achieving a goal that has been determined in advance. This ἔρως can thus also be said to be in possession of itself only through a lack of receptivity to what is revealed to it in the course of its movement toward achieving that goal. The supposed self-control of this ἔρως hinges on its remaining oblivious to the nature that it is, to the nature that both grounds and exceeds it.

Who is holding whom? Who is leading? Who has been carried off?[3] As the dialogue proceeds it becomes clear that Socrates must win his own release. But from whom? If Socrates is held captive, it cannot be denied that he also chooses to stay. After the reading of Lysias's speech, Phaedrus supposedly *compels* Socrates to stay, forcing him to offer a speech that will outdo the performance of Lysias. Yet this compulsion, supposedly imposed upon Socrates, arises only after Socrates himself has already tempted Phaedrus by disparaging the speech of Lysias and by mentioning others, "wise men and women," who have spoken in the past more persuasively about love and the benefits of gratifying the non-lover (*Phaedr.* 235b). It is Socrates who first suggests that because of what he has heard or received from others he might be able to outdo Lysias. And Phaedrus promptly expresses a great eagerness for such a competition, for such a display of prowess with words. And yet, during this competitive speech, which begins by invoking the Muses, Socrates will disavow all ownership of the things said, claiming in fact that he finds himself possessed, "suffering a divine passion" (θεῖον πάθος πεπονθέναι) (*Phaedr.* 238c). In this speech, if Socrates says the things a non-lover would say, he also nevertheless continues to act like a lover, and *betrays* the truth of his speech from the very beginning. After this speech is delivered, Socrates again finds it impossible to leave, now forbidden to do so by his own δαιμόνιον. Hearing this admonishing voice, this silent other who interrupts without speaking aloud, Socrates becomes aware of his transgressions against the divine and of the need to atone. This interruption occurs precisely at noon, at just that moment, says Phaedrus, when there is a standing still (*Phaedr.* 242a–d). But again, once the palinode has been offered, Socrates and Phaedrus keep at it, decide not to break off their discussion. The discussion continues, drawing on into the intense heat of the afternoon sun. This continuation, Socrates claims, is due in part to the presence of the cicadas, the lovers of the Muses who are able to grant to human beings the gift they themselves have received from the gods. They are now witnessing the conversation, taking notice of whether Phaedrus and Socrates continue to speak. If Socrates does not seek the admiration of humans, he does prize, it seems, the admiration of insects (Phaedr. 258e–259d). Throughout this dialogue, it is Socrates who repeatedly finds himself taken over and possessed by what surrounds and exceeds him. Such a loss of self-possession, which can be marked at every turning point in the dialogue, is possible, however, only by virtue of the peculiar *receptivity* that is characteristic of Socrates.

The inquiry into the erotic, undertaken here in the *Phaedrus* at first through an exchange of speeches aimed at seducing a beautiful youth, has to do initially with whether ἔρως is a human good, whether it benefits or harms the one loved (ἐρώμενος) and whether it benefits or harms the lover (ἐραστής). The answer to this question would seem to bear upon the possible good of seduction, upon the good of *being led* or even *carried off* by something beyond one's control. But is seduction, then, already to be understood as a form of compulsion? Can the distinction be sustained between force or necessity (ἀνάγκη) and being led or seduced, drawn forward, even persuaded? How can it be said that one *chooses* to love? But if ἔρως is simply a form of compulsion, does the erotic as such not indicate only the disaster of human life, the way in which that life is already exposed to overwhelming forces utterly beyond its own realm?

The human good seems to hang on gaining control over such dangerous erotic impulses, on taming this nature that erupts from within. But the dialogue interrupts precisely this narrow preoccupation with the human good, with the possibility of human life procuring for itself its own good, not in order to abandon the human good altogether but in order to transform the way in which it might be thought as a possibility, in order to transform the horizon within which such a possibility might appear. The possible good of ἔρως thus has to be rearticulated within the effects of this decisive transformation, a transformation that is first set into motion by the Socratic palinode, which praises love and the madness of love as the greatest of goods sent to humans by the gods. What is explicitly discussed at first can be seen to concern, therefore, simply the *ecstatic* character of human life, the way in which, in its desire (ἐπιθυμία), it is *always already beyond itself,* and the vulnerability or danger this inevitably must entail. And if, in the end, the dialogue can be said to affirm the *madness* of love, it also must be said that it does this without dismissing or making light of its inevitable dangers.

If the expertise in the erotic that Socrates professes on numerous occasions in the Platonic text proves difficult to characterize in any simple way, it is only as difficult as Socrates himself and the philosophical practice that he enacts and embodies. Such an expertise would have to be as strange and as difficult as the knowledge of one's own ignorance, since what is confronted here again has to do with the double difficulty articulated in the task of self-knowledge as it is posed by the Delphic inscriptions: to mark the limit without exceeding that limit. Is this not an *impossible* task, the tragic fate allotted to the monster? Does not the entire tradition of the tragic bear witness to precisely this monstrous impossibility? Yet, as Socrates makes such a doubling explicit, this neither yields nor results from a simple naturalism. Instead, in the doubling the task of self-knowledge turns on itself, and the inquiry into oneself becomes the encounter with oneself in relation to *the possibility of transgression that one is:* Socratic nature shows itself as a kind of *unnature,* lacking its proper place. But this very lack becomes itself a way of sustaining an original relation to nature. This reversal or perversion of nature is decisive, where the possibility of transgression itself first establishes the place of the transgression, first determines the limit. Socrates confirms this necessity again and again: what is only second also precedes the one. The supposed "knowledge" of the erotic of which Socrates speaks thus can be seen to open up the manifestation of nature in its very concealment, to open up that concealment as nature's way of manifestation, precisely in the refusal of place, of proper belonging. But as a movement that occurs *in such concealment,* the erotic can be neither mastered nor possessed. Thus, to speak here of a Socratic "expertise" is only to speak in riddles, as it returns us again to the same riddle, as it confirms and intensifies Socratic ignorance, as it enacts the encounter with a cryptic and impossible nature.

The *Phaedrus* addresses human life (as ψυχή, as βίος, and as ζῷον or ζωή) as a *movement,* as an occurrence in or through *time* that is caught up in its desire and longing, thus as a temporal movement of desire and longing that is also always *bound to others.* It thus takes up such communal human life as bound to "erotic necessities," but it reveals how this erotic movement, as something that is most proper to human life and to human interaction, has already opened that life to itself as *more than human,* led it beyond itself. The philosophical questioning of this self-surpassing movement of human life in its desire does not lead simply to the confrontation with something other, but must itself already be taken as the awakening to oneself as other, to the strange as it precludes any simple sense of propriety. One might wonder even whether taking up the philosophical task of self-knowledge, the *autognosis* that Socrates proclaims to be his ownmost task, does not also demand the affirmation of a certain *loss* of self, as the awakening to a tragic impossibility of recuperation, confirmed in a strange desire or love, in the love that would be nevertheless ownmost to the self, most proper to it. Such a task can thus have nothing whatsoever to do with a mere retreat into some sort of "inner self," if this is supposed to mean an

escape from the world, but is first of all taken up in the movement of dialogue, in the questioning that can occur only in and with another. It becomes apparent, in other words, that the task of self-knowledge demands
the risk of friendship, the risk within which Socratic dialogue lives and dies.
But if the dialogue can be said to address human life in such ecstatic dispossession, what I wish to show beyond this is how this occurs through the
making manifest of the way in which human desire is already grounded in
an excessive nature, in a nature which will have always exceeded the bounds
of merely human concerns, a nature, that is, which cannot be contained or
addressed within the walls of the city. Human community as such, and the
speech that is the life of that community, remain bound to undeniable
"erotic necessities"⁴ that already carry that community beyond itself.

The would-be seducer appears at first in the dialogue as a persuasive ma-
nipulator, as one who would wield speech as merely the means to his own
gratification and pleasure. Speech appears at first as a tool for the promotion
of what is thought to be a matter of self-interest, caring for what is one's
own: τὰ οἰκεῖα (Phaedr. 231a, 231b). This deceptive strategy of the seducer,
who wants to appear as the non-lover, thus depends upon the obviousness
of the good of such self-interest and obviousness of what such self-interest
in fact is. It is worth noting how Socrates' own relation to this good in its
obviousness is itself utterly in question. We saw that in the *Apology* Socrates
speaks of his neglect of his own affairs as something that appears inhuman
(Apol. 31b). And we have seen also how this interruption of the self-evident
good is confirmed in the *Gorgias, Meno,* and *Phaedo.* It is important to see
here exactly how the dialogical questioning that occurs in the encounter between Phaedrus and Socrates opens up this persuasive maneuver of the seducer, exposing and examining its operation and its pretense, since in this
way it effectively interrupts and breaks down the strategic position of the
seducer, his mendacious fortification, by raising the philosophical question
that concerns the prior possibility of such manipulative and deceptive
speech. This question, which can be said to concern the enabling ground of
rhetoric, thus can be heard to continue the same inquiry into the ground of
human desire with which the dialogue begins, but it does so by shifting the
focus of the questioning to the possible self-possession (or self-knowledge)
of the seducer and persuader, of the one who would merely persuade, who
would seek to produce convictions or opinions in others in order to pro-
mote his own advantage. What thus comes to be at issue in this way is the relation between a possible persuasive rhetoric—something employed or
deployed as a form of control—and the nature it would presume to be able
to exploit.

The connection between the two parts of the dialogue thus becomes
more explicit, between the first part, which concerns itself primarily with
ἔρως, whether it is a human good, and the second part, which concerns itself with the conditions of the possibility of rhetoric and, along with this,

the limits and dangers of writing. It is thus especially important to attend to how the Socratic question of erotic dispossession remains at issue in the second half of the dialogue, for it is in this way that this dialogue can be seen to address the concealing relation between speech and nature. Such an emphasis upon the decisiveness of erotic dispossession also works against the more dogmatic appropriations of dialectic as a λόγος of nature, of things articulated in their natural relations. In order to bring this out more fully, a careful examination is needed of the way in which the possibility of persuasion is shown to be bound to a *prior* relation to nature, to the nature that always must hide in the persuasive word. At issue here, then, is the very character of this priority itself, the limits of the way such priority might or might not show itself.

And yet, what is decisive here, from the very beginning, is not just that this conversation opens up the erotic dimension of speech as a question of speech in nature and of nature in speech. More decisive still is *where* such a conversation takes place, how it is determined by its topic, its radical τόπος, as the conversation itself takes Socrates and Phaedrus *outside* the city, leads them beyond its walls into the surrounding countryside, in all its resplendent and vibrant sensuous beauty.[5] As the dialogue proceeds, in fact, it becomes increasingly evident that the place itself—a place that proves to be "divine"—has to be regarded as if it were itself a participant in the conversation. But how could this be? What is decisive is that the conversation between Phaedrus and Socrates has *no human audience.* A discussion about persuasive speech, the most political phenomenon, occurs in a context that utterly lacks all public reception. Thus, Phaedrus believes that they are alone in an isolated place (Phaedr. 236c). If the power of speech lies in its ability to procure honor *among humans* (Phaedr. 242d), to gain prestige and the admiration of others, this place, in its total privacy, would be a good place to practice and rehearse, but certainly an utterly absurd place to seek to establish a reputation as an effective speaker. But if the philosophical ἔρως of Socrates is wholly different from the ἔρως that inhabits the φιλοτιμία of the speech writer (Phaedr. 257c), then perhaps this place offers an exceptional opportunity to question the limits of rhetoric, precisely because it lies outside the walls of the city.

But it has to be acknowledged that this dialogue, which ends with Socrates offering a prayer to Pan (Phaedr. 279b–c), is often enlisted in order to demonstrate the way in which Socratic practice constitutes itself in an exclusive emphasis upon or preoccupation with political and ethical concerns—*human* things, in other words. The dialogue is often taken to corroborate precisely the Socratic turn away from nature, as the denial of the primacy and even the importance of what occurs beyond the limits of human dwelling. And yet, *if* it can be said that the dialogue demonstrates how Socrates does *not* belong in nature, what must still be questioned carefully is the possible sense of this very non-belonging, the sense of such a being out of place. My contention will be that, far from showing simply a deficiency in relating to nature, an incapacity to experience even the *beauty* of the natural, the dialogue makes clear precisely how Socratic inquiry is grounded instead in an unmistakable *wonder* before nature but also therefore in an intimacy with nature. Such intimacy, however, does not abide in nature as the ordinary, but can be thought here at first only as a familiarity that opens up the extraordinary and strange, the clear as obscure and difficult—perhaps, then, we could say a *friendship* with nature, a friendship in and of the strange. Only in such an opening, therefore, the question of Socratic monstrosity arises, *his* appearance as a wonder, as a stranger, most out of place.⁶ This monstrosity of Socrates (and is it not also *our* monstrosity?) demands not the rejection of nature's primacy, but rather nothing less than rethinking the way that primacy or priority might manifest itself in human life, namely as a *doubling* from out of cryptic impossibility.

Near the beginning of the dialogue, at the end of a passage to which we shall return in a moment, where Socrates finds himself taken over by the divine beauty of this τόπος, taken outside himself by what he encounters, he praises Phaedrus for his excellence as one who would guide or lead the stranger, his excellence as a ξεναγός. Phaedrus's reply is also filled with astonishment, but not for the place itself. Phaedrus is taken by Socrates at this moment, by the very wonder of Socrates, as he agrees with what Socrates has just suggested:

And you, you wondrous one, you appear as one most out of place. Indeed you look like the stranger being guided, as you say, and not a native. Neither do you venture out of the city nor do you journey into the outland [οὕτως ἐκ τοῦ ἄστεος ὄυτ᾽ εἰς τήν ὑπερορίαν ἀποδημεῖς], and you even seem to me to go not at all outside the walls of the city. (Phaedr. 230c–d)

It is just as Socrates says, so it seems to Phaedrus. Wondrous Socrates does not belong here; he is not native, not ἐπιχώριος, not of the place, but ἀτοπώτατος, most out of place, most lacking place. It is important to ask at this point why Phaedrus supposes here that Socrates remains within the city, that he does not belong outside its walls. It seems that Phaedrus draws this conclusion not only because Socrates has in effect just called himself a stranger, but more decisively because of the wonder Socrates himself is expressing before the sensuous beauty of the surroundings. The description Socrates offers just prior to this remark is given to Phaedrus, given perhaps even *for* Phaedrus, one who is standing there with him and who can sense, who can see and feel for himself, the very same thing that Socrates now brings to word. We should ask: Why does this account of beauty, as it begins with an invocation of Hera, need to be given? The words draw out only what is already sensibly present, what shows itself most of all, showing itself in its beauty, as Socrates speaks to Phaedrus of that beauty: the sheltering shade of the wide tall tree under which they will converse, the pleasing fragrance of the spring flowers in full bloom, the delightfully refreshing cold water of the shallow river flowing by, which Socrates gently samples with his toes, the fresh breezes, which are "exceedingly sweet," the singing chorus of cicadas, the gentle welcoming slope of the grassy hill, which invites them to lie down, and, of course, the statues, which silently bear witness to the presence of divinities (Phaedr. 230b–c).

The attention now given to these things by Socrates, as he wonders at their beauty, causes Phaedrus to wonder at Socrates and to deem him out of place. This is what prompts the remark by Phaedrus. But it is important to consider here the different ways in which it might be said that Socrates is in fact now out of place by virtue of being outside the city. Socrates in his *Apology* will again speak of himself as a stranger, for example, but there the sense of the stranger has to do with an utter lack of experience with the courts. At seventy, he finds himself for the first time speaking in court (Apol. 17d). Here Phaedrus seems to assume that the comportment of Socrates can be caused only by this same kind of lack of experience, that this Socratic wonder before beauty is grounded in being wholly unaccustomed to venturing outside the city. This assumption must be questioned more closely. But before doing so, let us first consider Socrates' by-now famous reply to what Phaedrus has just said:

> Forgive me [please know me as I know myself, συγγίγνωσκέ μοι], you most excellent man, for I am a lover of learning. The countryside and the trees don't want to teach me anything, but humans in the city do [οἱ δ' ἐν τῷ ἄστει ἄνθρωποι]. But you seem to me to have found the potion for getting me out [τῆς ἐμῆς ἐξόδου τὸ φάρμακον ηὑρηκέναι]. Just as people lead hungry animals by shaking in front of them a branch of leaves or some fruit, it seems that you, by holding before me speeches in books, can lead me all around Attica and anywhere else you please. (Phaedr. 230d–e)

It appears that it is the Socratic love or friendship with learning which is responsible for his lack of engagement with what is τὰ χωρία, what is of the country or, we might say, proper to the place, simply in its place. The trees don't want to teach this φιλομαθής, but not so the humans, the city dwellers. But if it is fair to say that humans do *not* in fact teach Socrates, despite their *wanting* to, perhaps it is also premature to assume simply that the trees do not teach.[7] Perhaps the trees teach, even if not willingly. If Socrates is drawn to the humans in the city more than to the trees, this may have more to do with human *wanting* than with human teaching. In any case, it is highly problematic for Socrates to invoke διδάσκειν here as a way to account for his interactions with the humans in the city.[8] We saw in the *Meno*, for example, that Socrates questions the very possibility of teaching as it is typically understood, by speaking of learning as ἀνάμνησις. Likewise, the image of the cave in the *Republic,* as an image of human nature in its education and lack of education, suggests that learning occurs not through teaching but only as the soul comes to see what *is* with its own native power. There Socrates will conclude that education does not consist in transmitting knowledge, but only in turning the soul around, so that it might come to see for itself. And the mythic horizon of the palinode, as it is presented in the *Phaedrus,* will also confirm this same account of the soul's relation to the truth, an account that is echoed both in the so-called myth of Er and in the concluding myth in the *Phaedo.* Thus, it is even more questionable how such an account, the one given here by Socrates in the *Phaedrus* that concerns who or what shall "teach" Socrates, can put into relief the difference between Socrates in the city and his relation to what is now supposed to be other than or more than human.

The Socratic remark on the face of it is odd, to say the least: the trees here are singled out as the beings that, among all those that one finds as τὰ χωρία, hold the possibility of an encounter that is distinct from the human realm. But Phaedrus did not ask Socrates about trees at all. It is Socrates who volunteers an account of why he does not commune with trees. It should not be forgotten that already at this time these two, Phaedrus and Socrates, are standing in the shade of the tall plane tree, under which their entire conversation will unfold, and which, like the other divinities that inhabit the place, acts as a kind of silent witness to what transpires. One has to imagine the tree as it shelters these two humans from the overpowering brilliance and heat of the sun, actually giving to them the place of their conversation, the sheltering within which that conversation can transpire, without which it would not transpire, thus granting even the σχολή to follow the λόγος. Later Phaedrus will swear before this tree, precisely in order to compel or force Socrates to speak, threatening to withhold from him and never again to show or report to this "lover of speeches" another speech (Phaedr. 236d–e). It is this compulsion or necessity, this ἀνάγκη or ἀναγκάζειν, enacted by Phaedrus, that forces Socrates to give his first speech, praising the benefits of the non-lover and disparaging the supposed *hubris* of love.

One might wonder, in fact, whether it can simply be said that this tree does *not* speak, at least in its own way. It certainly is the case that it harbors the cicadas, who are singing the entire time Phaedrus and Socrates speak, who in fact sing and "converse with each other" (ἀλλήλοις διαλεγόμενοι) their entire life, without pause, forgoing even food and drink, and who continue to sing even during the intense heat of the midday sun, "looking down" (καθορᾶν) upon Socrates and Phaedrus, observing whether they might have fallen asleep (Phaedr. 258e–259a). The cicadas who in this way constantly praise the Muses, whom Socrates also loves, will inspire Socrates to tell the story of their origin, a story of pure seduction, death in ecstatic dispossession, the seduction of song itself.

It's said that before the Muses existed, these cicadas were humans, but after the Muses were born and singing made its appearance, some in those days were so overwhelmed by the pleasure of it that they were caught up in singing and forgot to eat or drink and died before they realized what was happening. The race of cicadas then developed from them, and they received from the Muses this gift of not needing any food from their birth, so that they sing continuously without eating or drinking until they die. (Phaedr. 259b–c)

Socrates tells here a story of translation and transformation. The cicadas, *who themselves were once human,* now open the human realm to divine nature. What is the gift the cicadas have received from the gods, which they in turn can bestow upon humans? For one who is not seduced by song, not overwhelmed by its pleasure (ἡδονή), it is only the gift of oblivion and death. Like Socrates, the cicadas seem to have forgotten their own affairs. They do not even eat or drink, caught up in song until they die, spending their whole life this way. And what the cicadas can give to humans is simply the power to be like themselves. The story about this gift that leads to death (this gift of death) is introduced by Socrates with the remark that there seems to be enough time to continue the conversation, that he and Phaedrus possess the σχολή that will allow them to continue (Phaedr. 258e).What is at issue here, then, is how Socrates and Phaedrus *pass the time.* And, in one sense, this is always the question. Socrates proposes to Phaedrus that these very cicadas will in fact relay their human conversation to the Muses, transporting it or translating it to the divine. To the oldest of the Muses, Calliope and Ourania, the cicadas report about "those who are *led* along (pass the time) in philosophy or in a friendship with wisdom [τοὺς ἐν φιλοσοφίᾳ διάγοντας], honoring the arts connected with these two [Muses], who most among the Muses are concerned with the heavens and with speeches divine and human and whose song is the most beautiful. So, there are many reasons why we should not take a midday nap" (Phaedr. 259d).

Here the tall plane tree shelters and harbors the divine nature, which looks down upon the human conversation and witnesses the love of wisdom, thereby inspiring the most beautiful songs, speeches *both human and divine.* It is this divine nature that also would seduce us to forgo all else, carrying us beyond ourselves, bestowing upon us the greatest gifts. Can the Socratic transgression against ἔρως, which is enacted in his first speech, be separated from such seduction? As his speech becomes "dithyrambic," Socrates attributes this to the divine place. A speech against ἔρως comes to be uttered by one who finds himself taken over, possessed by the Nymphs who dwell here, as Socrates proves thereby to be especially receptive to the divine nature that surrounds him.

Socrates will also speak later of another tree, one that clearly does speak, which is even said to have offered the "first prophetic speeches":

My friend, those at the temple of Zeus at Dodona said that the first prophetic speeches were those of an oak tree. Back then, since they weren't wise the way you young people are today, people were content in their simplicity to listen to an oak or a rock, if it spoke the truth. For you, perhaps it makes a difference who the speaker is and where he comes from. You don't just consider whether what's said is so or not. (Phaedr. 275b–c)

At this point, Socrates will have already mentioned the priestesses at Dodona and their divinely inspired madness (Phaedr. 244a). Zeus, the god of friendship,[9] but also the god of strangers,[10] plays an unusually prominent role in this dialogue, appearing even at the very beginning of the dialogue, as Phaedrus mentions his temple (Phaedr. 227b). In the palinode, Zeus appears as the *leader* of gods and humans, in a movement within a natural horizon, a movement that takes place in the play between what is weighty and what is light, between the earth and the heavens. And, for the gods, this is a movement that carries them even to a place beyond the heavens: "The mighty Zeus takes the lead in the journey through the heavens" (ὁ μὲν δὴ μέγας ἡγεμὼν ἐν οὐρανῷ Ζεύς) (Phaedr. 246e). The *hegemony* of Zeus, spoken of here, is thus also a leading, perhaps even a seduction. Those who follow Zeus also love those with a Zeus-like soul, whose nature it is to be a lover of wisdom, but also a ἡγεμονικὸς, a *leader* (Phaedr. 252e). Now, these speeches, the origin of all mantic λόγοι, given by an oak tree, are also received as the word of Zeus himself. The story of these speeches (the speeches of a tree) is the story of speeches that are thus translated and repeated by and for humans—thus translated oracularly from the realm of τὰ χωρία to the realm of humans, to those who are οἱ ἐν τῷ ἄστει ἄνθρωποι.[11]

Before continuing with the conversation at the earlier point in the text, it is worth mentioning that Socrates introduces this story about the tree at Dodona in response to Phaedrus's accusation that Socrates invents stories at will, or when convenient. At this later point in the dialogue, not far from its end, Phaedrus wants to challenge another story Socrates has just told about the conversation between Theuth and Thamus concerning the origin of writing. The story, which Socrates claims only to have *heard* from those who came before (τῶν προτέρων), those who know the truth, repeats the divine conversation that concerns whether and how writing is to be considered as a good in human life. As is well known, the lordly god Thamus strongly censures the inventive Theuth for his gift of writing, this work or product that he submits to the fatherly god for approval. The story ends with words said to have been spoken by Thamus himself, the non-writing god:

You've discovered a potion [φάρμακον] not for μνήμη but for ὑπόμνησις, not for memory but for reminding, and you offer to your students [τοῖς μαθηταῖς] apparent but not true wisdom [σοφία]. After hearing [or reading] many things from you without being taught [ἄνευ διδαχῆς], they will appear very knowledgeable [πολυγνώμονες] while being mostly ignorant [αγνώμονες], and they will be difficult to be with, since they will appear but not be wise. (Phaedr. 275a–b)

It is at this point that Phaedrus interrupts Socrates, accusing him of inventing the story. For Phaedrus, Socrates is the author of the story, and it matters *who* the author or owner is; it matters to whom one can assign this λόγος. But if Phaedrus did not already recognize himself in the harsh words of the Egyptian god, he cannot now be mistaken about Socrates' meaning in the rebuke that follows, about the young and "wise" who are no longer able to listen to the trees and the rocks, who cannot hear the truth wherever it is spoken. The same ones who are difficult to be with, because filled with mere book learning, are the young and "wise" who cannot hear the trees and the rocks, who thus *cannot be taught* by either trees or rocks. These youthful upstarts are the ones who are preoccupied with authority and reputation. They are the ones, like Phaedrus himself (but unlike the attendants at Dodona), for whom it matters *who* is the author of the speech. Yet the fixation upon this sense of authorship, as paternity and authority, promises only a sham wisdom, according to both Socrates and the Egyptian god. Precisely as non-writers, both Socrates and Thamus are now giving a lesson in how to read, in how to listen or receive the λόγος.

If we return now to the earlier point in the text, where Socrates seems to disavow the tutelage of trees, it seems impossible to take the remark at face value, to remove it from a sense of overpowering irony. Closely connected to this is the suggestive analogy with the way one *leads* hungry animals. If Socrates is like a hungry animal being led, the desire of this animal can be fulfilled only by the λόγος, which unlike the tasty treats that tempt other animals, cannot be easily contained and transported, even if this is precisely the seductive allure of the book itself. Phaedrus can hope to control Socrates, *lead* him wherever he wants, even all over Attica, only if he himself has already mastered the λόγος he carries with him. But what would such a mastery presuppose? The one who would deploy and administer this φάρμακον to another is equally susceptible to its effects. The potion or φάρμακον that would draw Socrates out, the elixir of his exodus (τῆς ἐξόδου τὸ φάρμακον), is irreducible to the means to his domestication, the way to transform the wild beast into a docile and gentle pet. On the contrary, what the dialogue demonstrates is that the pharmacological interaction between humans in speech only reveals an excessive nature that has already carried them beyond the city. But this, again, is only to ask whether Phaedrus knows himself, and whether he knows what he wants. It is to point to the way in which the task of self-knowledge is already posed in the λόγος as φάρμακον. The φάρμακον is thus always a sign of being led, of the possibility of being carried off by something beyond one's control, of the nature that one is. The uncontrollability of such an elixir or potion, its unruliness, opens up the nature at issue in the λόγος itself.

Moreover, it is necessary to account for the blatant falsity of the claim that Socrates is unaccustomed to leaving the city. The Socratic attachment to Athens—evidenced quite powerfully in the *Crito,* or, for example, at Theaetetus 143d—is nevertheless undeniable. To be sure, Socrates' curious allegiance to Athens, and even the preference that he gives to the Athenians, caring more for them, because they are closer, than for other Greeks or non-Greeks, is not at all to be taken as an incidental feature of his philosophical practice. This philosopher belongs to this city. But this friendship with Athens, the belonging together of Socrates and Athens, is also not to be confused with an inability to move beyond its boundaries. In fact, it is evident in the *Republic* that it is only the philosopher who can promise to save the city precisely because of the philosopher's ability to relate to what exceeds the city, to rupture the pretense to self-reliance and self-determination, to open up the city, in other words, to the nature that it is and that sustains it.

From the very beginning of the dialogue, it is also clear that Socrates is well acquainted with the place he and Phaedrus are visiting. Not only does Socrates unflinchingly corroborate the recommendation made by Acumenus, that walking on country roads is healthier and less exhausting than making laps in the city, it is Phaedrus who asks Socrates, after their initial encounter, to guide or lead him: πρόαγε δή (Phaedr. 227c). It is also telling that after a short exchange, Socrates recommends that they turn and follow the Ilissus, as if he already anticipates the peaceful place they are to find along their way (Phaedr. 228e). As Socrates then two times invites Phaedrus to lead, so that Phaedrus can decide upon a suitable place in which to read, Phaedrus spots the tree (Phaedr. 229a–b). It is at this point that Phaedrus has occasion to think of the story of Boreas abducting Oreithuia. It must not be overlooked, however, that Phaedrus asks Socrates, as they stroll alongside the river, whether it is "somewhere along here on the Ilissus" that the abduction is said to have occurred. And as Phaedrus questions whether where they now find themselves is the very place in which the abduction is reported to have happened, Socrates betrays a detailed knowledge of the area by stating that the supposed place of the abduction is a bit farther on (two or three stadia), where one finds an altar to Boreas, something that Phaedrus himself has not noticed (Phaedr. 229b–c). In one sense, then—and this sense is all-decisive—it is Phaedrus who seems more the stranger than Socrates.

There is no explanation given for why it occurs to Phaedrus to ask about the Boreas story. It seems only to occur to him because of where they happen to be at the moment. It is the place that prompts the question. But Phaedrus not only wants to know where the deed took place, he wants to know what Socrates thinks of it, how he relates to such stories. Phaedrus asks Socrates, "before Zeus" (πρὸς Διός), whether he believes or is persuaded (πείθη) that this story, this "mythologeme" (τὸ μυθολόγημα), that tells of an abduction or even of a rape, is true (Phaedr. 229c).

The Socratic reply to this question is well known and has been discussed many times. But it is remarkable that on occasion it has even been interpreted as the renunciation of myth and its relevance to philosophical inquiry: the emphatic χαίρειν of stories altogether.[12] One of the reasons the passage is difficult to interpret lies in the fact that what Socrates says in his reply to Phaedrus's question leads to no discussion whatsoever. Phaedrus, for whatever reason, simply passes by the provocative account Socrates offers about the status of myth and how it is or is not possible to relate to it. Phaedrus, obsessed with memorizing speeches, has no interest, it seems, in talking about the task of self-knowledge. In this regard, he is reminiscent of Meno and his fixation upon memorization, a talent that obstructs memory, that precludes the ability to think recollectively about the way one is already related to things, even already engaged with things in their manifest openness. Likewise, Phaedrus's overwhelming capacity for memorization becomes a liability. But for Phaedrus it is also an erotic disposition that obstructs his ability to be receptive to the recollective λόγος.

It is true that Socrates can even be heard discouraging Phaedrus's curiosity about the story, as he ends his reply by shifting attention away from the story of Boreas to Phaedrus's tree. At issue here, then, is the question of who is leading whom, who is guiding the conversation. It seems that Socrates, provocatively, wants Phaedrus to play this role, but it is the tree that interrupts the speeches: "But, my companion, in the midst of our speeches [μεταξὺ τῶν λόγων], is this not the tree to which you were leading us?" (Phaedr. 230a). Phaedrus confirms that this is indeed the tree. And Socrates will then go on to speak of the beauty of place, as Phaedrus will then remark at the strangeness and wonder of Socrates, his being out of place outside the city.

There is thus no elaboration of what Socrates says about the story, unless one takes the story of Boreas itself to be the repetition or the anticipation, in a mythic account, of the very same dramatic situation being presented in the encounter between Phaedrus and Socrates. Then the dialogue does not simply elaborate the story, but the story itself and, in particular, what Socrates says about it, what he says about how to relate to it, can also elaborate what is happening in the dialogue. Socrates' comments here about how he takes the story can then be taken as a guide for how one ought to read the dialogue. If *we* are tempted to ask, "Is this story about Phaedrus and Socrates true?" then we should listen carefully to what Socrates himself says.

The story is told about the nymph Oreithuia, the daughter of king Erechtheus, being carried off by the North Wind. The abduction of young girls, perhaps while they play with flowers, by marauding forces, foreigners passing by, divine or otherwise, is a motif that pervades the entirety of the Greek story. One might think of Europa and countless others, Persephone, Ariadne, and, of course, Helen.[13] It should be mentioned how Socrates will point out later that it is Helen of whom both Stesichorus and Homer speak, each poet suffering thereby in a different way a kind of blindness. Phaedrus's question, put to Socrates, about the "truth" of this exemplary story does not clarify at all what the story actually speaks of, what it is supposed to reveal or address. What would it mean for the story to be true, or to be not true? What is Phaedrus asking? Is this a violent abduction, even a rape? Or is it a seduction? Does it then open up something about the erotic dimension of human life? Did Oreithuia herself want to leave her home, even though (as it is also reported) her father refused to give her away? Was she persuaded to leave, perhaps with reluctance and hesitation? Or is it nothing at all like this, only an unfortunate accident, a girl playing with noxious herbs stumbles off a cliff in a strong gust of wind? Here I am intent upon stressing how this story can also be heard to speak about an encounter between the human and the natural, or at least what must be regarded as somehow other than the merely human. The altar mentioned by Socrates indicates that the Athenians were themselves somehow grateful to this divine wind and its potentially destructive power. Boreas, who originates from Thrace in the North, is also said to have come to the aid of the Athenians, saving them from the invading Persians by destroying their ships. Herodotus (and later Pausanias) even connects the two events: Boreas comes to the aid of the Athenians precisely *because* of his close connection to them through his marriage to Oreithuia. The abduction is bound also to a kind of loyalty and allegiance. When the Persian invasion was imminent, the oracle at Delphi is said to have spoken of Boreas as the "son-in-law" (γαμβρός) of Athens. Herodotus also links the altar spoken of in the *Phaedrus* to this event.[14] Who, then, is the Boreas for whom the altar is built, and to whom the Athenians are grateful because he saved them? Does Phaedrus, in putting his question to Socrates, ask this at all?

Socrates begins his reply by making a certain decisive assumption about what Phaedrus is after with his question. That Phaedrus does not object to this assumption suggests that Socrates has in fact caught on to Phaedrus's intent in asking the question. This assumption betrays that the story is thought, perhaps even by Phaedrus himself, to reveal something about the place of human life in the natural world. The assumption already betrays a certain powerful interpretation of nature. If Socrates were "like the wise" (ὥσπερ οἱ σοφοί), he would be unpersuaded, unconvinced, disbelieving, mistrustful. He would give another account of what happened, thus *translating* the story into terms not readily apparent in it. The story itself, according to the wise, is thus not true, but it does harbor within it a truth; a truth can nevertheless still be found in it for those who already know. The story deceives, which is to say, is persuasive, only for one who does not know such truth. Thus, it is important to see that for the so-called wise, *this truth itself does not depend at all upon the story*. The truth can be detached from the story, and the story is only an obstacle to the truth. Perhaps in the same way that dialectic would hope to remove itself from the necessities of persuasion, from the erotic engagement with nature, the truth here can remove itself from the disclosive power of the story as such. The translation, which would be enacted by the so-called wise, would only retranslate the story back into such truth, the truth that is prior to the story, thus making plain how the story is already itself a translation of the truth, or rather its distortion. What is decisive, then, is that the retranslation, enacted by the wise, would account for the story in terms that are radically foreign to it, imposing these terms upon the story, and insisting that the story is nothing but the aftereffect of a truth that does not need the story in order to be spoken. The story speaks of abduction or seduction, whereas the truth is only death. Love or death?[15] A girl "playing with drugs" came to her end by accident and "in this manner she was said to have been dragged off, snatched up by Boreas" (λεχθῆναι ὑπὸ τοῦ Βορέου ἀναρπαστὸν γεγονέναι) (229d). There are other versions of the story, of what Socrates calls here simply a λόγος (229d), but whether it happened here or at the Areios Pagos, the truth is not altered.

If Socrates *were* to be disbelieving in this way, like the wise, he would not be ἄτοπος, "out of place" (Phaedr. 229c). Yet, if Socrates is ἄτοπος, this also does not yet mean that he instead simply believes the story. The allegorical translation is carried out by one who can imagine the place from which it is enacted, who can thus already find himself compelled and claimed by it on some level, who is thus not wholly persuaded by the story. This stunning exercise, carried out by Socrates in the subjunctive, is thus both offered and taken back at once—a transgressive moment, then, but only the gesture of an assault upon the heavens. Here Socrates already anticipates, then, the offense he carries out in his first speech: the reduction of divine excess to petty human cunning and conniving. Socrates thus does not simply dismiss the allegorical account of the story, but instead actually shows its viability and its coherence. But are the wise then simply mistaken in their rejection and allegorizing translation of the story, as they would seek to supplant it with another, supposedly *more likely* story? Is their account more persuasive? Is this what Phaedrus is asking?

Socrates, having thus already entered into this debate, refuses to enter into this debate. Such things—namely, such allegorizing exercises—he says can be regarded at first as "refined" or perhaps "charming" (χαρίεντα), but in fact they belong to a man who is exceedingly terrible and clever, who is painfully overwrought, and who is not at all fortunate—λίαν δὲ δεινοῦ καὶ ἐπιπόνου καὶ οὐ πάνυ εὐτυχοῦς ἀνδρός (Phaedr. 229d). How close is Socrates to this man? Socrates, it seems, *would* be this man, this terrible transgressor, if he were to do what he has already done. Let me state most emphatically that it is precisely this allegorizing operation, and not myth itself, that Socrates will now dismiss. The χαίρειν here pertains not at all to the disclosive power of myth as such, but rather to such a possible transgression, both dangerous and utterly available, which would challenge the divine itself and claim instead, for itself, a nature devoid of divinities.

Why is the wise and clever master of allegoresis not at all fortunate? It seems that one cannot displace or unseat one divinity without taking on a whole world of monsters.[16] Here Socrates speaks of ἀνάγκη. After Boreas has been shown to be irrelevant, other natures appear, and it becomes *necessary* to deal with them, to give a similar account of them, setting them aright, *correcting* the divine world: "after this it is necessary to revise or correct [ἐπανορθοῦσθαι] the εἶδος of the Centaurs, and then later that of the Chimaera, and then a throng floods in upon him, Gorgons and Pegasuses, and a plethora of other inconceivable, strange and monstrously portentous natures" (καὶ ἐπιρρεῖ δὲ ὄχλος τοιούτων Γοργόνων καὶ Πηγάσων καὶ ἄλλων ἀμηχάνων πλήθη τε καὶ ἀτοπίαι τερατολόγων τινῶν φύσεων) (Phaedr. 229d–e). These natures are themselves monstrous and out of place. The Gorgon, who can be taken as the monstrous manifestation of Persephone, another girl abducted—whose name echoes Perseus and his glory or fame—and the horse, Pegasus, which emerges from her as Perseus cuts off her head, are only the beginning of what will now descend upon the clever hero, the heroic domesticator of monstrous nature, armed only with his brave operation of allegoresis.

But perhaps the allegory itself is the most monstrous, in its assault on divine nature. The merely human λόγος that would render the mythic world familiar and comprehensible is perhaps itself the most terrible and clever. But here there is then already the intimation of the necessity for a tragic recoil upon the hubris that overestimates its own power. Socrates states that one who disbelieves, unpersuaded by these natural monstrosities, who would employ such a rustic wisdom to bring them within the bounds of what is κατὰ τὸ εἰκός, what is likely, will need a great deal of time, an abundance of σχολή, in fact. But the suggestion here is that such σχολή would exceed the bounds of the humanly possible, would be a time in excess of human time. And Socrates himself does not have this time, or rather, in order to take upon himself the project of such a possible translation, the thorough "correcting" of the entire mythic world and its τερατολόγοι, this would have to come at the cost of forgoing another time, another more urgent σχολή. What are the consequences of such a forgoing?

What is at issue in the assertion of this economy, in which one time is replaced by another, and in which this other time threatens to make this time impossible, is a possible life that would be in accord with the Delphic inscription (κατὰ τὸ Δελφικὸν γράμμα), a life, however, that Socrates says he has not yet achieved, the life of self-knowledge (Phaedr. 229e). The Delphic inscription thus demands the σκοπεῖν into oneself as much as it precludes the σκοπεῖν into other things, the investigation that would attempt to translate mythic nature into a different and perhaps more likely account:

I myself have no leisure at all for these things, and the reason for that, my friend, is this: I'm not yet able, in accordance with the Delphic inscription, to know myself, and it seems ridiculous to me to investigate other things while still being ignorant. So, I leave those matters alone, and being persuaded by the customary beliefs about them [πειθόμενος δὲ τῷ νομιζομένῳ περὶ αὐτῶν], I investigate, as I was just saying, not those things but myself (Phaedr. 229e–230a)

Let me interrupt Socrates here to reiterate what is being abandoned. Not myth and what myth discloses but the project of *allegoresis* is what will be given over to the decisive Socratic send-off, to the χαίρειν that thus makes impossible the simplistic disjunction between story and the true account. What must be noted is how this very χαίρειν can also be thought as a turn away from a certain regionalized nature, and from the demythologizing λόγος through which that nature emerges in its region, restricted to that region as what is opposed to the human realm. This χαίρειν thus anticipates or repeats the same movement that Socrates speaks of in the *Phaedo,* as he recalls how it became necessary to take to the oars, to make a second sailing from out of the encounter with an impossible nature.

Here Socrates states that his lack of self-knowledge demands not being distracted by an investigation that, for its part, hangs on this very disjunction between myth and the truth. For the one who obeys Delphi, monstrous natures must be accepted. It is necessary not to be dismissive of such mythic monstrosity, because to do otherwise is to fail to take up the very inquiry into the self demanded by the god. This imperative from the god, which is itself already articulated and claimed within a mythic horizon, is thus bound also to Socratic ignorance, which here appears as the need for a kind of decisive receptivity, an ability to be persuaded. And, moreover, as long as he is ignorant, there is *no time* for other things. It is in this shortage of time that Socrates remains dependent upon the mythic. But also, it turns out, these other things—namely, the allegorical accounts themselves—as they would transgress the mythic world, correcting it and making it tame for human dwelling, would also already preclude the investigation into the self. The *autoscopy* of Socratic practice demands, then, the receptive encounter with monstrous nature, but this encounter is preserved and repeated in the νομίζειν (or νόμος) of myth, in the way things appear in what is customary. What this confirms is that nature does not appear in a simple disjunction, over and against human νόμος, but this νόμος itself already must be taken up as itself the very appearance of nature.

Socrates thus lacks σχολή, lacks the time to engage in an allegoresis of the stories concerning divine nature. But we should not take this to mean that he simply lacks σχολή altogether. Nothing would be further from the truth. But the question here concerns how σχολή itself is then to be opened up and preserved. As a word for a temporal space, it already bespeaks limits, and thus cannot be thought without a consideration of the exchange and interaction between what its limits would put into relief and keep separate. This open time also arises, then, as a question, as something not to be taken for granted. Such a time can be abused or perverted, just as the cicadas will praise only those who spend their time in a kind of love, devoted to the Muses, the very cicadas who spend their whole lives singing, carried off in the divine madness of song. If Socrates does not have time for entering into clever reductions of monstrous stories, and if he does not have this time so as to have another time, the time for something else, namely what is spoken of here explicity as the inquiry into or the examination of the self, as the question concerning what is *the same,* a task that appears as the promise but also as the very imperative of self-knowledge, then this time for self-knoweldge would be a decidedly different σχολή, a different time. Socrates says: σκοπῶ οὐ ταῦτα ἀλλὰ ἐμαυτόν—"I investigate not those things but rather myself."

This time, the time of philosophy, is already indicated at the very beginning of this dialogue, marking its opening, as the temporal space of the dialogue itself, as Phaedrus asks Socrates if he has the σχολή to hear about how Lysias and Phaedrus passed the time hearing and making speeches: "You shall learn [πεύσει], if you have the σχολή to come along and listen." Here the σχολή of Socrates is connected to a possible ἀκούειν, to the hearing or listening to the λόγος that defines Socratic ἔρως, the receptivity that Socrates speaks of at the beginning of the dialogue as his peculiar νόσος or sickness. The speeches introduced at the beginning of the dialogue are spoken of in terms of the διατριβή of Lysias and Phaedrus, and in order to repeat this *passing of time,* in order to hear about it, there is the further need for σχολή. This πρᾶγμα, this matter, which Socrates says, citing Pindar, is of greater importance than any ἀσχολία, involves, then, a peculiar "leisure," since it is in fact more urgent, more pressing than any serious business (Phaedr. 227b). The erotic sickness of Socrates is defined by a time that must abandon another time. It is also here that Phaedrus comments on the appropriateness of Socrates hearing the speech, precisely because it concerns the erotic. Socrates, it seems, does not have the leisure to explain stories away, because he is already claimed by this other time—what is therefore also a mythic time—in which it becomes possible to hear, to repeat and examine, the λόγος or μῦθος well worth hearing.

The σχολή that is said to be the privileged and necessary condition of philosophy at its origins, and to be necessary therefore to the recollective repetition of the λόγος, to that *ascending* repetition which is supposed to characterize the questioning movement of philosophical thinking—διάνοια as διαλέγεσθαι—will always have been, nevertheless, a *time* of mortal life. This freedom—no doubt free, to an extent, *from* the burdens of necessity, but then also *for* such recollective repetition—remains still caught in an inescapable economy, constrained within the limits of the possible, related to that which it will never do without, and so still determined decisively by an impossibility dictated by ἀνάγκη. How is it possible to open up the ground of these constraints, to do justice to this determining relation, to let this impossibility show itself?

The freedom of philosophy is so little the simple disregarding of necessity, that it is only in σχολή itself that such limits can first become manifest, precisely as they are imposed by necessity. The freedom of σχολή is thus free only as it opens itself to a certain constitutive impossibility, attending to it in its impossibility, running up against that impossibility, perhaps even suffering it in failure. But this is only to say also that this philosopher's time is erotic, an ecstatic movement that is led or carried off in its desire. Thus, at least in the context of the birth of philosophical inquiry, σχολή must not be confused with mere leisure, with namely a temporal space in which necessity has simply been suspended, set aside, forgotten. What is revealed in the awareness made possible in philosophical σχολή can first of all be spoken of only as a decisive lack, the lack that σχολή itself must harbor within itself, as a temporal space bespeaking limits and thus mortality.

It has already been pointed out that the task of self-knowledge is itself articulated here in terms that rely upon the very mythic world that Socrates refuses to allegorize. This refusal is already announced in the assertion that if one dispenses with the story of Boreas it becomes necessary then to take on an impossibility, something for which Socrates has little or no time, namely to confront a whole host of monstrous natures. But this refusal is then also made more emphatic as Socrates comes to elaborate more precisely what he takes the task of self-knowledge to involve. Here it becomes unmistakably clear that the question of human monstrosity is to open up the possibility of this self-knowledge—or rather, it becomes clear that the task of self-knowledge itself *is* precisely the attempt at deciding the question that concerns such monstrosity.[17] But this monstrosity has no sense outside of the stories told, and thus must be addressed through an inescapable mythic horizon, as if these very stories, the truth of which Phaedrus wants to question, are now to provide the language with which one might account for philosophical inquiry itself. The σχολή of philosophy, as the time opened up for the task of self-knowledge, depends upon the mythic, is a mythic time. How else to speak of monsters, except through stories? Socrates continues:

> So, I leave those matters alone, and being persuaded by the customary beliefs about them, I investigate, as I was just saying, not those things but myself, whether it is my fortune to be a beast more twisted and tangled, and more furious and raging than Typhon, or a more gentle and simple animal, possessing by nature a divine and quiet, un-Typhonic fate. But, my friend, in the midst of our speeches, is this not the tree to which you were leading us? (Phaedr. 229e–230a)

If one ever had an opportunity to ask Socrates what he is about, Phaedrus has now arrived at that moment. But it is as if the words just spoken by

Socrates fall on deaf ears. Phaedrus is either satisfied with what Socrates has said about the story, believing that he now understands what Socrates has said about the story and the priority given to the task of self-knowledge, or perhaps he is simply not at all interested in hearing more about this possibility of a Typhonic Socrates. In any case, the dialogue now seems to move on to other things, to the passages I have already discussed at some length. But as readers we can pause, freeze the action—if, that is, we have the time—and wonder about this strange account of himself Socrates has just put forward. For while Socrates may not yet know himself, it is certainly the case that he does know himself to be claimed by this question of self-knowledge. He knows himself well enough, in other words, to insist upon being so claimed, to not let himself get distracted by the project of allegoresis, for example. In the same way that Socrates is able to claim a knowledge of the erotic, it can be said that he does know himself precisely in the question of his own monstrosity, a question, however, that has to do, as it now becomes more apparent, with his place in nature. The question of self-knowledge, therefore, not only as it is posed by Socrates, but even as it comes to be enacted and lived by him as an ongoing question, raises the possibility that it is this very question—the way of being claimed by this question—that already in part constitutes the monstrosity at issue here. But this would also suggest that it is only a nature like that of Socrates—a nature that *could* perform the allegoresis that Socrates has just carried out, which he offers only as he takes it back—that is also capable of being claimed and even constituted in such a monstrous question, a question that then, in its monstrosity, turns on itself as a question, asking about the very monstrosity of the question as such.

The situation can also be considered dramatically. When Phaedrus asks if the story is true, Socrates can be heard to reply only with another question, but thereby also to enact that very question in the reply itself, to perform the question. Socrates is thus asking Phaedrus: What might this story (the story about the North Wind) tell you about yourself? Do you know what you want in asking this question about the truth? Are you able to keep your distance from this story and its truth? But how, then, can the Typhonic, even as a question, be introduced here precisely as a response to the story of Boreas? How can the memory of the most terrible monster of all time, still evident in the belching of Mount Aetna, a monster of the earth who sought violently to overthrow Zeus and his rule of the heavens, be related to the good son-in-law of Athens?

Both Boreas and Typhon appear as winds, one being (mostly) beneficent, the other being the most dreadful and destructive. Hesiod states that all the winds come from Typhoeus, but he excepts those winds that are a "blessing to humans," namely Notos, Boreas, and Zephyros. As for the others, there is "no remedy against this evil" (T 869–80). Herodotus tells us that for the Egyptians Typhon is the same as Set, the god who battles and murders Osiris, who, it is well known, is recognized by the Greeks as none other than Dionysus.[18] But if Osiris, according to the Egyptians, is also the father of Apollo, in both cases, Egyptian and Greek, Typhon battles the father of Apollo, whether this is Dionysus or Zeus. The Egyptian celebration of the rites of Osiris would lament the withdrawal of the Nile, but also the retreat of the cool wind from the North and, with this, the arrival of the hot wind Typhon.[19] Boreas and Typhon are thus linked together, as they stand in for each other, as alternates in a cyclic exchange, with the absence of one bringing about the presence of the other. Does the allegorizing dismissal of Boreas not already beckon the arrival of a Typhon? These same Egyptian rites were thought to correspond to the Dionysian festivals of Zagreus in Crete, which are associated with the origins of tragedy in Greece. It is also the case that Theuth, who appears later in the *Phaedrus,* as the god who brings the arts, especially writing, to mortal humans, is another manifestation of Osiris.[20]

The battle between Typhon and Zeus refers to the most violent and destructive encounter between the earth and the sky. Typhon is the "terrible, violent and lawless"—δεινός, ὑβριστής, ἄνομος[21]—says Hesiod. Typhoeus, whom Hesiod distinguishes from Typhon,[22] sought to do "a thing past mending," and would have been the "master of gods and mortals" had not Zeus intervened. The account of Apollodorus, which differs slightly from Hesiod's, is especially important in the context of the *Phaedrus.* Typhon, born of Ge and Tartarus, arises out of Ge's anger over the defeat of the Giants. Typhon, a god of the earth, thus arises in the wake of the Gigantomachy, in a retaliation for it and thus as a kind of continuation of it. He is said to be a "mixture of man and beast," with one hundred heads of serpents, arms extending from west to east, his body winged, his heads sometimes touching the stars. He hurled red-hot rocks at the sky itself. And when the gods saw him, they fled, changing themselves into animals as they went. Only Zeus challenged the monster. But for a time even Zeus was subdued, as Typhon cut out the sinews from his hands and feet. With the aid of Hermes, however, Zeus regained his strength and conquered the monster, appearing "from the sky in a chariot drawn by winged horses" and hurling thunderbolts. Typhon is finally buried in Tartarus or under Mount Aetna, the workshop of Hephaestus.

The turn away from one interpretation of nature, an interpretation that would extract nature from its mythic and divine horizon, thus seeking to produce a new nature, one devoid of the mythic and strange monsters, returns Socrates to another nature, to the question of his own nature, whether he is a gentler and simpler animal (ζῷον), whether "by nature" (φύσει) he does not possess a "divine dispensation" that is wholly ἄτυφος, wholly un-Typhonic. The connection between θεία μοῖρα and nature is repeated, as we have seen, in the *Meno* and elsewhere. But here both what arises by nature and what is sent by the gods are opposed to being some sort of θηρίον, a wild beast that is ἐπιτεθυμμέμον, more furious, but also *more Typhonic* than Typhon himself. Here the word translated as "more furious," ἐπιτεθυμμέμον, is also a participial form of the verb ἐπιτέφομαι, and thus is itself a word derived from the figure of Typhon. More Typhonic than Typhon himself, a wild beast? Or instead, perhaps a tame un-Typhonic animal, a life that by nature has a place, a place bestowed by the divine? This is the question, Socrates tells Phaedrus, taken up in the task of self-knowledge. But this also means—and this is decisive—that this is the question which that task itself brings about, since the task itself (or the question posed in it) already must open human life as possibly monstrous, as the life for which self-knowledge is still or can be a task. What is questioned in the task of self-knowledge is the way in which such a task itself can know itself, as the transgressive possibility that it is. Only monsters do not already know their place in nature, being monsters by virtue of being out of place, by virtue of lacking place.[23] What is thus at issue in the story is the way in which, precisely as a story, it already poses the question of self-knowledge, as it calls for interpretation. The possible allegoresis of the story is also an interpretation; but the rejection of the project of allegoresis is not at all the rejection of the task of interpretation, not at all the refusal to undertake the "hermeneutic adventure" occasioned by the story. In the supposed turn away from nature, in the resistance to the allegorizing reduction, undertaken without qualms by the so-called wise, there is already, on the part of Socrates, the more difficult confrontation with the very monstrosity of nature itself, of the monstrosity that is proper to nature's manifestation. The question of nature itself demands then the affirmation of the mythic, because nature itself already poses the question of self-knowledge.

In the context of the naturalistic causality of the so-called wise, the question of myth must be returned to the σχολή that is the temporal space within which this human monstrosity can first appear. And such monstrosity is already at issue in the very possibility of delimiting such a temporal space. It cannot be said, therefore, that such Socratic σχολή abandons nature. Such σχολή, on the contrary, sustains a relation to nature by establishing the temporal space through which nature appears as τὸ χαλεπόν, what verges on impossibility.[24] Socrates is not simply seduced by the story; he has not simply been carried off by Boreas. Rather, it is plainly evident that Socrates also already sees another time, another relation to nature: the death of a girl and the death of the story, the translation of seduction or of love into death. But in doing so, he confronts the *failure* of that other time, sees the monstrosity in it, and seeks to return it therefore to the limits of his own time, the time within which nature becomes manifest otherwise. The possible reconciliation with the monstrous, in which the ugly would be revealed as beautiful, thus bringing Socrates home, to the place assigned to him by a divine nature, always remains the hope, the love, and the courage of Plato's Socrates. Such a possibility is preserved for Socrates only in his turn to the disclosive movement of speech, as both λόγος and μῦθος.

Thus, we have to consider how such a return to the limits of σχολή also opens up the erotic madness of Socrates, an erotic madness that cannot be separated from an unyielding attachment or devotion to the disclosive power of speech. We recall that Socrates also speaks of his expertise in the erotic as a divine gift, but it is now more apparent how such a divine gift is also the possibility of the question of self-knowledge: it is erotic nature which poses the question of its own limits, which must ask that question through a tragic transgression of those very limits. In the same way that the causal accounts of Anaxagoras, as they are discussed in the *Phaedo,* prove inadequate, because they cannot address nature as it is bound to its manifestation in and through human life—in the limits of that life—the allegoresis of the story of Boreas cannot fully account for the encounter with nature in its *erotic* character. We have seen that Socrates betrays an ambiguous relation to the Boreas story, and therefore to the disclosive power of story as such. But this ambiguity only repeats or anticipates the way in which the question of the erotic comes to be addressed in the dialogue as a whole, whether and how ἔρως can be said to be a good in human life. The question of ἔρως always concerns transgression, involves the surpassing of the limits that would define the self and human life, the very rupture of one's self-relation in the excess that grounds human life. What is at issue here then, in the danger of being seduced or carried off by what is beyond one's own control, by what is not of one's own making, by the Typhonic unnature that one is, is not an excess or a strangeness that arises or arrives from the outside, first penetrating the sealed purity of what is held within. The self, always already a stranger to itself, is also the nature that exceeds it. If Boreas is a family member, the "son-in-law" of Athens, perhaps even Typhon belongs to the kinship of all things that is the whole of nature.

It is of the greatest importance, therefore, to consider how the dialogue raises the question of ἔρως in and through an examination of the disclosive power of persuasive speech. The question of the Typhonic nature of Socrates, as it must affirm and accept the mythic (but at its limits, already perhaps transgressing those limits), also enacts the question of the δεύτερος πλοῦς, enacts that very movement, as the turn that turns in a certain necessity to the λόγοι. Such a movement to the necessity of speech arises from out of a certain failed encounter with nature. Again and again in the dialogues Socrates reveals how he is compelled in such failure to take up the question of his own nature, to turn to the question of the nature that he is, as it is still bound to the manifestation of an impossible and cryptic nature, a demonic excess that surpasses the merely human.

8

Truth and Friendship

To be able to question along with Socrates, to be exposed to the dialogical questioning that is enacted with him, presupposes that one can rely upon a Platonic transmission, that one then will be able to experience the text also as a form of response, as the reception and repetition of an originally Socratic movement. The very belonging together of Plato and Socrates relies upon and presupposes this difference that is sustained through repetition. For this reason, it is worth considering how Socrates himself can be seen engaging the philosophical claims of his predecessors and contemporaries within the Platonic text. It is sometimes observed that the ancients freely adopt the words and thoughts of others to suit perhaps different purposes.[1] But this way of creatively appropriating and transforming what is asserted by others does not appear to have been taken as inconsistent or incompatible with a higher sense of fidelity and even friendship. This Greek sense of creative fidelity, a "friendship" sustained perhaps only through violation and overcoming, because it does constitute a tradition, should not be ignored at the level at which it might bear upon an interpretation of the Platonic text. I have said that *traditio* in this sense, as it preserves through delivery, by handing over and repeating, can be thought even as a form of betrayal. It is not to be overlooked, however, that such "betrayal" also has a positive character, since it consists in breaking down the pretense of an illusory meaning and in opening up the need for an originary and thoughtful reception and repetition. What is thus at issue here is the constitution or regeneration of tradition as the repetition of the *same*, but this sense of the "same" can be repeated only if first transposed into a more original difference.

In order to elaborate this strange liberating sense of betrayal as it is at issue in the Platonic text I will consider how Socrates articulates a suspicion of the written word by referring to it as the bastardly image of its legitimate brother, the living speech that, *as living*, meets its death in writing. This conflict, however, within speech, in which speech contends with its own death, is also connected to the Socratic censuring of poetry that takes place at the end of the *Republic.* The famous conflict between philosophy and poetry proves to be grounded in an intimacy or friendship that, as such, demands the conflict; this conflict itself thus opens up the "truth" of this intimacy or friendship. At issue here is not only the question of the origin of the λόγος, its supposed authorship and truth, but also nothing less than the question of how it is possible to speak for the dead—which is to say, the question of how the dead themselves continue to speak through the living and of what the living still owe the dead.

If for now we restrict ourselves to the way in which Socrates on numerous occasions engages the "wisdom" of past poets and thinkers, whether that wisdom presents itself in the form of stories or as a kind of teaching, what is noteworthy is that such an engagement on the part of Socrates almost always appears as a way of responding to the opinions presented by his interlocutor, whoever that might be, as those opinions show themselves to have already implicitly and perhaps unknowingly adopted and appropriated the wisdom of the tradition in a particular way. It is often rightly pointed out that Socratic dialogue is always directed to a concrete situation and context.[2] Socrates speaks in a way that addresses the particular *nature* of his interlocutor, the nature of that very soul, which is also to say, he speaks *pharmacologically.* The ψυχαγωγία of Socrates is always directed toward the individual, just as Aristotle reminds us that it is always the individual who is healed: "the physician does not heal the human being, except incidentally, but Callias, or Socrates, or any of the others called by such a name, who also happen to be human beings."[3] In a similar way, Socratic dialogue cannot be said to function by relying upon a simple typology of souls. The singular genius of Socrates, his daemonic "wisdom," shows itself only as it is able to respond to the singularity of his interlocutor. But this means also that Socrates can be found speaking always in response to actual interpretations of the tradition as they are already operative for that interlocutor in the given situation and context.

Even at those points where Socrates forecloses an engagement with the authority of prevailing wisdom, it is almost always for the sake of the one who has unquestioningly and superficially adopted that wisdom. Socrates will ask Meno, for example, not simply to repeat the teaching of Gorgias, but—since Gorgias is *absent*—to say what he himself believes ἀρετή to be.[4] And what is most remarkable in this passage is how Socrates has a difficult time recalling anything that Gorgias may have said about ἀρετή.[5] Socrates will also make a similar request of Phaedrus, but in a way that seems to be exactly opposite. After it is admitted that "Lysias himself is present" (Phaedr. 228e), that his written speech is in the possession of Phaedrus, and after his speech is then read aloud, repeated, Socrates will persuade Phaedrus to disengage himself from the authority of Lysias's professional writing concerning ἔρως and seduction. Thus, in a way that nevertheless echoes the *Meno,* Socrates asks Phaedrus that he stop reading for the sake of dumb memorization, that he stop repeating by rote and begin instead to think or recollect what is at issue in the speeches that are his obvious obsession. What is striking here is the peculiar way in which this is accomplished by Socrates, namely by letting Phaedrus speak through him, as Phaedrus himself becomes the "author" of the first speech Socrates gives (Phaedr. 243e–244a). In the encounter with Socrates, Phaedrus thus ends up confronting himself, confronting his own ἔρως, something that also demands that he rethink the traditional understanding of the art of rhetoric, that he now consider that art in terms of what it presupposes but does not itself make plain, namely, the difficulty of a dialectical knowledge of the natural relations of things, the possibility of articulating their unity and their difference. And, again, in still a different way, it is possible to see how the dialogue that comes to be recounted in the *Phaedo,* which takes place on the day of Socrates' death, becomes a sustained engagement with questions bound to tradition, but in that dialogue this means more precisely the materialist prejudices inherited by the late Pythagoreans, represented by Simmias and Cebes, as they pertain to the question of soul, death, and life.[6]

There are many occasions where Socrates will indeed appeal to the authority of the tradition, but he consistently does this as a way to interrupt the opinions of his interlocutor, by exposing the aporetic dimension of the tradition that otherwise could be taken for granted. It becomes evident in the *Republic,* for example, that Cephalus and his son, Polemarchus, in their utterly predictable assumptions about justice, as those assumptions inform and legitimate their way of life and even their relation to death, both rely in a certain way, and to varying degrees of explicitness, upon a poetic and tragic tradition that in the text is represented initially not only by Homer, but also by Simonides, Sophocles, and others. It is this same tradition, and its unbearable and oppressive univocity, that becomes the explicit counterpoint to Socratic discourse in Book II, as Socrates is prompted by Glaucon and Adeimantus to respond more thoroughly to the question of justice, as it is raised but left unresolved in the unruly encounter with Thrasymachus. The allegedly feigned speeches of Glaucon and Adeimantus, which praise the life of injustice, function as a retrieval of the most traditional views concerning the origin of νόμος, of custom (or law). And it becomes apparent that these views are intertwined with deeply trenchant assumptions about nature as a whole and our human relation to it. The task thus presented to Socrates by these two young men — in a way that again emphasizes his exceptional singularity —

consists in nothing less than an overturning of this entire tradition (Rep. 366e–367a).

One also might consider here how Theaetetus learns, when he says that knowledge is sensation or perception, is "nothing else than αἴσθησις" (οὐκ ἄλλο τί ἐστιν ἐπιστήμη ἢ αἴσθησις) (Theaet. 151e), that he is implicitly relying on a tradition running from Homer, through Heraclitus and others, to Protagoras. All the Greeks, all "the wise," in other words, excepting Parmenides, are gathered together at this point by Socrates: they are all saying "the same," that "nothing is itself one according to itself" (ἓν μὲν αὐτὸ καθ' αὑτὸ οὐδέν ἐστιν), that nothing is one alone by itself, and thus that nothing *is,* but rather is only at all times merely becoming, coming to be (e.g., Theaet. 152d–e). It is important to note here—precisely as it relates to the question of a possible knowledge of the self, or oneself as *the same*—how this talk of the αὐτός is connected to the possible unity of being, to the very sense of being as and in its unity.[7] At the same time, it is also clear that this account of the Heracliteanism of the tradition has to be taken more as a caricature than as an actual report concerning Heraclitean doctrine. In the *Sophist,* the Eleatic Stranger, for example, will speak of the "Ionic Muses," whose thought could never be reduced to the mere paradox of things in constant flux, since there it is said that being is "both many and one." "Held together by enmity and friendship," the Stranger says, being "continuously comes together in differing with itself" (Soph. 242e). Gadamer has pointed out how this statement, as it appears at an utterly crucial juncture in the dialogue, can be recognized as Heraclitean, especially since in another Platonic text (Sym. 187a) a very similar statement is directly attributed to him.[8] The Eleatic Stranger in this passage is also, in Socratic fashion, quite reluctant to offer an account that would conclusively sum up this supposed wisdom of the tradition: "Whether any of them spoke truly about these things or not, it is harsh and discordant to censure so heavily such famous and ancient men" (Soph. 243a). Instead, what is taken up here explicitly is nothing other than the very obscurity and difficulty of the tradition, the question of "access" through repetition. Those who came before, and who spoke about being, all of them *tell us a story* as if we were children (Soph. 242c). But, he continues, "they overlooked and made too little of us ordinary people. For without caring whether we follow them as they speak or are left behind, each of them goes on to reach his own conclusion" (Soph. 243a–b).[9] The question arises that concerns why such stories are relied upon in this way, and how they are to be received. It must be emphasized, however, that this passage does not at all decide whether dialectic and the dialectical λόγος can now, with this Stranger, succeed in leaving these obscure stories behind, thus overcoming their very obscurity. From this passage alone it cannot be concluded that Plato's text is engaged in a demythologizing of its own tradition.

The case of Parmenides, especially as he is mentioned in the *Theaetetus,* proves to be of great importance, because he is said in this way to mark such an exception to the Heraclitean tradition and its account of nature (Theaet. 183e–184b). But Socrates, like the Eleatic Stranger in the *Sophist,* will express a great reluctance to engage in a questioning examination of the meaning of Parmenidean thought. It is remarkable here that Socrates simply insists on the need to pass by: "So I'm afraid that we'll fail as much to understand what he was saying as we'll fall far short of what he thought when he spoke" (Theaet. 184a). But why does Socrates avoid Parmenides? And how is it that this task is more appropriately reserved for the stranger who appears unexpectedly at the beginning of the *Sophist*? The characterization of Parmenides, which occurs as he is placed in stark opposition to the rest of the Greeks, as singular as Socrates himself, if simply accepted at face value, becomes deeply misleading and no less reductive than the account that heaps all the other "wise" Greeks together. What Socrates says is that he is *less ashamed* before the other wise Greeks, whom he does engage and examine, no doubt in a reductive manner, but also in a way that provokes questioning. Citing Homer, Socrates speaks of Parmenides in distinctly heroic terms, saying he is both αἰδοῖος, awesome, and δεινός, terrible, clever, uncanny (Theaet. 183e). But at the same time Socrates also gives another reason here for not entering into a lengthy confrontation with Parmenides. In this passage Socrates continues to justify his avoidance of Parmenides by speaking of what amounts to a shortage of time, a restricted temporal economy: to take up Parmenides now will lead to the neglect of the question at issue (which he says is ἐπιστήμη) and, in particular, as this question arises for Theaetetus. This remark is especially striking when one considers that in the *Theaetetus* one also finds the most extensive discussion concerning the σχολή that belongs necessarily to philosophical life. It is evident that the *Theaetetus,* like the *Phaedo,* is framed by the question of σχολή, as this sense of an interstitial time points to the mortality of human life.[10] In both dialogues σχολή does not appear as simply the alleviation from the constraints of time; the paradox is rather that only with σχολή does one first confront the necessity of σχολή as a lack or absence. In this case, strangely, one can know what is missing only once one has it. What is important to see is that it is also this same necessity that also bears upon the possible engagement with and repetition of Parmenides, an engagement and repetition that at this point amounts to its postponement or deferral. It is all the more significant, therefore, that the "greater" λόγος concerning the philosopher's lack of place in the city, as it interrupts the dialogue precisely by privileging the σχολή of philosophy, comes to an end with Socratic speaking of a certain necessity. Socrates reminds Theodorus of what will be neglected if the speech is allowed to continue unabated (Theaet. 177b–c).

Socrates enforces again and again a questioning that cannot take the meaning of its tradition for granted. But to depart from this mere acceptance is to enter into a questioning movement that takes time. In the course of the dialogue, Theaetetus is asked to give an account not only of *his own* opinion but also of how the wisdom of Protagoras is to be interpreted in its relation to those opinions, elaborated through a questioning examination that continues to ask itself if it is persuaded. In other words, this questioning engagement with Theaetetus and with the tradition invoked by him, as he appeals to the authority of αἴσθησις, also performatively demonstrates precisely the necessity of the δεύτερος πλοῦς that Socrates discusses most thematically in the *Phaedo*. From the very beginning Socrates asks Theaetetus not whether he knows what knowledge is but that he give a λόγος of knowledge, an account of what it is (Theaet. 146a). It is thus assumed from the beginning of the inquiry that a knowledge of knowledge would have to include the ability to *say* what it is. This has to be considered along with the way in which the primacy Theaetetus initially wants to grant αἴσθησις is grounded first of all in a certain traditional *interpretation* of nature, stretching from Homer, through Heraclitus, to Protagoras. The turn to the λόγος thus would seem to demand likewise an overturning, a revolution from within that tradition represented most explicitly by Protagoras and his statement about the human as the measure for what is and what is not. It is all the more telling in this regard that the *Theaetetus*, a dialogue that throughout concerns itself with finding a definition or λόγος of knowledge, leaves off puzzling over the difficulty of attaining a λόγος of the λόγος itself.

These Socratic engagements with the tradition, as they arise within the dramatic and mythic contexts of the dialogues, deserve to be scrutinized with care and in detail, and I intend to return to them. What is important for now is only to see how Socrates at such moments is never at all simply dismissive of such traditional wisdom. He does not simply disregard or categorically refute the λόγος handed down. On the contrary, he almost always accords it in advance an unconditional status, conceding to it, however ironically, a certain unquestionable "truth." Nevertheless, in doing so he also makes clear how this presumption of truth at the same time poses an immense task of interpretation and interrogation: the λόγος received only presents and opens up, precisely in the form of the aporetic or enigmatic, something that calls for interrogation. When Phaedrus, for example, declares that he has heard that one who speaks about justice (or what is good or beautiful) does not have to know justice as it *is* but only as it *seems,* namely, as it appears for the audience, Socrates replies, again citing Homer: "Anything wise men say, Phaedrus, is definitely 'not a word to be cast aside.' We must examine it, in case they're saying something worthwhile, and in particular we mustn't dismiss what's just been said" (Phaedr. 260a). Socrates responds in a similar way when Polemarchus cites Simonides. Socrates relays his own words: "'Well, it certainly isn't easy to disbelieve a Simonides,' I said. 'He is a wise and divine man. However, you, Polemarchus, perhaps know what on earth he means, but I don't understand'" (Rep. 331e).

Whatever is viable about the tradition consists in its being first of all a provocation that, as a point of difficulty, offers a way to interrupt and interrogate the commonplace opinions of the interlocutor. The story handed down to us by Diogenes Laertius about Socrates' assessment of the aphoristic riddles of Heraclitus only confirms this way of responding to the tradition: "what I understand I find to be excellent, and what I don't, I take to be even more so. But I suspect it would take a Delian diver to get to the bottom of them."[11]

Socratic questioning is thus not simply interruptive or refutative, because it actually inhabits and repeats the discourse it examines. This is brought to exquisite tension at those points in the text where Socrates appears almost to advocate and endorse the tradition he is supposedly only assessing. At the point in the *Theaetetus* where the traditional λόγος (or μῦθος)[12] is brought to an extreme formulation, Socrates states that, according to the tradition, to speak "according to nature" (κατὰ φύσιν) amounts to the very denial of all *being*. It is to assert that all things are at all times only coming to be, in generative and degenerative change and instability. I have just indicated that this discourse that concerns nature, and that concerns the traditional discourse that concerns nature, finally leads in the dialogue to an interruption, as a "greater" λόγος overtakes the conversation. But what is decisive here is that this interruption takes place precisely as the question of nature's doubling, as the philosophical inquiry into nature, defined by the tradition that is exemplified by Thales, appears to be irreconcilable with the life of political persuasive speech. As Socrates puts it, just before he introduces the greater speech, hardly anyone would insist that justice and the like exist "by nature" (Theaet. 172b).

But all of this serves only to make Theaetetus aware of the burden of interpretation he must assume, as he learns that the possibility of appropriating such a traditional λόγος is intimately bound to the limits of his knowledge of his own opinions. If Theaetetus can be said to be "with child," and Socrates wants to help him find out whether he is, what is first of all in question is the identity of the father. And it turns out that Socratic midwifery not only challenges the supposed identity of the father; it undermines the very patriarchy of thought, by revealing what must be called simply the wonder of regeneration, the wonder of birth itself as it is opened up in a repetition of the same. It becomes clear that Theaetetus himself may still be looking to Socrates to play the role of father to his child. When Socrates asks Theaetetus what he thinks of this traditional λόγος that establishes a strict correlation between "nature" and a supposed utter denial of being, asserting only pure "becoming," Theaetetus at first simply replies: "I do not know, Socrates, for I'm not even capable of understanding how it is with you, whether you're speaking your very own opinions or you're testing me"

(Theaet. 157c). The Socratic response, however, can be seen once again to force Theaetetus back upon his own opinion and away from patriarchal authority and the search for dogma, including that of Socrates himself as teacher:

> You don't remember, my friend, that it's not I who neither know nor adopt (produce) anything of the sort as mine, for I am incapable of generating them. But I midwife you and for the sake of this I sing incantations and serve up for you to get a taste of the several wise things until I may help to lead out into the light your very own opinion. And then, when it is led out, I'll go ahead and examine whether it will show up as a wind-egg or fruitful. But be confident and persistent, and in a good and manly fashion answer whatever appears to you about whatever I ask. (Theaet. 157c–d)

Thus, if the Socratic engagement with the prevailing tradition does seem to offer an actual account of that tradition and its claims, as that tradition repeats and regenerates itself (even in the "barren" soul of Socrates), it does so not by simply summing up its dogmatic content, but by releasing what is at issue in it as a question still unresolved, as a task to be taken up, and always with reference to a possible self-knowledge.

The account of the opinions of the Greeks that Socrates receives, presented in Plato's text by Socrates himself, thus provides an invaluable way to begin to think what occurs historically with the event of Socrates. And it is crucial here, above all, to consider how this tradition also comes to be articulated through the account it offers of nature and the human relation to nature. The Platonic text does not free us from the encounter with these moments as aporetic, nor does it simply replace them with a new coherent and improved doctrine. On the contrary, the engagement with the tradition only makes the aporetic and riddling character of that tradition more emphatic and inescapable, as it embeds its very discourse in that tradition. One sees this even in those passages that have lent themselves most readily to the establishment of a Platonic doctrine. These moments arise consistently as intense provocations toward the most rigorous and exacting interrogation. Rather than being acceptable in any straightforward way, they can be said to enact a questioning, to have an effect that is less dogmatic and more oracular or pharmacological, as they refuse simplistic appropriations and compel the reader to take up questions and to respond to them.

This same manner of reception, while Socratic, can be recognized as it is taken over in a distinctive way in Aristotelian dialectic. This is an important point because of the commanding position of Aristotle's account of philosophy as it precedes him. In his discussion of the pre-Socratics and their preoccupation with "nature," but also in his several engagements with Plato and the so-called "friends of the forms," Aristotle can be seen to be repeating or enacting the same kind of transformative appropriation that is found already in Plato's Socrates. The difficulty can thus be said to lie in the way this Aristotelian account is at once both indispensable and deeply misleading, as he provides a sure way of access to his predecessors and at the same time the greatest obstacle to a thoughtful encounter with them. Yet it should be possible to view Aristotle's account of his predecessors less dogmatically and *more Socratically*. The reductive simplification deployed by Aristotle then would serve to intensify and heighten the aporetic character of dialectical inquiry: it would be precisely a direct provocation to give an account of what in the earlier tradition exceeds the dogmatic reduction and its gross simplification.[13]

The reluctance Aristotle expresses at the beginning of his account of the Platonic good in the *Ethics* is especially revealing in this regard, since it can be heard as a direct imitation of Socrates, as Plato has him engage Homer and the poetic tradition in Book X of the *Republic*. As he introduces the necessity of expelling the poets from the city he has made in the λόγος, Socrates will also express a certain reluctance. And this reluctance is also grounded in a certain old friendship, a friendship with Homer that goes back to childhood, and, as in the passage just read concerning Parmenides, a certain *shame*. But before reading the Platonic text, let us first look at Aristotle. The passage in the *Ethics* runs:

> although such an inquiry is made with reluctance because those who introduced the forms are friends. Yet it would perhaps be thought better, and also necessary [δεῖν], to forsake even what is close to us [τὰ οἰκεῖα] in order to preserve the truth, especially as we are philosophers; for while both are friends [dear, beloved, φίλοιν], it is sacred to honor truth above friendship. (Nic. Ethics 1096a12–17)[14]

The need to forsake or betray τὰ οἰκεῖα, our own interests, what is properly our own, is invoked in the name of philosophy, as what is proper to philosophy. As with Socrates, the propriety of philosophy demands a certain impropriety, or loss of propriety, a dispossession. Aristotle thus seems here to place truth above friendship, or the honoring of truth above the honoring of friendship. But one cannot pass over this point without also accepting the need to consider more deeply what is at stake in such friendship precisely in its connection to philosophical inquiry (or truth), since it is evident that truth and friendship do not here stand in a simple opposition, as if it were a matter of deciding between the two, of choosing one over the other. It becomes necessary, that is, to contend with the way in which they are in conflict and yet still intimately bound together. This becomes clear, above all, as Aristotle in this passage speaks of a *friendship* with the truth, thus implicitly appealing to the original sense of philosophy, as of a kind of friendship or love. Such an approach to the Aristotelian text would lead to a more complex and nuanced understanding of his "critique." This supposed critique would be carried out, in other words, not simply for the sake of the truth—not only because the truth here is to be honored above the love of Plato—but rather also because Plato, *precisely as a friend,* already himself demands this very betrayal, precisely in the name of the truth, in the name of what is inseparable from the truth, namely, the love of truth. For the love of Plato, then, we must honor the truth. In this context it is worth remembering how Aristotle is said to have attacked those who wished to defend Plato, saying that it is not right for the bad even to praise him.[15] Here, in the *Ethics,* Aristotle can be seen to encourage us for the sake of the truth and as philosophers, to be prepared to abandon what we take to be closest to us, most our own, most akin to us, τὰ οἰκεῖα, precisely because it is this kinship itself that already demands such a possible abandonment or betrayal. To betray Plato is to betray what is one's own, but this is a demand that we ourselves, in our love of truth, as philosophers, impose upon ourselves. The question of the friendship with Plato thus already opens the question of self-knowledge, precisely in one's relation to what is τὰ οἰκεῖα.

Nothing less than the need to speak the truth also dictates to Socrates that he undertake a still more rigorous account of how the λόγος itself necessitates the exclusion of the tragic poets and the imitative from the righteous city. This is just what he declares at the very beginning of the last book of the *Republic.* The truth must be told, which is that imitative ποίησις, "more than anything" (Rep. 595a), must be excluded from the city made in the λόγος, the same city that Socrates and Glaucon have just agreed does not exist anywhere "on earth." How can one be excluded from a city that does not exist, that has yet to be founded? The extreme measures that have been entertained in order to account for the mere possibility of such a city, while they have not ruled out entirely the possible coming to be of such a city, have nevertheless convinced Glaucon that this city in fact does not exist, is not to be found as an ἔργον. And Socrates too agrees that such a city, while not impossible, and thus not a mere prayer or pipe dream (εὐχή), remains utterly difficult, stands at the very limits of the possible. The extremity of the difficulty, its way of verging even on impossibility, is perhaps made nowhere more evident than when, at the end of Book VII, Socrates finds it necessary for the rulers, in order to achieve a break with the parental ἦθος that would work against the proper founding of the city, to send out into the country all those in the city who happen to be older than ten years (Rep. 540e–541a). No discussion takes place of how the founders would manage to carry out this drastic but necessary exportation of the adult population. And it is indeed remarkable that Glaucon and the others simply accept this extreme measure as necessary for the generation of the city. The paradoxical coming to be of the best city, of which it is now said that it could begin only as a city of children—a city that begins, then, in the banishing or betrayal of its own tradition—becomes persuasive only at the very limits of the possible, at a point at which it must also begin to threaten and even undermine its own possibility.

And although such a paradoxical city does not exist *on earth,* as Glaucon puts it, and is thus not to be found anywhere *as a city,* Socrates does state in response to this point that "perhaps [ἴσως] there is a παράδειγμα [or model] laid up in heaven for the one who wants to see and on the basis of what is seen to found a city in oneself." Socrates, in other words, in the face of the factical absence of such a city, preserves this "eidetic" possibility, but only for the singular exception, the one who would found oneself as such a city, transforming oneself, so as to make such a city proper to oneself and to make oneself proper to it: ἑαυτὸν κατοικίζειν (Rep. 592b). The entire questioning of the *Republic* culminates at this point at the end of Book IX in the possibility of this extreme self-relation, and thus has to be viewed as an interrogation of the difficulties of self-knowledge, precisely as those difficulties can be opened up only in the intractable difference between city and soul, between what is held in common and what must remain excluded from such community, as utterly private. What Socrates says is that for such a one who desires to see such a city, so that *through such seeing* a certain self-relation might come to be established, it matters little whether this city has ever been or ever will be. *This* is the city that now, he says at the beginning of Book X, must not admit anything of the imitative. And he declares that the need for this apparently outrageous exclusion is even more apparent, now that the forms of soul (τὰ τῆς ψυχῆς εἴδη) have been distinguished, something that has emerged through the account of the generation and destruction of the four kinds of bad cities.

As he introduces this need to speak the truth, which is that the poetic as imitative must be utterly excluded from the best city, Socrates thus appeals again to the most questionable but fundamental inference of the entire *Republic,* the pervasive logic that would connect city and soul, and that would interpret each of these as if it were the other, interpreting each through a likeness, through a mimetic relation that nevertheless still must harbor the most abyssal difference. Thus, it is indeed curious that Socrates finds it necessary to return to the discussion of the best city in order to make more plain how it would have to be constituted, when already at the end of Book VII, immediately after the problematic expulsion of those older than ten years is asserted, it is agreed that the account of the best city has reached its end, its completion and fulfillment. It is worth noting in this regard that Socrates and Glaucon at the end of Book VII also decide to pass by the discussion of exactly how the best soul might be made more visible through what becomes manifest in the account of the best city (Rep. 541b). It is already plain what kind of human this would be, they say, presumably because of what became apparent in accounting for the best city, the city that leads to the most paradoxical and scandalous necessity: that philosophy (or the philosophers) must rule. But if Glaucon (along with his brother) is already persuaded at the end of Book VII that the just city is the best and happiest city, and thus that only philosophy can promise the best life, why then does Socrates find it necessary now to return to the question of the constitution of that city in its relation to the tragic and the imitative? What Socrates says at this point at the beginning of Book X, provocatively enough, is simply that the truth must be told. We thus find ourselves confronting at the end of the *Republic* the same question that is raised at the beginning of the *Apology:* how is it possible for Socrates to speak his truth?

But precisely as this appeal is made to truth, to the need for speaking or telling the truth, Socrates will also issue at that very moment a certain demand for discretion. He asks that his words not simply be made available to others, that he not be repeated indiscriminately, that he not be denounced publicly to the tragic poets and all the other imitators, in other words, that he not be *betrayed,* handed over. Socrates would like what is said here to remain to an extent a private discourse, singularly addressed to those of us who are present, that it remain for us, said *between us*, πρὸς ὑμᾶς εἰρῆσθαι (Rep. 595b).

What is to be withheld in this way—and what Socrates now claims to be even more convinced of—he says at first in a general way, that tragic poetry and the other forms of imitation disable or maim thought (διάνοια), unless the listeners, Socrates adds, "possess as a φάρμακον the knowledge of how these things are" (Rep. 595b). Such an addendum may be of great importance, since it already suggests that what is actually needed is not simply the exclusion of the imitative—something that, in fact, turns out to be both undesirable and even impossible—but rather a certain knowledge of imitation itself that would have a pharmacological effect against its *unhealthy* enactment. The decisive question, then, would be: How can such a pharmacological knowledge come about, as it would interrupt the deleterious effects of tragedy and imitation? Does this knowledge share at all in the pathos of tragedy? In what way is it still bound to imitation, dependent upon it? What is provocative here is that the more serious charge that Socrates would bring against any poetry cannot, in the end, rely simply upon the opposition between philosophy and imitation as such, but has to do more importantly with a conflict that arises within philosophical life itself in its relation to the excesses of tragic art, of which Homer is said to be first of all emblematic.

With this demand for confidentiality, however, it seems that Socrates already appeals to a community that would shelter the truth, that would protect the truth by withholding it, by restricting or inhibiting the simple telling of that truth to others, especially the poets. There is thus already the gesture toward a possible community of those who would be willing to withhold the truth at that very moment at which Socrates also insists that such truth cannot be withheld. "It must be said . . ." (ῥητέον). Socrates repeats himself, saying the word twice (Rep. 595b–c). He will share the secret—because he must—that the imitative deforms the thinking of the one who experiences it naively, without the right φάρμακον. And yet, what is also evident, although not pursued here any further, is that this is not the only secret by which philosophy must now define itself, even by which it would come to rule over the city (or soul). The more powerful and constitutive secret of philosophy, the secret much more closely guarded, which Socrates merely indicates in passing, is that there is a long-standing kinship, an ancient friendship even, of philosophy with poetry and imitation.[16]

It is not simply that the seductive beauty of tragedy leads to a corrupted life, if not countered by the λόγος of philosophy, as if this λόγος were thus able to stand apart from such seduction and such beauty, wholly unaffected, as if it were already able to be in possession of itself in and through a certain purity. Instead, it becomes clear that philosophy, as it confesses to sharing with tragic poetry a deep affinity, has already been seduced and charmed precisely by the tragic. This seduction demands the most careful consideration, as it marks a constitutive or formative moment, something indispensable to the coming to be of Socrates and philosophy itself, the very passage into philosophy. Philosophy, *in one sense,* thus defines itself, can first establish itself, precisely in an attempted exclusion of poetry, but only as the antidote to a seductive charm that has *already* claimed the philosophical λόγος from its very beginning. But what makes the attempted exclusion of the poetic so difficult is that it has to be regarded as a movement within the same or from out of the same, an attempt to prohibit something that has already laid its claim upon the one who would enact the prohibition. It amounts to the impossible attempt to forbid something that would make the forbidding itself possible, as if one could kill the father before one's own birth. The paradoxical turn against the seductive charm of tragedy can be understood, therefore, precisely as a manifestation of the same reversal that is at issue in the historical event of Socrates, as the descent or reversal through which the same becomes other to itself, in its own doubling, the doubling that also must be thought as the doubling of nature.

What Socrates reveals here is that philosophy as such comes to be in the seductive charm of tragic poetry. And so, if it also must be said that poetry departs from nature, remains removed from nature, such departure or removal does not consist simply in its not being true, but in that it also, by being untrue, presents thereby a great danger to *health,* to the human good. But this is also only to admit that such health would always have to begin in and with a tragic affirmation of its own sickness, in the need for a certain recovery. It can easily be shown how the λόγος of the *Republic* as a whole can itself only be taken as a pharmacological text, since it remains at least as untrue as any other poetic discourse. But this means then, *in another sense,* that precisely the danger of the sickness has to be regarded as the natural movement of philosophy itself, in the way that one must concede that nothing is more natural to nature and health than the sickness that constantly and already demands a kind of self-healing movement. But then, from such a perspective, it is also the case that poetic discourse itself, as tragic, takes up here its own possible self-healing movement through and as the turn to the philosophical λόγος. Or, to say the same thing in a different way, human life, insofar as it is thoroughly bound to the poetic and the tragic, regenerates itself only *through its own betrayal,* the betrayal that becomes explicit as poetry turns on itself, now masquerading as philosophy. This is the truth that now must be told, that compels Socrates to speak. It must be said (ῥητέον), he says, but also not passed on indiscriminately, *repeated,* at least not to just anyone. Let it then remain between us.

If, for now, we attend only to what Socrates says here at the beginning of the concluding book of the *Republic,* then already it is necessary to hesitate precisely at the point at which Socrates himself finds it necessary to articulate his own hesitation and shame. Socrates, before he proceeds with his interrogation against the poets, presents himself as deeply conflicted. This conflict seems to arise in a certain space between the friend and the truth. While there is, on the one hand, the loyalty owed to the old friend, there is, on the other hand, the truth. And this is what he says now makes it difficult, although in the end not impossible, to speak. Presumably, it is also what prompts Socrates to ask his "friends," the ones now addressed, that they not spread the word to the poets indiscriminately, that he not be denounced to them. What Socrates says is remarkable: A certain *friendship* or φιλία for Homer (and therefore shame before him) is said to originate in a bond that goes back to *childhood.*

Speaking in a way that repeats what he says about his own δαιμόνιον, that most private and silent voice, Socrates says he has grown up in this friendship, emerged from it, being *possessed* by it since his childhood (ἐκ παιδός). He thus concedes that he in a certain way is like any Greek, educated by Homer, the foremost teacher and guide concerning what is beautiful and tragic. Socrates, reared by Homer, is therefore also the philosopher who comes to be from out of this tradition of tragic poetry. This same Homer, who has possessed Socrates since childhood, is now said by Socrates himself to have failed as an educator, and is now indicted as a corruptor and deceiver of youth. Socrates thus turns against this old friend, the beloved teacher, and he does so, it seems, for the sake of truth. While he grants a place of honor to his friendship with Homer, such friendship is to be subordinated, if not to say forsaken, for the sake of another friendship. Again, one might suppose on this basis that one kind of friendship comes before another. But one then also has to concede that the loyalty that is now given up, however discreetly, undergoes such betrayal precisely for the sake of friendship, in the name of friendship. Although both friend and the truth are to be honored, Socrates says: "Still and all, a man must not be honored before the truth, but, as I say, the truth must be said [ῥητέον]" (Rep. 595c). What is especially worth noting here is how the transmission or preservation of this truth, its very opening, demands both the friendship and the betrayal of the friend, the betrayal of the very friend who also grounds and grants that transmission and opening, as if the friend as friend is the very one who demands such betrayal: the truth both is revealed and remains hidden precisely in and by the betrayal. One thus betrays the friend, not simply for the cold truth, but for the sake of the friendship itself, for that community which can continue only in the disruption of its sense of its own propriety, and which thereby demands, as Aristotle says, forsaking even τὰ οἰκεῖα, what is most our own.

This supposed community of truth, addressed by Socrates, which would form itself in this betrayal, *for* the friend *against* the friend, defines philosophy itself, that community or friendship that would be philosophy; it can be said to define the self-defining gesture of philosophy. This is therefore an *original* conflict, the turn against the other that gives rise to the same, the turn out of which a certain origin of philosophy can thus be marked, as it emerges from out of its childhood, from out of its friendships, as it also would overcome a *childish* love for myth and poetry, for images, and as it would resist falling back into this love, resisting the seductive charm of the poetic story that continues to give it its life. How then might we encounter the limits of this community or this friendship that defines philosophy through exclusion, through which philosophy would define itself, such that it also might become possible for such truth to be kept within the circle of friends? How shall it remain between us? How would one begin to measure and to delimit the scope or range of the question of friendship and community as it arises in the *Republic,* to say nothing of the way this question reverberates throughout the dialogues as a whole?

Would this community not be defined by Socratic dialogue? But such dialogue would itself then be defined also by the necessity of a very precise sense of betrayal. One could read the Platonic text itself as it attests to precisely this most difficult sense of friendship, the friendship between Plato and Socrates, in which each finds himself both preserved (conveyed) and covered over, lost. No doubt what is decisive is that philosophy, as this community or this friendship (in and with the truth), is such that it allows itself to be determined in and by the movement of the speech, in the turn to the λόγοι. But such a turn to speech, in dialogue, also already demands the other, the dialogical partner with which the inquiry may proceed. Socrates often insists upon this need for another. In the middle of the retelling of the story of Er, for example, he interrupts himself and his story in order to impress upon those present and listening how the story makes evident the most decisive moment, the κίνδυνος, the great *danger* of human life. What Socrates is concerned with here is what he calls "the most important choice . . . in life and death" (Rep. 618d). In this passage, to which we must return, he states how it is necessary to be able "to look off toward the nature of the soul" (πρὸς τὴν τῆς ψυχῆς φύσιν ἀποβλέποντα) so as to be able to make the better choice. But this great danger, the inevitable choice in and of human life, Socrates also states, without explanation, not only demands that one be a seeker of the knowledge of what distinguishes the good and the bad life, but also that one find out *who* would be able to provide such knowledge (Rep. 618b–c). Similarly, in the *Phaedo* Socrates recommends to his friends that after he is gone they spare no expense searching Greece and beyond for the one who will be able to sing and charm away their childish fears of death, suggesting also that among themselves they might find such a one (Phaedo 77e–78a).

Would this one also be the friend? In the *Meno*, for example, Socrates asks Meno to agree that it is the friend, as opposed to the eristic sophist, who is said to make possible a dialogical interaction that will open up the truth (Meno 75c–d). In Book I of the *Republic* one finds a similar passage, where Socrates asks Glaucon how he would like the inquiry to proceed, whether by "setting speech against speech," where there will be a need for judges, or by "coming to agreement with one another" and examining together (Rep. 348a–b; also, Theaet. 154d–e). A philosophical conversation can take place only among friends, even if at the same time the very sense of what makes the friend the friend remains utterly elusive. It must be acknowledged that nowhere in the Platonic text does one find a viable resolution to the aporia of friendship as it is presented in the *Lysis*. If, as the *Lysis* demonstrates, friendship can be accounted for only in its way of being grounded aporetically in nature, then friendship confirms precisely the tragic relation human life sustains with nature. We have already seen how the Socratic affirmation of friendship points to the *daemonic* or excessive character of his practice, since he continually relies and insists upon the language of friendship despite the lack of clarity concerning who and what the friend is.

But let it remain "between us." In a written text Socrates is thus portrayed as attempting to preserve a propriety of transmission, to preserve his ownership over his own words, to restrain and direct the way in which he shall come to be repeated. In order not to be misunderstood, he asks that he not be repeated (or imitated) at all, at least not to the tragic poets and the other imitators. Why does the censuring of the imitative deserve to be treated as a confidential matter? This question becomes more puzzling as it is clear that such censuring occurs in a way that obviously violates such confidentiality. We are asked at the beginning of this discussion concerning the poetry to imagine the possibility of something that has already become impossible, that became impossible at the moment it was said, the moment it was *written*.

In the *Second Letter*, in the passage that concerns Socrates, the author become young and beautiful, and that concerns the non-existence of any writing belonging to Plato, it is written "that it is not possible for things written not to be divulged" (L2 314c). The author of that letter also asks the recipient to take care that the letter does not fall into the hands of the uneducated (L2 314a), recommending, in fact, that the letter be destroyed

(L2 314c), a recommendation that obviously does not get carried out. We thus read and repeat such a letter, as it speaks of inappropriate readers, always through a kind of impropriety, as intruders, since it is not addressed to us. In the *Phaedrus,* it is the way in which writing allows itself to be dumbly repeated that Socrates says makes it especially incapable of rendering anything "clear and reliable" (Phaedr. 275c). In that text, however, it is not simply that writing often, or even always, bungles the transmission of truth. Instead, writing is taken up as something both terrible and clever, as what is δεινόν, precisely because of its similarity to ζωγραφία, a word that refers to the painted image, but that says also the "writing of life." Writing itself is as graphic as painting, which is itself a kind of writing. Why does the painted image deserve to be spoken of as terribly uncanny, as a monstrosity? And how does painting in this way, as itself a kind of writing, make especially clear the terribly uncanny character of writing as such? What Socrates says is that painted images stand there "as though they were alive [ὡς ζῶντα] but if you ask them anything, they maintain a quite solemn silence" (Phaedr. 275d). In this passage, therefore, Socrates seems to complain of not being able to converse with paintings, the same Socrates who has just insisted (on the previous page) that it is possible to listen to a stone or a tree, if it would speak the truth (Phaedr. 275b). The failing of the written λόγος is articulated here, then, precisely through a similarity with a graphics of life, a failing that thus has to do not only with its continual or constant speaking, but also with its way of keeping silent, its failure to respond when addressed. Writing is unreceptive because utterly receptive. Like painted images, the written λόγος keeps silent when one would like it to answer questions, and keeps on talking when one would like it to keep silent.

> Speeches [οἱ λόγοι] are the same way. You might expect them to speak like intelligent beings [as if they had φρόνησις, ὥς τι φρονοῦντας], but if you question them with the intention of learning something about what they're saying, they always just continue saying the one same thing [ἕν τι σημαίνει μόνον ταὐτόν ἀεί]. Every speech, once it's in writing, is bandied about everywhere equally among those who understand and those who've no business having it. It doesn't know to whom it ought to speak and to whom not. When it's ill-treated and unjustly abused, it is always in need of its father for help, since it isn't able to defend [ἀμύνασθαι] or to help itself by itself. (Phaedr. 275d–e)

The maltreatment of written speech has to do, presumably, with its way of being received and repeated, with the way in which such reception or repetition may not do justice to the writing *itself,* with what would be properly at issue in it. Once written the λόγος can no longer be attentive to the context, to whom it is being addressed. And this lapse can alter the λόγος itself, allow it to be altered. Thus, writing cannot ward off inappropriate appropriations, cannot defend itself against such abuse. And it is suggested that it is the *absence* of the father that lets writing, as such an errant bastard or orphan, be taken up or taken over in a way that actually violates not only the writing, but the father also, violating, then, the presumed origin of the λόγος through the violation of what is supposedly only derived from that origin. From this perspective, then, Socrates can speak of the written λόγος as an εἴδωλον, as a mere phantom or image of the speech that is *living* and is the legitimate brother of writing (Phaedr. 276a). The written word would be repeated always as the *dead* word, no longer living, and thus no longer able to defend *itself*.

But it is necessary, then, to ask: What is this dead word, precisely as *itself*, as the self it can no longer defend and live up to, if as what is merely dead it can only mark its own impropriety and failure to be alive? For to speak of the propriety of writing, of preserving such propriety, which is what the possible abuse of writing must presume, is also already to grant a peculiar life to the dead word. The more one pursues this question, and the more that the difficulty of this question is released, the more obvious it is that here there can be only the appearance of a simple privileging of life and of the living—in its *purity* (as Heidegger might say), as what is not at all in need of writing or death in order to be. For one has to wonder how such a purity can even be imagined or spoken of, since the moment that it is spoken of, even if at the same time one asks for the utmost discretion— let it remain *between us*, in the intimacy of a friendship or love—it already must also call for its defense, its repetition, even its own imitation. The father is thus *already* absent, or perhaps dead, as speech itself marks not simply life, but also and inevitably the *death* of the father. The problem of writing, therefore, as it is posed in this way through the question of repetition and the image, serves only to put into relief in the *Phaedrus*—in an extreme way—a difficulty that already pertains to the λόγος as such, whether written or spoken. This becomes unmistakable as Socrates finally has occasion to speak of living speech as the speech that is *written* in the soul (Phaedr. 278a).

What the problem of writing reveals, through a *reductio* to impossibility, is the utter indispensability of imaging and imitation. The appearance of this "supplemental logic"—as the priority and necessity of what would be only second—is not at all, however, only a function of interpretation, of the way in which one might choose to repeat or appropriate the λόγος. We could say that the λόγος *itself* demands this doubling, perhaps by its refusal to defend itself, *through its letting itself be repeated and received*, as it comes to itself in the Platonic text. This doubling and this refusal, then, is what already will have necessitated the second sailing. What occurs for the reader in such a passage is not the realization that the text allows itself to be appropriated to one's desires, but rather that the appropriation of the text has already taken one outside oneself. We should be prepared to abandon, forsake, or even betray what is τὰ οἰκεῖα, most our own. Yet it is clear that this abandonment occurs, has *already* occurred, the moment one begins to speak.

This discussion in the *Phaedrus* that deals with the limits of writing thus turns out to be especially relevant to the discussion in the *Republic* that deals with poetry as imitative. Asserting the imaginal character of writing amounts to speaking of writing as a kind of imitation. But, as Socrates says, the *truth* concerning the imitative must be told, because it is only this very truth, or rather the knowledge of it, that supposedly can work as an antidote to the debilitating effects of imitation, work against the λώβη of imitation, its deleterious effects upon thought as διάνοια, thought as it is bound to the λόγος. And yet, it is first of all questionable whether such knowledge, spoken of here at the opening of Book X of the *Republic* as a φάρμακον, is actually available to us. For it cannot be overlooked how, before anything more comes to be said about imitation and the truth of imitation, Socrates begins with an admission of ignorance, even if he does so ironically. He states that he himself lacks a knowledge of imitation. "Could you tell what imitation in general is? For I myself scarcely comprehend what it wants to be [τί βούλεται εἶναι]" (Rep. 595c). It is indeed remarkable that almost immediately after he declares his strong conviction—namely that only the knowledge concerning the truth of imitation will be able to thwart the degenerative influence imitation would have upon thinking—Socrates then proceeds to tell Glaucon that he himself, in fact, still lacks this very φάρμακον.

The reader may want to take this Socratic admission of ignorance as insincere or disingenuous, and thus as *merely* ironic. Thrasymachus himself would provide an excellent model of how to apprehend Socratic ignorance in this way, as a coyness that only hides a more entrenched dogmatism.[17] But it should at least be admitted that at the point at which such an interpretive decision is made, then arguably one has also refused to encounter the deeply aporetic character of imitation itself as it comes to be articulated here by Socrates, and as it proves to bear upon the entire *Republic* as a text. Above all, it becomes questionable how the difference between philosophy and poetry, a supposedly *ancient difference,* could ever be sustained through the account of imitation that is offered here. For it is undeniable that philosophy itself, the very movement of its inquiry, will never have been in a position to undo, abandon, or overcome all mimetic operations. I have been emphasizing from the beginning of this study that this dependency of philosophy upon imitation and repetition is most powerfully demonstrated first of all in the way that the Platonic dialogues themselves dramatically portray the life of Socrates, presenting an *image* of him, or perhaps, alternatively—speaking to us as if we were children—presenting him through a μῦθος.

Aristotle designates the Σωκρατικοί λόγοι precisely as a kind of imitation.[18] But the speeches of Socrates have to be taken as mimetic not only because

they come to be written by Plato (and others), as transformative appropriations of the things said, to begin with, by Socrates. They are also mimetic in
a more original sense, as Socrates himself returns us again and again to the
doubling occurrence that is indispensable to myth and image, in his descent.
And what could be further from the truth, when Socrates says here, at the
beginning of Book X, that the imitative has been excluded from the righteous city from the very beginning? On the contrary, the founding of the
righteous city, the making of it in the λόγος, proves again and again to call for
the dissembling operation of imitation and imaging. The lie, Socrates repeatedly argues, remains an indispensable resource for the founding of the best
city, a φάρμακον to be employed carefully and cautiously. To undertake now
to exclude imitation as unjust, because false (or merely imitative), seems to
overlook the fact that justice itself has repeatedly demanded falsehood, and
even a kind of betrayal. This demand for falsehood is articulated by Socrates
from the very beginning, at the very point where the question of justice is
first broached, as Cephalus implies that justice is a kind of truth telling and
paying of debts. Socrates proposes, and Cephalus finds it necessary to agree,
that even the friend *as a friend,* demands at times a justice that would violate
the truth. One must lie even to a friend, if the lie might save the friend, save
that friend from his or her own madness (Rep. 331c). It is, perhaps, the
friendship itself that demands such a lying justice.

Moreover, the very production of this city, its production in the λόγος,
is itself repeatedly likened by Socrates to the work of a painter or sculptor.
How is the Socratic city, his *logical* city, produced as it is through a continuous ἀποβλέπειν πρός, not itself an image, derived then from something
that is supposedly more original? Does not Socrates speak at the end of
Book IX of the exemplar laid up in heaven for the one who would found
a city in himself, "on the basis of what he sees" (ὁρῶντι) (Rep. 592b)? But
then, to state the matter with still greater abruptness, how is this city, the
one that is made, not itself a kind of falsehood, a dim thing when compared to the truth?

But the greatest perplexity of the Socratic account of imitation as it is presented here lies in the way in which the originals, the forms or ideas that
supposedly ground the possibility of their own (degenerate) replication, can
be spoken of, apparently, only as coming to be through a production that is
itself still a kind of imitation. Or, at the very least, it is left entirely unclear
how such a production is to be distinguished from the imitative. The question here seems at first to concern the very *making* of nature. It is agreed that
the imitative poet can be distinguished from the craftsman, in that the latter
makes, for example, an actual bed or couch, while the former renders only
an image, something that looks like a bed, only *appears* to be a bed, something that is therefore less true and more false. Socrates admits, however,
that even the production of the craftsman yields a work that "turns out to be
a dim thing when compared to the truth" (Rep. 597a). What Socrates says is

that none of the craftsmen produces or manufactures the ἰδέα or εἶδος, the idea or "look" itself, the model that would guide every production, because it provides the measure and model for the ἔργον to be produced (Rep. 596b, 597a). Thus, even the activity of the carpenter, for example, has to be seen as a kind of imitation at this point, an imitation of an origin that is not produced by carpentry itself. Still, this imitation of the carpenter must be held apart from the still more degenerate form of production that is merely imitative, that is therefore almost not a production at all. Yet it is also important to see that it is *necessary* that carpentry *not* be able to produce its own measure, that such necessity is tied to its very productive ability. If carpentry is to be the craft that it is, if it is to be able to produce what is proper to it, it must take its bearings from a measure that is external to the production itself.

But the origin of the origin itself, the idea that would inform the work of the carpenter, is something that Socrates does not leave here unaddressed. This originary "look" or idea comes to be for its part returned to another, prior *productive* activity, the production undertaken by a god. It should be noted how Socrates introduces this divine δημιουργός, namely with a certain questioning tentativeness, giving Glaucon the opportunity to disagree or to offer another possibility (Rep. 597b). For it is precisely this production of the idea—which Socrates also says amounts to the production of nature itself—that seems to undermine the entire account of imitation as it is presented thus far.

The making of nature would have to be the production of an original. But given that production is first of all defined precisely as a kind of mimetic operation that is always dependent upon something else, something *external* to the production itself, a prior measure that would provide it with the sense of what is to be produced, how can it be said, exactly, that the god then *produces* nature?[19] Such divine ποίησις would have to rupture the very sense of production, since the original is precisely what is not and cannot be produced. What seems to be the immeasurable difference here, the difference between what would be a *divine* production—which could not be like any other production, because it would make production possible, as the very making of the possibility of making itself—and the production undertaken by *humans,* is, however, a difference that is grounded in a still greater difficulty, the difficulty that concerns the difference, namely, between the way things come to be *by nature* and the way things come to be *through artifice.* This difficulty concerns, more precisely, the way in which artifice must ground itself in nature, must presuppose a certain unquestionable relation to nature and what comes to be by nature. This soon becomes unmistakable, as Socrates introduces the distinction between making and using, and subordinates making to the knowledge that first comes with use (Rep. 601c–e). It seems that it is the limits of utility that most of all determine the idea of the thing to be made. But this distinction and the hierarchy of the arts it introduces are not mentioned during the discussion of the divine craftsman.

The difference between divine and human production must be established and maintained, precisely because this difference enables the difference that Socrates wants most of all to insist upon, so as to justify the expulsion of poetry, namely the difference between the craftsman (as carpenter) and the (mere) imitator (as poet or painter). But what comes to be left out of the account—or rather only inserted and relied upon without being explicitly addressed—is the way in which *nature does not depend upon production at all in order to be.* The Socratic account of imitation simply passes by the distinction between, on the one hand, the generation proper to growth and birth and, on the other hand, the bringing forth through making. What, in other words, the account of imitation achieves, quite conspicuously, is the utter reduction of all genesis to production, the loss of nature to the order of τέχνη, to an activity that can be likened to that of a carpenter or painter. It should be noted that one does not hear Socrates speak here, in the discussion of imitation, of physicians, farmers, or pilots, although these are referred to regularly in the context of political questions. The absurd consequence of this reduction, however, can be seen most clearly in the way in which the bed or table of the carpenter has to be considered, then, as a thing of nature. It is worth recalling in this context how Aristotle tells us repeatedly that there can be Platonic ideas or forms only of natural beings.[20] But if it is a strangely paradoxical claim to speak of a natural idea of an artifact, this paradox only makes explicit, again through a form of *reductio,* the aporetic character of all talk of originary forms. Of the three kinds of beds or couches, the first kind, the kind that is made by the god, is "in nature," says Socrates (Rep. 597b). Thus, the impossibility of accounting for divine production is grounded in the same difficulty that belongs to accounting for what comes to be by nature, or in the difficulty of accounting for nature at all. This connection becomes more evident as Socrates at first speaks of the production of the god as itself something that occurs φύσει, as something that occurs, that is, *by nature,* as a natural movement, but then almost at once also speaks of the divine craftsman as a φυτουργόν, as the maker or craftsman of nature (Rep. 597d). The making of this god then would already span the insuperable difference between birth or growth and making, as a making of nature by nature, as if nature were to make itself, or as if the most appropriate way to speak of nature were through such an impossible likeness with making, as *self*-making, in which making as such comes thereby to be ruptured.

The Socratic reception of the tradition of poetry and thought that precedes it proves to be grounded in the possibility of receiving and repeating the λόγος, whether in speech or in writing. But this transmission in and through the λόγος cannot be isolated from the tragic necessity that thoroughly determines Socratic practice. The concealment of nature, nature's own refusal in human life, leads to a dialogical engagement through which that same nature would be nevertheless addressed. The danger of misology is opened up, then, in the difficulty of a human community or friendship, as that friendship also points to the same tragic alienation that determines the human good—if, that is, the possibility of friendship is grounded in the possibility of dialogue. But the question of the reception and repetition of what is handed down or handed over, as a tradition, also has to bear no less upon the Platonic reception of Socrates. At such a point it is necessary to gain as much clarity as possible concerning what it might mean to be *persuaded* by Socrates, to receive the λόγος put forward by him. The Platonic text, without doubt, both repeats and *questions* this λόγος—the λόγος that could be said to be properly Socratic but that we all have in common. But this text also makes clear that Socrates himself, the one who is now dead, also must question his own λόγος. Socrates asks himself whether and how he is to be persuaded.

The turn to the disclosive power of speech, which in the *Phaedo* is said to arise out of a certain failed engagement with nature, is also what would shelter the human soul from the blinding brilliance that in that dialogue is presented through the image of the sun. But in this turn to speech and its disclosive sheltering, it is clear that it is also necessary to affirm precisely a certain risk, which Socrates addresses by comparing it to the risk of friendship and betrayal. The comparison consists in the fact that venturing friendship already means assuming the risk of betrayal, since it is friendship itself that can lead to misanthropy, to the incapacity for friendship. Friendship is thus only possible in the affirmation of such risk or danger. The affirmation of the friend demands an openness to betrayal, the betrayal that threatens to eradicate friendship altogether. Socrates presents this risk as a way to think the turn to speech, which likewise must remain open to a possible betrayal precisely in its own movement. The movement of the λόγος, its aporetic and dialectical difficulty, presents the possibility, that is, of misology, the danger that one will begin to mistrust and even hate speech itself.

To be on guard against misology, as Socrates advocates, requires nothing less than the capacity to be persuaded while also remaining open to refutation, to follow a movement that withholds what is at issue in it, that withdraws as it discloses. Such a capacity is what Socrates characterizes as a "healthy" relation to speech and dialogue, even in the courage that is the affirmation of death as a human good. The risk of misology is great precisely because one *wants* to be persuaded. This desire, the desire that already claims one before one begins to speak, is itself already indicative of the great risk Socrates refers to: that we might proceed "without art" in the λόγος and come to mistrust its disclosure altogether. That Socrates describes his own desire in this context as the difficulty of a "health" only returns us again to the necessity of dialogue as itself a movement of nature's manifestation. And Socrates, at his imminent departure, asks us in the name of such health to be willing, in fact, to affirm even the possibility of forsaking him. He says this because, as he puts it, he is also in danger of believing himself simply "for the sake of death itself" (Phaedo 91a). For this reason, he says, it becomes all the more necessary to pay heed to the λόγος as such, rather than "Socrates" himself. Socrates himself, recollected by Phaedo—through the writing of Plato—asks us to honor the truth above all, perhaps in a friendship that already demands a certain betrayal.

"Thus prepared, Simmias and Cebes," he said, "I give myself over to the λόγος. But as for all of you, *if you are persuaded by me* and give little thought to Socrates and much more to the truth, you must agree with me if I seem to say to you what's true; and if I don't, you must strain against me with every λόγος you possess, taking care that I don't, out of eagerness, go off, having deceived both myself and you, like a bee that's left its stinger behind. But we must get going," he said. (Phaedo 91c)

An Ending

This book began by asking how the sense of the friendship between Socrates and Plato, as the tradition they establish, can be transformed by attending to the strangeness and singularity of Socrates as he appears in Plato's text, a strangeness that reveals their way of belonging together in a difference or doubling. It has ended with an account of Socratic friendship as an ecstatic affirmation of what exceeds the λόγος only by becoming manifest through the λόγος, namely, in the exceeding as such, as a prior excess. Friendship thus proves to be grounded in a truth that must take friendship beyond itself, imposing limits upon it by demanding even that the possibility of betrayal be preserved precisely as the confirmation of the friendship itself. But this demand is also only the rupturing of one's self-relation, as the forsaking of what is τὰ οἰκεῖα, as Aristotle says, but for the sake of the truth and the friendship that would be grounded in that truth. The forsaking of this sense of what is most familiar is, however, precisely what sets Socrates apart and, as he puts it, does not even seem to be human. We have seen that the Socratic task of self-knowledge as a possible friendship with oneself, modulated through an emphatic ignorance, returns us to an originary doubling, the necessity of nature's manifestation in its withdrawal. It is the concealed kinship of nature, the belonging together of all things, that shows itself in the limit that is affirmed again and again through Socratic ignorance. The affirmation of refutation and the delimitation of the regionalized knowledge of τέχνη are inseparable from Socratic wisdom and irony. His ironic wisdom is not simply a mask that hides his true intentions or his true self, and certainly not his true teaching, but is rather only indicative of nature's own concealing necessity, the same aporetic necessity that launches the second sailing. This ironic wisdom can be said to be

194

a secret that has nothing to hide except only nature and love, and nature's love of hiding.

No discussion of the strangeness of Socrates can afford to neglect his appearance in the *Symposium,* particularly as that strangeness is refracted through the honesty and longing of Alcibiades' drunken speech, as it offers a kind of censuring praise of Socrates. There can be no question here of dealing with this text in an adequate way. I would, however, like to raise a question that I think will demonstrate how the reading developed in this book might lead to an interpretation of the "truth" (Sym. 213a, 214e) spoken by the beautiful Alcibiades.

This intoxicated truth of the friend and lover needs to be set alongside the "truth" Socrates promises to speak in his own *Apology,* as he accounts for his practice and his reputation in the city. And just as the *Apology* accounts for the genesis of Socrates through his relation to an Apollonian imperative, in the *Symposium* Socrates has just given another account of his own emergence as it takes place under the tutelage of the wise Diotima. But Alcibiades appears as a speaker in a series of speakers who have been attempting to praise ἔρως, and so one cannot but take his speech also as such a praising eulogy of ἔρως. What does it mean, then, that his speech is entirely directed at the question that concerns the nature of Socrates, that he praises ἔρως through his praise of Socrates?

The wondrous Socrates who triumphs over every human being when it comes to speeches (Sym. 213e), whose manners do not alter with drink (is he already drunk?) (Sym. 214a, 220a), who is constantly ironic and playful (Sym. 216e), who needs no sleep, who remains impervious to the cold, who always speaks of things contrary to their way of being (Sym. 214d), who cannot be seduced even by the physical beauty of an Alcibiades (219b–d), who is singularly distinguished by the fact that he is the only one who has ever brought Alcibiades to a sense of shame (Sym. 216b), who as an ugly old man can captivate the most beautiful youths, who bewitches humans with his words (Sym. 215c), who is courageous and generous in the midst of the greatest dangers of battle (Sym. 220d–221b)—this Socrates is a human who is utterly unlike every other human, exceeding even the heroes, from Achilles to Pericles (Sym. 221c). There is nothing like him, says Alcibiades, speaking of Socrates as an ἄνθρωπος but as one marked by his complete strangeness, his being wholly and utterly out of place, his ἀτοπία (Sym. 221d). Only Silenus, or the Satyr Marsyas, who rivaled the beauty of Apollo's flute and paid for it by being flayed, offers a reasonable likeness. But Silenus is never as he appears; there are treasures hidden within Socrates. What is decisive is that Alcibiades ends his praise by speaking of himself and of the effect Socrates has had upon him: the truth Alcibiades reveals is not simply that philosophy is madness or Dionysian frenzy (Sym. 218b), but rather that the question of Socrates must recoil upon the one who confronts it and that in that encounter one is thrown back upon oneself as a task.

The genius of Plato is also his love, that he discovers the beautiful Socrates, that he finds himself in a beauty that is not simply the opposite of what is ugly or even shameful. The irony of Socrates is nothing less than this strange appearance of beauty in its withdrawal, the monstrous example of a Socrates that remains the non-relational appearance of human singularity and individuation, even in its destruction and loss. And just as Plato writes only through the strangeness of Socrates, the truth of ἔρως is that one can confront oneself only in a friendship that is able to preserve the intimate strangeness of the friend.

Notes

Preface

1. μέτρον δέ γ’, ἔφη, ὦ Σώκρατες, ὁ Γλαύκων, τοιούτων λόγων ἀκούειν ὅλος ὁ βίος νοῦν ἔχουσιν. I have made free use of Alan Bloom’s translation of the *Republic,* although at times it has also been necessary to depart from this fine translation in order to draw out more explicitly certain interpretive points.
2. See Gadamer’s discussion of this passage in *The Enigma of Health,* pp. 39–41, and elsewhere. Gadamer insists upon preserving the text as it has been bequeathed to us on the basis of interpretation. But, as he points out, it is not an insignificant fact that scholars, commentators, and translators have often been reluctant to let the text stand as it has been handed down to us. There is, in other words, a tendency to have the nature spoken of here refer back to the nature of the body or soul, as a particular region, rather than to let it point to an indeterminate *whole* that, precisely as a whole, already grounds or sustains the body and soul. More recently see Gill, “Plato’s *Phaedrus* and the Method of Hippocrates,” and Brown, “Knowing the Whole: Comments on Gill, ‘Plato’s *Phaedrus* and the Method of Hippocrates.’”
3. Jacob Klein speaks against the “developmentalist” reading by insisting that each dialogue be read on its own terms and as a self-sufficient whole. See Klein, *A Commentary on Plato’s Meno,* p. 9, and *Plato’s Trilogy: Theaetetus, The Sophist and The Statesman,* p. 2. For a discussion that makes a similar point but through a very different strategic orientation, see the opening passages of Derrida’s “Plato’s Pharmacy” in *Dissemination,* p. 63 ff.
4. See, for example, Rep. 347e; Gorg. 447b, 447c, 449b–c; Statesman 258a.
5. What Lacan says of Antigone, I take to apply no less to (Plato’s) Socrates. “This line of sight focuses on an image that possesses a mystery which up till now has never been articulated, since it forces you to close your eyes at the very moment you look at it. Yet that image is at the center of tragedy, since it is the fascinating image of Antigone herself. We know very well that over and beyond the dialogue, over and beyond the question of family and country, over and beyond the moralizing arguments, it is Antigone herself who fascinates us, Antigone in her unbearable splendor. She has a quality that both attracts us and startles us, in the sense of intimidates

197

us; this terrible, self-willed victim disturbs us." Lacan, *The Seminar of Jacques Lacan,* Book VII: *The Ethics of Psychoanalysis, 1959–60,* p. 247.

1. Reading Plato with a Difference

1. "His influence was such that very few philosophers in Greek, Hellenistic and Roman worlds (at least until the rise of Christianity and of Neo-Platonism) did not consider him a predecessor in some significant manner." Tarrant, *Plato's First Interpreters,* p. 2. For an interpretation of Socrates as a turning point that appropriates its current trends, see Cropsey, "The Dramatic End of Plato's Socrates," esp. p. 174. On the question of the legacy of Socrates, see also Amory, "Socrates: The Legend," and, for a treatment dealing more extensively with the interpretations of Socrates beyond antiquity, see Hulse, *The Reputations of Socrates: The Afterlife of a Gadfly,* and Kofman, *Socrates: Fictions of a Philosopher.*

2. For an informative and thoughtful account of the emergence of the title *philosophy* and Plato's role in the establishment of the word's significance, see Nightingale's discussion of the "property" of philosophy, in *Genres in Dialogue: Plato and the Construct of Philosophy,* pp. 13–21, 47–59. For a reading that proceeds by taking the limits of philosophy to be at stake in the dialogues, see Chance, *Plato's Euthydemus: An Analysis of What Is and What Is Not Philosophy.*

3. Kofman, p. 250, cites the bibliography of Francis Wolff, *Socrate,* which lists 16,000 titles dealing with the problem of Socrates. For an anthologized collection of interpretations of Socrates stretching beyond antiquity, see Spiegelberg, *The Socratic Enigma.* But it is necessary only to mention a few names in order to see the contemporary diversity of the appropriations of Socrates: Vlastos, Kahn, Kofman, Derrida, Gadamer, Figal, Sallis, Heidegger, Hegel, Nietzsche, Straus, etc.

4. See Lachterman, *The Ethics of Geometry,* pp. 1–7, 124–41.

5. This view is thus to be sharply distinguished from any form of historicism, since it does not claim to have something like a "theoretical" perspective from which the operation of history's influence can be considered.

6. Remi Brague states that "today Socrates would do history." See "History of Philosophy as Freedom," p. 50.

7. This is the claim of Kofman, p. 8 et passim: "Is it not the atopia of the *Janus bifrons* that fascinates and enchants us in Socrates, that makes him relevant to us even today? . . . And what matters to us in all these interpretations is not the possibility that we might cut through their diversity to find a single interpretation, the 'true' one, that finally gives us the 'real Socrates,' bound over hand and foot; what is important to us is that these interpretations make manifest the impossibility of any reading that is not, no matter what approach it takes, a reappropriating fiction."

8. Heidegger, *Der Satz vom Grund,* p. 171.

9. I return to this issue in chapter 8 of this study in order to elaborate how it shows itself in Plato's text.

10. In *Chorology: On Beginning in Plato's "Timaeus,"* John Sallis develops an interpretation of the speeches of Timaeus by attending to the "palintropic" necessity these speeches encounter in their progression.

11. Rep. 424a, 449c; Phaedr. 279c; Lysis 207c.

12. I have in mind here the analogy that Thrasymachus introduces between shepherd and ruler as it leads to a kind of *reductio* to impossibility (Rep. 343b–346e). See especially the statement made by Socrates at 346c: "Then whatever benefit all the craftsmen derive in common is plainly derived from their additional use of something that is common and the same for all" [ἥντινα ἄρα ὠφελίαν κοινῇ ὠφελοῦνται πάντες οἱ δημιουργοί, δῆλον ὅτι κοινῇ τινι τῷ αὐτῷ προσχρώμενοι ἀπ' ἐκείνου

ὠφελοῦνται]. What is at issue in the analogy is both the singularity of each of the arts and the fact that this singularity seems to be already caught up in an economy that cannot be accounted for in any one of the arts. Socrates already broaches this question at 342a–b as he poses to Thrasymachus the array of questions that concern the self-sufficiency of the arts. But at that point Thrasymachus turns away from the issue.

13. Perhaps one thinks of Empedoclean love at this point. But one also hears this friendship in the Heraclitean fragment that speaks of nature's contradictory love. This love, as the most intimate of all loves, is also a love that refuses itself. In perfect Heraclitean fashion, one sees the intense contradiction of a unity: φύσις κρύπτεσθαι φιλεῖ (fr. 123). One hears: Nature, the love that loves not to love, that loves by holding itself back. For a discussion of Heraclitean style in this vein, see Gadamer's "Heraclitus Studies." For a discussion of this radical sense of friendship or φιλία (*Gunst*) in fragment 123, see Heidegger, *Heraklit: Gesamtausgabe Band 55*, pp. 85–90, 109–40. My reference to a "cryptic" nature should thus be heard as it refers to this Heraclitean κρύπτεσθαι, a word that also speaks paradoxically of nature's love or friendship.

14. On the question of Socrates' descent, see Krell, "Socrates' Body," esp. p. 451.

15. See Nails, *Agora, Academy, and the Conduct of Philosophy*, pp. 28–29: "What were Socrates' and Plato's respective philosophical doctrines and methods?—though important to philosophers, is not itself a philosophical problem. Rather, it is an issue within the history of ideas." See also pp. 32–43.

16. Diskin Clay puts the matter clearly: "Without Socrates there could have been no Plato. . . . it is fair to say too that without Plato there could have been no Socrates. For better or worse, our Socrates is Plato's Socrates." See *Platonic Questions: Dialogues with the Silent Philosopher*, p. 5. See also Woodbridge, *The Son of Apollo*, pp. 254–72.

17. Phaedo 60b–c.

18. Emerson, "Plato, or the Philosopher," pp. 39–40. See Hyland, *Finitude and Transcendence in the Platonic Dialogues*, p. 91.

19. Since this has been the implicit obsession of scholarship for the past two hundred years, any reference here is partial. For an overview of the history and bibliography of interpretation through this question, see Tigerstedt, *Interpreting Plato;* Griswold's Introduction in *Platonic Writings: Platonic Readings*, pp. 1–15; Gonzalez's Introduction in *The Third Way: New Directions in Platonic Studies*, pp. 1–22; and Press's Introduction in *Who Speaks for Plato? Studies in Platonic Anonymity*, pp. 1–11.

20. While this way of reading is usually returned to Schleiermacher, one finds it anticipated in Schlegel. Ast, *Platons Leben und Schriften*, is critical of Schleiermacher, although he is also nevertheless a significant interlocutor in the emergence of this interpretive tradition. And also Schelling, e.g., *Initia Philosophiae Universae. Erlanger Vorlesungen WS 1820/21*, pp. 55–56, speaks of Socrates in such a way that in the encounter with him one is thrown back upon the task of philosophical thinking as such, which he interprets through the paradigmatic conversation of questioning and answering. See also Heidegger, *Vom Wesen der Wahrheit. Zu Platons Höhlengleichnis and Theätet*, p. 149: we are to take ourselves as "*mitfragende* Zuhörer." For the most straightforward account of the assumptions of this way of reading, see the outlines at the beginning of the books by Jacob Klein, cited above. See also Dorter, "The Dramatic Aspect of Plato's *Phaedo*," p. 580; Miller, *Plato's Parmenides: The Conversion of the Soul*, pp. 4–12; and Moors, "Plato's Use of Dialogue," p. 92. See also Ausland's thorough account of the history of this way of reading and his masterful defense of it, "On Reading Plato Mimetically." For an attempted critique of Klein's approach, see Gould, "Klein on Ethological Mimes: For

Example, the *Meno.*" Strauss takes things one step further and concludes that because Platonic writing, like Socratic irony, is able to say different things to different
people (with differing natures), this writing is able therefore to negotiate successfully between the different natures that take it up, thus "speaking" intelligently, and
remaining silent when necessary. But this conclusion assumes that Plato is able to
anticipate the possible ways in which he might be received. Such an assumption is
based upon a determination of speech, however, that the dialogues themselves both
establish and yet also undermine. See Strauss, *The City and Man,* pp. 53–54.

21. Socrates speaks of himself this way at Theaet. 149a; but see also Phaedrus's use of
the word at Phaedr. 230c. Also, Sym. 175a, in reference to Socrates. Compare Glaucon's sense of the strangeness of the philosophical vision at Rep. 515a. Also, articles
by Eide, "On Socrates' ἀτοπία." Also, Barabas, "The Strangeness of Socrates," and
Turner, "Atopia in Plato's *Gorgias.*" Also see Kofman, pp. 18–21.

22. See Clay, pp. 54–55.

23. Such an approach thus already has to impose a decisive interpretation upon the numerous passages within the dialogues where thought and opinion are returned instead to a διαλέγεσθαι, as a movement in speech in which what is same proves to be
in need of an other in order to be itself. See, for example, Theaet. 189e–190a, and
Soph. 263e, where it is said that thinking is a silent conversation within and with
oneself as something self-same.

24. Recently, see the essays gathered together in Gerald A. Press, *Who Speaks for
Plato?* But also see the earlier discussion by Edelstein, "Platonic Anonymity," and
Plass, "Philosophic Anonymity and Irony in the Platonic Dialogues."

25. Ausland, p. 399.

26. See Ausland, pp. 407–408. Ausland also points to Friedländer's helpful overview of
the ways in which this passage has been taken. See Friedländer, *Plato: The Dialogues, Second and Third Periods,* p. 36.

27. For a historical discussion dealing with ancient accounts of the difference between
the poet who writes the poem and the poet who appears within it, see Clay, "The
Theory of the Literary Persona in Antiquity." See also the discussion by Cherniss,
"The Biographical Fashion in Literary Criticism," which is suspicious of an excessive reliance upon historical biography for understanding the work and the "per-
sonality" of its author.

28. Maranhao, *The Interpretation of Dialogue,* p. 14, hovers before the difficulty I am
raising without actually engaging it: "As in the case of narrative, in which the nar-
rated story was composed by someone else or was present in the collective memory
of the tradition, represented dialogue also depends on a deus ex machina: that author as superspeaker. But are omniscience and omnipresence (or omniabsence) of
author and of central speaker not identical? In relation to narrative, represented dialogue opens an additional fold in the fan of representation by adding the character
of the leader to that of the author." See also Blondell, *The Play of Character in
Plato's Dialogues,* p. 43.

29. It should not be overlooked that Derrida always speaks of the singularity of the signature, as an origin (what I am calling here authority), as something that also must
demand its iterability or repetition. See "Signature, Event, Context" in *Margins of
Philosophy,* p. 328: "By definition, a written signature implies the actual or empiri-
cal nonpresence of the signer. But, it will be said, it also marks and retains his hav-
ing-been present in a past now, which will remain a future now, and therefore in a
now in general, in the transcendental form of nowness (maintenance). This general
maintenance is somehow inscribed, stapled to present punctuality, always evident
and always singular, in the form of the signature. This is the enigmatic originality of
every paraph. For the attachment to the source to occur, the absolute singularity of
an event of the signature and of a form of the signature must be retained: the pure

reproducibility of a pure event." See also Burke, "The Textual Estate: Plato and the Ethics of Signature," who draws out the ethical dimension of this elusive erasure of the origin in the signature as it pertains to the reading of Plato.

30. Foucault raises the same suspicion, although draws entirely different conclusions than those developed here: "To imagine writing as absence seems to be a simple repetition, in transcendental terms, of both the religious principle of an inalterable and yet never fulfilled tradition, and the aesthetic principle of the work's survival, its perpetuation beyond the author's death, and its enigmatic excess in relation to him." Foucault, "What Is an Author?" *Foucault Reader*, p. 105. Diskin Clay also sees the remarkable contrast between the author's absence and a reassertion of authorial position with regard to Plato: "The interest of present-day philosophy in making Plato its contemporary is a manifestation of the overwhelming authority of a philosopher who abjured authoritative modes of discourse but who, despite his failure to appear or to speak in any of his dialogues, has been recognized as the final authority for what his 'spokemen'—Socrates, the Eleatic Stranger, Timaeus, Critias, the Athenian Stranger—have to say." Clay, *Platonic Questions*, p. xii.

31. Mention is often made of Whitehead's remark in *Process and Reality* about the history of philosophy as only a footnote, but Heidegger is both more severe and yet more subtle, since he states that philosophy is metaphysics and metaphysics is Platonism. Heidegger, *Zur Sache des Denkens*, p. 61 and p. 63. For a thoughtful discussion of Whitehead's footnote imagery, see Blondell, p. 46.

32. Consider the way in which Derrida in his essay "Plato's Pharmacy" still finds himself able to speak for Plato and Plato's desire. Heidegger in his lectures on Parmenides says that "since Plato" it has been assumed that philosophers express their own thoughts. He is asking here whether it is appropriate to make such an assumption when reading the mythic and poetic discourse of Parmenides. But why can it be assumed when reading Plato? See my discussion of Heidegger's claim in "Reading Plato before Platonism (after Heidegger)." Also, this question of Plato's ownership is taken up by Nails, "Mouthpiece Schmouthpiece," in Press.

33. If we are to listen to Alcibiades, Socrates never means what he says: "his entire life is occupied with being ironic and playing games with people" (εἰρωνευόμενος δὲ καὶ παίζων πάντα τὸν βίον πρὸς τοὺς ἀνθρώπους διατελεῖ) (Sym. 216e).

34. See Hartland-Swann, "Plato as Poet: A Critical Interpretation," and Rossetti, "Where Philosophy and Literature Merge in the Platonic Dialogues."

35. See Hoffman, "Die literarische Voraussetzungen des Platonverständnisses," esp. p. 472. But see also Nancy, "Myth Interrupted," in *The Inoperative Community*, pp. 43–70. And Lacoue-Labarthe, "The Fable," in *The Subject of Philosophy*, pp. 1–13. Yet Detienne, *The Creation of Mythology*, whom Nancy enlists and adduces to support his subversive logic, does not let the difficulty infiltrate his reading of Plato's text. See also Gerard Naddaf's Translator's Introduction to Luc Brisson's study, which assembles the textual evidence for the sense of myth prior to Plato. Brisson, *Plato the Myth Maker*, pp. vii–liii.

36. Gadamer, following Heidegger, has raised this question in his reading of Platonic-Aristotelian philosophy in order to show how the εἶδος as a Platonic innovation bears upon Arisotle's twofold determination of nature (μόρφη and ὕλη) as it is articulated in his physics. See especially Phys. B1. See Gadamer, *The Idea of the Good in Platonic-Aristotelian Philosophy*, p. 21 et passim: "The task is to get back to the common ground upon which both Plato and Aristotle base their talk of the εἶδος." Gadamer, however, takes the Aristotelian appropriation of Platonic thought as a translation from metaphor to concept. But then the question arises concerning how there can be "metaphor" in Plato, if Aristotle marks the very passage of philosophy itself into the concept? As Derrida shows in "White Mythology," the concept of metaphor as philosopheme always remains caught up in the concept of the concept.

See Gasché's discussion in *The Tain of the Mirror: Derrida and the Philosophy of Reflection,* pp. 293–318. See also Kirby, "Aristotle on Metaphor." Thus, Gadamer's numerous remarks in this regard become highly provocative, precisely as he indicates a pre-Aristotelian Plato will always elude us: "All scientific philosophy is Aristotelianism insofar as it is conceptual work, and thus if one wants to interpret Plato's philosophy philosophically, one must necessarily interpret it via Aristotle. The historical realization that this will always be a projection cannot be made productive by trying to dissolve or avoid this projection. The firsthand discovery that Plato is more than what Aristotle and conceptual analysis can extract from him cannot, itself, be conveyed secondhand. It stands at the limit of all Plato interpretation." Gadamer, *Plato's Dialectical Ethics,* p. 8.

37. While it is certainly the case that a few others have been making this point already for a long time now, my emphasis falls upon something that I believe has not received sufficient emphasis, even by those who also begin with the difficulty of the operative metaphysical legacy that already asserts itself in the reading of Plato. It is precisely the question of the "placeless place" of the figure of Socrates in the Platonic text that allows for the most decisive interruption of the metaphysical reading of Plato. But see Sallis, *Being and Logos: Reading the Platonic Dialogues,* p. 7: "Either directly or indirectly the presentation of philosophical activity accomplished by the dialogues is mostly, if not entirely, a presentation of Socrates' practice. This is to say that in its most immediate form our first question is: Who is Socrates?" Nails, et passim, but esp. pp. 205–12, gives a concise account of some of the more prevalent ways of attempting to settle this question.

38. Diogenes Laertius 3.5: "Afterwards as he was about to compete with a tragedy he heard Socrates in front of the theater of Dionysus and then with these words burned his poetry, 'Come here, Hephaestus. Plato needs you.'" See Riginos, *Platonica: The Anecdotes Concerning the Life and Writings of Plato,* pp. 43–49.

39. See Patzer, "Die philosophische Bedeutung der Sokratesgestalt in den platonischen Dialogen." See also Kahn's citation and discussion of Patzer in Kahn, *Plato and the Socratic Dialogue,* p. 71.

40. And even in those dialogues where Socrates recedes into the background to let these other more fictional speakers take center stage—such as the unnamed and mysterious Eleatic Stranger, the wise Diotima, or the most astronomical Timaeus of Locri—it is clear that the original Socratic provocation still remains decisive for what comes to be said. The *Sophist, Statesman,* and *Timaeus* are dialogues thoroughly determined by the peculiar *receptivity* of Socrates and by the way in which the questions taken up are initiated by him in a distinctively Socratic way. The *Laws* might be seen here to offer an interesting counterexample. Still the question arises concerning the extent to which the *Laws* are to be taken *programmatically.*

41. This is one of consequences to be drawn from Nightingale, passim, but see pp. 193–95.

42. For a discussion of the ethical dimension of the tragic, as it is interpreted by Aristotle, see Schmidt, *On Germans and Other Greeks: Tragedy and Ethical Life,* pp. 46–72, esp. p. 60.

43. Benardete and Davis, *Aristotle—On Poetics,* p. 27, connect this passage to the passage in the *Phaedrus,* 271c–272b. I am indebted to this fine translation of the *Poetics.*

44. Aristotle uses Socrates to name the *hypokeimenon* that endures through change. See, for example, Met. 1007b.

45. According to Plutarch, that is. See Hadas, *Ancilla to Classical Reading,* p. 43.

46. In fact, Thucydides' critique of Herodotus parallels in a remarkable way Aristotle's admonishing of the poets. For a careful discussion of Thucydides over and against the inquiries of Herodotus, especially as it bears upon the so-called mythic dimension of historical inquiry, see Benardete, *Herodotean Inquiries,* pp. 29–30, 63. See p.

30: "From Thucydides' point of view, Herodotus sacrifices the advantage of fable without grounding his account on the literal truth."

47. Lacoue-Labarthe, *Typography: Mimesis, Philosophy, Politics,* p. 247.
48. This sense of propriety returns us to the question of metaphor, given the inaugurating Aristotelian determination of the concept of metaphor, as it relies on the proper name: a metaphor, Aristotle states, consists in giving a name that belongs to something else (Poetics 1457b9). Again, see Derrida's analysis in "White Mythology." But see Ricouer's challenge to this analysis as it relies upon this sense of propriety in *Rule of Metaphor,* pp. 284–94.
49. L 7, 344c.
50. This, of course, does not have to mean that what is not beautiful is already therefore ugly. In fact, I wish to show how the Platonic dialogues overturn this naive and simplistic opposition. The strangeness of Socrates has to do, in other words, with a beauty that belongs to his ugliness. I return to this question at the end of this study. See Sym. 201e–202a. Consider this tension as it raised in the *Theaetetus.* The "beauty" of Theaetetus emerges only through the thought of the incommensurable that exceeds a geometric knowledge of ratio or proportion. Theodorus, the geometer, is no portraitist, and thus is in no position to assess the beauty of Theaetetus.
51. The oft-cited passage is found in Aristotle's *Poetics* at 1447b9–13.
52. Aristotle is always talking about the written Socrates. Tarrant, p. 48. Kahn, pp. 83–87, and Vlastos, *Socrates: Ironist and Moral Philosopher,* pp. 97–98, emphasize that others had written Socratic dialogues and this informs Aristotle's Socrates; they do this as a way to give Plato's text back to him, as his own work. For a discussion of the mimetic interpretation of Plato as it was referred to in antiquity and as it can inform a reading of the dialogues, see Reich, *Der Mimus,* pp. 354–413.
53. Deleuze's reading might be worth considering here in *The Logic of Sense,* "Plato and the Simulacrum," pp. 253–65, esp. 256: "Was it not Plato himself who pointed out the direction for the reversal of Platonism?"
54. Phaedo 99e–100a.
55. Consider Cicero's remark (On the Orator 3.60), cited and discussed by Clay, p. xi: "Plato has made his genius and varied conversations immortal to posterity in his own writings."
56. My point here is that the dialogues as they are written by Plato would be unthinkable without the fact of Socrates' death. And it is precisely the fact that we listen to Socrates as members of *Plato's* audience that bears upon the words of Socrates as they bear upon his fate. Diskin Clay has developed this sense of Platonic irony, as it exceeds Socratic irony, by fruitfully comparing it to the irony found in the tragedies. See Clay, pp. 33–40.
57. See Chapter 6, below.

2. Socrates and the Retreat of Nature

1. This is admittedly a strange claim. Consider, for example, the self-evidence in the assertion made by Nightingale, p. 14: "The discipline of philosophy emerged at a certain moment in history. It was not born, like a natural organism. Rather, it was an artificial construct that had to be invented and legitimized as a new and unique cultural practice."
2. This is the first thesis of Vlastos, pp. 47–48. The difference between the Socrates of the early dialogues and the Socrates of the later middle dialogues hangs, according to Vlastos, on the way in which the early Socrates is exclusively a "moral philosopher" and thus does not engage in metaphysics, epistemology, philosophy

of science, education, language, art. The Socrates one finds in the later dialogues has the "whole encyclopedia of philosophical science" as his domain.

3. As Strauss in *Socrates and Aristophanes*, p. 4, et passim, does, for example.

4. John Sallis, *Force of Imagination: The Sense of the Elemental*, p. 24, speaks about a turn to "wild nature" in the context of the second sailing of Socrates, which he articulates without reference to this Socratic relation to the earth and sky. But in an unpublished paper Sallis develops a reading of the *Phaedo* around the figure of Socrates with his feet planted firmly on the earth: "Speaking of the Earth: Figures of Transport in Plato's *Phaedo.*" The paper was delivered at the meeting of the Ancient Philosophy Society as a satellite group for the Society for Phenomenology and Existential Philosophy (at the Pennsylvania State University, 2002). See also Langiulli, "On the Location of Socrates' Feet; or, the Immanence of Transcendence."

5. For attempts to resolve this enigma, see, for example, Beardslee, "The Use of φύσις in Fifth-Century Greek Literature"; Hardy, *Der Begriff der Physis in der Griechischen Philosophie;* Patzer, *Physis: Grundlegung zu einer Geschichte des Wortes;* Lovejoy, *The Meaning of* φύσις *in the Greek Physiologers.*

6. In his famous Munich Lectures Schelling states that Hegel's philosophy remains a mere episode, because it remains merely negative, which is to say, determined thoroughly by the paradigm *speculative* thinking or reflection. Schelling, *Zur Geschichte der Neueren Philosophie*, pp. 109–10. I have tried to question this speculative legacy in Arisotle's *nous noeton* as it asserts itself in Hegel's sense of history's completion. See Warnek, "Once More for the First Time . . . : Aristotle and Hegel in the Logic of History."

7. This is starting point, for example, of Merleau-Ponty's lectures on nature that he gave at the Collège de France from 1956 to 1960.

8. Sallis, *Chorology*, p. 54.

9. Phys. A2, 184b27–185a1: "Now to examine if being is one and motionless is not to be examining nature."

10. Walter Brogan's article "Is Aristotle a Metaphysician?" develops this point through a reading of Heidegger's interpretation of Aristotle.

11. See Kahn's commentary in *The Art and Thought of Heraclitus*, p. 105. See also Gadamer, "Heraclitus Studies."

12. Phys. B1, 193a2–6.

13. Θαλῆς δὲ πρῶτος παραδέτοται τὴν περὶ φύσεως ἱστορίαν τοῖς ῞Ελλησιν ἐκφῆναι, πολλῶν μὲν καὶ ἄλλων προγεγονότων, ὡς καὶ τῷ καὶ τῷ Θεωφράστῳ δοκεῖ, αὐτὸς δὲ πολὺ διενεγκὼν ἐκείνων, ὡς ἀποκρύψαι πάντας τοὺς πρὸ αὐτοῦ. Simplicius, *Commentaria in Aristotelum Graeca*, vol. 9, ed. Herman Diels (Berlin, 1882), p. 23. Cited in Reale, *From the Origins to Socrates: A History of Ancient Philosophy*, p. 36.

14. I am suggesting that the aporetic interruptions as they appear in the dialogues consistently enact this same covering over. I am claiming that the appearing of what is original requires such a moment of failure, takes place only in the aporetic refutation that confirms that the original is already lost, and that as lost it is interrupting the assumptions that previously prevailed, which were sustained by it and yet which kept it hidden. For this reason, such interruptive failures, as they pervade the dialogues, cannot be regarded as setbacks or as circuitous detours, even if their disclosure is such that it cannot be transmitted directly and explicitly through doctrinaire formulations. As I take it, this is the sense of the phrase that is repeated throughout the Platonic dialogues, and raised often as an injunction, namely, that it is necessary to begin *again,* to repeat the beginning, to proceed ἐξ ἀρχῆς, which is to say, *from* it. To list only some notable examples: Phaedo 59c, 207c, and throughout; Apol. 19a; Rep. 348b, 366e, 369c, 433a, 450a, 490c, 502e; Statesman 268d, cf. 267a; Euth. 11b, 15c; Theaet. 164c, 179e, 187b, 200d; Sym. 174a, 223c; Charm. 167b; Laches 198a; Crito. 119c; Gorg. 488b, 492b.

15. When, in a famous passage (Met. A2 982b11–28), Aristotle speaks of the origin of philosophy, he will also point to myth. Both begin in ignorance and aporia, by wondering (διὰ τὸ θαυμάζειν): "whence a lover of myth, too, is in a sense a philosopher, for a myth is composed of wonders." Whether one does so philosophically or philomythically, one turns to the "generation of all things" (γένεσις τοῦ παντός) in wonder, and only by being freed from the "necessities" of life. Or rather, the lover of myth is already a philosopher both because the wonder of each cannot be subordinated to any production—it is "for its own sake"—and because in that wonder both turn to the same matter. The assertion of the common origin of myth and philosophy demands, then, the inevitable translation of myth into philosophy, because the turn to φύσις from out of myth is the further liberation of an originally free movement. The turn to φύσις, as the upsurge of philosophy, continues the movement of myth as it also demythologizes that movement. Thus, the mythic legacy itself that lingered and even prevailed in all early engagements with φύσις can be read (as it indeed it has been read) as a testimony to this allegorizing, demythologizing progression. Thales, as the "first" to turn to φύσις, is also reported to have said that "all things are full of gods." Diels-Kranz, 11A22; de an A5, 4111a7; Laws, X, 899b. And Xenophanes, for example, himself regarded by antiquity as a poet, and described in Plato's *Sophist* as one who bears and perpetuates a *mythical* tradition (Soph. 242d), clears his way to φύσις by reinterpreting or reappropriating the divine and the human relation to the divine. See Fr. 11, 14, 15, 16. Xenophanes, remarkably, entertains cattle and horses with *hands,* as if to say that this is what is distinctly human. But it is worth noting that contemporary scholarship remains divided on the question of where to situate the inquiry of Xenophanes. The question goes back at least to Simplicius and Theophrastus, who focus upon the question whether Xenophanes is to be understood as a "physicist" or a "theologian." For our purposes, what is most significant is the fact that this question is posed at all, since it takes for granted the distinction between the regions designated by theology and physics. What must first be considered is how the inquiry into φύσις would require destroying the anthropomorphic interpretation of the divine. It becomes possible to reinterpret the divine by confronting the question of the place of human life within φύσις as a whole, and it is this project that dominates Aristotelian questioning. Both φύσις and the divine come to be considered precisely as they impose limits on human life.

16. Met. A3 983b6.

17. Met. A3 983b20.

18. Diels-Kranz, 11A22; de an A5, 4111a7; Laws X, 899b.

19. Met. A3 983b27–984a3.

20. Met. B4 1000a9–19.

21. See Met. Λ8 1074b1–14.

22. Again, this awakens a suspicion of myth as it is already anticipated in the third book of the *Republic*. The seductive power of myth is connected to the fact that the poets—in this case, primarily Homer—speak so as to make the listener forget it is they who speak; they speak as if they were another, as if their voice came from somewhere else.

23. "Socrates autem primus philosophiam devocavit de caelo et in uribus conlocavit et in domus etiam introduxit et coegit de vita et moribus rebusque bonis et malis quaerere." Cicero *Tusc. Disp.* v. 4, 10.

24. Lives, II, 21. Cf. III, 56.

25. Mem. I.i.11–16.

26. See, for example, Mem. IV.vii.5–6.

27. Mem. I.i.12

28. Met. M4, 1078b17–20.

29. See Gigon, *Mus. Helv.* 1959, p. 192.
30. The word is badly translated as "induction." According to Heidegger, ἐπαγωγή has to be thought as the opening up of the being of beings in a productive *Entwurf,* and thus involves a decisive insight arising through a turn away from beings.
31. See also *De partibus animalium* 642a28: "in Socrates' time an advance was made as to the method, but the study of φύσις was given up, and philosophers turned their attention to practical goodness and political science."
32. Our age—taking itself to be more historically minded—will tend to see any statement that gives credit to a single individual for such monumental shifts in history as an oversimplification of an event that has to be considered along many lines. Modern scholars and classicists, when considering the question of the emergence of Socratic-Platonic inquiry, have become much more willing, for example, to consider the contributions made by the sophistic and Pythagorean traditions and the environment that was created by the "political" events of the time. Yet the conviction that something decisive erupts with Socrates is still present. See Guthrie, *Socrates,* pp. 97–105. Jaeger, *Paideia II,* pp. 23, 31. Strauss, *City and Man,* p. 13. Also Sallis, *Being and Logos,* p. 36 ff. Also Guthrie, *The Greeks and Their Gods,* where he speaks of sophistry in the context of the rise of a "moral relativism" bound to "naturalism." Nestle, *Vom Mythos zum Logos: Die Selbstentfaltung des Griechischen Denkens von Homer bis auf die Sophistik und Sokrates,* speaks of the "new epoch" introduced by Socrates, pp. 529 ff., 539.
33. "*der Geist der Welt fängt hier, mit Sokrates, eine Umkehr an.*" Hegel, *Werke* 18, p. 468. Hegel affirms the traditional interpretation of Socratic inquiry, relying upon the language of regional inquiry, while also repeating the Aristotelian characterization of the matter or concern of Socratic inquiry: the ethical. But the Socratic relation to the "universal" remains one-sided, precisely because it has yet to subsume "nature" into the ethical. Ethics here remains subjective; it remains "*Moralität,*" not yet "*Sittlichkeit.*" But while Socrates does not yet establish the systematic philosophy that involves both a return to nature and, precisely therefore, the ethical in a higher sense, he does prepare the way for it in Plato and Aristotle. Hegel also repeats Aristotle's assessment in that he finds in Socrates a distinctive advance in the dialectic and thus indicates here a critical moment in the development or becoming of science and system: "Socrates took up the good at first only in the particular sense of the practical: What is substantial to me for action, that is what I am concerned with. Plato and Aristotle took the good in a higher sense: it is the universal, not only for me. This is only *one* form or mode of the idea, the idea for the will. [Another version adds: ". . . which nevertheless is only one mode of the substantial idea; the universal is not only for me, but also, as an end existent in and for itself, the principle of the philosophy of nature, and in this higher sense it was taken by Plato and Aristotle."] Of Socrates it is thus said, in the older histories of philosophy, that his main distinction was having added ethics as a new concept to philosophy, which formerly only took nature into consideration." *HW 18,* 144; *Lectures on the History of Philosophy,* vol. 1, p. 387.
34. Diogenes Laertius, III, 56. Loeb Library, vol. 1, p. 327.
35. My emphasis. Schleiermacher, *Introductions to the Dialogues of Plato,* p. 7.
36. Schleiermacher, p. 19.
37. Sextus Empiricus refers to Aristotle's finding dialectic already in Zeno and others. There is also evidence that Heraclitus would stand as an exception to this account of the genesis of philosophy. Sextus Empiricus states that Heraclitus, while he is to be included among the exponents of the physical orientation in philosophy, also confronts us with "the question whether he was not merely a physicist but ethical philosopher as well" (I, 7). See also DK. Diodotos, another stoic, states that Heraclitus was not concerned with φύσις at all, but rather the *politeia,* the question of

how the city is constituted. But here the question is not whether this is an "accurate" conception of Heraclitus, but rather first of all how such a confusion or controversy concerning the difference between φύσις and politeia can arise. See Gadamer's essay, "Heraclitus Studies."

38. *Against the Logicians,* I, 16. Loeb Library, Sextus Empiricus, vol. 2, pp. 8–9.
39. *Against the Logicians,* I, 8–10. Loeb Library, Sextus Empiricus, vol. 2, p. 7.
40. This question, too, begins with Aristotle, who, for example, finds it necessary to identify the Athenian stranger as Socrates (Politics 1265a12). For a defense of Aristotle's interpretation, see Strauss, *What Is Political Philosophy?* p. 31 ff. The difficulty of this paradox is in part due to the way in which the ethical turn of Socrates finds its confirmation by adducing nothing other than the dialogues, or at least certain dialogues, as evidence. The same group of texts are supposed to yield both the pre-Platonic advance of Socrates and what is held to be the more comprehensive project of Plato. In this way it becomes important to ask about the chronology of the dialogues and to consider the extent to which the earlier dialogues, such as the *Apology of Socrates,* can be relied upon as "historical documents," as historically accurate portrayals of Socrates, and to what extent later dialogues can be read as departures from Socratic doctrine. To the extent that Socrates speaks in the later dialogues, one wants to know whether Plato imposes upon him his own philosophical project. It then also becomes important to know whether the main protagonists of the later dialogues, such as the Eleatic Stranger, Timaeus, or the Athenian Stranger, are speaking directly for Plato, and maybe even against Socrates.
41. In *The Idea of the Good in Platonic-Aristotelian Philosophy,* Gadamer argues that in this way Aristotle's *Physics,* too, must be taken as the extension or the execution of the basic Platonic project, insofar as that project is to be understood most basically as the turn to dialectic or as the "flight into the speeches."

3. The Purest Thinker of the West and the Older Accusations in the *Apology*

1. Heidegger, *Was Heisst Denken?* p. 52. The German text reads: "Sind wir auf das Sichentzeihende bezogen, dann sind wir auf dem Zug in das Sichentzeihende, in die rätselvolle und darum wandelbar Nähe seines Anspruchs. Wenn ein Mensch eigens auf diesem Zug ist, dann denkt er, mag er noch so weit von dem Sichentzeihende entfernt sein, mag der Entzug wie immer auch verschleiert bleiben. Sokrates hat zeit seines Lebens, bis in seinen Tod hinein, nichts anderes getan, als sich in den Zugwind dieses Zuges zu stellen und darin sich zu halten. Darum ist er der reinste Denker des Abendlandes. Deshalb hat er nichts geschrieben. Denn wer aus dem Denken zu schreiben beginnt, muß unweigerlich den Menschen gleichen, die vor allzu starkem Zugwind in den Windschatten flüchten. Es bleibt das Geheimnis einer noch verborgenen Geschichte, daß alle Denker des Abendlandes nach Sokrates, unbeschadet ihrer Größe, solche Flüchtlinge sein mußten. Das Denken ging in die Literatur ein."
2. But see the remarkable early statement by Heidegger, *Der Grundbegriffe der antiken Philosophie,* pp. 92–93: "Sokrates war nicht Ethiker und verschmähte die Naturphilosophie, sondern ihm ging es um das *Verständnis des Wissens und Handelns des Daseins überhaupt.* Ebensowenig auf bestimmte Gebiete der Naturerkenntnis wie auf bestimmte inhaltliche ethische Sätze oder gar auf besonderes Wertsystem mit besonderer Wertrangordnung. Sokrates dachte viel zu radikal, als daß er sich auf eine solche Zufälligkeit festgelegt hätte: Theoretiker, Praktiker, Dialektiker, Ethiker, Prophet, Philosoph, religiöse Persönlichkeit. Sokrates wird deutlich aus der Arbeit von Plato und Aristoteles und dem Vergleich ihrer philosophischen Problematik

gegenüber der vorangegangenen Philosophie viel mehr, als wenn wir versuchen, von ihm ein Bild zusammenzubauen."

3. Heidegger speaks of Socrates as a soldier. Clay, *Platonic Questions,* pp. 50–59, demonstrates how the Platonic Socrates appropriates and transforms the paradigm of the 'hero.' See also Eisner, "Socrates as Hero."

4. For a helpful discussion of the nuanced sense of this word in antiquity, including its appearance in Plato's and Aristotle's texts, see Anastasiadis, "Idealized ΣΧΟΛΗ and Disdain for Work: Aspects of Philosophy and Politics in Ancient Democracy."

5. See, however, that Heidegger's apparent privileging of speech over writing cannot be taken simplistically, as he complicates this relation. At the beginning of his "Letter on Humanism," he apparently privileges the spoken word that takes place in conversation. But he then offers a subtle addendum in which distinctive advantages belonging to writing are mentioned. Heidegger, "Brief über den Humanismus," *Wegmarken,* p. 147: "Aber das Schriftliche bietet andererseits den heilsamen Zwang zur bedachtsamen sprachlichen Fassung."

6. See the essays collected in Benson, *Essays on the Philosophy of Socrates.*

7. Schleiermacher, *Introductions to the Dialogues of Plato,* p. 134.

8. See Kahn, "Why Did Plato Write Socratic Dialogues?" pp. 37, 47.

9. For more recent and more skeptical views on this point, see Morrison, "On the Alleged Historical Reliability of Plato's *Apology,*" and Prior, "The Historicity of Plato's *Apology.*" For yet another alternative, see Seeskin, "Is the *Apology of Socrates* a Parody?"

10. See Gadamer, "Plato als Porträtist," and Figal, *Sokrates,* pp. 16–21.

11. The origins of this account go back to Hermann, *Geschichte und System der Platonischen Philosophie.* See also Raeder, *Platons Philosophische Entwicklung,* and Charles Kahn's discussion of this history, *Plato and the Socratic Dialogue,* pp. 42–48. For succinct criticisms of the project of reconstructing a Platonic chronology, see Theslef, "Platonic Chronology," and Howland, "Re-reading Plato: The Problem of Platonic Chronology." Nails, *Agora, Academy, and the Conduct of Philosophy,* pp. 53–68, takes the chronology controversy very seriously but wishes to delimit its philosophical importance. See also her critical assessment of Theslef's contribution, pp. 115–35.

12. "But in different sets of dialogues he pursues philosophies so different that they could not have been depicted as cohabiting the same brain throughout unless it had been the brain of a schizophrenic." Vlastos, p. 46.

13. See Brickhouse and Smith on this question, "The Origin of Socrates' Mission."

14. Diskin Clay rightly points out how Socrates in cross-examining Meletus conducts a "perfect Socratic interrogation," although he too says that the *Apology* is "not strictly a dialogue." Clay, pp. 41, 46. Burnyeat, "The Impiety of Socrates," states that the *Apology* is "decidedly not a dialogue," yet he also bases his reading on the premise that the text challenges us to make a judgment concerning Socrates.

15. See, for example, Reeve, *Socrates in the "Apology,"* pp. 15–19, who cites Zeller, *Socrates and the Socratic Schools,* p. 175, and Lacey, "Our Knowledge of Socrates," p. 27, and who also turns to the *Phaedo* as a way to corroborate this kind of interpretation. The question for Reeve in this context leads to a consideration of the Socrates portrayed in Aristophanes' *Clouds.*

16. Peter Ahrensdorf proposes that we find these charges explicitly articulated in the *Phaedo.* See Ahrensdorf, *The Death of Socrates and the Life of Philosophy: An Interpretation of Plato's "Phaedo,"* p. 2 et passim.

17. This same reversal is carried out in the *Republic* as Adeimantus challenges Socrates to take up the fact of philosophy, its ἔργον as opposed to its "mere" λόγος. This factical actuality of the "failure" of philosphy in the city demands, according to Socrates, that an account be given of the city in its reception of a philosophical nature. Before pre-

senting the image of the ship, Socrates states: "So hard is the condition suffered by the most decent men with respect to the cities that there is no single other condition like it." Rep. 488a. On this point in the *Apology*, see Burnyeat, p. 12: "Yes, Socrates was guilty as charged of not believing in the traditional gods and introducing new divinities. But what is shown by the fact that so good a man as Socrates was guilty of impiety under Athenian law? The impiety of Athenian religion."

18. Howland, *The Paradox of Political Philosophy*, makes this the starting point for his reading of the *Apology*, pp. 23–38, and even the dialogues as a whole.

19. See Brann, "The Offense of Socrates: Apology," in *The Music of the Republic*, p. 44.

20. The Greek here suggests a word play: ὥσπερ μειρακίῳ πλάττοντι λόγους. To fabricate means to "Platonize" speech? Here, at the beginning of the *Apology*, Socrates speaks of his way of speaking as a kind of improvisation, over and against the premeditated and constructed speech that relies on style and fancy turns of phrase to achieve its effect. In the *Symposium* Socrates makes the same contrast between the beautiful speech of Agathon and his own "shameful" speech that only speaks the truth: "do you want to hear the truth spoken about love, with the turns and the ordering of the phrases presented in whatever manner they happen to emerge?" (Sym. 199b). The irony here, of course, is the remarkable beauty of this self-deprecating speech as it is translated into the logographic necessity of Platonic writing.

21. See, however, Meletus's appeal to the "laws" in his initial response to the Socratic question of who it is, exactly, that is able to improve the youth of Athens (Apol. 24e).

22. Again, this is reflected in the response of Meletus, when he claims that Socrates takes the sun and moon to be not gods but stone and earth (Apol. 26d).

23. In the *Nicomachean Ethics,* Aristotle speaks of "defending a thesis" in decidedly ethical terms. Such an action, even if it leads to great suffering, may still preserve the human good. It is difficult to read this passage and not think of Socrates, as if Aristotle is also suggesting that Socratic practice as a whole, his life as deed, is itself the extension of a single great hypothesis, the hypothesis through which Socrates can also be said to be "happy" (Nic. Ethics 1095b32–1096a2).

24. See Aristotle's criticism of the way the gods are put to work for the city, at the end of *Nicomachean Ethics* VI. "This would be like someone saying that the political commands the gods because it gives orders about all things in the city." Nic. Ethics 1145a10–11. See also Euripides' *Bacchae;* Cadmus tells Pentheus to act as if he believes, to say the god exists even if it is a lie. "Even if Dionysus is not a god, as you claim, persuade yourself that he is. The lie is a noble one" (Bacchae 333–35).

25. Strauss, p. 56.

26. Sallis, *Being and Logos,* p. 26.

27. Again, ibid., 7.

28. See Langiulli.

------

4. The Good, the Bad, and the Ugly

1. Aristotle's account of sophistic argumentation is in *Refutations of the Sophists,* 173a7–18. For an account of the historical emergence of the opposition, see the study by Heinimann, *Nomos und Physis.* See especially Kerferd's discussion, "The Nomos-Physis Controversy," in *The Sophistic Movement.*

2. See Gorg. 449b, 461d. But Socrates himself at times finds it necessary to speak at length and even remarks upon his own having done so, for example, at 465e–466a.

3. One frequently sees this assumption guiding the interpretation. See, for example, "In Defence of Reason: Plato's Gorgias," in Wardy, *The Birth of Rhetoric: Gorgias, Plato and Their Successors,* pp. 52–85, esp. pp. 74–77. Also, McComiskey, "Disassembling

Plato's Critique of Rhetoric in the *Gorgias* (447a–466a)," in *Gorgias and the New Sophistic Rhetoric,* pp. 17–31.

4. Herodotus 1.6–15.

5. Apol. 26d; Phaedr. 270a; Phaedo 72c, 97b–d; Crat. 400a, 409a, 413c.

6. Richard McKim, "Shame and Truth in Plato's *Gorgias,*" makes this very point when he concludes that what is persuasive about the dialogue is that those who are refuted discover that their shame is grounded in a kind of "honesty" with regard to oneself and what one takes to be harmful.

7. Jeffrey Turner, "Atopia in Plato's *Gorgias,*" makes the point that this contradictory character of human desire finds itself expressed by the dialogue itself in its way of leaving its questions unresolved.

8. For a discussion of the limits of this characterization, see Allen, "The Socratic Paradox."

9. For a discussion that begins with this passage, see Edmonds, "Socrates the Beautiful: Role Reversal and Midwifery in Plato's *Symposium.*"

10. At times, Socrates, the exception, is spoken of as a form of mockery. See Sym. 173d.

11. See White, "The Good in Plato's *Gorgias,*" for an account of the good in the dialogue as it relates to a natural harmony.

12. See in this context Cholbi, "Dialectical Refutation as a Paradigm of Socratic Punishment," who contrasts the Socratic sense of just punishment with the punishment of Socrates by the Athenian court. See also Berman, "How Polus Was Refuted: Reconsidering Plato's *Gorgias* 474c–475c," and Johnson, "Socrates' Encounter with Polus in the Plato's *Gorgias.*"

13. See Klein's remarks on this passage, where he insists that this phrase should be distanced from the modern sense of natural law. Klein, *Lectures and Essays,* pp. 232–33. Dodds makes the same point. See Dodds, *Plato's Gorgias,* p. 268. See also Fussi, "Callicles' Examples of νόμος τῆς φύσεως in Plato's *Gorgias,*" who develops the interpretation of the statement by considering it as it emerges in the refutation of rhetorical speech. For a reading that elaborates the complexity of the character of Callicles and locates his failure in the unwillingness I am taking up here, see Stauffer, "Socrates and Callicles: A Reading of Plato's *Gorgias.*"

14. For an account of how the concluding myth repeats the movement of the dialogue, see Kaatman, "The Role of the Myth in Plato's *Gorgias,*" and Fussi, "The Myth of the Last Judgment in the *Gorgias.*"

5. Silenic Wisdom in the *Apology* and *Phaedo*

1. The *Gorgias* and the *Phaedrus* thus do not offer opposite views on rhetoric. Heidegger makes the questionable claim that one sees in the *Phaedrus* the influence of the young Aristotle and that the *Gorgias* gives us the properly Platonic conception of rhetoric as the production of convictions. The development of rhetoric from Plato to Aristotle is taken up in *Platon: Sophistes,* pp. 308–10, 337–39. Rhetoric is recognized as a legitimate *art* only first by Aristotle, something that Plato did not achieve, because Aristotle is able to think the logos in its everydayness. Aristotle's advance, and his influence upon Plato, is that the *logos* is no longer limited to the predicative, scientific, or *apophantic* logos. But this claim is possible only if one disregards the *persuasive* movement of Socratic speech as it seeks to refute even itself. I shall return to this question of the self-relation at issue in persuasion in chapter 7 in the reading of the *Phaedrus.* See Lewis, "Refutative Rhetoric as True Rhetoric in the *Gorgias,*" who argues that the *Gorgias* and the *Phaedrus* are both attempting to distinguish authentic rhetoric from a less philosophical sense of rhetoric.

2. This is evident, for example, at Gorg. 489e. But Thrasymachus's view of Socrates in Book I of the *Republic* is the most blatant example of this interpretation, in which irony is taken to be merely a way to hide what one knows (Rep. 337a). It is telling also that Thrasymachus speaks of this irony as a wisdom or σοφία (Rep. 338b). Socratic ignorance is not thought to lie in nature's refusal but is taken instead as a mere ploy. Thrasymachus also returns Socratic refutation to a love of honor, because he believes that it is easier to ask than to answer (Rep. 336c–d). Thus, just as in *Gorgias,* the disagreement over justice is enacted through the demonstration of an insuperable difference between two different ways of comporting oneself in speech.

3. For an account of tragic poetry that begins with this assumption, compare Schelling, *System of Transcendental Idealism,* pp. 219–36, and especially pp. 231–32: "The view of nature, which the philosopher frames artificially, is for art the original and natural one. What we speak of as nature is a poem lying pent in mysterious and wonderful script."

4. Strauss, p. 60: "one cannot take seriously enough the law of logographic necessity. Nothing is accidental in a Platonic dialogue; everything is necessary at the place where it occurs. Everything which would be accidental outside the dialogue becomes meaningful within the dialogue. In all actual conversations chance plays a considerable role: all Platonic dialogues are radically fictitious. The Platonic dialogue is based on a fundamental falsehood, a beautiful or beautifying falsehood, *viz.* on the denial of chance." Compare this to Diskin Clay's consideration of "logographic necessity" as it refers us to nature's purpose, especially as it is spoken of aphoristically by Aristotle. Clay, *Platonic Questions,* pp. 10, 110–12.

5. This point only confirms that all talk of a Platonic "fiction" returns us to the fundamental structure of Platonism. Every fiction is taken as it emerges from the noetic vision into the truth and is structurally bound to this other. Tim. 27d–28a: "Now then, in my opinion, one must first distinguish the following. What is it that always *is* and has no becoming; and what is it that comes to be and never *is*? Now the one is grasped by intellection accompanied by speech, since it's always in the same condition; but the other in its turn is opined by opinion accompanied by irrational sensation, since it comes to be and perishes and never genuinely is. Again, everything that comes to be, of necessity comes to be by some cause; for apart from a cause, it's impossible for anything to have come to be." (I have slightly modified Kalkavage's translation.) For a discussion of this decisive passage, see Sallis, *Chorology,* pp. 46–50.

6. Here one obviously can look to the *Timaeus* for an example of this interruptive disclosure, as the purely noetic movement recoils on itself. In the *Timaeus,* one sees this take place as Timaeus finds it necessary to make another beginning through a turn to another kind of "errant" causality. Sallis, *Chorology,* p. 90ff. But other dialogues, if read with this sense of interruptive disclosure in view, perform exactly the same operation. For example, the *Republic* is marked throughout by such interruptions that alter the anticipated progression of the dialogue. Many times these transformative moments even go unaddressed as such.

7. One might think here of Herodotus's account of Solon's response to Croesus. But the questionable possibility of the "happy tyrant," as it is modulated through the necessity of mortality, comes up in the *Republic* and, as we have seen, is also in play in the *Gorgias.* Listen to what the chorus says at the very end of Sophocles' OT: "one should never call a mortal happy while he still waits to see his final day, until he passes life's ultimate limit free from misery."

8. Nic. Ethics 1100a10ff.

9. I address this question more thoroughly in chapter 6. But see the careful studies by Kube, *TEXNH und APETH: Sophistisches und Platonisches Tugendwissen,* and Roochnik, *Of Art and Wisdom: Plato's Understanding of Techne.*

10. See Heidegger, *Einführung in die Metaphysik,* pp. 11–14 and 138–39.

11. In addition to the story of his second sailing, as it is told in the *Phaedo,* the youthful conversation with the wise Diotima and the complex dialectical interrogation the young Socrates undergoes in the *Parmenides* also offer obvious opportunities to take up this question. For a discussion that considers this question of the genesis of Socrates through a reading of the passage recounting his experience with women, see also Blair, "Women: The Unrecognized Teachers of the Platonic Socrates." For another account of the legacy of the feminine in the *Symposium,* see also Saxenhouse, *Fear of Diversity,* pp. 173–84. Cavarero, *In Spite of Plato,* approaches the role of women in the dialogues as they undermine the pretense of the philosopher.

12. Timaeus confronts this moment directly as his speech confronts the necessity of a "third kind," the necessity even of necessity itself as it strangely precedes the purely noetic cosmogony he first presents. On the way χώρα displaces Platonistic metaphysics, see Sallis, *Chorology,* esp. p. 99. See also Derrida's essay "Khora" in Derrida, *On the Name.*

13. See Sallis, *Being and Logos,* pp. 46–49.

14. The disturbing effects of this question can be taken as the very starting point for the entire *Republic.* Polemarchus interrupts the *ascent* of Socrates in precisely this way: ἢ καὶ δύναισθ' ἄν, ἦ δ' ὅς, πεῖσαι μὴ ἀκούοντας (Rep. 327c). But this interruption of the ascent confirms that Socrates is still making his way down, already returning to a dialogical doubling.

15. Contrast this claim with the interpretation of Brickhouse and Smith.

16. We shall see in the next chapter that this naive disjunction between knowledge and ignorance, as it is proposed by Meno, also refuses nature's doubling.

17. See chapter 1.

18. Here, of course, one has to mention the *Theaetetus.* I return to this dialogue in chapter 8.

19. For a discussion of Evenus's appearance in the Phaedo, see Ebert, "Why Is Evenus Called a Philosopher at Phaedo 61c?"

20. For a discussion of the sense of this phrase, see Dorter, *Plato's* Phaedo: *An Interpretation,* pp. 193–203.

21. Naas, "Philosophy Bound: The Fate of the Promethean Socrates," deals with this same question of a Socratic temporality, but through a reading that takes the *Protagoras* as its starting point and through a connection between Socrates and the mythic tragic figure of Prometheus.

22. For a reading of the dream in the dialogue that proceeds based upon very different assumptions, but that in the end draws many of the same conclusions that I am drawing, see Roochnik, "The Deathbed Dream of Reason: Socrates' Dream in the *Phaedo.*" The dream is taken to challenge in a healthy way the exaggerated expectations of the project of a pure philosophy by returning it to the necessity of myth.

23. See Klein's essay "Plato's *Phaedo,*" in *Lectures and Essays,* pp. 375–93.

24. Calasso makes this very point. See *The Marriage of Cadmus and Harmony,* p. 19.

25. Scholars have debated ad nauseam the "adequacy" of the so-called proofs while largely ignoring the question of what this failure reveals. I am claiming that the breakdown of eidetic knowledge, as it is exhibited in the dialogue, displays and confirms nature's concealment in speech and in the task of self-knowledge. For other readings that also emphasize the radically disclosive character of this failure, see Bolotin, "The Life of Philosophy and the Immortality of the Soul"; Burger, *The* Phaedo: *A Platonic Labyrinth*; Gadamer, "The Proofs of Immortality in Plato's *Phaedo,*" in *Dialogue and Dialectic: Eight Hermeneutical Studies on Plato;* Roochnik, "The Deathbed Dream of Reason"; Ahrensdorf, *The Death of Socrates and the Life of Philosophy;* Ausland, "On Reading Plato Mimetically"; Dorter, "The Dramatic Aspect of Plato's *Phaedo,*" and *Plato's* Phaedo: An Interpretation;

Madison, "Have We Been Careless with Socrates' Last Words? A Rereading of the *Phaedo.*" See also Prufer, "The Dramatic Form of Phaedo."

26. One finds the clearest account of this "wisdom" at *Oedipus at Colonus,* 1224–28. But it also appears in various guises elsewhere. Consider again the very end of OT (1528–30): "one should never call a mortal happy while he still waits to see his final day, until he passes life's ultimate limit free from misery" (ὥστε θνητὸν ὄντα κείνην τὴν τελευταίαν ἰδεῖν ἡμέραν ἐπισκοποῦντα μηδέν' ὀλβίζειν, πρὶν ἂν τέρμα τοῦ βίου περάσῃ μηδὲν ἀλγεινὸν παθών).

27. "die fragwürdigste Erscheinung des Altertums." *Die Geburt der Tragödie:* §13, 90. Nietzsche also speaks of Socrates as a monstrosity: "Monstrosität per defectum!"

28. Hegel, *Werke* 18, p. 447: "Sein Schicksal ist nicht bloß sein persönliches individuell romantisches Schicksal, sondern ist die Tragödie Athens, die Tragödie Griechenlands, die darin aufgeführt wird, in ihm zur Vorstellung kommt."

29. Nietzsche, p. 34. See also Lacan's mention of this "wisdom." Lacan, p. 250.

30. See Klein's "Plato's *Phaedo,*" p. 378.

6. Teiresias in Athens

1. "We shall have clear knowledge of this when, before we investigate how it comes to be present in humans, we first try to find out what ἀρετή in itself is. But now the time has come for me to go" (100b). I consulted the translation by Grube (Indianapolis: Hackett Publishing, 1976). But it has also been necessary to depart from this translation at many points.

2. See Rep. 506c.

3. Others have thematically developed such an interpretive approach to the dialogues, as protreptic philosophical dramas that necessarily involve the reader: most notably, Schleiermacher, Gadamer, Strauss, Klein, Benardete, Sallis.

4. It is worth noting how the question of the φύσις of Socrates is raised here in this much-discussed passage. The Socratic dismissal of stories that is thought to be voiced here is clearly ironic, and is much more the dismissal of the project of *allegoresis,* of the demythologizing interpretive project that already assumes and promotes a certain highly restricted relation to φύσις and, it must be emphasized, to that φύσις as divine. But this turn away from allegoresis is also said to be connected to the task of self-knowledge. Such a reading of the *Phaedrus* thus opens up an affinity between the task of self-knowledge, as Socrates enacts it, and the necessary philosophical relation to the excessive φύσις that is at the center of the myth in the *Meno,* as it speaks of the kinship of all with all.

5. Hom. Od. 10, 490–95.

6. See Phaedo 69c–d, where being initiated into the Mysteries is identified with practicing philosophy.

7. Cf. Cleit. 407b, Euthyd. 282b.

8. It is worth noting that Socrates when he first rephrases the question put to him by Meno places an undeniable emphasis upon the question of the limits of teaching: "so far am I from knowing whether it can be taught or not, that I actually do not even know what ἀρετή itself is" (Meno 71a).

9. See Meno 98d; but also, for example, Rep. 618d, Phaedr. 237d.

10. For example, Protagoras 80 B3, B10; Diss Log. VI; Democritus, 68B 242; Antiphon 87B 60; Hippocrates: π. ἀέρ ὑδ, τόπ. II 58, IV 264; Isocrates, 15, 209ff.; Theognis 429. See especially Aristotle, *Sophistici Elenchi,* 173a7–18. But also Nic. Ethics 1179b20–26 and Politics 1332a38–40. For secondary literature on this question, Heinimann, *Nomos und Physis;* Kube, TEXNE *und* APETH; Shorey, "Φύσις, Μελέτη, Ἐπιστήμη"; Kerferd, especially the chapters entitled "The Nomos-Physis

Controversy" and "Can Virtue be Taught"; Pohlenz, "Nomos und Physis"; Beardslee. See also Heidegger, "Vom Wesen und Begriff der Φύσις Aristoteles Physik B 1 (1939)," in *Wegmarken.* In the Platonic text, Φύσις is at times opposed to what is produced by humans through τέχνη: Rep. 596c, 597b, 601d. But see also Soph. 268c–e, where the Stranger seems to undermine the difference between φύσις and τέχνη by attributing what is by φύσις to a *divine* τέχνη. Almost always τέχνη itself must begin by φύσις: Phaedr. 269d and throughout the *Republic.* Physis is also repeatedly opposed to or complemented by τροφή, and sometimes παιδεία: Rep. 424a, 491d, 491e, 495a, 520b; also Rep. 430a, 441a; Tim. 20a; Phaedr. 270a–b, 272d; Gorg. 524c. See also where γένεσις is contrasted to τροφή: Laws 631d; Rep. 451d, 509b; Crito. 50d; Theaet. 169e, 210b; Statesman. 261d, 274a. Also, τροφή is often aligned with *paideia*: Rep. 445e, 451e, 552e; Phaedo 107d; Phil. 55d; Tim. 19c, 86e. At Rep. 591c τροφή is aligned with ἕξις, but then see Theaet. 153b, where it is suggested that the ἕξις in the soul comes through μελέτη and μάθησις. For references to the problem of what is "teachable" (διδακτός), see Rep. 488b; Euth. 274e, 282c; Prot. 319a and throughout; Cleit. 408b. On the theme of φύσις/νόμος: Rep 359c; Laws 888e ff.; Prot. 320c ff.; Gorg. 482c ff. For secondary literature on this question in Plato, see Kube; Roochnik, *Of Art and Wisdom;* Mannsperger, *Physis bei Platon;* Muth, "Zum Physis-Begriff bei Platon." Also, Hoerber, "Plato's Meno."

11. Sallis has developed this theme of whole and parts in his reading of the *Meno,* in *Being and Logos,* pp. 64–103.
12. Socrates uses the verb ἀποβλέπειν (Meno 72c). See also Rep. 618d, 472c, 484c, 501b, 540a, 591e.
13. Callicles, in the *Gorgias,* in fact reproaches Socrates for exploiting just this difference without addressing the fact that he is doing so (Gorg. 482c ff.). I have already mentioned that Aristotle tells us that such a ploy is the mark of sophistical argumentation (Soph. Elench. 173a7–18). But, perhaps most notably, the need to make clear how human political affairs relate to φύσις can also be seen as the basic task posed in the *Republic,* as Socrates finds it necessary there to respond to the accounts of justice presented in the first two Books.
14. See, for example, Rep. 353b.
15. Meno 71b. Klein addresses the question of the different ways in which we might be said to "know" something, *A Commentary on Plato's* Meno, p. 42.
16. μὴ μόνον γε, ὦ ἑταῖρε, ἀλλὰ καὶ ὅτι οὐδ' ἄλλῳ πω ἐνέτυχον εἰδότι, ὡς ἐμοὶ δοκῶ.
17. "Why has Meno not learned his lesson? Is he perhaps altogether incapable of learning? And is not his inability to learn the very consequence of his powerful memory? Why should his memory interfere with his learning? Is it not because something is missing in his memory? It is true that we could not learn anything if we did not remember. But it is equally true that remembering or 'memorizing' with learning leads to nothing. What Meno lacks is the *effort* of learning. Mythically speaking, he is not capable of recollecting. This is revealed to us by the action presented in the dialogue." Jacob Klein, "On the Platonic Meno in Particular and Platonic Dialogues in General," p. 366.
18. See Rep. 473a, 487c.
19. πολλάκις γοῦν ζητῶν εἴ τινες εἶεν αὐτῆς διδάσκαλοι, πάντα ποιῶν οὐ δύναμαι εὑρεῖν. καίτοι μετὰ πολλῶν γε ζητῶ, καὶ τούτων μάλιστα οὓς ἂν οἴωμαι ἐμπειροτάτους εἶναι τοῦ πράγματος.
20. Another such remark is found, for example, in the *Republic* at 497b: "not one city today is in a condition worthy of the philosophic nature." See Bloom's translation.
21. Sayre, *Plato's Literary Garden: How to Read a Platonic Dialogue,* pp. 56–57, and Arieti, *Interpreting Plato: The Dialogues as Drama,* p. 201 ff., develop this reversal.
22. See Gadamer, *Plato's Dialectical Ethics,* esp. pp. 51–100.

23. It is especially important to attend to the region of inquiry from which these examples are taken and to note how far they lie from the questioning concerned with the genesis of human ἀρετή.

24. Klein points out that Meno at 71e–72a emphasizes four times in rapid succession the non-difficulty of the question: οὐ χαλεπόν, ῥᾴδιον, οὐκ ἀπορία εἰπεῖν. Klein, *Commentary on Plato's* Meno, p. 46.

25. Some, however, want to sharply qualify the sense of this kind of statement. See Belfiore, "Elenchus, Epode, and Magic: Socrates as Silenus."

26. See also, for example, Laches 200e, Rep. 337d ff.

27. Klein and others have pointed out that Meno's name already refers to a being stuck. Klein, *Commentary on Plato's "Meno,"* p. 44.

28. Arieti, p. 202, argues that Meno's motives are not sincere but eristic.

29. "Plato takes a new step here. He shows that reaching the aporia in which Meno's attempts to determine the nature of ἀρετή end is the precondition for raising the question of ἀρετή in the first place. But here, raising the question means questioning oneself. The knowledge in question can only be called forth." Gadamer, *The Idea of the Good in Plato and Aristotle,* p. 52.

30. See ibid., pp. 50–61, esp. pp. 50–51.

31. See also Meno 76d.

32. The *Republic* and the dialogues in general repeatedly connect the movement of dialogue to filiation and friendship. Friendship calls for dialogue, just as dialogue would seem to presuppose friendship. See Rep. 328d, 348a–b, Theaet. 146a, and the *Phaedo* 89c–e, where misology is said to arise in the same way that an inability to have friends would arise. It is as if the possibility of philosophy, or at least of a philosophical conversation, actually hangs on the possibility of friendship. It is worth remembering that the *Republic* demonstrates that the possibility of justice and of the just city hang on the sense of the saying that "friends have all things in common."

33. Sallis, *Being and Logos,* p. 82.

34. The myth hangs on this assertion. See Klein, *Commentary on Plato's Meno,* p. 96. Gadamer, "Dialektik ist nicht Sophistik," in *Plato im Dialog,* p. 340. Sallis, pp. 80–82.

35. Klein, *Commentary on Plato's "Meno,"* p. 93.

36. Cf. Tim. 41e; Phaedr. 246a ff. Also, Sophist 242d, where the Eleatic thesis concerning the unity of things is referred to as a μῦθος.

37. Gadamer takes this "being reminded of something forgotten" as "completely contrived." The actual point being made here is that one comes to know only what one in some sense already knows. *The Idea of the Good in Plato and Aristotle,* p. 58. But such an assertion can be made only by the means of the concomitant privileging of a certain demythologizing agenda, whereby philosophy progresses from myth to concept. Thus, according to Gadamer Aristotle is to be read accordingly as the more developed (conceptual) formulation of what Plato already said (mythically and metaphorically). "In Aristotle's thought, what Plato intended is transferred to the cautious and tentative language of philosophical concepts." P. 178, and also pp. 114–15.

38. Platonic myth in this sense repeatedly functions so as to defy all allegoresis. Far from being the sensual or imaginative means to philosophical thought (Hegel), myth addresses the very limits of that thought *in the λόγος.* The lethic character of the myth of Er has been emphasized by Heidegger, in his lectures on *Parmenides,* pp. 130–93. Schelling's attempt to think myth as tautegory attests to this lethic necessity. Also, Derrida, "White Mythology" in *Margins of Philosophy* and especially "Khora" in *On the Name,* addresses the disclosive concealing movement of myth. I have already cited a number of French thinkers who want to read Plato as producing the first philosophical containment of myth: Deleuze, for example, states that

myth does not interrupt at all, but is part of the method of division that connects myth and dialectic, forming a systematic whole. Nancy in "Myth Interrupted" in *The Inoperative Community*, who follows Detienne, *The Creation of Mythology,* and Lacoue-Labarthe, *The Subject of Philosophy.* The status of mythic discourse in the dialogues is taken by these thinkers as unproblematic. Also Vernant, "The Reason of Myth" in *Myth and Society,* and the essays collected in *Terror und Spiel,* ed. Manfred Fuhrman, follow this line of inquiry. Nietzsche, in his *Birth of Tragedy,* insists upon the creative power of myth as an artistic impulse of nature. Hegel states that what is decisive is Plato's *thought,* but also concedes that what Plato had to express nevertheless demanded myth. He also criticizes those who fail to think beyond Aristotle's analogies, to the speculative greatness of Aristotle's thought. Schleiermacher does subordinate myth to a means in his account of the Platonic "system." Cassirer, *Philosophy of Symbolic Forms,* vol. 2: *Mythical Thought,* and *Myth of the State,* still rationalizes myth, even while granting its historical power. See Heidegger's review of Cassirer's book, as an Appendix in *Kant and the Problem of Metaphysics* (Bloomington: Indiana University Press, 1997), pp. 180–90. Gadamer, "Plato and the Poets" in *Dialogue and Dialectic,* characterizes the Platonic myths as projections of psychic structure, writ large, with ethical import; they are not cosmology. Nestle gives a comprehensive reading of antiquity according to a demythologizing teleology. Friedländer and Klein, however, attempt to allow for the productivity of myth in its own right.

39. This injunction, as it is made explicit by Timaeus, speaks of the importance of beginning every matter at the beginning that begins κατὰ φύσιν (Tim. 29b). The rejoinder to begin "from the beginning" occurs, however, throughout the dialogues. For example: Phaedo 59c, 207c and throughout. But in the *Phaedo* the *antilogikoi* are the ones who dispute over the ἀρχή and what follows it. Apol. 19a: Socrates proposes to take things up from the beginning; Rep. 348b, 366e, 369c, 433a, 450a, 490c, 502e; Statesman 268d, cf. 267a; Euth. 11b, 15c; Theaet. 164c, 179e, 187b, 200d; Sym. 174a, 223c; Charm. 167b; Laches 198a; Crito. 119c; Gorg. 488b, 492b.

40. Klein, *Commentary on Plato's "Meno,"* p. 97.

41. The situation resembles, then, the situation in which Socrates finds himself in the *Republic* in the conversation with Thrasymachus, Glaucon, and Adeimantus. Without his knowing *what* justice is, without being able to say what it is *as such,* ἁπλῶς, it nevertheless becomes necessary for Socrates to make very definite claims about justice: it becomes necessary namely to defend in the λόγος the life of justice as the best life, to affirm the good of justice.

42. Cf. Rep. 510b, 511b–d, 532c–d; Phaedo 100a.

43. See Gadamer, *Plato's Dialectical Ethics,* p. 75.

44. J. T. Bedu-Addo, "Recollection and the Argument 'From a Hypothesis' in Plato's *Meno,"* correctly identifies the crucial hypothesis to be that ἀρετή is knowledge, rather than the preliminary claim that asserts that ἀρετή is teachable if and only if it is knowledge.

45. Compare what Socrates says to Protagoras on this subject (Prot. 319a–320c). This question is also developed in the *Gorgias* and *Theaetetus.*

46. Although Socrates later, at Meno 98e, will claim that it has been agreed that ἀρετή was not φρόνησις, such a question is never taken up explicitly in the dialogue. Socrates, again, is attempting to slip things by unnoticed. It is also the case that Socrates seems to equivocate between σοφία and φρόνησις at 99b. And in the *Republic,* Socrates will argue that φρόνησις cannot be "taught," since it is instead a power, like sight, that must be *turned* to the light. See also Aristotle's discussion in Nic. Ethics VI, where the distinction is developed between σοφία and φρόνησις.

47. Edward Warren argues that living must be taken as a kind of τέχνη in "The Craft Argument: An Analogy?" Richard D. Parry makes a similar argument in *Plato's*

Craft of Justice. Strauss also seems to indicate that philosophy can be regarded as a τέχνη: "the art of arts will prove to be philosophy," p. 97. For a reading that insists upon the inadequacy of τέχνη see both Roochnik, *Of Art and Wisdom,* and Kube. Also see C. D. C. Reeve, *Philosopher-Kings,* pp. 8, 19, but also pp. 82–85.

48. The same claim is made by Meletus in the *Apology.* See the discussion at 24c ff. One could also consider the myth of Prometheus that Protagoras tells at Prot. 320c ff., where—after having identified ἀρετή with πολιτικὴ τέχνη, which is the knowledge of how to best arrange one's house—Protagoras distinguishes the political art from the other arts precisely by affirming its *generic* character. The arts are said to have their origin in a gift from the gods, in "divine dispensation" (θεία μοίρα) (Prot. 322a). But each of the arts, other than the political art, is distributed only to a few: "only one possessing the medical is able to treat many others, and so with the other craftsmen" (Prot. 322c). And yet, the political art is distributed to all by Zeus in order to save the human race. The myth is designed to show that such a political art as ἀρετή is teachable because one need not be distinguished in any way in order to become just; it is a *sine qua non* of one's kinship with humankind (Prot. 323c). And yet, the myth, while attempting to account for the origin of ἀρετή, does not yet account for the *teacher* of ἀρετή.

49. *Physics* II, 193b8–22.

50. See Prot. 326e ff., where the unreliability of the transmission or generation of ἀρετή, from generation to generation, is attributed, strangely, to φύσις (Prot. 327c). Again, Protagoras assumes ἀρετή to be like the arts (e.g., flute playing).

51. This emphasis upon the search for a teacher in the search for self-knowledge is repeated in other dialogues. See, for example, Rep. 618c; Phaedo 78a.

52. Much of the *Republic* deals with the force of this "belief," both as it makes possible and as it precludes. Often, the dialogue progresses by appealing to such belief, as the operative assumption upon which further possibilities can be considered or pursued. The word can be aligned together with the group of words that, in general, refer to the originally productive *showing* that can also cover over, such as δόξα, δοκεῖν, and even νομίζειν. Cf. the men "one *believes* to be good, one loves" (Rep. 334c); "Thrasymachus evidently desired to speak . . . since he *believed* he had a very fine answer" (Rep. 338a); "The advantage of the stronger is what the stronger *believes* to be his advantage" (Rep. 340b); "Do you suppose anyone who *believes* Hades' domain exists and is full of terror will be fearless in the face of death and choose death in battles above defeat and slavery?" (Rep. 386b); "And wouldn't he surely love something most when he *believed* that the same things are advantageous to it and to himself" (Rep. 412d); "the sort of men who look as if they were entirely eager to do what they *believe* to be advantageous to the city" (Rep. 412e); "Isn't it charming in them that they *believe* the greatest enemy of all is the man who tells the truth" (Rep. 426a); "Won't such a man also *believe* that death is not something terrible?" (Rep. 486b); "because they won't be willing to act, *believing* they have emigrated to a colony on the Isles of the Blessed while they are still alive" (Rep. 519c); "he will willingly partake of and taste those that be *believes* will make him better" (Rep. 592a).

53. Cf. Euth. 11b–e, 15b.

54. This recourse to the λόγος in the *Meno* is strikingly parallel to the "second sailing" described in the *Phaedo,* where Socrates relates his own recourse to the λόγος from out of the youthful encounter with an aporetic φύσις.

55. It is worth considering the first passage in which Socrates rejects φύσις, at 89b: "if the good were good by φύσις, we surely should have had men able to discern who among the young were good by φύσις; we would take those whom they had pointed out and keep them safe in the Acropolis, setting our mark on them much more so than on our gold, so that none might corrupt them, and when they came to

be of age, they might be useful to their cities." It would be worthwhile to attempt to reconcile this passage with what is attempted in the *Republic* in the making of the best city.

56. The same point is in the *Apology* with regard to the poets, but there such divine inspiration, such *mantic mania* is also said to be grounded in φύσις. Apol. 22c. See also the role of θεία μοίρα for the poets in the *Ion* as it is opposed to τέχνη, 534c, 535a, 536c–d, 542a. Above all, the *Phaedrus* must be considered, since poetic madness (mania) is also there explicitly said to be a divine gift: θεία μοίρα, 244c.

57. And yet, one could compare, for example, the passage in the *Symposium*, where Diotima states that giving birth is divine and that "everything, *by* φύσις, esteems its own offspring" (207c) and then speaks of the soul giving birth to *phronesis* and ἀρετή (Sym. 208e ff.).

58. Thus, Aristotle will affirm the life of θεωρία as the highest praxis.

59. It could be shown that the dialogues repeatedly demonstrate that the productive power of each τέχνη becomes possible only in its being restricted to the region proper to it.

60. "Subtle interpreters of Plato see in this divine dispensation an indication that Socrates himself is the only true teacher of ἀρετή. . . . [But] Plato's concern is not to sanctify this charismatic Socrates. Rather, he is much more concerned with overcoming the false conception of learning and knowing that prevails in the young Meno, as it does in his teacher Gorgias. It is to this end that he adverts to divine dispensation." Gadamer, *The Idea of the Good in Plato and Aristotle*, p. 51.

61. See Gorg. 521d–522a.

7. Typhonic Eros and the Place of the *Phaedrus*

1. At Rep. 485b–c: the necessity of the erotic, that those who love by nature care for everything related to the beloved; this is related to philosophical natures. In the *Republic*, Book IX, there is an alliance between madness and eros in the tyrannical soul (572e–573c, 587a).

2. The original sense of psychagogy is the *leading* of souls down to Hades. Socratic psychagogy is itself still a form of descent.

3. See Griswold, *Self-knowledge in Plato's* Phaedrus, pp. 29, 251.

4. Rep. 458d.

5. Sallis makes this the guiding thread of his interpretation in *Being and Logos*, pp. 104–75. See also Griswold, *Self-knowledge in Plato's* Phaedrus, pp. 33–36.

6. Ferrari discusses the sense of this multiple reference to what is out of place, *Listening to the Cicadas: A Study of Plato's* Phaedrus, pp. 12–15.

7. Griswold, *Self-knowledge in Plato's* Phaedrus, p. 35, seems to take the statement at face value.

8. Sym. 201d, where Socrates says: "Diotima taught me about the erotic"—ἐμὲ τὰ ἐρωτικὰ ἐδίδαξεν.

9. Phaedrus speaks of him this way at 234e.

10. Consider here the beginning of the *Sophist*.

11. Consider here the passage at Apol. 34d and elsewhere: I do not come from an oak tree or a rock.

12. See Derrida, "Plato's Pharmacy," in *Dissemination*, p. 69. Against such an interpretation, see Sallis, *Being and Logos*, p. 116, as well as Nicholson, *Plato's* Phaedrus: *The Philosophy of Love*, p. 22.

13. See the opening pages of Calasso's brilliant study, *The Marriage of Cadmus and Harmony*, for an elaboration of this feature of Greek myth.

14. Herodotus 7.189; Pausanias 1.19.

15. See Burger, *Plato's* Phaedrus: *A Defense of a Philosophic Art of Writing*, pp. 14–15, 42, 74. Also, Brogan, "Socrates' Tragic Speech," in *Retracing the Platonic Text*, p. 38.
16. See Nicholson, pp. 19–22.
17. Ferrari, p. 11: "That mythological monsters should continue to stalk Socrates' phraseology even after he had 'said goodbye' to myth (230a1–2) is not just a pleasant irony, but anticipates and exhibits a situation of epistemological significance."
18. Herodotus 2.156; also, 3.5.
19. Plutarch, *De Iside et Osiride,* 32. Aelian, *De Nat. Animalium,* 10, 46.
20. See Derrida, "Plato's Pharmacy" in *Dissemination,* p. 90.
21. Theogony, 306.
22. Hesiod distinguishes Typhaon and Typhoeus, the former being the son of the latter. Typhaon is also the father (by grisly Echidna) of, among others, the Sphinx. See Theogony 295–332, 820–80. Apollodorus gives an account of Typhon that corresponds to Hesiod's Typhoeus (Apollodorus 1.39–45). Some accounts link Typhoeus to Hera, as the maternal origin of the monster, with no father, since Hera was angry at Zeus for having fathered Athena.
23. Griswold suggests indirectly that this question is raised by the story. Griswold, *Self-Knowledge in Plato's* Phaedrus, p. 42.
24. In its adverbial form, σκολῇ, the word can mean "when possible," or "at one's leisure," but it often also has the sense of "hardly," or "not at all." See, for example, Phaedo 106d.

8. Truth and Friendship

1. This is particularly evident with Aristotle. See, for example, Gadamer, "Aristotle's Doxographical Approach," in *The Beginning of Philosophy*, pp. 71–82. See also Benardete, "The First Crisis in First Philosophy," in *The Argument of the Action*, pp. 3–14. Also, Kofman, "Aristotle and the 'Presocratics'," in *Freud and Fiction*, pp. 9–19. See also Klein, "Aristotle, an Introduction," in *Lectures and Essays,* pp. 171–95.
2. For a reading of the dialogues that is opened up through this assumption, see Hyland. The point is also made in passing by Roochnik, *Beautiful City*, pp. 107–108.
3. Metaphysics, 981a18–20.
4. "Then let us pass him by, since in fact he is absent. But tell me, by the god, Meno, what do you say ἀρετή to be." Meno 71d.
5. Sallis, *Being and Logos,* pp. 67–68.
6. Gadamer, "Three Proofs of Immortality in Plato's *Phaedo*" in *Dialogue and Dialectic,* pp. 22–23.
7. Roochnik, "Self-Recognition in Plato's *Theaetetus,*" reads the dialogue through this question.
8. See Gadamer, "Heraclitus Studies," pp. 207–208.
9. I am making use of Eva Brann's fine translation here.
10. One might also consider here how the *Theaetetus* raises again the question of a Socratic writing. Does the shortage of time, as it is haunted by death's inevitability, not also bear upon this turn to writing? The dialogue begins with Euclides recalling how Socrates selects him as a kind of transcriptionist to record in writing the conversation that took place with Theaetetus, when Theaetetus was only a youth, a conversation that is said to be "well worth hearing" (Theaet. 142d). In the account given by Euclides, Socrates also acts as a collaborator and even as a sort of ghostwriter, as he participates in the revisions of this written work that is dependent upon the memory of Socrates, but also of Euclides himself. Now, however, Euclides admits that he has become dependent upon the writing, since he insists that he would be unable to narrate

from memory what was said. At the time that Euclides relays this to Terpsion, Socrates is already dead and Theaetetus, returning home from battle, sick and wounded, is now dying, soon to be dead. One can take the dying of Theaetetus to be the decisive provocation for the conversation between Euclides and Terpsion as it leads to the reading of this old text. The promising future of Theaetetus's nature, the promise of his goodness and his beauty as a youth, emphasized by Socrates, is now marked and put into relief by the finality of Theaetetus's life but also through the reading of this written record that Euclides was able to write and recollect because of σχολή (Theaet. 143a). This written record—first recalled at leisure but now itself serving to remind and sustain the very contact that has been lost—concludes with Socrates finding it necessary to break off the discussion, with the question at issue in that discussion left unanswered, because there is no more time, because it is time for him to go to the porch of the king and to hear the charges that have been brought against him. The σχολή of the philosopher thus finds itself again claimed by a certain interruptive finality. And yet, an awareness of this interruption is already conveyed through the Socratic desire that the conversation, arising in σχολή and recorded through σχολή, be translated, repeated, and recorded in written form. Like the *Phaedo*, the *Theaetetus* is framed also by both σχολή and death, as if this philosophical σχολή is only the insistence upon its own limit, that time is short and that, perhaps, it is even already too late.

11. Diogenes Laertius, ii, 22: ἃ μὲν συ·ῆκα, γενναῖα. οἶμαι δὲ καὶ ἃ μὴ συνῆκα. πλὴν Δηλίου γέ τινος δεῖται κολυμβητοῦ.

12. See for example, Theaet. 156c, 164d, 164e, where Protagoras's is referred to in this way.

13. The Aristotelian critique of the Platonic good has to do with the necessity of addressing the manifold sense of the good. But Aristotle's own discussion begins with an affirmation of precisely the *unity* of this manifold. And his discussion of the form of the good returns to the necessity of such a unity. It thus can be read just as much as a clarification of how not to read Plato as a supposed "critique" of him.

14. See also Gadamer's essay, "Amicus Platon Sed Magis Amicus Veritas," in *Dialogue and Dialectic.*

15. See Aristotle, Fr. 623 1583a12. The statement concerns an altar that is dedicated to friendship. See Klein, "Aristotle, an Introduction," in *Lectures and Essays*, p. 174. Klein refers to Jaeger, *Aristotle,* p. 106 ff., who interprets the statement to mean that those who praise Plato are the same ones who believe they are defending him by opposing Aristotle's criticism.

16. Consider how at Theaet. 180d Socrates speaks of the origins of the philosophical tradition as "ancient" and as "concealed in poetry," a passage that relates to the Eleatic Stranger's statement at Soph. 242c that the early thinkers tells us stories as if we are children. In chapter 2 I have discussed how similar remarks are found in Aristotle's work.

17. See note at the beginning of chapter 5.

18. Poetics 1447b9–13. See chapter 1.

19. Rosen's discussion of this problem, *The Quarrel between Philosophy and Poetry,* p. 7.

20. See, for example, Met. 1070a18–20, 1080a5–6, 991b6.

Bibliography

Translations of Platonic Dialogues, and Other Classical Authors

Loeb Classical Library. Cambridge: Harvard University Press.
Benardete, Seth. 1986. *Plato's Theaetetus.* Chicago: University of Chicago Press.
Benardete, Seth, and Michael Davis. 2002. *Aristotle—On Poetics.* South Bend: St. Augustine's Press.
Bloom, Allan. 1968. *The Republic of Plato.* New York: Basic Books.
Brann, Eva T. H., Peter Kalkavage, and Eric Salem. 1996. *Plato's Sophist.* Newburyport: Focus Classical Library.
———. 1998. *Plato's Phaedo.* Newburyport: Focus Classical Library.
Cobb, William S. 1993. *The Symposium and the Phaedrus: Plato's Erotic Dialogues.* Albany: SUNY Press.
Cooper, John, ed. 1997. *Plato: Complete Works.* Indianapolis: Hackett Publishing.
Diels, Hermann, and Walther Kranz. 1960. *Die Fragmente der Vorsokratiker.* 3 vols. Berlin: Weidmannsche Verlagsbuchhandlung.
Kalkavage, Peter. *Plato's Timaeus.* Newburyport: Focus Classical Library.
Sachs, J. 1998. *Aristotle's Physics: A Guided Study.* New Brunswick: Rutgers University Press.
———. 1999. *Aristotle's Metaphysics.* Santa Fe: Green Lion Press.
———. 2002. *Nicomachean Ethics: Aristotle.* Newburyport: Focus Publishing.

Secondary Materials

Ahrensdorf, Peter J. 1995. *The Death of Socrates and the Life of Philosophy: An Interpretation of Plato's* Phaedo. Albany: SUNY Press.
Allen, R. E. 1960. "The Socratic Paradox." *Journal of the History of Ideas* 21.2: 256–65.
Amory, F. 1984. "Socrates: The Legend." *Classica et Medievialia* 35: 19–56.
Anastasiadis, V. I. 2004. "Idealized ΣΧΟΛΗ and Disdain for Work: Aspects of Philosophy and Politics in Ancient Democracy." *Classical Quarterly* 54: 58–79.

Arieti, James A. 1991. *Interpreting Plato: The Dialogues as Drama.* Savage, Md.: Rowman and Littlefield.

Ast, Friedrich. 1816. *Platons Leben und Schriften.* Leipzig: Weidmann.

Ausland, Hayden W. 1997. "On Reading Plato Mimetically." *American Journal of Philology* 118: 371–416.

Barabas, Marina. 1986. "The Strangeness of Socrates." *Philosophical Investigations* 9.2: 89–110.

Beardslee, J. W. 1987. "The Use of φύσις in Fifth-Century Greek Literature." In *Early Greek Thought: Three Studies.* New York: Garland.

Bedu-Addo, J. T. 1984. "Recollection and the Argument 'From a Hypothesis' in Plato's *Meno.*" *Journal of Hellenic Studies* 104: 1–14.

Belfiore, Elizabeth. 1980. *"Elenchus, Epode,* and Magic: Socrates as Silenus." *Phoenix* 34: 128–37.

Benardete, S. 1999. *Herodotean Inquiries.* South Bend: St. Augustine's Press.

———. 2000. *The Argument of the Action.* Chicago: University of Chicago Press.

Benson, Hugh H., ed. 1992. *Essays on the Philosophy of Socrates.* Oxford: Oxford University Press.

Berman, Scott. 1991. "How Polus was Refuted: Reconsidering Plato's *Gorgias* 474c–475c." *Ancient Philosophy* 11: 265–84.

Blair, E. D. 1996. "Women: The Unrecognized Teachers of the Platonic Socrates." *Ancient Philosophy* 16: 333–50.

Blondell, Ruby. 2002. *The Play of Character in Plato's Dialogues.* Cambridge: Cambridge University Press.

Bolotin, David. 1987. "The Life of Philosophy and the Immortality of the Soul." *Ancient Philosophy* 7: 39–56.

Brague, Remi. 2002. "History of Philosophy as Freedom." *Epoché* 7.1: 39–50.

Brann, Eva. 2004. *The Music of the Republic.* Philadelphia: Paul Dry Books.

Brickhouse, T. C., and N. D. Smith. 1983. "The Origin of Socrates' Mission." *Journal of the History of Ideas* 44.4: 657–66.

Brisson, Luc. 1998. *Plato the Myth Maker.* Trans. Gerard Naddaf. Chicago: University of Chicago Press.

Brogan, Walter. 1984. "Is Aristotle a Metaphysician?" *Journal of the British Society of Phenomenology* 15: 249–61.

———. "Socrates' Tragic Speech." In *Retracing the Platonic Text,* ed. John Russon and John Sallis. Evanston: Northwestern University Press.

Brown, Eric. 2003. "Knowing the Whole: Comments on Gill, 'Plato's *Phaedrus* and the Method of Hippocrates.'" *Modern Schoolman* 80.4: 315–23.

Burger, Ronna. 1980. *Plato's Phaedrus: A Defense of a Philosophic Art of Writing.* University: University of Alabama Press.

———. 1984. *The Phaedo: A Platonic Labyrinth.* New Haven: Yale University Press.

Burke, S. 1996. "The Textual Estate: Plato and the Ethics of Signature." *History of the Human Sciences* 9.1: 59–72.

Burnyeat, Myles. 1997. "The Impiety of Socrates." *Ancient Philosophy* 17.1: 1–12.

Calasso, Roberto. 1994. *The Marriage of Cadmus and Harmony.* New York: Vintage Books.

Cassirer, Ernst. 1955. *Philosophy of Symbolic Forms.* Vol. 2: *Mythical Thought.* New Haven: Yale University.

———. 1974. *The Myth of the State.* New Haven: Yale University.

Cavarero, Adriana. 1995. *In Spite of Plato.* New York: Routledge.

Chance, Thomas H. 1992. *Plato's Euthydemus: An Analysis of What Is and What Is Not Philosophy.* Berkeley: University of California Press.

Cherniss, Harold. 1943. "The Biographical Fashion in Literary Criticism." In *Selected Papers,* 1–13. Leiden: E. J. Brill.

Cholbi, Michael. 2002. "Dialectical Refutation as a Paradigm of Socratic Punishment." *Journal of Philosophical Research* 27: 371–79.

Clay, Diskin. 1998. "The Theory of the Literary Persona in Antiquity." *Materiali e discussioni per l'analisi dei test classici* 40: 9–40.

———. 2000. *Platonic Questions: Dialogues with the Silent Philosopher.* University Park: Pennsylvania State University Press.

Cropsey, Joseph. 1986. "The Dramatic End of Plato's Socrates." *Interpretation* 14: 155–75.

———. 1995. *Plato's World: Man's Place in the Universe.* Chicago: University of Chicago Press.

Deleuze, Gilles. 1990. *The Logic of Sense.* New York: Columbia University Press.

Detienne, Marcel. 1981. *The Creation of Mythology.* Trans. Margaret Cook. Chicago: University of Chicago Press.

Derrida, J. 1972. *Margins of Philosophy.* Trans. Alan Bass. Chicago: University of Chicago Press.

———. 1981. *Dissemination.* Trans. Barbara Johnson. Chicago: University of Chicago Press.

———. 1995. *On the Name.* Trans. David Wood. Stanford: Stanford University Press.

Dodds, E. R. 1959. *Plato's Gorgias.* London: Oxford University Press.

Dorter, Kenneth. 1970. "The Dramatic Aspect of Plato's *Phaedo.*" *Dialogue* 8: 564–80.

———. 1982. *Plato's* Phaedo: *An Interpretation.* Toronto: University of Toronto Press.

Ebert, T. 2001. "Why Is Evenus Called a Philosopher at Phaedo 61c?" *Classical Quarterly* 51.2: 423–34.

Edelstein, Ludwig. 1962. "Platonic Anonymity." *American Journal of Philology* 83: 1–22.

Edmonds, Radcliffe G. III. 2000. "Socrates the Beautiful: Role Reversal and Midwifery in Plato's *Symposium.*" *Transactions of the American Philological Association* 130: 261–85.

Eide, Tormod. 1996. "On Socrates' ἀτοπία." *Symbolae Osloenses* 71: 59–67.

Eisner, Robert. 1982. "Socrates as Hero." *Philosophy and Literature* 6: 106–18.

Emerson, R. W. 1971. "Plato, or the Philosopher." In *Collected Works of R. W. Emerson.* Vol. 4: *Representative Men.* Cambridge: Harvard University Press.

Ferrari, G. R. F. 1987. *Listening to the Cicadas: A Study of Plato's* Phaedrus. Cambridge: Cambridge University Press.

Figal, Günter. 1998. *Sokrates.* München: Beck.

Foucault, Michel. 1984. *Foucault Reader.* New York: Pantheon Books.

Friedländer, Paul. 1969. *Plato: The Dialogues, Second and Third Periods.* Trans. H. Meyerhoff. New York: Pantheon.

Fuhrman, Manfred, ed. 1971. *Terror und Spiel.* München: Wilhelm Fink.

Fussi, Alessandra. 1996. "Callicles' Examples of νόμος τῆς φύσεως in Plato's *Gorgias.*" *Graduate Faculty Philosophy Journal* 19: 119–49.

———. 2001. "The Myth of the Last Judgment in the *Gorgias.*" *Review of Metaphysics* 54: 529–52.

Gadamer, Hans-Georg. 1980. *Dialogue and Dialectic: Eight Hermeneutical Studies on Plato.* Trans. P. C. Smith. New Haven: Yale University Press.

———. 1986. *The Idea of the Good in Platonic-Aristotelian Philosophy.* Trans. P. C. Smith. New Haven: Yale University Press.

———. 1991. "Dialektik ist nicht Sophistik." In *Griechische Philosophie III: Plato im Dialog,* 338–69. Tübingen: J. C. B. Mohr (Paul Siebeck).

———. 1991. "Plato als Porträtist." In *Griechische Philosophie III: Plato im Dialog,* 228–57. Tübingen: J. C. B. Mohr (Paul Siebeck).

———. 1991. *Plato's Dialectical Ethics.* Trans. Robert Wallace. New Haven: Yale University Press.

————. 1996. *The Enigma of Health.* Trans. Jason Gaiger and Nicholas Walker. Stanford: Stanford University Press.

————. 1998. *The Beginning of Philosophy.* Trans. Rod Coltman. New York: Continuum.

————. 1999. "Heraclitus Studies." In *The Presocratics after Heidegger,* ed. David Jacobs. Albany: SUNY Press.

Gasché, Rudolphe. 1986. *The Tain of the Mirror: Derrida and the Philosophy of Reflection.* Cambridge: Harvard University Press.

Gill, Marie Louise. 2003. "Plato's *Phaedrus* and the Method of Hippocrates." *Modern Schoolman* 80.4: 295–314.

Gonzalez, Francisco J., ed. 1995. *The Third Way: New Directions in Platonic Studies.* Lanham, Md.: Rowman and Littlefield.

Gould, Josiah M. 1969. "Klein on Ethological Mimes: For Example, the *Meno.*" *Journal of Philosophy* 66: 253–65.

Griswold, Charles L., Jr. 1986. *Self-Knowledge in Plato's* Phaedrus. University Park: Pennsylvania State University Press.

Griswold, Charles L., Jr., ed. 1988. *Platonic Writings: Platonic Readings.* New York: Routledge.

Guthrie, W. K. C. 1955. *The Greeks and Their Gods.* Boston: Beacon Press.

————. 1971. *Socrates.* Cambridge: Cambridge University Press.

Hadas, M. 1999. *Ancilla to Classical Reading.* Pleasantville: Akadine Press.

Hardy, E. 1884. *Der Begriff der Physis in der Griechischen Philosophie.* Berlin: Weidmannsche Buchhandlung.

Hartland-Swann, John. 1951. "Plato as Poet: A Critical Interpretation." *Philosophy* 26: 3–18, 131–41.

Hegel, G. W. F. *Werke.* 20 vols. Frankfurt am Main: Suhrkamp.

Heidegger, Martin. 1953. *Einführung in die Metaphysik.* Tübingen: Max Niemeyer.

————. 1954. *Was Heisst Denken?* Tübingen: Max Niemeyer.

————. 1957. *Der Satz vom Grund.* Pfullingen: Neske.

————. 1967. *Wegmarken.* Frankfurt (Main): Vittorio Klostermann.

————. 1969. *Zur Sache des Denkens.* Tübingen: Max Niemeyer.

————. 1979. *Heraklit. Gesamtausgabe Band 55.* Frankfurt (Main): Vittorio Klostermann.

————. 1982. *Parmenides. Gesamtausgabe Band 54.* Frankfurt (Main): Vittorio Klostermann.

————. 1988. *Vom Wesen der Wahrheit. zu Platons Höhlengleichnis und Theätet. Gesamtausgabe Band 34.* Frankfurt (Main): Vittorio Klostermann.

————. 1992. *Platon: Sophistes. Gesamtausgabe Band 19.* Frankfurt (Main): Vittorio Klostermann.

————. 1993. *Der Grundbegriffe der antiken Philosophie. Gesamtausgabe Band 22.* Frankfurt (Main): Vittorio Klostermann.

Heinimann, Felix. 1965. *Nomos und Physis.* Basel: Friedrich Reinhardt.

Hermann, Karl Friedrich. 1839. *Geschichte und System der Platonischen Philosophie.* Vol. 1. Heidelberg: Winter.

Hirzel, Rudolf. 1895. *Der Dialog: Ein literarhistorische Versuch.* Leipzig: S. Hirzel.

Hoerber, Robert. 1960. "Plato's Meno." *Phronesis* 5: 78–102.

Hoffman, Ernst. 1947. "Die literarische Voraussetzungen des Platonverständnisses." *Zeitschrift für philosophische Forschung* 2: 465–80. Also published in *Platon* (Zürich: Artemis, 1950), 7–28.

Howland, Jacob. 1991. "Re-reading Plato: The Problem of Platonic Chronology." *Phoenix* 45: 189–214.

————. 1998. *The Paradox of Political Philosophy.* Lanham, Md.: Rowman and Littlefield.

Hulse, James. 1995. *The Reputations of Socrates: The Afterlife of a Gadfly.* New York: P. Lang.

Hyland, Drew. 1995. *Finitude and Transcendence in the Platonic Dialogues*. Albany: SUNY Press.

Jaeger, W. 1961. *Aristotle*. Oxford: Oxford University Press.

———. 1971. *Paideia: The Ideals of Greek Culture*. Vols. 1–3. Trans. G. Highet. Oxford: Oxford University Press.

Johnson, Curtis. 1989. "Socrates' Encounter with Polus in Plato's *Gorgias*." *Phoenix* 43: 196–216.

Joseph, H. W. B. 1935. *Essays in Ancient and Modern Philosophy*. Oxford: Oxford University Press.

Kaatman, David. 1995. "The Role of Myth in Plato's *Gorgias*." *Dialogue* 38: 15–20.

Kahn, Charles. 1979. *The Art and Thought of Heraclitus*. Cambridge: Cambridge University Press.

———. 1981. "Did Plato Write Socratic Dialogues?" *Classic Quarterly* 31 (1981): 305–20. Reprinted in Benson, *Essays on the Philosophy of Socrates*, 35–52.

———. 1992. "Why Did Plato Write Socratic Dialogues?" In Benson, *Essays on the Philosophy of Socrates*.

———. 1996. *Plato and the Socratic Dialogue*. Cambridge: Cambridge University Press.

Kerferd, G. B. 1981. *The Sophistic Movement*. Cambridge: Cambridge University Press.

Kirby, John T. 1997. "Aristotle on Metaphor." *American Journal of Philology* 118: 517–54.

Klagge, James C., and Nicholas D. Smith, eds. 1992. *Methods of Interpreting Plato and His Dialogues*. Suppl. vol., Oxford Studies in Ancient Philosophy. Oxford: Oxford University Press.

Klein, Jacob. 1965. *A Commentary on Plato's* Meno. Chapel Hill: University of North Carolina Press.

———. 1977. *Plato's Trilogy: Theaetetus, The Sophist and The Statesman*. Chicago: University of Chicago Press.

———. 1985. *Lectures and Essays*. Annapolis: Saint John's College Press.

———. 2001. "On the Platonic Meno in Particular and Platonic Dialogues in General." In *New Yearbook for Phenomenology and Phenomenological Philosophy*, no. 1 (2001): 357–67.

Kofman, Sarah. 1991. *Freud and Fiction*. Boston: Northeastern University Press.

———. 1998. *Socrates: Fictions of a Philosopher*. Ithaca: Cornell University Press.

Kosman, Aryeh. 1992. "Silence and Imitation in the Platonic Dialogues." In Klagge and Smith, *Methods of Interpreting Plato and His Dialogues*, 73–92.

Krell, David F. 1972. "Socrates' Body." *Southern Journal of Philosophy* 10: 443–51.

Kube, Jörg. 1969. *TEXNH und APETH. Sophistisches und Platonisches Tugendwissen*. Berlin: Walter de Gruyter and Co.

Lacan, Jacques. 1992. *The Seminar of Jacques Lacan*. Book VII: *The Ethics of Psychoanalysis, 1959–60*. Trans. Dennis Porter. New York: W. W. Norton and Company.

Lacey, A. R. 1971. "Our Knowledge of Socrates." In *The Philosophy of Socrates*, comp. Gregory Vlastos. Garden City: Anchor Books.

Lachterman, David. 1989. *The Ethics of Geometry*. London: Routledge.

Lacoue-Labarthe, P. 1989. *Typography: Mimesis, Philosophy, Politics*. Cambridge: Harvard University Press.

———. 1993. *The Subject of Philosophy*. Minneapolis: Minnesota University Press.

Langiulli, Nino. 1993. "On the Location of Socrates' Feet; or, The Immanence of Transcendence." *Telos* 96: 143–48.

Lewis, Thomas. 1986. "Refutative Rhetoric as True Rhetoric in the *Gorgias*." *Interpretation* 14: 195–210.

Lovejoy, Arthur. 1909. "The Meaning of φύσις in the Greek Physiologers." *Philosophical Review* 18.4: 369–83.

Madison, L. 2002. "Have We Been Careless with Socrates' Last Words? A Rereading of the *Phaedo.*" *Journal of the History of Philosophy* 40.4: 421–36.

Mannsperger, Dietrich. 1969. *Physis bei Platon.* Berlin: Walter de Gruyter.

Maranhao, T., ed. 1990. *The Interpretation of Dialogue.* Chicago: University of Chicago Press.

McComiskey, Bruce. 2002. *Gorgias and the New Sophistic Rhetoric.* Carbondale: Southern Illinois University Press.

McKim, Richard. 1988. "Shame and Truth in Plato's *Gorgias.*" In Griswold, *Platonic Writings,* 34–48.

Merleau-Ponty, Maurice. 2003. *Nature: Course Notes from the Collège de France.* Evanston: Northwestern University Press.

Michelini, Ann N. 2000. "Socrates Plays the Buffoon: Cautionary Protreptic in *Euthydemus.*" *American Journal of Philology* 121: 509–35.

Miller, Mitchell H. 1980. *The Philosopher in Plato's Statesman.* The Hague: Martinus Nijhoff Publishers.

———. 1984. *Plato's Parmenides: The Conversion of the Soul.* Princeton: Princeton University Press.

Moors, Kent F. 1978. "Plato's Use of Dialogue." *Classical World* 72: 77–93.

Morrison, Donald. 2000. "On the Alleged Historical Reliability of Plato's *Apology.*" *Archiv für Geschichte der Philosophie* 82.3: 235–65.

Muth, Robert. 1949. "Zum Physis-Begriff bei Platon." *Wiener Studien* 64: 53–70.

Naas, Michael. 1995. "Philosophy Bound: The Fate of the Promethean Socrates." *Research in Phenomenology* 25: 121–41.

Nails, Debra. 1995. *Agora, Academy, and the Conduct of Philosophy.* Dordrecht: Kluwer Academic Publishers.

———. 2000. "Mouthpiece Schmouthpiece." In *Who Speaks for Plato? Studies in Platonic Anonymity,* ed. Gerald A. Press. Lanham, Md.: Rowman and Littlefield.

Nancy, Jean-Luc. 1991. *The Inoperative Community.* Minneapolis: Minnesota University Press.

Nestle, Wilhelm. 1966. *Vom Mythos zum Logos. Die Selbstentfaltung des Griechischen Denkens von Homer bis auf die Sophistik und Sokrates.* Stuttgart: Aalen.

Nicholson, Graeme. 1999. *Plato's* Phaedrus: *The Philosophy of Love.* West Lafayette: Purdue University Press.

Nightingale, A. W. 1995. *Genres in Dialogue: Plato and the Construct of Philosophy.* Cambridge: Cambridge University Press.

Nietzsche, Friedrich. 1988. *Die Geburt der Tragödie.* Vol. I of the Kritische Studienausgabe. München: Walter de Gruyter.

Parry, Richard D. 1996. *Plato's Craft of Justice.* Albany: SUNY Press.

Patterson, Richard. 1982. "The Platonic Art of Comedy and Tragedy." *Philosophy and Literature* 6: 76–93.

Patzer, Harald. 1965. "Die philosophische Bedeutung der Sokratesgestalt in den platonischen Dialogen." In *Parusia: Studien zur Philosophie Platons und zur Problemgeschichte des Platonismus. Festgabe für Johannes Hirschberger,* ed. Kurt Flash. Frankfurt/Main: Minerva, 21–43.

———. 1993. *Physis: Grundlegung zu einer Geschichte des Wortes.* Stuttgart: Franz Steiner Verlag.

Plass, Paul. 1964. "Philosophic Anonymity and Irony in the Platonic Dialogues." *American Journal of Philology* 85: 254–78.

Pohlenz, Max. 1953. "Nomos und Physis." *Hermes* 81: 418–38.

Press, Gerald A., ed. 2000. *Who Speaks for Plato? Studies in Platonic Anonymity.* Lanham, Md.: Rowman and Littlefield.

Prior, William. 2001. "The Historicity of Plato's *Apology.*" *Polis* 18: 41–57.

Prufer, Thomas. 1986. "The Dramatic Form of Phaedo." *Review of Metaphysics* 39: 547–51.

Raeder, Hans. 1905. *Platons Philosophische Entwicklung.* Leipzig: Teubner.

Reale, Giovanni. 1987. *From the Origins to Socrates: A History of Ancient Philosophy.* Albany: SUNY Press.

Reeve, C. D. C. 1988. *Philosopher-Kings.* Princeton: Princeton University Press.

———. 1989. *Socrates in the* Apology. Indianapolis: Hackett Publishing.

Reich, Hermann. 1903. *Der Mimus.* Berlin: Weidmannsche Buchhandlung.

Ricouer, Paul. 1977. *The Rule of Metaphor.* Toronto: University of Toronto Press.

Riginos, Alice Swift. 1976. *Platonica: The Anecdotes concerning the Life and Writings of Plato.* Leiden: Brill.

Roochnik, David. 1996. *Of Art and Wisdom: Plato's Understanding of Techne.* University Park: Pennsylvania State University Press.

———. 2001. "The Deathbed Dream of Reason: Socrates' Dream in the *Phaedo.*" *Arethusa* 34: 239–58.

———. 2002. "Self-Recognition in Plato's *Theaetetus.*" *Ancient Philosophy* 22: 37–50.

———. 2003. *Beautiful City: The Dialectical Character of Plato's* Republic. Ithaca: Cornell University Press.

Rosen, Stanley. 1993. *The Quarrel between Philosophy and Poetry.* New York: Routledge.

Rossetti, Livio. 1993. "Where Philosophy and Literature Merge in the Platonic Dialogues." *Argumentation* 6: 433–43.

Sallis, John. 1996. *Being and Logos: Reading the Platonic Dialogues.* Bloomington: Indiana University Press.

———. 1999. *Chorology: On Beginning in Plato's* Timaeus. Bloomington: Indiana University Press.

———. 2000. *Force of Imagination: The Sense of the Elemental.* Bloomington: Indiana University Press.

Saxenhouse, Arlene. 1992. *Fear of Diversity: The Birth of Political Science in Ancient Greek Thought.* Chicago: University of Chicago Press.

Sayre, Kenneth M. 1995. *Plato's Literary Garden: How to Read a Platonic Dialogue.* Notre Dame: Notre Dame Press.

Schelling, F. W. J. 1959. *Zur Geschichte der Neueren Philosophie.* Darmstadt: Wissenschaftliche Buchgesellschaft.

———. 1969. *Initia Philosophiae Universae. Erlanger Vorlesungen WS 1820/21.* Ed. H. Fuhrmans. Bonn: H. Bouvier u. Co. Verlag.

———. 1978. *System of Transcendental Idealism.* Trans. Peter Lauchlan Heath. Charlottesville: University Press of Virginia.

———. 1997. *Philosophische Untersuchungen über das Wesen der menschlichen Freiheit und die damit zusammenhängenden Gegenstände.* Ed. Thomas Buchheim. Hamburg: Felix Meiner.

Schlegel, Friedrich. [1795–1804] 1958. *Wissenschaft der europäischen Literatur: Vorlesungen, Aufsätze und Fragmente aus der Zeit von 1795–1804.* Ed. Ernst Behler. Munich: Schöningh.

Schleiermacher, Friedrich. [1804] 1996. *Über die Philosophie Platons.* Hamburg: Felix Meiner. Schleiermacher's introductions to his famous translations are translated in William Dobson's *Schleiermacher's Introductions to the Dialogues of Plato.* New York: Arno Press.

———. 1826. *Platons Werke.* Vol. II.3. 2nd ed. Berlin: Reimer.

Seeskin, Kenneth. 1982. "Is the *Apology of Socrates* a Parody?" *Philosophy and Literature* 6: 94–105.

Schmidt, Dennis J. 2001. *On Germans and Other Greeks: Tragedy and Ethical Life.* Bloomington: Indiana University Press.

Shorey, Paul. 1909. "Φύσις, Μελέτη, ᾽Επιστήμη." *Transactions and Proceedings of the American Philological Association* 40: 185–201.

Spiegelberg, H., ed. 1964. *The Socratic Enigma.* New York: Bobbs-Merrill Company.

Stauffer, Devin. 2002. "Socrates and Callicles: A Reading of Plato's *Gorgias.*" *Review of Politics* 64: 627–57.

Strauss, Leo. 1964. *The City and Man.* Chicago: Rand McNally.

———. 1966. *Socrates and Aristophanes.* Chicago: University of Chicago Press.

———. 1988. *What Is Political Philosophy?* Chicago: University of Chicago Press.

Tarrant, Harold. 2000. *Plato's First Interpreters.* Ithaca: Cornell University Press.

Theslef, Holger. 1989. "Platonic Chronology." *Phronesis* 34: 1–26.

Tigerstedt, E. N. 1977. *Interpreting Plato.* Uppsala: Almquist and Wiksell.

Turner, Jeffrey. 1993. "Atopia in Plato's *Gorgias.*" *International Studies in Philosophy* 25: 69–77.

Vernant, Jean Pierre. 1990. "The Reason of Myth." In *Myth and Society in Ancient Greece.* New York: Zone Books.

Vlastos, Gregory. 1991. *Socrates: Ironist and Moral Philosopher.* Ithaca: Cornell University Press.

Wardy, Robert. 1996. *The Birth of Rhetoric: Gorgias, Plato and Their Successors.* London: Routledge.

Warnek, P. 1997. "Reading Plato before Platonism (after Heidegger)." *Research in Phenomenology* 27: 61–89.

———. 2002. "Saving the Last Word: Heidegger and the Concluding Myth of Plato's *Republic.*" *Philosophy Today* 46.3: 255–73.

———. 2003. "Teiresias in Athens: Socrates as Educator and the Kinship of Physis in Plato's *Meno.*" *Epoché* 7.2: 261–89.

———. 2004. "Once More for the First Time . . . : Aristotle and Hegel in the Logic of History." *Research in Phenomenology* 34: 160–80.

Warren, Edward. 1989. "The Craft Argument: An Analogy?" In *Essays in Ancient Greek Philosophy III: Plato,* ed. John P. Anton and Anthony Preus. Albany: SUNY Press.

White, F. C. 1990. "The Good in Plato's *Gorgias.*" *Phronesis* 35.2: 117–27.

Wolff, Francis. 1985. *Socrate.* Paris: Presses Universitaires de France.

Woodbridge, Frederick J. E. 1929. *The Son of Apollo.* Boston: Houghton Mifflin.

Zeller, Eduard. 1962. *Socrates and the Socratic Schools.* Trans. Oswald J. Reichel. New York: Russell and Russell.

Index

Index of Greek Words

About the Author

PETER WARNEK is Associate Professor of Philosophy at the University of Oregon. He is co-translator (with Walter Brogan) of Heidegger's *Aristotle's Metaphysics Theta 1–3* (Indiana University Press, 1995). He is a founding member of the Ancient Philosophy Society.